The Complete Air Fryer Co Beginners 2022

1000 Quick, Easy & Affordable Air Fryer Recipes - Tips & Tricks - Fry, Grill, Roast, and Bake Your Favorite Foods

Elena Baker

8

Breakfast & Brunch

Bread Rolls With Potato Stuffing
Serves: 4
- Bread - white part only (8 slices)
- Potatoes (5 large)
- Oil - frying and brushing (2 tbsp.)
- Finely chopped coriander (1 small bunch)
- Seeded chopped green chilies (2)
- Turmeric (.5 tsp.)
- Curry leaf sprigs (2)
- Mustard seeds (.5 tsp.)
- Finely chopped small onions (2) Salt (as desired)

1. Set the Air Fryer at 392° Fahrenheit.
2. Remove the edges of the bread. Peel the potatoes and boil. Mash the potatoes using one teaspoon of salt.
3. On the stovetop, prepare a skillet using one teaspoon of oil. Toss in the mustard seeds and onions. When the seeds sputter, continue frying until they become translucent. Toss in the curry and turmeric.
4. Fry the mixture a few seconds and add the mashed potatoes. Mix well and let it cool. Shape eight portions of dough into an oval shape. Set them aside for now.
5. Wet the bread with water and press it in your palm to remove the excess water. Place the oval potato into the bread and roll it around the potato mixture. Be sure they are completely sealed.
6. Brush the potato rolls with oil and set aside.
7. Set the timer for 12 to 13 minutes. Cook until crispy and browned.

Cheesy Garlic Bread
Serves: 4
- Bread slices
- Round or baguette (5 rounds)
- Sun-dried tomato pesto (5 tsp.)
- Garlic cloves (3)
- Melted butter (4 tbsp.)
- Grated Mozzarella cheese (1 cup)
  Garnish Options:
- Chili flakes
- Chopped basil leaves Oregano

1. Set the Air Fryer to reach 356° Fahrenheit.
2. Slice the bread loaf into five thick slices.
3. Spread the butter, pesto, and cheese over the bread.
4. Put the slices in the air Fryer for six to eight minutes.
5. Garnish with your choice of toppings.
6. Note: Round or baguette bread was used for this recipe.

Quick & Easy Poached Eggs
Serves: 4
- Boiling water (3 cups)
- Large egg (1)

1. Set the Air Fryer at 390° Fahrenheit.
1. Pour boiling water into the Air Fryer basket.
2. Break the egg into a dish and slide it into the water. Set the basket into the fryer.
3. Set the timer for 3 minutes. When ready, scoop the poached egg into a plate using a slotted spoon.
4. Serve with a serving of toast to your liking.

Baked Apple & Walnuts
Serves: 2
- Apple or pear (1 medium)
- Chopped walnuts (2 tbsp.)
- Raisins (2 tbsp.)
- Light margarine (1.5 tsp. - melted)
- Cinnamon (.25 tsp.)
- Nutmeg (.25 tsp.)
- Water (.25 cup)

1. Set the Air Fryer temperature at 350° Fahrenheit.
2. Cut the apple/pear in half around the middle and spoon out some of the flesh.
3. Place the apple or pear in the pan (to fit in the Air Fryer).
4. In a small mixing container, combine the cinnamon, nutmeg, margarine, raisins, and walnuts.
5. Add the mixture into the centers of the fruit halves.
6. Pour water into the pan.
7. Air-fry for 20 minutes.

Baked Eggs In A Bread Bowl
Serves: 4
- Large eggs (4)
- Crusty dinner rolls (4)
- Heavy cream (4 tbsp.)
- Mixed herbs - ex. Chopped tarragon, chives, parsley, etc. (4 tbsp.each)
- Grated parmesan cheese (to your liking)

1. Set the Air Fryer at 350° Fahrenheit.
2. Use a sharp knife to remove the top of each of the rolls – setting them aside for later. Use a glass or cookie cutter to make a hole in the bread large enough for the egg.
3. Place the rolls in the fryer basket. Break an egg into the roll and top with the cream and herbs. Sprinkle using a portion of the parmesan.
4. Bake for about 20-25 minutes until the egg is set. The bread should be toasted.
5. After 20 minutes, arrange the tops of the bread on the egg and bake a few more minutes to finish the browning process.
6. Remove from the Air Fryer and wait for five minutes. Serve warm.

Banana Fritters
Serves: 8
- Vegetable oil (3 tbsp.)
- Breadcrumbs (.75 cup)
- Corn flour (3 tbsp.)
- Ripe peeled bananas (8) Egg white (1)

1. Warm the Air Fryer to reach 356° Fahrenheit.
2. Use the low-heat temperature setting to warm a skillet. Pour in the oil and toss in the breadcrumbs. Cook until golden brown.
3. Coat the bananas with the flour. Dip them into the whisked egg white and cover with the breadcrumbs.
4. Arrange the prepared bananas in a single layer of the basket and place thefritter cakes onto a bunch of paper towels to drain before serving.

Cheesy Mushroom Onion Frittata
Serves: 2
- Olive oil (1 tbsp.)

- Mushrooms (2 cups)
- Onion (1 small)
- Eggs (3)
- Grated cheese (50 g or .5 cup)
- Salt (1 pinch)
- 1 Skillet

1.Warm the Air Fryer at 320º Fahrenheit.
2.Prepare a skillet (medium heat) and pour in the oil.
3.Chop the mushrooms and onions. Toss into the pan and sauté for about five minutes before adding them to the Air Fryer.
4.Whisk the eggs and salt. Dump it into the fryer with a sprinkle of cheese.
5.Set the timer for 10 minutes and remove to serve.

Chicken Breakfast Burrito
Serves: 1-2
- Eggs (2)
- Chicken or turkey breast (3-4 slices)
- Avocado (.25 of 1)
- Bell pepper (.25 of 1)
- Mozzarella cheese (.125 cup - grated) Pepper and salt (1 pinch each)
- Salsa (2 tbsp.)
- Tortilla (1)

1.Heat the fryer to reach 392º Fahrenheit.
2.Slice the bell pepper and avocado; and set aside. In a small mixing container, whisk the eggs, pepper, and salt.
3.Fold the fixings into a small pan and arrange it in the Air Fryer basket.
4.Set the timer for 5 minutes.
5.When done, transfer the egg from the pan, add the fixings, and load the tortilla. Combine all of the fixings and wrap it.
6.Add a piece of foil to the Air Fryer tray and add the burrito. Heat for three minutes at 356º Fahrenheit.
7.Garnish as desired and serve.

Chocolate & Avocado Muffins
Serves: 7
- Apple cider vinegar (1 tsp.)
- Almond flour (1 cup) Baking soda (.5 tsp.) Stevia powder (3 scoops)
- Egg (1)
- Melted dark chocolate (1 oz.) Butter (4 tbsp.)
- Pitted avocado (.5 cup)

1.Heat the Air Fryer at 355º Fahrenheit.
2.Whisk the baking soda, almond flour, and the vinegar. Melt and add in the chocolate and stevia powder.
3.Whisk the egg in another bowl and add to the mixture along with the butter.
4.Peel, cube, and mash the avocado and add. Blend using a hand mixer until smooth. Pour into the muffin forms (halfway full). Cook them for nine minutes.
5.Reduce the heat (340º Fahrenheit) and cook for another nine minutes.
6.Chill before serving for the best results.

Churros
Serves: 6
- Butter (.25 cup)
- Milk (.5 cup) Salt (1 pinch salt)

- All-purpose flour (.5 cup) Eggs (2)
- White sugar (.25 cup)
- Ground cinnamon (.5 tsp.)

1.Heat the Air Fryer at 340º Fahrenheit.
2.Melt the butter in a saucepan using the med-high heat setting. Pour in milk and add salt. Lower heat to medium and let it boil, continuously stirring with a wooden spoon.
3.Quickly add flour all at once. Keep stirring until the dough comes together.
4.Remove from the heat and cool it for 5-7 minutes. Mix in eggs with a wooden spoon until the choux pastry comes together.
5.Spoon the dough into a pastry bag that is fitted with a large star tip. Pipe the dough into strips straight into the Air Fryer basket.
6.Air-fry the churros a for five minutes.
7.In a small mixing container, whisk the cinnamon and sugar (shallow is best).
8.Remove the fried churros from fryer and roll in the cinnamon- sugar mixture.

Delicious Doughnuts In A Jiffy
Serves: 4
- Flaky jumbo refrigerated dough biscuits (1 can) Ground cinnamon (1.5 tsp.)
- White granulated sugar (.5 cup) Coconut oil or ghee (as needed)

1.Prepare the fryer to 350º Fahrenheit.
2.Arrange the biscuits on a cutting board. Use a one-inch biscuit cutter to remove the centers.
3.Grease the basket with the oil/ghee.
4.Whisk the sugar and cinnamon.
5.Air-fry for five to six minutes. Fry the holes for three to four minutes.
6.Transfer to a dish and brush using the butter, garnishing using a cinnamon/sugar mixture's sprinkle.

French Toast Soldiers
Serves:2
- Wholemeal bread (4 slices)
- Large eggs (2) Whole milk (.25 cup)
- Brown sugar (.25 cup)
- Honey (1 tbsp.)
- Cinnamon (1 tsp.)
- Nutmeg (1 pinch) Icing sugar (1 pinch)

1.Chop the bread slices into "soldiers." Each slice should make four soldiers.
2.Combine and mix the rest of the fixings (apart from the icing sugar) into a mixing bowl.
3.Dip each one into the mixture. You'll have 16 pieces.
4.Place them on 320º Fahrenheit for 10 minutes or until they're crispy like toast. Halfway through cooking, flip them over so that both sides of the soldiers will be evenly cooked.
5.Garnish using fresh berries and a dusting of icing sugar.

Ham - Egg - Mushroom & Cheese Croissant
Serves: 1
- Egg (1)
- Mozzarella or cheddar cheese (1.8 oz.) Honey shaved ham (3 slices) Croissant (1)
- Halved cherry tomatoes (4)

- Small quartered button mushrooms (4) Optional: Roughly chopped rosemary sprig (half of 1)

1. Help prevent the batter from sticking by lightly greasing the baking dish. Set the Air Fryer temperature to reach 320° Fahrenheit.
2. Measure and add half of the cheese in the bottom of the dish. Add the sliced ham. Leave a space in the center portion of the ham. Break and add the egg with a sprinkle of the rosemary, salt, and pepper.
3. Sprinkle with the last of the cheese.
4. Arrange in the basket and air-fry for eight minutes.
5. Air fry the croissant for about four minutes. Serve when the egg is set.

Ham Hash
Serves: 3
- Ham (10 oz.)
- Parmesan (5 oz.)
- Onion (.5 of 1)
- Butter (1 tbsp.)
- Egg (1)
- Black pepper (1 tsp.) Paprika (1 tsp.)
- Also Needed: 3 ramekins

1. Set the Air Fryer at 350° Fahrenheit.
2. Peel and dice the onion. Shred the parmesan cheese and slice the ham into small strips.
3. Whisk and mix in the egg, salt, pepper, and paprika.
4. Combine all of the fixings and add to the ramekins with a sprinkle of parmesan.
5. Air Fryer for 10 minutes.
6. Transfer to your plate, and lightly scramble to serve.

Loaded Hash Browns
Serves: 4
- Russet potatoes (3)
- Red & green peppers (.25 cup each) Onions (.25 cup)
- Garlic (2 cloves)
- Paprika (1 tsp.) Olive oil (2 tsp.)
- Salt & pepper (as desired)

1. Warm the Air Fryer at 400° Fahrenheit,
2. Prep the fixings. Chop the onions, garlic, and peppers. Use the biggest holes of a cheese grater to prepare the potatoes.
3. Toss into a bowl of cold water to remove the starchiness and make them crunchy (20-25 min.).
4. Drain the water and dry in a towel. Place in a bowl and mix with the fixings. Toss them into the Air Fryer for 10 minutes.
5. Chill slightly before serving.

Pepperoni - Egg & Cheese Pizza
Serves: 1
- Oregano (.5 tsp.)
- Basil (.5 tsp.)
- Eggs (2)
- Shredded mozzarella cheese (2 tbsp.)
- Thinly sliced pepperoni (4 pieces)
- Also Needed: 1 ramekin

1. Whisk the eggs, basil, and oregano.
2. Pour the eggs into the ramekin, and add the pepperoni and cheese.
3. Arrange the ramekin in the Air Fryer for three minutes and serve.

Sausage Patties
Serves: 4
- Sausage patties (12 oz pkg.)
- Cooking oil spray

1. Warm the Air Fryer at 400° Fahrenheit.
2. Arrange the patties in a single layer, working in batches if needed. Set the timer for five minutes.
3. Flip the sausage over and cook until they reach 160° Fahrenheit on an instant- read thermometer or about three minutes.

Sausage Wraps
Serves: 8
- Crescent roll dough (1 can - 8-count)
- American cheese (2 slices)
- Heat & Serve Sausages (8)
- Wooden skewers (8)
- Optional for Dipping: BBQ sauce, ketchup or syrup

1. Set the Air Fryer to 380° Fahrenheit. Open the sausages, and separate the rolls.
2. Slice the cheese into quarters and add the pieces starting on the triangle's widest part to the tip. Add the sausage.
3. Gather each end and roll-over the sausage and cheese. Pinch each side together. Add these in two batches to the fryer.
4. Cook for 3-4 minutes.
5. Remove from the fryer and add a skewer. Set it out for serving with the desired garnish.

Scrambled Eggs
Serves: 1
- Butter (for the fryer basket)
- Eggs (2)
- Salt & black pepper (to your liking)
- Optional: Cheese & tomatoes

1. Warm the Air Fryer at 285° Fahrenheit for about five minutes. Melt a small portion of butter, spreading it out evenly.
2. Whisk and dump the eggs and any other desired fixings desired. Open the fryer every few minutes to whisk the eggs.
3. Serve with a serving of toast or have a scrambled egg sandwich.

Sweet Potato Hash
Serves: 6
- Large sweet potato (2)
- Bacon (2 slices - cut into small pieces) Olive oil (2 tbsp.)
- Smoked paprika (1 tbsp.) Sea salt (1 tsp.)
- Ground black pepper (1 tsp.) Dried dill weed (1 tsp.)

1. Set the Air Fryer at 400° Fahrenheit.
2. Dice the sweet potatoes and combine with the bacon, olive oil, paprika, salt, pepper, and dill in a large bowl.
3. Toss the mixture into the Air Fryer. Air-fry for 12-16 minutes.
4. Check and stir after ten minutes, and then every three minutes until crispy and browned.

Western Omelet
Serves: 4
- Eggs (5)

- Cream cheese (3 tbsp.) Cilantro (1 tsp.)
- Oregano (1 tsp.)
- Shredded parmesan cheese (3 oz.) Green pepper (1)
- Yellow diced onion (1.5) Olive oil (1 tsp.)
- Butter (1 tsp.)
- Also Needed: 1 Skillet

1.Whisk the eggs, cilantro, oregano, and parmesan. Mix in the cream cheese. Set the Air Fryer at 360° Fahrenheit.
2.Pour the eggs into the fryer basket. Set the timer for 10 minutes.
3.Chop the onions and peppers. Pour oil into a skillet using the medium heat temperature setting. Sauté for 8 minutes.
4.When the eggs are done, serve and garnish with the sautéd veggies.

Sweet Potato Hash

Serves: 6
- 2 slices bacon, chopped
- 2 sweet potatoes, cubed
- 1 tablespoon smoked paprika 2 tablespoons olive oil
- 1 teaspoon dried dill weed Salt and pepper to taste

1.Preheat your ninja air fryer to 400 degrees f.
2.Toss all the in a bowl.
3.Transfer to the air fryer.
4.Cook for 15 minutes, stirring every 3 minutes.

Breakfast Frittata

Serves: 2
- 4 eggs, beaten
- 1 green onion, chopped
- 2 tablespoons bell pepper, chopped 1/2 cup cheddar cheese
- 1/4 lb. Breakfast sausage, cooked, removed from casing and crumbled
- Cooking spray

1.Mix all the in a bowl.

2. Preheat your air fryer to 360 degrees f and spray with oil.
3.Pour the egg mixture into a small cake pan.
4.Place inside the air fryer.
5.Cook for 20 minutes.

Mexican Hash Browns

Serves: 4
- 2 lb. Potatoes, cubed and soaked in water for 20 minutes 1 tablespoon olive oil, divided
- 1 red bell pepper, chopped
- 1 jalapeno pepper, sliced into rings 1 onion, chopped
- 1/2 teaspoon ground cumin
- 1/2 teaspoon taco seasoning mix Salt and pepper to taste

1.Preheat your air fryer to 320 degrees f.
2.Toss the potatoes in half of the oil.
3.Cook in the air fryer for 20 minutes, shaking every 5 minutes.
4.In a bowl, add the rest of the .

5.Mix well.
6.Add to the air fryer and cook for another 5 minutes.

French Toast Sticks

Serves: 2
- 1/4 cup almond milk - 2 eggs, beaten 1 teaspoon cinnamon
- 1 teaspoon vanilla extract
- 4 slices bread, sliced into sticks

1.Preheat your ninja air fryer to 360 degrees f.
2.Mix all the in a bowl except the bread.
3.Dip the bread sticks into the mixture.
4.Cook in the air fryer basket in batches, for 10 minutes each batch,turning halfway through.

Breakfast Sausage

Serves:4
- 12 oz. Sausage patties
- Cooking spray

1.Preheat your air fryer to 400 degrees f.
2.Add the patties in the air fryer basket and spray with oil.
3.Cook for 5 minutes.
4.Turn and cook for another 4 minutes.

Ham & Egg Tarts

Serves: 4
- 1 sheet puffy pastry
- 4 tablespoons cheese, shredded
- 4 tablespoons ham, cooked and diced 4 eggs

1.Preheat your air fryer to 400 degrees f.
2.Slice puffy pastry into 4.
3.Place in the air fryer basket for 6 minutes.
4.Make an indentation in the puffy pastry.
5.Add cheese and ham on top.
6.Add the egg on top.
7.Cook for 5 minutes.

Churros V2

Serves:6
- 1/2 cup milk
- 1/4 cup butter, melted Salt to taste
- 1/2 cup all-purpose flour 2 eggs - 1/4 cup Sugar
- 1/2 teaspoon ground cinnamon

1.Mix milk, butter and salt in a pan over medium heat.
2.Add the flour and egg and mix well.
3.Transfer mixture into a pastry bag.
4.Pipe the dough to create strips and cook in the air fryer for 5 minutes.
5.Combine cinnamon and Sugar in a bowl.
6.
7.Sprinkle the churros with this mixture.

Bacon

Serves: 6
- 16 oz. Bacon

1.Preheat your air fryer to 390 degrees f.
2.Add the bacon to the air fryer basket.
3.Cook for 7 minutes.

4.Flip and cook for 8 minutes.

Scotch Eggs
Serves: 6
Sauce:
- 3 tablespoons mango flavored yogurt 1 tablespoon mayonnaise
- Salt and pepper to taste Pinch curry powder

Eggs:
- 1 lb. Pork sausage
- 6 hard-boiled eggs, peeled 1/4 cup flour
- 2 eggs, beaten
- 1 cup panko breadcrumbs Cooking spray

1.Mix the sauce and refrigerate.
2.Create 6 patties from the ground pork.
3.Wrap the hardboiled eggs with the patties.
4.Dip in the beaten eggs and cover with breadcrumbs.
5.Place these in the air fryer.
6.Cook at 390 degrees f for 12 minutes or until crispy.
7.Serve with the sauce.

Potato Latkes
Serves: 5
- 16 oz. Hash browns
- 1/2 cup onion, grated 1 egg, beaten
- Salt and pepper to taste
- 2 tablespoons breadcrumbs
- Cooking spray

1.Preheat your air fryer to 375 degrees f.
2.Squeeze moisture out of the onion and hash browns.
3.Season the egg with the salt and pepper.
4.Add the potatoes and the breadcrumbs.
5.Mix well.
6.Form patties from the mixture.
7.Spray air fryer basket with oil.
8.Transfer patties in the air fryer basket.
9. Cook for 10 minutes or until golden.

Salmon Patties
Serves: 4
Sauce:
- 1/2 teaspoon lemon juice
- 1/2 cup light mayonnaise
- 2 pinches cajun seasoning
- 1 teaspoon garlic, minced

Patties:
- 12 oz. Salmon, flaked or chopped 1 tablespoon chives, chopped
- 1 teaspoon parsley, chopped 1 teaspoon garlic, minced Salt to taste
- 1 tablespoon flour Cooking spray

1.Combine sauce in a bowl.
2.Refrigerate until ready to use.
3.Mix the for the patties in a bowl.
4.Form patties from this mixture.
5.Preheat your air fryer to 350 degrees f.
6.Cook the patties for 15 minutes.
7.Serve with the sauce.

Breaded Shrimp
Serves: 4

Sauce:
- 1 tablespoon hot sauce
- 1/4 cup sweet chili sauce
- 1/2 cup light mayonnaise

Shrimp:
- 1 lb. Shrimp, peeled and deveined
- 1 egg, beaten
- 1 cup breadcrumbs

1.Blend hot sauce, sweet chili sauce and mayo in a bowl.
2.Cover and refrigerate.
3.Dip the shrimp in egg and then cover with breadcrumbs.
4.Add to the ninja air fryer basket.
5.Cook at 350 degrees f for 12 minutes or until golden and crispy.
6.Serve with the spicy sauce.

Roasted Cauliflower & Broccoli
Serves: 6
- 2 tablespoons olive oil
- 1/4 teaspoon paprika
- 1/2 teaspoon garlic powder Salt and pepper to taste
- 3 cups cauliflower florets
- 3 cups broccoli florets, steamed

1.Preheat your air fryer to 400 degrees f.
2.Mix the oil, paprika, garlic powder, salt and pepper in a bowl.
3.Toss the veggies in the mixture.
4.Cook for 10 to 12 minutes, shaking once or twice.

Garlic Cheese Bread
Serves: 2
- 1 egg, beaten
- 1/4 cup parmesan cheese, grated
- 1 cup mozzarella cheese
- 1/2 teaspoon garlic powder

1.Cover the air fryer basket with parchment paper.
2.Mix all the in a bowl.
3.Form a round shape from the mixture.
4.Add to the air fryer basket.
5.Cook for 10 minutes.

Buttermilk Fried Chicken
Serves: 4
- 1/2 teaspoon hot sauce
- 1 cup buttermilk
- 1/2 teaspoon garlic
- Salt
- 1/4 cup tapioca flour
- Salt and pepper to taste 1 egg, beaten
- 1/2 cup all-purpose flour
  - /2 teaspoons brown Sugar 1/2 teaspoon onion powder
- 1 teaspoon garlic powder 1/2 teaspoon paprika
- 1/4 teaspoon oregano 1 lb. Chicken thighs

1.Mix hot sauce and milk in a plate.
2.Combine the garlic salt, tapioca flour, salt and pepper in another dish.
3.Transfer the egg to a bowl.
4.Blend the rest of the except the chicken.

5.Dip each chicken in the milk mixture, tapioca mixture, egg and seasoned flour. Cook in the air fryer at 380 degrees f for 10 minutes.

6.Turn and cook for another 10 minutes.

Air-Fried Scotch Eggs

Serves:6

- 1 egg, lightly beaten
- 1 lb. Bulk sausage, uncooked 5 hard-boiled eggs
- 1 tbsp. Mustard or hot sauce Oil spray, for coating
- 1 cup almond flour or coconut flour

1.Peel the hard-boiled eggs and set aside.

2.Meanwhile, divide the sausage into 6 equal parts and flatten to form a 4-inch wide patty. Lay the boiled eggs in the center and wrap the patty around it. Repeat the process until you have used up all the eggs and sausage patties.

3.Dip each sausage-wrapped patty in the beaten egg and then into almond flour for coating. Spray evenly all sides with oil.

4.Place wrapped patties in the air fryer, making sure they aren't overcrowded. You may use the second layer of the air fryer basket to accommodate all patties. Attach the instant pot duo crisp air fryer lid and air fry at 400 degrees f for 12-16 minutes, turning halfway through Cooking.

5.Once done, cut in halves and serve with mustard on top. You may also serve it with hot sauce.

Pepperoni Pasta

Serves:8

- 16 oz. Rigatoni pasta
- 1 lb. Italian sausage
- oz. Pepperoni, sliced
- 1 (28 oz.) Can diced italian tomatoes, with juice 1 (28 oz.)
- Can tomato puree
- oz. Mozzarella cheese, shredded 2 cups chicken stock
- 1 cup red wine
- 1 medium onion, chopped 2 tbsps. Garlic, minced
- ½ tsp. Oregano
- ½ tsp. Basil
- ¼ tsp. Red pepper, crushed
- ¼ tsp. Ground black pepper
- ½ tsp. Salt

1. Set the instant pot to saute then cook the onions, sausage and garlic until browned.

1.Stir in the spices, salt, pepper, the chicken stock, red wine, and half of the pepperoni. Make sure that everything is well combined.

2.Add the tomato puree and tomatoes and stir lightly.

3.Pour in the pasta, gently pressing down to ensure that it's covered with liquid. Don't stir so that the pasta will be kept at the bottom of the pot.

4.Pressure cook on high for about 6 minutes or until al dente.

5.Quick-release and remove the lid.

6.Add in ⅓ of the cheese then stir well. Add the remaining cheese on top and layer the rest of the pepperoni on top of the cheese.

7.Attach the air fryer lid to the instant pot and air-fry at 400 degrees f for 5 minutes.

8.Once cooked, remove the lid and serve the pepperoni pasta.

Cheesy Air Fryer Spaghetti

Serves:6

- 1 lb. Ground beef
- 1 (24 oz.) Jar spaghetti sauce
- 8 oz. Spaghetti noodles, broken into thirds
- 1½ cups mozzarella cheese, grated and divided
- ½ cup parmesan cheese grated 2 cups beef broth
- 1 onion, diced
- 1 green onion, diced (optional) 2 tbsps. Olive oil
- ¼ tsp. Salt

1.Set the instant pot to saute then drizzle the bottom of the steel pot with olive oil.

2.Sauté the onions and ground beef then season with salt. Continue to cook until the ground beef is no longer pink.

3.Evenly spread the cooked meat to cover the bottom of the pot entirely.

4.Pour the spaghetti sauce then add the broth into the jar. Put the lid back on and shake the jar to mix the meat and broth with the remaining sauce. Pour the broth into the pot but do not stir.

5.Sprinkle the broken spaghetti noodles on top of the liquid.

6.Using a spoon spatula, gently submerge the noodles into the sauce but do not stir.

7.Place the pressure cooker lid and close the steam valve.

8.Pressure cook on high for 9 minutes.

9.Quick-release and remove the lid.

10.Stir in one cup of mozzarella cheese until it melts.

11.Sprinkle the remaining half cup of the mozzarella

12.cheese plus the parmesan on top of the spaghetti. Top with the diced green onions then closes the pot with air fryer lid.

13.Air fry at 400degrees f for 5 minutes, until the cheese melts and gets golden brown on top.

14.Serve and enjoy.

Healthy Breakfast Bake

Serves: 2

- 1 slice whole grain bread, torn into pieces 4 eggs
- 1½ cups baby spinach
- ¼ cup + 2 tbsps. Shredded cheddar cheese, divided
- ½ cup bell pepper, diced 2 tbsps. 1% low-Fat milk 1 tsp. Hot sauce
- ½ tsp. Kosher salt

1.Preheat your air fryer to 250 degrees f.

2.Spritz a 6-inch soufflé dish with nonstick spray and set aside.

3.In a medium bowl, add the beaten Waffle Omelette

Recipe

4. Gently fold in the spinach, ¼ cup cheddar, bread pieces and bell peppers.

5. Pour the egg mixture into the prepared soufflé dish and place the dish into the air fryer basket.

6. Set up the trivet to the inner pot of the cooker and place the basket on top.

7. Cook at 250 degrees f for 20 minutes. Sprinkle the top with the remaining cheese and cook for another 5 minutes or until the eggs are set and the edges are golden brown.

8. Remove from the air fryer basket and set aside for about 10 minutes before serving.

Perfect Bacon & Croissant Breakfast

Serves: 2

- bacon-croissant sandwiches
- 4 pieces thick-cut bacon 2 croissants, sliced
- 2 eggs
- 1 tbsp. Butter

For the bacon barbecue sauce:

- ½ cup ketchup
- 2 tbsps. Apple cider vinegar 1 tbsp. Brown Sugar
- 1 tbsp. Molasses
- ½ tbsp. Worcestershire sauce
- ¼ tsp. Onion powder
- ¼ tsp. Mustard powder
- ¼ tsp. Liquid smoke

1. Preheat your air fryer to 390 degrees f.

2. Meanwhile, incorporate all the barbecue sauce in a small saucepan. Place the pan over medium heat and bring it to a simmer until the sauce thickens slightly.

3. Place the bacon cuts flat on a tray and brush them with barbecue sauce on one side.

4. Transfer to the air fryer basket with the brushed side up. Cook for about 4-5 minutes then flip the bacon. Brush the other side with bacon sauce and cook for another 5 minutes (or until your desired doneness is achieved).

5. In a medium-size frying pan, melt the butter and fry the eggs according to your preference.

6. Once done, place the eggs at the bottom of each croissant. Top

7. them with two bacon slices each and close with the croissant on top.

8. Serve with your favorite breakfast beverage.

Ranchero Brunch Crunch Wraps

Serves:2

- 2 Servings tofu scramble (or vegan egg) 2 large flour tortillas
- 2 small corn tortillas
- ⅓ cup pinto beans, cooked
- ½ cup classic ranchero sauce
- ½ avocado, peeled and sliced
- 2 fresh jalapeños, stemmed and sliced

1. Assemble the large tortillas on a work surface. Arrange the crunch wraps by stacking the following in order: tofu or egg scramble, jalapeños, ranchero sauce, corn tortillas, avocado, and pinto beans. You can add more ranchero sauce if desired.

2. Fold the large flour tortilla around the fillings until sealed completely.

3. Place one crunch wrap in the air fryer basket and set the basket on top of the trivet.

4. Air-fry each crunch wrap at 350 degrees f (or 180°c) for 6 minutes. Remove from the basket and transfer to a plate.

5. Repeat step 3 and 4 for the other crunch wrap.

Crunchy Breakfast Nuggets

Serves: 4

- 1 lb. Boneless, skinless chicken breasts
- ⅔ cup whole wheat panko breadcrumbs
- ⅓ cup parmesan cheese, freshly grated
- ¼ cup whole wheat flour 1 large egg
- 2 tsps. Dried parsley flakes
- Olive oil spray
- ¼ tsp. Salt or to taste
- ¼ tsp. Black pepper

1. Preheat your air fryer 400 degrees f for about 8-10 minutes.

2. Meanwhile, slice the chicken breasts into 1-inch cubes.

3. Prepare three shallow bowls; mix the flour, salt, and pepper in the first bowl. Lightly beat the egg in the second and combine the parmesan, panko, and parsley flakes in the third.

4. Working one piece at a time, dredge the chicken in the flour

5. mixture and press lightly to adhere. Next, dip it into the egg, removing the excess egg as needed. Finally, coat with the panko mixture, pressing lightly to help evenly coat the chicken.

6. Arrange the nuggets in the air fryer basket in a single layer. Liberally spritz them with Cooking spray to help them get crispy and golden brown.

7. Air-fry each batch for about 7 minutes or until the internal temperature reaches 165 degrees f (or 74°c). Monitor them to make sure that they're not overcooked.

8. Serve with your favorite dip and your favorite side dish.

Air Fryer Garlic Bread

Serves:4

- 4 slices ciabatta
- ¼ cup parmesan, freshly grated
- 1 tbsp. Salted butter
- 3 cloves garlic, crushed
- A few pinches of dried parsley

1. Preheat your air fryer to 360 degrees f.

2. Put the butter in a small bowl and microwave for 10 seconds or until softened.

3. Add the cheese, garlic and dried parsley to the bowl of butter.

4. Spread the garlic mixture to both sides of ciabatta slices.

5. Assemble the slices in the air fryer basket and air-fry for about 3-5 minutes.

6. Serve warm.

Salsa Eggs

Serves: 2

- ½ green bell pepper, chopped
- ½ red bell pepper, chopped 2 eggs, whisked
- 1 tablespoon mild salsa Cooking spray
- ½ tablespoon chives, chopped
- Salt and black pepper, to taste
- ¼ cup cheddar cheese, grated

1.Grease 2 ramekins with Cooking spray and divide the bell peppers into each.
1.In a bowl, mix the eggs with the salsa, chives, salt, and pepper and whisk well.
2.Divide the egg mixture between each ramekin and sprinkle thecheese on top.
3.Preheat the air fryer at 360f. Arrange the ramekins in the frying basket.
4.Cook for 20 minutes at 360f.
5.Serve.

Banana Oats
Serves: 2

- 1 cup old fashioned oats
- ½ teaspoon baking powder 2 tablespoons Sugar
- ½ teaspoon vanilla extract
- 1 banana, peeled and mashed
- ½ cup milk
- ½ cup heavy cream
- 1 egg, whisked - 1 tablespoon butter Cooking spray

1.In a bowl, mix the oats with the baking powder, Sugar, and other except for the Cooking spray and whisk well. Divide the mixture into 2 ramekins.
2.Grease the air fryer with Cooking spray and preheat at 340f.
3.Place the ramekins in the air fryer and cook for 20 minutes.
4.Serve.

Jalapeno Popper Egg Cups
Serves: 2

- 4 eggs
- ¼ cup pickled jalapenos, chopped 2 ounces full-Fat cream cheese
- ½ cup shredded sharp cheddar cheese

1.Beat the eggs in a bowl, then pour into four silicon muffin cups.
2.In a bowl, add cream cheese, jalapenos, and cheddar. Microwave for 30 seconds and stir.
3.Take about ¼ of the mixture and place it in the center of one egg cup.
4.Repeat with the remaining mixture.
5.Place egg cups into the air fryer basket.
6.Cook at 320f for 10 minutes.
7.Serve.

Cheese Sandwich
Serves: 2

- 4 cheddar cheese slices
- 4 teaspoons butter
- 4 bread slices

1.Place 2 cheese slices between the 2 bread slices and spread the butter on the outside of both pieces of bread.

2.Repeat to assemble the remaining sandwich.
3.Place sandwiches in the air fryer basket and cook at 370f for 8 minutes. Turn halfway through.
4.Serve.

French Toast
Serves: 2

- 4 bread slices
- 1 tablespoon powdered cinnamon 1 teaspoon vanilla extract
- ⅔ cup milk
- 2 eggs

1.In a bowl, combine eggs, vanilla, cinnamon, and milk. Mix well.
2.Dip each bread slice into the egg mixture and shake off excess.
3.Place bread slices in a pan.
4.Place pan in the air fryer and cook at 320f for 3 minutes. Flip and cook for 3 more minutes, then serve.

Breakfast Sausage Frittata
Serves: 2

- 2 eggs
- 1 tablespoon butter, melted
- 2 tablespoons cheddar cheese
- 1 bell pepper, chopped
- 1 tablespoon spring onions, chopped
- 1 breakfast sausage patty, chopped
- Salt and pepper, to taste

1.Spray a 4-inch mini pan with Cooking spray and set aside.
2.Add chopped sausage patty to a prepared dish and air fry at 350f for 5 minutes.

3. Meanwhile, in a bowl, whisk the eggs, pepper, and salt.
4.Add bell peppers, spring onions, and mix well.
5.Once the sausage is done, add them to the egg mixture and mix well, then pour it into the 4-inch pan.
6.Sprinkle with cheese and air fry at 350f for 5 minutes.
7.Serve.

Scrambled Eggs With Toasted Bread
Serves: 2

- 4 eggs
- 2 bread slices
- Salt and pepper, to taste

1.Warm bread slices in the air fryer at 400f for 3 minutes.
2.Add eggs t a pan and season with salt and pepper. Mix well.
3.Place pan in the air fryer and cook at 360f for 2 minutes. Stir quickly and cook for 4 more minutes.
4.Stir well and transfer the scrambled eggs over the toasted bread slices.
5.Serve.

Egg, Spinach, And Sausage Cups
Serves: 2

- ¼ cup eggs, beaten

- 4 teaspoons shredded jack cheese
- 4 tablespoons spinach, chopped
- 4 tablespoons sausage, cooked and crumbled Salt and pepper

1. Whisk everything together in a bowl and mix well.
2. Pour batter into muffin cups and place them in the air fryer basket.
3. Bake at 330f for 10 minutes.
4. Cool and serve.

Turkey Burrito
Serves: 2

- 4 slices turkey breast, cooked
- ½ red bell pepper, sliced
- 2 eggs
- 1 small avocado, peeled, pitted, and sliced
- 2 tablespoons salsa
- Salt and black pepper, to taste
- ⅛ cup mozzarella cheese, grated
- Tortillas for serving

1. In a bowl, whisk the eggs with salt and pepper. Pour them in a pan and place in the air fryer's basket.
2. Cook at 400f for 5 minutes. Remove from the fryer and transfer
3. eggs to a plate.
4. Arrange tortillas on a working surface. Divide eggs, turkey meat, bell pepper, cheese, salsa, and avocado between them.
5. Roll the burritos. Line the air fryer basket with tin foil and place the burritos inside.
6. Heat the burritos at 300f for 3 minutes.
7. Serve.

Breakfast Bread Pudding
Serves: 2

- ¼ pound white bread, cubed
- tablespoons milk
- tablespoons water
- 1 teaspoon cornstarch
- ¼ cup apple, peeled, cored, and chopped 2 ½ tablespoons honey
- ½ teaspoon vanilla extract
- 1 teaspoon cinnamon powder
- ¾ cup flour - ⅓ cup brown Sugar 1 ½ ounces soft butter

1. In a bowl, combine bread, apple, cornstarch, vanilla, cinnamon, honey, milk, and water. Whisk well.
2. In another bowl, combine butter, Sugar, and flour and mix well.
3. Press half of the crumble mixture into the bottom of the air fryer,
4. add bread and apple mixture, then add the rest of the crumble. Cook at 350f for 22 minutes.
5. Divide bread pudding onto plates and serve.

Eggs In Avocado Boats
Serves: 2

- 1 large avocado, cut in half lengthwise
- 2 eggs
- Salt and pepper, to taste
- 1 cup cheddar, shredded
- 1 teaspoon parsley

1. Preheat the air fryer at 300f.

2. In a bowl, crack the eggs and mix with the pulp of avocado after de-seeding it.
3. Add salt, pepper, and shredded cheddar.
4. Pour the mixture into the empty avocado halves.
5. Cook in the air fryer for 5 minutes.
6. Sprinkle with chopped parsley and serve.

Ham Egg Cups
Serves: 2

- (1-ounce) slices deli ham 4 eggs
- 2 tablespoons full-Fat sour cream
- ¼ cup green bell pepper,
- 2 tablespoons red bell pepper, diced 2 tablespoons white onion, diced
- ½ cup shredded cheddar cheese

1. Place 1 slice of ham on the bottom of 4 baking cups.
2. In a bowl, whisk eggs with sour cream. Stir in onion, red pepper, and green pepper.
3. Pour the egg mixture into the baking cups.
4. Top with cheddar and place cups into the air fryer basket.
5. Cook to 320f for 12 minutes.
6. Serve.

Breakfast Cal Zone
Serves: 2

- ¾ cup shredded mozzarella cheese
- ¼ cup almond flour
- ½ ounce full-Fat cream cheese 1 whole egg
- 2 eggs, scrambled
- ¼ pound breakfast sausage, cooked and crumbled
- 4 tablespoons shredded cheddar cheese

1. Add almond flour, mozzarella, and cream cheese to a bowl. Microwave for 1 minute.
2. Stir until the mixture is smooth and forms a ball. Add the egg and stir until dough forms.
3. Place the dough between two sheets of parchment and roll out to a
4. ¼-inch thickness.
5. Cut the dough into four rectangles.
6. In a bowl, mix cooked sausage and scrambled eggs.
7. Divide the blend between each piece of dough, placing it on the lower half of the rectangle. Sprinkle each with cheddar.
8. Fold to cover and seal the edges. Cover the air fryer basket with parchment paper and cook at 380f for 15 minutes. Flip the Cal zones halfway through the Cooking time.
9. Serve.

Cheese Broccoli Frittata
Serves: 2

- 3 eggs
- 2 tbsp parmesan cheese, grated 1/4 tsp garlic powder
- 1/4 tsp onion powder
- 2 tbsp milk
- 1/2 cup bell pepper, chopped 1/2 cup broccoli florets Pepper
- Salt

1. Spray baking dish with cooking spray.

2.Place bell peppers and broccoli in the prepared baking dish.
3.In a bowl, whisk together eggs, milk, and seasoning.
4.Pour egg mixture over vegetables and sprinkle cheese on top.
5.Place steam rack into the instant pot then place baking dish on top of the rack.
6.Seal pot with air fryer lid and select air fry mode then set the temperature to 380 f and timer for 10 minutes.
7.Serve and enjoy.

Cranberry & Cinnamon Oatmeal

Serves: 4

- 2 cups old-fashioned oatmeal
- ¼ cup plain vinegar
- ½ tsp nutmeg powder
- 1 tbsp cinnamon powder
- ½ tsp vanilla extract 3¾ cups water
- ½ cup dried cranberries, plus more for garnish 2 raspberries, sliced
- ⅛ tsp salt
- Honey, for topping

1.Combine the oatmeal, water, vinegar, nutmeg, cinnamon, vanilla, cranberries, and salt in the pot. Seal the pressure lid, choose pressure cook mode and cook for 10 minutes on high. Press start.
2.When the timer has ended, perform a natural pressure release for 10 minutes, then carefully open the lid.
3.Stir the oatmeal, drizzle with honey and decorate with raspberries.
  1. Serve immediately.

Gruyere & Bacon Grits

Serves: 4

- slices smoked bacon, diced
- 1 ½ cups grated gruyere cheese 1 cup ground grits
- 2 tsp butter
- Salt and black pepper
- ½ cup water
- ½ cup milk

1.To preheat the cooker, select sear/sauté mode and set to high pressure. Cook bacon until crispy, about 5 minutes. Set aside.
2.Add the grits, butter, milk, water, salt, and pepper to the pot and stir using a spoon. Close the pressure lid and secure the pressure valve.
3.Choose the pressure mode and cook for 3 minutes on high. Press start.
4.Once the timer has ended, turn the vent handle and do a quick pressure release. Add in cheddar cheese and give the pudding a good stir with the same spoon.
5.Close crisping lid, press bake button and cook for 8 minutes on 370 f.
6.Press start key.
7.When ready, dish the cheesy grits into serving bowls and spoon over the crisped bacon.
8.Serve right away with toasted bread.

Speedy Pork Roast Sandwich With Slaw

Serves: 8

- 2 lb. Chuck roast
- ¼ cup Sugar
- 1 tsp spanish paprika
- 1 tsp garlic powder
- 1 white onion, sliced
- 2 cups beef broth
- Salt to taste
- 2 tbsp apple cider vinegar

Assembling:

- buns, halved
- 1 cup white cheddar cheese, grated 4 tbsp mayonnaise
- 1 cup red cabbage, shredded
- 1 cup white cabbage, shredded

1.Place the pork roast on a clean flat surface and sprinkle with paprika, garlic powder, Sugar, and salt. Use your hands to rub the seasoning on the meat.
2.Open the cooker, add beef broth, onions, pork, and apple cider vinegar.
3.Close the lid, secure the pressure valve, and select pressure mode on high pressure for 12 minutes. Press start.
4.Once the timer has ended, does a quick pressure release. Remove the roast to a cutting board and use two forks to shred them. Return to the pot, close the crisping lid, and cook for 3 minutes on air fry at 300 f.
5.In the buns, spread the mayo, add the shredded pork, some cooked
6.onions from the pot, and shredded red and white cabbage. Top with the cheese.

Bell Pepper & Salmon Cakes

Serves: 4

- 2 (5 oz) packs steamed salmon flakes 1 red onion, chopped
- Salt and black pepper to taste 1 tsp garlic powder
- 2 tbsp olive oil
- 1 red bell pepper, seeded and chopped 4 tbsp butter, divided
- eggs, cracked into a bowl 1 cup breadcrumbs
- tbsp mayonnaise
- 2 tsp worcestershire sauce
- ¼ cup chopped parsley

1.Turn on the cooker and select sear/sauté on high pressure. Heat oil and add half of the butter. Once it has melted, add the onions and
2.the chopped red bell peppers. Cook for 6 minutes while stirring occasionally. Press start.
3.In a mixing bowl, add salmon flakes, sautéed red bell pepper and onion, breadcrumbs, eggs, mayonnaise, Worcestershire sauce, garlic powder, salt, pepper, and parsley.
4.Use a spoon to mix well while breaking the salmon into the tiny

5.pieces. Use your hands to mold 4 patties out of the mixture.
6.Add the remaining butter to melt, and when melted, add the patties. Fry for 4 minutes, flipping once.
7.Close the crisping lid, select bake mode and bake for 4 minutes on 320 f.
8.Remove them onto a wire rack to rest. Serve.

Cheese Eggs With Prosciutto

Serves: 4

- 4 eggs, beaten
- 1 cup milk
- 1 orange bell pepper, seeded and chopped Salt and black pepper to taste
- 1 cup shredded Monterey jack cheese 8 ounces prosciutto, chopped
- 1 cup water

1. Put the almond milk, eggs, pink salt, and black pepper and whisk in a bowl until evenly combined and a creamy color has formed. Stir in the Monterey jack cheese.
2. Arrange the bell pepper and prosciutto onto a baking dish. Then, pour over the egg mixture, cover the pan with aluminum foil and put on the reversible rack.
3. Add the water into the pot, put the rack with the dish in the pot.
4. Then, seal the pressure lid, choose pressure and set to high. Set the time to 20 minutes. Choose start.
5. When done Cooking , perform a quick pressure release and carefully remove the lid.
6. Take out the dish from the pot and place it on a cooling rack. Cool for 5 minutes and serve.

Homemade Giant Pancake

Serves: 6

- cups all-purpose flour
- ¾ cup Sugar 5 eggs
- ⅓ cup olive oil
- ⅓ cup sparkling water
- ⅓ tsp salt
- 1 ½ tsp baking soda 2 tbsp maple syrup
- A dollop of whipped cream to serve

1. Start by pouring the flour, Sugar, eggs, olive oil, sparkling water, salt, and baking soda into a food processor and blend until smooth.
2. Pour the batter into the cooker and let it sit in there for 15 minutes. Close the lid and secure the pressure valve.
3. Select the pressure mode on low pressure for 10 minutes. Press start.
4. Once the timer goes off, press cancel, quick release the pressure valve to let out any steam and open the lid.
5. Gently run a spatula around the pancake to let lose any sticking.
6. Once ready, slide the pancake onto a serving plate and drizzle with maple syrup. Top with the whipped cream to serve.

Hash Browns With Pancetta

Serves: 3

- slices pancetta, chopped
- 1 white onion, diced
- 2 potatoes, peeled and grated 1 tsp sweet paprika
- 1 tsp pink salt
- 1 tsp ground black pepper 1 tsp garlic powder
- 3 eggs

1. Choose sear/sauté and set too high to preheat your cooker. Place in the pancetta and cook for 5 minutes, or until crispy.
2. Stir in the onion, potatoes, eggs, the sweet paprika, pink salt, black pepper, and garlic powder. Press the hash brown mixture.
3. Close the crisping lid, choose bake and cook for 25 minutes at 350 f.
4. Once the timer goes off, ensure the hash brown is perfectly golden brown on top. Serve immediately.

Easy Poached Eggs On Heirloom Ripe Tomatoes

Serves: 4

- large eggs
- 1 cup water
- 2 large heirloom ripe tomatoes, halved crosswise
- Salt and black pepper to taste
- 1 tsp chopped fresh herbs, of your choice 2 tbsp grated parmesan cheese
- Cooking spray

1. Pour the water into the cooker and fit the reversible rack.
2. Grease the ramekins with the Cooking spray and crack each egg into them.
3. Season with salt and pepper. Cover the ramekins with aluminum foil.
4. Place the cups on the trivet. Seal the lid.
5. Select steam mode for 3 minutes on high pressure. Press start.
6. Once the timer goes off, do a quick pressure release.
7. Use a napkin to remove the ramekins onto a flat surface.
8. In serving plates, share the halved tomatoes and toss the eggs in the ramekin over each tomato half.
9. Sprinkle with salt and pepper, parmesan, and garnish with chopped herbs.

Honey-Mustard Sausage Weenies

Serves: 4

- 20 hot dogs, cut into 4 pieces
- Salt and black pepper to taste
- 1 tsp dijon mustard
- 1 ½ tsp soy sauce
- ¼ cup honey
- ¼ cup red wine vinegar
- ½ cup tomato puree - ¼ cup water

1. Add the tomato puree, red wine vinegar, honey, soy sauce, Dijon mustard, salt, and black pepper in a medium bowl. Mix them with a spoon.
2. Put sausage weenies in the crisp basket and close the crisping lid.
3. Select air fry mode. Set the temperature to 370 f and the timer to 4 minutes. Press start. At the 2-minute mark, turn the sausages.
4. Once ready, open the lid and pour the sweet sauce over the sausage weenies.
5. Close the pressure lid, secure the pressure valve, and select pressure mode on high for 3 minutes. Press start.
6. Once the timer has ended, do a quick pressure release. Serve and enjoy.

Delicious Egg Brule

Serves: 8

- 8 large eggs
- 1 tsp Sugar Salt to taste
- 1 cup water for ice bath

1.Open the cooker, pour the water in, and fit the reversible rack in it. Put the eggs on the rack in a single layer, close the lid, secure the pressure valve, and select pressure on high pressure for 5 minutes. Press start. Once the timer has ended, do a quick pressure release, and open the pot.

2.Remove the eggs into the ice bath and peel the eggs. Put the peeled eggs in a plate and slice them in half.

3.Sprinkle a bit of salt on them and then followed by the Sugar. Lay onto your crisp basket fryer basket. Select air fry mode, set the temperature to 390 f and the time to 3 minutes.

Tasty Ham With Collard Greens

Serves: 4

- 20 oz collard greens, washed and cut
- 2 cubes of chicken bouillon
- cups water
- ½ cup diced sweet onion
- 2 ½ cups diced ham

1.Place the ham at the bottom of the inner pot. Add collard greens and onion.

2.Then, add chicken cubes to the water and dissolve it.

3.Pour the mixture into the pot. Close the lid, secure the pressure valve, to seal properly.

4.Select steam mode on high pressure for 5 minutes. Press start.

5.Once the timer has ended, do a quick pressure release, and open the lid.

6.Spoon the vegetables and the ham with sauce into a serving platter.

7.Serve with a side of steak dish of your choice.

Delicious Kale And Sausage

Serves: 4

- 1 medium sweet yellow onion
- medium eggs
- sausage links
- 2 cups kale, chopped
- 1 cup mushrooms
- Olive oil as needed

1.Take your ninja foodi grill and open lid, arrange grill grate and close top

2.Pre-heat ninja foodi by pressing the "grill" option and setting it to "high" and timer to 5 minutes

3.Let it pre-heat until you hear a beep

4.Arrange sausages over grill grate, lock lid and cook for 2 minutes, flip sausages and cook for 3 minutes more

5.Take sausages out

6.Take a baking pan and spread onion, kale, mushrooms, sausages and crack eggs on top

7.Arrange pan inside the grill and used the "bake" option to bake it at 350 degrees f for 5 minutes

8.Once done, open lid and serve

9.Enjoy!

Baked Eggs And Stuffed Pepper

Serves: 4

- 1 cup cheddar cheese, shredded
- slices bacon, cooked and chopped
- bell peppers, seeded and tops removed 4 large eggs
- Salt and pepper to taste Chopped parsley for garnish

1.Take your bell peppers and divide cheese and bacon between them, crack an egg into each of the bell peppers. Season them with salt and pepper

2.Pre-heat ninja foodi by pressing the "air crisp" option and setting it to "390 degrees f" and timer to 15 minutes

3.Let it pre-heat until you hear a beep

4.Transfer bell pepper to your Cooking basket and transfer to foodi grill, lock lid and cook for 10-15 minutes until egg whites are cooked well until the yolks are slightly runny

5.Remove peppers from the basket and garnish with parsley, serve and enjoy!

Grilled Maple Broccoli

Serves: 4

- 2 heads broccoli, cut into florets 4 tablespoons balsamic vinegar 2 teaspoons maple syrup
- tablespoons soy sauce 2 tablespoons canola oil
- Red pepper flakes and sesame seeds, to garnish

1.Take a mixing bowl and add soy sauce, oil, balsamic vinegar, maple syrup

2.Whisk well and add the broccoli and toss well

3.Arrange the grill grate and close the lid

4.Pre-heat ninja foodi by pressing the "grill" option and setting it to "max" and timer to 10 minutes

5.Let it pre-heat until you hear a beep

6.Arrange the broccoli over the grill grate, lock lid and cook until the timer reads zero

7.Serve warm with red pepper and enjoy!

Onion, Pepper And Mushroom Frittata

Serves: 4

- 4 large eggs
- 1/2 bell pepper, seeded and diced
- cremini mushrooms, sliced 1/2 onion, chopped
- 1/2 cup cheddar cheese, shredded 1/4 cup whole milk
- sea salt Black pepper

1.Take a medium bowl, add eggs and milk, then whisk them together

2.Season with salt and pepper

3.Add bell pepper, mushrooms, onion, and cheese mix to combine well

4.Preheat by selecting the "bake" option and setting it to 400 degrees f for 10 minutes

5.Pour the egg mixture into the baking pan and spread evenly

6.You will hear a beep after it pre-heated, then close the lid

7.Cook for 10 minutes

8.Serve and enjoy!

Regano Squash

Serves: 4

- 1 medium squash peeled, seeded butternut, cut into 1/2-inch slices 1 tablespoon olive oil
- 1 and 1/2 teaspoons oregano, dried 1 teaspoon thyme, dried
- 1/2 teaspoon salt
- 1/4 teaspoon black pepper

1.Take a mixing bowl and add all **,** combine well
2.Arrange the grill grate while closing the lid
3.Pre-heat ninja foodi by pressing the "grill" option and setting it to "med" and timer to 16 minutes
4. Let it pre-heat until you hear a beep
5.Arrange the squash slices over the grill grate, lock lid and cook for 8 minutes
6.Flip them and close the lid, cook for 8 minutes more
7.Serve warm and enjoy!

Awesome Peanut Butter And Banana Chips

Serves: 4

- **2** bananas, sliced into ¼ inch rounds
- 2 tablespoons creamy peanut butter

1.Take a medium-sized bowl and add banana slices with peanut butter, toss well until coated
2.If the butter is too thick, add 1-2 tablespoons water
3.Place banana slices flat on your crisper basket and arrange them in a single layer
4.Transfer basket to your grill grate
5.Pre-heat ninja foodi by pressing the "dehydrate" option and setting it to "135 degrees f" and timer to 15 minutes
6.Let it pre-heat until you hear a beep
7.Let them dehydrate until the default timer runs out
8.Once done, store them in airtight container and serve when needed
9.Enjoy!

Bacon And Tomato Omelet

Serves: 4

- whole eggs, whisked
- 1 tablespoon cheddar, grated
- 1/4-pound bacon, cooked and chopped
- 4 tomatoes, cubed
- 1 tablespoon parsley, chopped
- 1 tablespoon olive oil
- Salt and pepper to taste

1.Take a small pan and place it over medium heat, add bacon and sauté for 2 minutes until crisp
2.Take a bowl and add bacon, add remaining and gently stir. Sprinkle cheese on top
3.Pre-heat ninja foodi by pressing the "bake" option and setting it to "400 degrees f" and timer to 10 minutes
4.Let it pre-heat until you hear a beep
5.Pour mixture into a baking dish and transfer baking dish inside ninja foodi grill, let it bake for 8 minutes
6.Serve and enjoy!

Potato Pancakes

Serves: 4

- medium potatoes, peeled and cleaned 1

medium onion, chopped
- 1 beaten egg 1/4 milk
- 2 tablespoons unsalted butter 1/2aspoon garlic powder 1/4aspoon salt
- tablespoons all-purpose flour Pepper as needed

1.Peel your potatoes and shred them up
2. Soak the shredded potatoes under cold water to remove starch
3.Drain the potatoes
4.Take a bowl and add eggs, milk, butter, garlic powder, salt, and pepper
5.Add in flour
6.Mix well
7.Add the shredded potatoes
8.Pre-heat ninja foodi by pressing the "air crisp" option and setting it to "390 degrees f" and timer to 24 minutes
9.Let it pre-heat until you hear a beep
10.Add ¼ cup of the potato pancake batter to your
11.Cooking basket and cook for 12 minutes until the golden-brown texture is seen
12.Enjoy!

Cheesy Turkey Rice With Broccoli

Serves: 4

- 1 cup cooked, chopped turkey meat 1 and 1/2 tablespoons butter, melted
- 1/20 (10-ounce package) broccoli, frozen
- 1/2 (7 ounces package) whole wheat crackers, crushed 1/2 cup cheddar cheese, shredded
- 1/2 cup white rice, uncooked

1.Insert the crisper basket and close the hood
2.Pre-heat ninja foodi by pressing the "air crisp" option and setting it to 360 degrees f for 15 minutes
3.Bring boil 2 cups of water in a saucepan, stir in rice and simmer for 20 minutes
4.Grease the baking pan of the air fryer with Cooking spray
5.Mixed cooked rice, cheese, turkey and broccoli
6. Toss well to mix
7.Take a small bowl and mix melted butter and crushed crackers
8.Air fry for 20 minutes
9.Serve and enjoy!

Lunch Recipes

Chicken Fried Rice

Serves: 5-6
- Packed cooked chicken (1 cup)
- Cold cooked white rice (3 cups)
- Frozen carrots and peas (1 cup)
- Vegetable oil (1 tbsp.)
- Soy sauce (6 tbsp.)
- Diced onion (.5 cup)
- Also Needed: 7 by 2-inch cake pan

1. Set the Air Fryer at 360° Fahrenheit.
2. Cook and dice the chicken. Prepare the rice. Dice the onion.
3. Add the chilled rice, soy sauce, and oil into a mixing bowl. Stir well.
4. Toss in the onion, chicken, peas, and carrots. Combine the fixings in the Air Fryer and fry for 20 minutes.
5. Enjoy as a luncheon treat or serve as a side with your favorite dinner time meal.

Fried Tortellini

Serves: 6
- Cheese tortellini (9-oz. pkg.)
- Panko breadcrumbs (1 cup)
- Freshly grated parmesan (.33 cup)
- Dried oregano (1 tsp.)
- Garlic powder (.5 tsp.)
- Crushed red pepper flakes (.5 tsp.)
- Kosher salt & freshly ground black pepper
- All-purpose flour (1 cup)
- Large eggs (2)
- For Serving: Marinara sauce

1. Set the Air Fryer at 370° Fahrenheit.
2. In a large pot of boiling salted water, prepare the tortellini until al dente and drain.
3. Use three shallow dishes for prep. Combine the panko, parmesan, oregano, garlic powder, salt, pepper, and red pepper flakes in one. In another, beat the eggs, and in the third bowl, add flour.
4. Coat the tortellini in the flour, then dredge in eggs, and panko mixture. Continue until all of the tortellini are coated.
5. Place in the Air Fryer and fry until crispy (10 min.).
6. Serve with the marinara.

Grilled Cheese Sandwiches

Serves: 2
- Sharp cheddar cheese (.5 cup)
- White bread or brioche (4 slices)
- Melted butter (.25 cup)

1. Set the Air Fryer at 360° Fahrenheit.
2. Butter all slices of bread (both sides). Assemble each sandwich and arrange them in the fryer basket.
3. Prepare for 5-7 minutes and serve immediately for the best taste results.

Loaded Twice-Baked Air-Fried Potatoes

Serves: 2
- Olive oil (1 tsp.)
- Potato (14-16 oz.)
- Bacon bits (3 slices)
- Finely chopped green onion (1 tbsp. + .25 cup)
- Unsalted butter (1 tbsp.)
- Salt (.25 tsp.)
- Black pepper (.125 tsp.)
- Heavy cream (2 tbsp.)

1. Set the temperature to 400° Fahrenheit.
2. Fry the bacon about ten minutes in a skillet - reserving the fat - and chop into ½-inch pieces.
3. Finely chop the onions.
4. Coat the potato with the oil and add it to the Air Fryer basket for 30 minutes. Turn the potato (spritzing with oil if needed), and cook for another 30 minutes. Cool for a minimum of 20 minutes.
5. Slice the potato length-ways. Scoop out the pulp leaving about
6. ¼-inch borders to support the filling.
7. Whisk the scooped potatoes, bacon fat, bacon bits, .25 of a cup of the cheese, 1.5 tsp. of onions, pepper, salt, butter, and cream. Combine well.
8. Scoop the mixture into the prepared skins. Garnish with the cheese and place them in the Air Fryer.
9. Set the timer for 20 minutes or until the tops are browned.
10. Sprinkle the rest of the onions on top of the potato and serve.

Mac N Cheese Balls

Serves: 2
- Macaroni and cheese – leftovers are good (2 cups)
- Shredded cheddar cheese (.33 cup)
- Milk (2 cups)
- Eggs (3)
- White flour (.75 cup)
- Plain breadcrumbs (1 cup)

1. Heat the Air Fryer at 360° Fahrenheit.
2. Combine the leftovers with the shredded cheese.
3. Add the breadcrumbs into a dish.
4. Measure the flour into another bowl.
5. Combine the milk and eggs.
6. Make two balls from the mac n cheese.
7. Roll the balls in the flour, eggs, and lastly the breadcrumbs.
8. Arrange the balls in the fryer basket. Press 'M' and go to the chicken icon.
9. Set the timer for 10 minutes – rotating halfway through the cooking cycle.

Pigs In A Blanket

Serves: 4
- Crescent rolls (8 oz. can)
- Cocktail franks (12 oz. pkg.)

1. Warm the Air Fryer at 330° Fahrenheit.
2. Rinse and dry the franks using paper towels.
3. Slice the dough into rectangular strips (1.5 inches x 1-inch).
4. Roll the dough around the franks, but leave the ends open.
5. Place them in the freezer for approximately five minutes.
6. Transfer them to the fryer for 6-8 minutes.
7. Raise the temperature setting to 390° Fahrenheit. Continue cooking for approximately three more minutes.

Pita Bread Pizza - Pepperoni Sausage & Onion

Serves: 1

- Pizza sauce (1 tbsp.)
- Pita bread (1)
- Mozzarella cheese (.25 cup)
- Olive oil (1 spritz)
- Needed - The Toppings:
- Pepperoni (7 slices)
- Garlic (.5 tsp.)
- Sausage (.25 cup)
- Onions (1 tbsp.)

1. Warm the Air Fryer to 350° Fahrenheit.
2. Spoon the sauce onto the bread.
3. Mince the garlic. Thinly slice the onions. Toss on the toppings and spritz using a drizzle of oil.
4. Arrange the bread in the Air Fryer and place it on the trivet/rack.
5. Set the timer for six minutes. Serve when it's browned.

Pizza Dogs

Serves: 2

- Hot dogs (2)
- Pepperoni (4 slices - halved)
- Pizza sauce (.5 cup)
- Hot dog buns (2)
- Mozzarella cheese (.25 cup)
- Sliced olives (2 tsp.)

1. Warm the Air Fryer at 390° Fahrenheit.
2. Make four slits down each hot dog and place them in the Air Fryer basket. Set the timer for 3 minutes. Transfer to a cutting board.
3. Place a pepperoni half in each slit of the hot dogs. Portion the pizza sauce between buns and fill with the hot dogs, mozzarella cheese, and olives.
4. Return the hot dogs into the fryer basket and cook until buns are crisp and cheese is melted (2 min.).

Portobello Stuffed Mushrooms

Serves: 3

- Portobello mushrooms (3)
- Minced garlic (1 tsp.)
- Medium diced onion (1)
- Grated mozzarella cheese (3 tbsp.)
- Chopped ham (2 slices)
- Diced tomato (1)
- Diced green pepper (1)
- Sea salt (.5 tsp.)
- Pepper (.25 tsp.)
- Olive oil (1 tbsp.)

1. Heat the Air Fryer temperature setting at 320° Fahrenheit.
2. Rinse, dry, and discard the stems from the mushrooms. Drizzle with oil and set aside for now.
3. Mix the cheese, tomato, onion, pepper, salt, garlic, bell peppers, and ham. Stuff the mixture into the mushroom caps.
4. Arrange the mushrooms in the Air Fryer to cook for eight minutes.
5. Serve with your favorite main dish or for a delicious lunch treat.

Ravioli

Serves: 4-5

- Olive oil (as needed)
- Cheese or meat ravioli (1 pkg.)
- Marinara sauce (1 jar)
- Buttermilk (1 cup)
- Breadcrumbs - Italian-style (2 cups)
- Parmesan cheese (.25 cup)

1. Set the Air Fryer temperature at 200° Fahrenheit.
2. Add the buttermilk into a dish and dip in the ravioli.
3. Mix a spoonful of oil with the breadcrumbs and coat the ravioli using the breadcrumbs.
4. Arrange the ravioli in the fryer using a layer of parchment baking paper for approximately five minutes.
5. Note: It is best to use ready-made ravioli and sauce.

Reuben Roasted Turkey Sandwiches

Serves: 2

- Rye bread (4 slices)
- Skinless – roasted turkey breast (8 slices)
- Coleslaw (4 tbsp.)
- Swiss cheese (8 slices)
- Salted butter (2 tbsp.)
- Russian dressing (2 tbsp.)

1. Prepare two slices of bread on one side with butter and place them, butter side down, on the cutting board.
2. In layers, arrange the turkey, cheese, coleslaw, and Russian dressing on top of the two slices of bread. Fold them together to make one sandwich.
3. Add the sandwich to the Air Fryer basket.
4. Select the bake icon setting (310° Fahrenheit for 12 min.).
5. After 6 minutes, flip the sandwich and continue until browned.
6. Slice and serve.

Roasted Veggie Pasta Salad

Serves: 6

- Yellow squash (1)
- Brown mushrooms (4 oz.)
- Zucchini (1)
- Red - Green - Orange bell peppers (1 each)
- Red onion (1)
- Freshly cracked black pepper and salt (1 pinch each)
- Italian seasoning (1 tsp.)
- Grape tomatoes (1 cup)
- Pitted Kalamata olives (.5 cup)
- Cooked Rigatoni or Penne Rigate (1 lb.)
- Olive oil (.25 cup)
- Freshly chopped basil (2 tbsp.)
- Balsamic vinegar (3 tbsp.)

1. Set the Air Fryer temperature to 380° Fahrenheit.
2. Cut the peppers into large chunks and slice the red onion. Slice the tomatoes and olives into halves. Cut the squash and zucchini into half-moons.
3. Toss the red onion, mushrooms, peppers, squash, and zucchini in

4.a large mixing container. Drizzle with a spritz of oil, tossing well using the black pepper, salt, and Italian seasoning.

5.Prepare in the Air Fryer until the veggies are softened - not mushy (12 to 15 min.). Toss the fixings in the basket about halfway through the cooking cycle for even frying.

6.Combine the cooked pasta, roasted veggies, olives, and tomatoes into a large container. Pour in the vinegar, and toss.

7.Keep it refrigerated until ready to serve. Garnish using the fresh basil as serving time.

Simple Hot Dogs & Cheese
Serves: 2

- Hot dogs (2)
- Hot dog buns (2)
- Grated cheese (2 tbsp.)

1.Heat the Air Fryer for four (4) minutes at 390° Fahrenheit.

2.Arrange the hot dogs in the Air Fryer and cook for five minutes.

3.Place the hot dog on the bun and top it off with cheese.

4.Place in the fryer for about two minutes to melt the cheese and serve.

Mozzarella Cheese Sticks
Serves: 5

- Mozzarella string cheese (10 pieces)
- Italian breadcrumbs (1 cup)
- Egg (1)
- Flour (.5 cup)
- Marinara sauce (1 cup)
- Pepper and salt (as desired)

1.Warm the Air Fryer at 400° Fahrenheit.

2.Toss the breadcrumbs, salt, and pepper.

3.Prepare three dishes. Dip each piece of cheese in flour, egg, and lastly the breadcrumbs.

4.Chill the sticks for one hour to help them hold the stick shape during frying.

5.Lightly spritz the sticks with coconut oil using a baking brush.

6.Arrange the prepared sticks in the Air Fryer. Set the timer for 8 minutes. At that point, turn them over using tongs and air-fry for another 8 minutes.

7.Wait for 5 minutes and remove from the pan and serve.

Yellow Squash Fritters
Serves: 4

- 1 (3-ounce) package cream cheese, softened 1 egg, beaten
- ½ teaspoon dried oregano
- Pinch salt
- Freshly ground black pepper
- 1 medium yellow summer squash, grated
- ⅓ cup grated carrot
- ⅔ cup breadcrumbs
- 2 tablespoons olive oil

1.In a medium bowl, combine the cream cheese, egg, oregano, and salt and pepper. Add the squash and carrot and mix well. Stir in the breadcrumbs.

2.Form about 2 tablespoons of this mixture into a patty about ½ inch thick. Repeat with remaining mixture. Brush the fritters with olive oil.

3. air-fry until crisp and golden, about 7 to 9 minutes.

Lunch Special Pancake
Serves: 2

- 1 tablespoon butter
- eggs, whisked
- ½ cup flour
- ½ cup milk 1 cup salsa
- 1 cup small shrimp, peeled and deveined

1.Preheat your air fryer at 400 degrees f, add fryer's pan, add 1 tablespoon butter and melt it.

2.In a bowl, mix eggs with flour and milk, whisk well and pour into air fryer's pan, spread, cook at 350 degrees for 12 minutes and transfer to a plate.

3.In a bowl, mix shrimp with salsa, stir and serve your pancake with this on the side.

Fish And Chips
Serves: 2

- 2 medium cod fillets, skinless and boneless Salt and black pepper to the taste
- ¼ cup buttermilk
- cups kettle chips, cooked

1.In a bowl, mix fish with salt, pepper and buttermilk, toss and leave aside for 5 minutes.

2.Put chips in your food processor, crush them and spread them on a plate.

3.Add fish and press well on all sides.

4.Transfer fish to your air fryer's basket and cook at 400 degrees f for 12 minutes.

Chicken Sandwiches
Serves: 4

- 2 chicken breasts, skinless, boneless and cubed 1 red onion, chopped
- 1 red bell pepper, sliced
- ½ cup italian seasoning
- ½ teaspoon thyme, dried 2 cups butter lettuce, torn 4 pita pockets
- 1 cup cherry tomatoes, halved
- 1 tablespoon olive oil

1.In your air fryer, mix chicken with onion, bell pepper, italian seasoning and oil, toss and cook at 380 degrees f for 10 minutes.

2.Transfer chicken mix to a bowl, add thyme, butter lettuce, cherry tomatoes, and toss well, stuff pita pockets with this mix.

Fresh Chicken Mix
Serves: 4

- 2 chicken breasts, skinless, boneless and cubed 8 button mushrooms, sliced
- 1 red bell pepper, chopped 1 tablespoon olive oil
- ½ teaspoon thyme, dried 10 ounces alfredo sauce 6 bread slices
- 2 tablespoons butter, soft

1.In your air fryer, mix chicken with mushrooms, bell pepper and oil, toss to coat well, and cook 350 degrees f for 15 minutes.

2.Transfer chicken mix to a bowl, add thyme and alfredo sauce, toss, return to air fryer and cook at 350 degrees f for 4 minutes more.
3.Spread butter on bread slices, add it to the fryer, butter side up and cook for 4 minutes more.
4.Arrange toasted bread slices on a platter, top each with chicken mix.

Hot Bacon Sandwiches

Serves: 4

- 1/3 cup bbq sauce
- 2 tablespoons honey
- bacon slices, cooked and cut into thirds 1 red bell pepper, sliced
- 1 yellow bell pepper, sliced 3 pita pockets, halved
- 1 and ¼ cup butter lettuce leaves, torn 2 tomatoes, sliced

1.In a bowl, mix bbq sauce with honey and whisk well.
2.Brush bacon and all bell peppers with some of this mix, place them in your air fryer and cook at 350 degrees f for 4 minutes.
3.Shake fryer and cook them for 2 minutes more.
4.Stuff pita pockets with bacon mix, stuff with tomatoes and lettuce, and spread the rest of the bbq sauce.

Scal Lops And Dill

Serves: 4

- 1-pound sea sCal lops, debearded 1 tablespoon lemon juice
- 1 teaspoon dill, chopped 2 teaspoons olive oil
- Salt and black pepper to the taste

1.In your air fryer, mix sCal lops with dill, oil, salt, pepper and lemon juice, cover and cook at 360 degrees f for 5 minutes.
2.Discard unopened ones, divide sCal lops and dill sauce on plates and serve for lunch.

Macaroni And Cheese

Serves: 3

- 1 and ½ cups favorite macaroni Cooking spray
- ½ cup heavy cream 1 cup chicken stock
- ¾ cup cheddar cheese, shredded
- ½ cup mozzarella cheese, shredded
- ¼ cup parmesan, shredded

1.Spray a pan with Cooking spray, add macaroni, heavy cream, stock, cheddar cheese, mozzarella and parmesan but also salt and pepper, toss well, place pan in your air fryer's basket and cook for 30 minutes.
2. Divide among plates and serve for lunch.

Chicken Pie

Serves: 4

- chicken thighs, boneless, skinless and cubed 1 carrot, chopped
- 1 yellow onion, chopped
- 2 potatoes, chopped
- 2 mushrooms, chopped 1 teaspoon soy sauce

- Salt and black pepper to the taste 1 teaspoon italian seasoning
- ½ teaspoon garlic powder
- 1 teaspoon worcestershire sauce 1 tablespoon flour
- 1 tablespoon milk 2 puff pastry sheets
- 1 tablespoon butter, melted

1.Heat a pan over medium high heat, add potatoes, carrots and onion, stir and cook for 2 minutes.
2.Add chicken and mushrooms, salt, soy sauce, pepper, italian
3.seasoning, garlic powder, worcestershire sauce, flour and milk, stir well and take off heat.
4.Place 1 puff pastry sheet on the bottom of your air fryer's pan and trim edge excess.
5.Add chicken mix, top with the other puff pastry sheet, trim excess
6.as well and brush pie with butter.
7.Place in your air fryer and cook at 360 degrees f for 6 minutes.
8.Leave pie to cool down, slice and serve for breakfast.

Lunch Fajitas

Serves: 4

- 1 teaspoon garlic powder
- ¼ teaspoon cumin, ground
- ½ teaspoon chili powder
- Salt and black pepper to the taste
- ¼ teaspoon coriander, ground
- 1-pound chicken breasts, cut into strips 1 red bell pepper, sliced
- 1 green bell pepper, sliced 1 yellow onion, chopped 1 tablespoon lime juice Cooking spray
- tortillas, warmed up Salsa for serving
- Sour cream for serving
- 1 cup lettuce leaves, torn for serving

1.In a bowl, mix chicken with garlic powder, cumin, chili, salt, pepper, coriander, lime juice, red bell pepper, green bell pepper and onion, toss, leave aside for 10 minutes, transfer to your air fryer and drizzle some Cooking spray all over.
2.Toss and cook at 400 degrees f for 10 minutes.
3.Arrange tortillas on a working surface, divide chicken mix, also add salsa, sour cream and lettuce, wrap and serve for lunch.

Lunch Chicken Salad

Serves: 4

- ears of corn, hulled
- 1-pound chicken tenders, boneless Olive oil as needed
- Salt and black pepper to the taste 1 teaspoon sweet paprika
- 1 tablespoon brown Sugar
- ½ teaspoon garlic powder
- ½ iceberg lettuce head, cut into medium strips
- ½ romaine lettuce head, cut into medium strips 1 cup canned black beans, drained
- 1 cup cheddar cheese, shredded 3 tablespoons cilantro, chopped 4 green

- onions, chopped
  - cherry tomatoes, sliced
  - ¼ cup ranch dressing
  - tablespoons bbq sauce

1.Put corn in your air fryer, drizzle some oil, toss, cook at 400 degrees f for 10 minutes, transfer to a plate and leave aside for now.
2.Put chicken in your air fryer's basket, add salt, pepper, brown Sugar, paprika and garlic powder, toss, drizzle some more oil, cook at 400 degrees f for 10 minutes, flipping them halfway, transfer tenders to a cutting board and chop them.
3.Cur kernels off the cob, transfer corn to a bowl, add chicken, iceberg lettuce, romaine lettuce, black beans, cheese, cilantro, tomatoes, onions, bbq sauce and ranch dressing, toss well and serve for lunch.

Delicious Beef Cubes
Serves: 4
  - 1-pound sirloin, cubed
  - 16 ounces jarred pasta sauce 1 and ½ cups breadcrumbs 2 tablespoons olive oil
  - ½ teaspoon marjoram, dried
  - White rice, already cooked for serving

1.In a bowl, mix beef cubes with pasta sauce and toss well.
2.In another bowl, mix breadcrumbs with marjoram and oil and stir well.
3.Dip beef cubes in this mix, place them in your air fryer and cook at 360 degrees f for 12 minutes.
4.Divide among plates and serve with white rice on the side.

Pasta Salad
Serves: 6
  - 1 zucchini, sliced in half and roughly chopped
  - 1 orange bell pepper, roughly chopped 1 green bell pepper, roughly chopped 1 red onion, chopped
  - ounces brown mushrooms, halved Salt and black pepper to the taste
  - 1 teaspoon italian seasoning
  - 1-pound penne frigate, already cooked 1 cup cherry tomatoes, halved
  - ½ cup kalamata olive, pitted and halved
  - ¼ cup olive oil
  - tablespoons balsamic vinegar 2 tablespoons basil, chopped

1.In a bowl, mix zucchini with mushrooms, orange bell pepper, green bell pepper, red onion, salt, pepper, italian seasoning and oil, toss well, transfer to preheated air fryer at 380 degrees f and cook them for 12 minutes.
2.In a large salad bowl, mix pasta with cooked veggies, cherry tomatoes, olives, vinegar and basil, toss and serve for lunch.

Sweet Potato Lunch Casserole
Serves: 6
- 3big sweet potatoes, pricked with a fork 1 cup chicken stock
- Salt and black pepper to the taste
- A pinch of cayenne pepper

- ¼ teaspoon nutmeg, ground 1/3 cup coconut cream

1.Place sweet potatoes in your air fryer, cook them at 350 degrees f
2.for 40 minutes, cool them down, peel, roughly chop and transfer to a pan that fits your air fryer.
3.Add stock, salt, pepper, cayenne and coconut cream, toss, introduce in your air fryer and cook at 360 degrees f for 10 minutes more.
4.Divide casserole into bowls and serve.

Ground Chicken Meatballs
Serves: 2
  - 1-lb. Ground chicken 1/3 cup panko
  - 1 teaspoon salt
  - teaspoons chives
  - 1/2 teaspoon garlic powder 1 teaspoon thyme
  - 1 egg

1.Toss all the meatball in a bowl and mix well.
2.Make small meatballs out this mixture and place them in the air fryer basket.
3.Press "power button" of air fry oven and turn the dial to select the "air fry" mode.
4.Press the time button and again turn the dial to set the Cooking time to 10 minutes.
5.Now push the temp button and rotate the dial to set the temperature at 350 degrees f.
6.Once preheated, place the air fryer basket inside and close its lid. Serve warm.

Lamb Potato Chips Baked
Serves: 2
  - ½ lb. Minced lamb
  - 1 tbs parsley chopped
  - teaspoon curry powder
  - 1 pinch salt and black pepper 1 lb. Potato cooked, mashed 1 oz. Cheese grated
  - 1 ½ oz. Potato chips crushed

1.Mix lamb, curry powder, seasoning and parsley.
2.Spread this lamb mixture in a casserole dish.
3.Top the lamb mixture with potato mash, cheese, and potato chips.
4.Press "power button" of air fry oven and turn the dial to select the "bake" mode.
5.Press the time button and again turn the dial to set the Cooking time to 20 minutes.
6.Now push the temp button and rotate the dial to set the temperature at 350 degrees f.
7.Once preheated, place casserole dish in the oven and close its lid.
8.Serve warm.

Delicious Creamy Green Beans
Serves: 2
  - ½ cup heavy cream
  - 1 cup mozzarella, shredded 2/3 cup parmesan, grated
  - Salt and black pepper to the taste 2 pounds green beans
  - teaspoons lemon zest, grated A pinch of red pepper flakes

1.Put the beans in a dish that fits your air fryer, add heavy cream, salt, pepper, lemon zest, pepper flakes, mozzarella and parmesan, toss, introduce in your air fryer and cook at 350 degrees f for 15 minutes.

2.Divide among plates and serve right away.

3.Enjoy!

Parmesan Chicken Meatballs

Serves: 2

- 1-lb. Ground chicken 1 large egg, beaten
- ½ cup parmesan cheese, grated
- ½ cup pork rinds, ground 1 teaspoon garlic powder 1 teaspoon paprika
- 1 teaspoon kosher salt
- ½ teaspoon pepper

Crust:

- ½ cup pork rinds, ground

1.Toss all the meatball in a bowl and mix well.

2.Make small meatballs out this mixture and roll them in the pork rinds.

3.Place the coated meatballs in the air fryer basket.

4.Press "power button" of air fry oven and turn the dial to select the "bake" mode.

5.Press the time button and again turn the dial to set the Cooking time to 12 minutes.

6.Now push the temp button and rotate the dial to set the temperature at 400 degrees f.

7.Once preheated, place the air fryer basket inside and close its lid.

8.serve warm.

Lunch Broccoli Mix

Serves: 2

- broccoli heads, florets separated 2 teaspoons sweet paprika
- Juice of ½ lemon
- 1 tablespoon olive oil
- Salt and black pepper to taste 1 tablespoon sesame seeds
- garlic cloves, minced
- ½ cup bacon, cooked and crumbled

1.In your air fryer's pan, mix all except the bacon, toss, cover, and cook at 360 degrees f for 15 minutes.

2.Add the bacon and cook for 5 more minutes.

3.Divide between plates and serve.

Tasty Okra

Serves: 2

- 1/2 lb. Okra, ends trimmed and sliced 1 tsp olive oil
- 1/2 tsp mango powder 1/2 tsp chili powder
- 1/2 tsp ground coriander 1/2 tsp ground cumin 1/8 tsp pepper
- 1/4 tsp salt

1.Preheat the air fryer to 350 f.

2.Add all into the large bowl and toss well.

3.Spray air fryer basket with Cooking spray.

4.Transfer okra mixture into the air fryer basket and cook for 10 minutes. Shake basket halfway through.

5.Toss okra well and cook for 2 minutes more.

6.Serve and enjoy.

Air Fried Asparagus

Serves: 2

- pounds fresh asparagus, trimmed
- ¼ cup olive oil
- Salt and black pepper to the taste 1 teaspoon lemon zest
- garlic cloves, minced
- ½ teaspoon oregano, dried
- ¼ teaspoon red pepper flakes
- ounces feta cheese, crumbled
- 2 tablespoons parsley, finely chopped Juice from 1 lemon

1.In a bowl, mix oil with lemon zest, garlic, pepper flakes and oregano and whisk.

2.Add asparagus, cheese, salt and pepper, toss, transfer to your air fryer's basket and cook at 350 degrees f for 8 minutes.

3.Divide asparagus on plates, drizzle lemon juice and sprinkle parsley on top and serve.

4.Enjoy!

Mint Lamb With Roasted Hazelnuts

Serves: 2

- ¼ cup hazelnuts, toasted
- 2/3 lb. Shoulder of lamb cut into strips 1 tablespoon hazelnut oil
- tablespoon fresh mint leaves chopped
- ½ cup frozen peas
- ¼ cup of water
- ½ cup white wine
- Salt and black pepper to taste

1.Toss lamb with hazelnuts, spices, and all the in a baking pan.

2.Press "power button" of air fry oven and turn the dial to select the "bake" mode.

3.Press the time button and again turn the dial to set the Cooking time to 25 minutes.

4.Now push the temp button and rotate the dial to set the temperature at 370 degrees f.

5.Once preheated, place the baking pan in the oven and close its lid.

7.Slice and serve warm.

Cabbage Wedges

Serves: 2

- 1 small cabbage head, cut into wedges 3 tbsp olive oil
- 1/4 tsp red chili flakes 1/2 tsp fennel seeds
- 1 tsp garlic powder 1 tsp onion powder Pepper
- Salt

1.Spray air fryer basket with Cooking spray.

2.In a small bowl, mix garlic powder, red chili flakes, fennel seeds, onion powder, pepper, and salt.

3.Coat cabbage wedges with oil and rub with garlic powder mixture.

4.Place cabbage wedges into the air fryer basket and cook at 400 f for 8 minutes.

5.Turn cabbage wedges to another side and cook for 6 minutes more.

6.Serve and enjoy.

Simple Beef Curry

Serves: 2

- pounds cubed beef
- 2 tablespoons olive oil 3 potatoes, diced
- 1 tomato, cubed
- 2½ tablespoons curry powder 2 yellow onions, chopped
- 2 garlic cloves, minced 10 ounces coconut milk
- Salt and black pepper to taste

1.In a pan that fits your air fryer, heat the oil over medium heat.
2.Add the meat and brown it for 2-3 minutes.
3.Then add the potatoes, tomato, curry powder, onions, garlic, salt, and pepper; toss, and cook for 2 more minutes.
4.Transfer the pan to your air fryer and cook at 380 degrees f for 25 minutes.
5.Add the coconut milk, toss, and cook for 5 minutes more.
6.Divide everything into bowls, serve, and enjoy.

Healthy Mama Meatloaf

Serves: 2

- 1 tablespoon olive oil
- 1 green bell pepper, diced 1/2 cup diced sweet onion 1/2 teaspoon minced garlic 1-lb. Ground beef
- 1 cup whole wheat breadcrumbs 2 large eggs
- 3/4 cup shredded carrot 3/4 cup shredded zucchini
- Salt and ground black pepper to taste 1/4 cup ketchup, or to taste

1.Thoroughly mix ground beef with egg, onion, garlic, crumbs, and in a bowl.
2.Grease a meatloaf pan with oil or butter and spread the minced beef in the pan.

3.Press "power button" of air fry oven and turn the dial to select the "bake" mode.
4.Press the time button and again turn the dial to set the Cooking time to 40 minutes.
5.Now push the temp button and rotate the dial to set the temperature at 375 degrees f.
6.Once preheated, place the beef baking pan in the oven and close its lid.
7.Slice and serve.

Beef Short Ribs

Serves: 2

- 1 2/3 lbs. Short ribs
- Salt and black pepper, to taste 1 teaspoon grated garlic
- 1/2 teaspoon salt
- 1 teaspoon cumin seeds
- ¼ cup panko crumbs
- 1 teaspoon ground cumin 1 teaspoon avocado oil
- ½ teaspoon orange zest 1 egg, beaten
- Place the beef ribs in a baking tray and pour the whisked egg on top.
- Whisk rest of the crusting in a bowl and spread over the beef.

- Press "power button" of air fry oven and turn the dial to select the "air fry" mode.
1.Press the time button and again turn the dial to set the Cooking time to 35 minutes.
2.Now push the temp button and rotate the dial to set the temperature at 350 degrees f.
3.Once preheated, place the beef baking tray in the oven and close its lid.
4.Serve warm.

Tarragon Beef Shanks

Serves: 2

- tablespoons olive oil 2 lbs. Beef shank
- Salt and black pepper to taste 1 onion, diced
- 2 stalks celery, diced
- 1 cup marsala wine
- 2 tablespoons dried tarragon

1.Place the beef shanks in a baking pan.
2.Whisk rest of the in a bowl and pour over the shanks.
3.Place these shanks in the air fryer basket.
4.Press "power button" of air fry oven and turn the dial to select the "air fry" mode.
5.Press the time button and turn the dial to set the Cooking time to 1 hr. 30 minutes.
6.Now push the temp button and rotate the dial to set the temperature at 400 degrees f.
7.Once preheated, place the air fryer basket in the oven and close its lid.
8.Serve warm.

Tomato Kebabs

Serves: 12

- tablespoon balsamic vinegar
- 24 cherry tomatoes
- 2 tablespoon olive oil 3 garlic cloves; minced
- 1 tablespoon thyme; chopped Salt and black pepper to the taste For the dressing:
- 2 tablespoon balsamic vinegar 4 tablespoon olive oil
- Salt and black pepper to the taste

1.Take a medium bowl and add 2 tablespoon oil, 3 garlic cloves, thyme, salt, 2 tablespoon vinegar, and black pepper in it. Mix well, then toss in tomatoes and coat them liberally. 2.Thread 6 tomatoes on each skewer. Place these skewers in the air fryer basket inside the instant pot.
3.Put on the instant air fryer lid and cook on air fry mode for 6 minutes at 360 degrees f. 4.Once done, remove the lid and serve warm. 5.Meanwhile, whisk 2 tablespoon vinegar with pepper, salt, and 4 tablespoon oil.
6.Place the cooked skewers in the serving plates.
7.Pour the vinegar dressing over them.

Corn Okra Medley

Serves: 4

- 1pound okra; trimmed
- 28oz. Canned tomatoes; chopped 6 sCal lions; chopped
- tablespoon olive oil 1 teaspoon Sugar
- 1 cup of corn

- green bell peppers; chopped Salt and black pepper to the taste

1.Take a baking dish suitable to fit in your instant pot. Place it over medium heat and add oil, bell peppers, sCal lions, and sauté for 5 minutes. Stir in salt, pepper, okra, Sugar, corn, and tomatoes.
2.Transfer the dish to the instant pot. Put on the instant air fryer lid and cook on bake mode for 7 minutes at 360 degrees f. Once done, remove the lid and serve warm.

Saucy Artichokes

Serves: 4

- artichokes; trimmed
- 1 tablespoon lemon juice 2 garlic cloves; minced A drizzle olive oil

For The Sauce:

- anchovy fillets
- 1/4 cup extra virgin olive oil 1/4 cup coconut oil
- garlic cloves

1.Toss artichokes with lemon juice, oil and 2 garlic cloves in a large bowl. Place the seasoned artichokes in the air fryer basket inside the instant pot.
2.Put on the instant air fryer lid and cook on air fry mode for 6 minutes at 350 degrees f.
3.Blend coconut oil with olive oil, anchovy and 3 garlic cloves in a food processor. Place the artichokes in the serving plates. Pour the anchovy mixture over the artichokes.

Parmesan Green Beans

Serves: 6

- 2pound green beans 1/2 cup heavy cream
- 1 cup mozzarella; shredded 2/3 cup parmesan; grated
- teaspoon lemon zest; grated Salt and black pepper to the taste A pinch red pepper flake

1.Take a baking dish suitable to fit in your instant pot. Add beans and toss them with salt, cream, pepper, pepper flakes, parmesan, lemon zest, and mozzarella in the dish.
2. Place the beans dish in the instant pot.
3.Put on the instant air fryer lid and cook on bake mode for 15 minutes at 350 degrees f. Once done, remove the lid and serve warm.

Turkey Wings With Collard Greens

Serves: 2

- 1 sweet onion; chopped 2 smoked turkey wings
- 1/2 teaspoon crushed red pepper 2 tablespoon apple cider vinegar 1 tablespoon brown Sugar
- tablespoon olive oil 3 garlic cloves; minced
- 2 ½pound collard greens; chopped Salt and black pepper to the taste

1.Add oil and onions to the dish and place it over medium heat to sauté for 2 minutes.
2.Add vinegar, greens, salt, pepper, garlic, red pepper, smoked turkey and Sugar.
3.Mix well then transfer to the instant pot.
4.Put on the instant air fryer lid and cook on bake mode for 15 minutes at 350 degrees f.
5.Once done, remove the lid and serve warm.

Zucchini Noodles With Tomato Sauce

Serves: 4

- tablespoon olive oil
- zucchinis; cut with a spiralizer 1/4 cup sundried tomatoes; chopped 1 teaspoon garlic; minced
- 1/2 cup cherry tomatoes; halved 16oz. Mushrooms; sliced
- 2 cups tomatoes sauce 2 cups spinach; torn
- Salt and black pepper to the taste Handful basil; chopped

1.Place zucchini noodles in a colander then sprinkle salt and black pepper over them.
2.Leave it for 10 minutes.
3.Add garlic to a greased pan and sauté for 1 minute. 4.Stir in mushrooms, cherry tomatoes, sundried tomatoes, cayenne, spinach, tomato sauce, and drained zucchini noodles.
5.Transfer this mixture to the instant pot.
6.Put on the instant air fryer lid and cook on bake mode for 10 minutes at 320 degrees f.
7.Once done, remove the lid. Garnish with basil. Enjoy.

Mediterranean Eggplant Satay

Serves: 4

- 1 red onion; chopped
- garlic cloves; chopped 1 bunch parsley; chopped 1 teaspoon oregano; dried
- 2 eggplants; cut into medium chunks 2 tablespoon olive oil
- 2 tablespoon capers; chopped
- 1 handful green olives; pitted and sliced Salt and black pepper to the taste
- tomatoes; chopped
- tablespoon herb vinegar

1.Add oil to a greased skillet and place it over medium heat. Stir in oregano, eggplant, salt, and pepper.
2.Cook for 5 minutes then add parsley, onion, garlic, capers, vinegar, tomatoes, and olives.
3.Mix well then transfer this mixture to the instant pot. 4.Put on the instant air fryer lid and cook on bake mode for 15 minutes at 360 degrees f.
5.Once done, remove the lid and serve warm.

Mushroom Cream Pie

Serves: 6

- 6 eggs
- 2 tablespoon parmesan cheese, grated 2 oz fresh spinach
- 2 teaspoon olive oil
- 1 teaspoon garlic, minced 4 oz mushrooms, sliced
- 1/2 cup mozzarella cheese, shredded 1/4 teaspoon nutmeg
- 1/2 teaspoon pepper 1/2 cup heavy cream 16 oz cottage cheese 1 teaspoon salt

1.Heat oil in a suitable pan over moderate heat.
2.Toss in garlic and mushrooms and sauté until soft. 3.Stir in salt, black pepper, nutmeg, and spinach.
4.Drain this mushrooms spinach mixture then adds spread it into a suitable pie dish.
5.Whisk eggs with cream and cottage cheese in a bowl.
6.Pour this egg mixture over the mushrooms and top it with cheese.
7.Place the mushroom pie in the instant pot.
8.Put on the instant air fryer lid and cook on bake mode for 50 minutes at 350 degrees f.
9.Once done, remove the lid and serve warm.

Chicken Zucchini Casserole

Serves: 6

- ½ lbs. Chicken breasts, boneless and cubed
- 12 oz roasted red peppers, drained and chopped
- 2 garlic cloves, minced 2/3 cup mayonnaise
- 1 zucchini, cut into cubes 1 teaspoon xanthan gum 1 tablespoon tomato paste 2 oz coconut cream
- 1 teaspoon salt

1. Spread the chicken and zucchini in a baking dish. 2.Cover them with foil sheet and place it in the instant pot.
3.Put on the instant air fryer lid and cook on bake mode for 25 minutes at 350 degrees f.
4.Once done, remove the lid and toss again.
5.Continue baking for another 10 minutes.
6.Mix leftover in a separate bowl.
7.Pour this sauce over this chicken and put on the instant air fryer lid and cook on broil mode for 5 minutes at 350 degrees f.
8.Once done, remove the lid and serve warm.

Cauliflower Cream Casserole

Serves: 6

- 1 cauliflower head, cut into florets and boil 2 oz cream cheese
- 1 cup heavy cream
- 1 teaspoon garlic powder
- cups cheddar cheese, shredded 2 teaspoon dijon mustard
- 1/2 teaspoon pepper
- 1/2 teaspoon salt

1. Heat the cream to a simmer in a saucepan.
2.Stir in cream cheese, and mustard then stir cook until it thickens.
3.Remove this sauce from the heat and add seasoning and 1 cup cheese.
4.Spread the cauliflower florets in the greased baking pan.
5.Top these florets with the sauce and remaining cheese.
6.Place this baking dish in the instant pot.
8.Put on the instant air fryer lid and cook on bake mode for 15 minutes at 350 degrees f.
9.Once done, remove the lid and serve warm.

Italian Casserole

Serves: 4

- eggs
- 2/3 cup parmesan cheese, grated 2/3 cup chicken broth
- 1 lb. Italian sausage 2 egg whites
- 1 teaspoon pine nuts, minced
- ¼ cup roasted red pepper, sliced
- ¼ cup pesto sauce 1/8 teaspoon pepper
- ¼ teaspoon of sea salt

1. Place a pan over moderate heat and add sausage to the pan.
2.Stir cook until golden brown then drain the excess Fat.
3.Spread the sautéed sausage in a greased baking dish.
4.Beat the rest of the in a bowl.
5.Pour this sauce over the sausage and place this pan in the instant pot.
6.Put on the instant air fryer lid and cook on bake mode for 35 minutes at 400 degrees f.
7.Once done, remove the lid and serve warm.

Herbed Pork Tenderloin

Serves: 2

- thyme sprigs
- rosemary sprigs
- 1/3 teaspoon soy sauce 1 ½ tablespoon olive oil
- 2 tablespoon balsamic vinegar 3 tablespoon butter
- 1 minced shallot
- 1 peeled garlic clove 1/3 lb. Pork tenderloin

1. Rub the pork with salt and black pepper.
2.Place a skillet over moderate heat and add olive oil and butter.
3.Stir in garlic and shallot, then sauté for 5 minutes. 4.Toss in the leftover , including the pork.
5.Mix well, then spread this mixture in a baking pan. 6.Place the pan in the instant pot.
7.Put on the instant air fryer lid and cook on bake mode for 5 minutes at 350 degrees f.
8.Once done, remove the lid and serve warm.

Glazed Baby Potatoes

Serves: 4

- 1 ½pound baby potatoes; halved 2 thyme springs; chopped
- 9oz. Cherry tomatoes 3 tablespoon olive oil
- garlic cloves; chopped 2 red onions; chopped
- 1 ½ tablespoon balsamic vinegar
- Salt and black pepper to the taste

1.Add garlic, oil, onions, thyme, vinegar, salt, and pepper to the food processor.
2.Pulse well to blend them.
3.Toss the potatoes and tomatoes with the prepared sauce.
4.Mix well then spread the veggies in the instant pot.
5.Put on the instant air fryer lid and cook on roast mode for 20 minutes at 380 degrees f.
6.Once done, remove the lid and serve warm.

Ginger Broccoli Luncheon

Serves: 4

- 28oz. Canned tomatoes; pureed A pinch red pepper; crushed
- 1 small ginger piece; chopped
- 1 garlic clove; minced
- 1 broccoli head; florets separated 2 teaspoon coriander seeds
- 1 tablespoon olive oil
- 1 yellow onion; chopped
- Salt and black pepper to the taste

1. Add oil to a greased pan and place it over medium heat.
2.Stir in onions, pepper, salt, and red pepper.
3.Sauté for 7 minutes then add garlic, ginger, tomatoes, coriander seeds, and broccoli.
4.Transfer this mixture to the instant pot.
5.Put on the instant air fryer lid and cook on bake mode for 12 minutes at 360 degrees f.
6.Once done, remove the lid and serve warm.

Dinner Recipes

Air Fried Beef & Potato

Serves: 4

- Mashed potatoes (3 cups)
- Ground beef (1 lb.)

- Eggs (2)
- Garlic powder (2 tbsp.)
- Sour cream (1 cup)
- Freshly cracked black pepper (as desired)
- Salt (1 pinch)

1.Set the Air Fryer to reach 390° Fahrenheit.
2.Combine all of the fixings in a mixing container.
3.Scoop it into a heat-safe dish.
4.Arrange in the fryer to cook for two minutes.
5.Serve for lunch or a quick dinner.

Beef & Bacon Taco Rolls

Serves: 2
- Ground beef (2 cups)
- Bacon bits (.5 cup)
- Tomato salsa (1 cup)
- Shredded Monterey Jack Cheese (1 cup)

As desired - with the beef taco spices:
- Garlic powder Chili powder Black pepper
- Turmeric coconut wraps/your choice (4)

1.Warm the Air Fryer to reach 390° Fahrenheit.
2.Mix the beef and chosen spices, and add it to each of the fixings into the wraps.
3.Roll up the wraps and arrange them in the Air Fryer.
4.Set the timer for 15 minutes and serve.

Beef Empanadas

Serves: 4
- Onion (1 small)
- Cloves of garlic (2) Olive oil (1 tbsp.) Ground beef (1 lb.) Empanada shells (1 pkg.) Green pepper (.5 of 1)
- Cumin (.5 tsp.) Tomato salsa (.25 cup) Egg yolk (1)
- Pepper and sea salt (to your liking)

1.Peel and mince the garlic and onion. Deseed and dice the pepper.
2.Pour the oil to a skillet using the high-heat temperature setting.
3.Fry the ground beef until browned. Drain the grease and add the onions and garlic. Cook for 4 minutes. Combine the remainder of fixings (omitting the milk, egg, and shells for now). Cook using the low setting for 10 minutes.
4.Make an egg wash with the yolk and milk.
5.Add the meat to half of the rolled dough, brushing the edges with the wash. Fold it over and seal using a fork, brushing with the wash, and adding it to the basket.
6.Continue the process until all are done. Set the timer for 10 minutes in the Air Fryer at 350° Fahrenheit. Serve.

Beef Stew

Serves: 6
- Butter (2 tsp.)
- Beef short ribs (10 oz.) Salt (.25 tsp.)
- Turmeric (1 tsp.)
- Chili flakes (.5 tsp.) Green pepper (1)
- Kale (4 oz.)
- Chicken stock (1 cup) Onion (half of 1) Green peas (4 oz.)

1.Heat the Air Fryer at 360° Fahrenheit.
2.Measure the two teaspoons of butter to melt in the fryer basket. Add the ribs. Sprinkle with the salt, turmeric, and chili flakes. Set the timer to air- fry for 15 minutes.
3.Remove the seeds and chop the kale and green pepper. Dice the onion.

4.When the timer buzzes, pour in the stock, peppers, onions, peas, and the peeled garlic clove.
5.Stir well and add the chopped kale. Set the timer for eight more minutes before serving.

Black Peppercorns Meatloaf

Serves: 4
- Parsley (1 tbsp.)
- Oregano (1 tbsp.)
- Basil (1 tbsp.)
- Salt and pepper (to your liking) Ground beef (4.5 lb.)
- Large onion (1 diced) Worcestershire sauce (1 tsp.) Tomato ketchup (3 tbsp.)
- Breadcrumbs (1 slice of bread if homemade)

1.Set the temperature setting at 356° Fahrenheit.
2.Toss the beef, herbs, onion, Worcestershire sauce, and ketchup together and mix well (5 min.). Mix in the breadcrumbs.
3.Scoop the meatloaf into the baking dish and arrange it in the Air Fryer basket. Air-fry for 25 minutes.

Breaded Beef Schnitzel

Serves: 1
- Olive oil (2 tbsp.)
- Thin beef schnitzel (1)
- Gluten-free breadcrumbs (.5 cup)
- Egg (1)

1.Heat the Air Fryer a couple of minutes (356° Fahrenheit).
2.Combine the breadcrumbs and oil in a shallow bowl. Whisk the egg in another mixing container.
3.Dip the beef into the egg, and then the breadcrumbs.
4.Arrange in the basket of the Air Fryer.
5.Air-fry 12 minutes and serve.

Cheesy Beef Enchiladas

Serves: 4
- Ground beef (1 lb.)
- Regular/Gluten-free taco seasoning (1 pkg.) Gluten-free tortillas (8)
- Black beans (1 can) Diced tomatoes (1 can)
- Mild chopped green chilies (1 can) Red enchilada sauce (1 can) Shredded Mexican Cheese (1 cup) Chopped fresh cilantro (1 cup) Sour cream (.5 cup)

1.Set the Air Fryer temperature ahead of cooking time at 355° Fahrenheit. Line the fryer with a layer of foil if you choose.
2.Drain and rinse the beans. Drain the tomatoes and chiles.
3.Brown the ground beef in a skillet. Add in the taco seasoning.
4.Prepare four tortillas by adding beans, tomatoes, beef, and chilies.
5.Arrange the prepared tortillas in the basket of the Air Fryer.
6.After they are prepared, pour the enchilada sauce evenly over them, and garnish using the cheese.
7.Cook for five minutes in the Air Fryer.
8.Carefully remove, add the desired toppings, and serve.

Country Fried Steak

Serves: 1
- Sirloin steak (1 - 6 oz.)

- Eggs (3)
- Panko (1 cup)
- Flour (1 cup)
- Pepper & salt (1 tsp. each) Garlic powder (1 tsp.) Onion powder (1 tsp.) Ground sausage (6 oz.) Pepper (1 tsp.)
- Flour (2 tbsp.)
- Milk (2 cups)

1. Warm the Air Fryer to reach 370° Fahrenheit.
2. Use a meat mallet to beat the steak until thin. Add the seasonings with the panko.
3. Dredge the beef through the flour, egg, and panko.
4. Arrange the prepared steak in the basket. Set the timer for 12 minutes. Remove the steak.
5. Prepare the gravy. Cook the sausage and drain on a few paper towels, saving two tablespoons in the pan. Blend in the flour and sausage.
6. Pour in the milk and pepper, mixing until thickened.
7. Air-fry for three more minutes before serving.

Easy Rib Steak

Serves: 2
- Steak rub - your preference (1 tbsp.)
- Rib steaks (2 lb.) Olive oil (1 tbsp.)

1. Before it is time to cook, set the Air Fryer at 400° Fahrenheit.
2. Dust the steak using the oil and rub.
3. Place it in the basket to fry for 14 minutes, flipping after seven minutes.
4. Wait for at least 10 minutes before you slice to serve.

Inside Out Cheeseburgers

Serves: 5
- Cheddar cheese (4 slices)
- Lean ground beef (.75 lb. or 12 oz.) Ketchup (4 tsp.)
- Minced onion (3 tbsp.)
- Salt & black pepper (as desired) Yellow mustard (2 tsp.)
- Dill pickle chips (8)

1. Heat the Air Fryer at 370° Fahrenheit.
2. Dice the cheese into small pieces.
3. In a large mixing container, combine the ground beef, ketchup, pepper, salt, and mustard. Make four patties.
4. Place two burgers, side by side. Flatten the patty and add four pickle chips, and a layer of cheese.
5. Mash a patty on top, pressing the meat together tightly to enclose all of the fixings.
6. Arrange the burgers in the basket and cook for twenty minutes. Turn them over after about 10 minutes.
7. Serve the cheeseburgers on a bun with lettuce and tomatoes.

Mongolian Beef

Serves: 4
- Flank steak (1 lb.)
- Cornstarch (.25 cup) The Sauce:
- Vegetable oil (2 tsp.)
- Ginger (.5 tsp.) Minced garlic (1 tbsp.)
- Soy sauce or Gluten-free soy sauce (.5 cup) Water (.5 cup)
- Brown sugar - packed (.75 cup)

Extras:
- Cooked rice Green beans Green onions

1. Set the temperature at 390° Fahrenheit.

2. Thinly slice the steak in long strips, then coat using the cornstarch.
3. Arrange in the Air Fryer and cook for 5 minutes per side.
4. While you're waiting for the steak cook, heat all of the sauce fixings in a medium-sized saucepan using the med-high heat setting.
5. Whisk each of the fixings together until it gets to a low-boil.
6. Once both the steak and sauce are cooked, place the steak in a bowl with the sauce and let it marinate in it for about 5 to 10 minutes.
7. When it's time to eat, use a set of tongs to remove the steak and let the excess sauce drip off.
8. Place the steak over the cooked rice and green beans, top with additional sauce if desired.

Roast Beef

Serves: 6
- Garlic powder (.5 tsp.)
- Oregano (.5 tsp.)
- Dried thyme (1 tsp.)
- Olive oil (1 tbsp.)
- Round roast (2 lb.)

1. Set the Air Fryer at 330° Fahrenheit.
2. Combine the spices. Brush the oil over the beef, and rub it using the spice mixture.
3. Add to a baking dish and arrange it in the Air Fryer basket for 30 minutes. Turn it over and continue cooking 25 more minutes.
4. Wait for a few minutes before slicing.
5. Serve on your choice of bread or plain with a delicious side dish.

Steak & Mushrooms

Serves: 4
- Beef sirloin steak (1 lb.)
- Button mushrooms (8 oz./.25 cup) Worcestershire sauce (.25 cup) Olive oil (1 tbsp.)
- Parsley flakes (1 tsp.)
- Paprika (1 tsp.)
- Crushed chile flakes (1 tsp.)

1. Slice the mushrooms. Cut the steak into one-inch cubes and
2. combine with the mushrooms, Worcestershire sauce, olive oil, parsley, paprika, and chile flakes in a bowl.
3. Place a lid on the container and chill in the fridge for a minimum of four hours to overnight. About a half of an hour before you plan on preparing the steak, take it out of the fridge.
4. Warm the Air Fryer to 400° Fahrenheit.
5. Drain and discard the marinade from the steak mixture. Arrange the steak and mushrooms in the basket of the Air Fryer.
6. Set the timer for 5 minutes. Toss and cook for five more minutes.
7. Transfer the meal to a plate and wait for 5 minutes before serving.

Pineapple Pizza

Serves: 3
- 1 large whole wheat tortilla
- ¼ cup tomato pizza sauce
- ¼ cup pineapple tidbits
- ¼ cup mozzarella cheese, grated
- ¼ cup ham slice

1.Preheat your air fryer to 300°fahrenehit.
2. Place the tortilla on a baking sheet then spread pizza sauce over tortilla.
3.Arrange ham slice, cheese, pineapple over the tortilla.
4.Place the pizza in the air fryer basket and cook for 10-minutes. Serve hot.

Air Fryer Tortilla Pizza

Serves: 6
- 1 large whole wheat tortilla 1 tablespoon black olives
- Salt and pepper to taste
- tablespoons tomato sauce 8 pepperoni slices
- tablespoons of sweet corn
- 1 medium, tomato, chopped
- ½ cup mozzarella cheese, grated

1. Preheat your air fryer to 325°fahrenheit.
2.Spread tomato sauce over tortilla.
3.Add pepperoni slices, olives, corn, tomato, and cheese on top of the tortilla.
4.Season with salt and pepper.
5.Place pizza in air fryer basket and cook for 7-minutes.
6.Serve and enjoy!

Air Fried Pork Apple Balls

Serves: 8
- cups pork, minced
- basil leaves, chopped
- 2 tablespoons cheddar cheese, grated 4 garlic cloves, minced
- ½ cup apple, peeled, cored, chopped 1 large white onion, diced
- Salt and pepper to taste
- 2 teaspoons dijon mustard 1 teaspoon liquid stevia

1.Add pork minced in a bowl, add diced onion and apple into a bowl and mix well.
2.Add the stevia, mustard, garlic, cheese, basil, salt and pepper and combine well.
3.Make small round balls from the mixture and place them into air fryer basket.
5.Cook at 350°fahrenheit for 15-minutes. Serve and enjoy!

Rosemary Citrus Chicken

Serves: 2
- 1 lb. Chicken thighs
- 1/2 teaspoon rosemary, fresh, chopped 1/8 teaspoon thyme, dried
- ½ cup tangerine juice
- tablespoons white wine 1 teaspoon garlic, minced Salt and pepper to taste
- 2 tablespoons lemon juice

1.Place the chicken thighs in a mixing bowl.
2.In another bowl, mix tangerine juice, garlic, white wine, lemon juice, rosemary, pepper, salt, and thyme. 3.Pour the mixture over chicken thighs and place in the fridge for 20-minutes.
4.Preheat your air fryer to 350°fahrenheit and place your marinated chicken in air fryer basket and cook for 15-minutes. Serve hot and enjoy!

Air Fried Garlic Popcorn Chicken

Serves: 6
- 1 lb. Chicken breasts, skinless, Boneless, cut into

bite-size chunks
- ¼ teaspoon garlic powder Salt and pepper to taste
- ¼ teaspoon paprika
- ¼ cup of buttermilk 1 tablespoon olive oil
- ½ cup gluten-free flour 2 cups corn flakes
- 2 tablespoons parmesan cheese, grated

1. Preheat your air fryer to 350°fahrenheit. In a bowl, mix garlic, chicken, pepper, and salt.
2.Add cornflakes, parmesan cheese, pepper, paprika, and salt into food processor and process mix until it forms a crumble.
3.In a shallow dish add flour. In another bowl add the crumbled cornflake mixture.
4.Add chicken pieces to the flour and coat well.
5.Drizzle buttermilk over the coated chicken pieces and mix well.
6.Coat chicken pieces with cornflakes mixture.
7.Add coated chicken pieces onto a baking sheet and place in the air fryer basket.
8.Drizzle the olive oil over popcorn chicken. Bake in preheated air fryer for 15-minutes. Serve warm!

Macaroni Cheese Toast

Serves: 2
- 1 egg, beaten
- tablespoons cheddar cheese, grated Salt and pepper to taste
- ½ cup macaroni and cheese 4 bread slices

1. Spread the cheese and macaroni and cheese over the two bread slices.
2.Place the other bread slices on top of cheese and cut diagonally.
3.In a bowl, beat egg and season with salt and pepper. Brush the egg mixture onto the bread.
4.Place the bread into air fryer and cook at 300°fahrenehit for 5-minutes.

Cheeseburger Patties

Serves: 6
- 1 lb. Ground beef
- cheddar cheese slices Pepper and salt to taste

1. Preheat your air fryer to 390°fahrenheit.
2. Season beef with salt and pepper.
3.Make six round shaped patties from the mixture and place them into air fryer basket.
4.Air fry the patties for 10-minutes.
5.Open the air fryer basket and place cheese slices on top of patties and place into air fryer with an additional cook time of 1-minute.

Grilled Cheese Corn

Serves: 2
- whole corn on the cob, peel husks and discard silk
- 1 teaspoon olive oil 2 teaspoons paprika
- ½ cup feta cheese, grated

1. Rub the olive oil over corn then sprinkle with paprika and rub all over the corn.
2.Preheat your air fryer to 300°fahrenheit.
3.Place the seasoned corn on the grill for 15-minutes. 4.Place corn on a serving dish then sprinkle with grated cheese over corn. Serve and enjoy!

Eggplant Fries

Serves: 4

- 1 eggplant, cut into 3-inch pieces
- ¼ cup of water
- 1 tablespoon of olive oil 4 tablespoons cornstarch Sea salt to taste

1. Preheat your air fryer to 390° fahrenheit. In a bowl, combine eggplant, water, oil, and cornstarch. Place the eggplant fries in air fryer basket, and air fry them for 20-minutes. Serve warm and enjoy!

Light & Crispy Okra
Serves: 4
- cups okra, wash and dry
- 1 teaspoon fresh lemon juice 1 teaspoon coriander
- tablespoons gram flour
- 2 teaspoons red chili powder 1 teaspoon dry mango powder 1 teaspoon cumin powder
- Sea salt to taste

1. Cut the top of okra then cut a deep horizontal cut in each okra and set aside. In a bowl, combine gram flour, salt, lemon juice, and all the spices. Add a little water in gram flour mixture and make a
thick batter.
2. Fill batter in each okra and place in the air fryer basket.
3. Spray okra with Cooking spray.
4. Preheat your air fryer to 350° fahrenheit for 5-minutes.
5. Air fry the stuffed okra for 10- minutes or until lightly golden brown. Serve and enjoy!

Chili Rellenos
Serves: 5
- cans of green chili peppers
- 1 cup of Monterey jack cheese
- ½ cup milk
- 1 can tomato sauce
- 2 tablespoons almond flour 1 can evaporated milk
- 1 cup of cheddar cheese, shredded 2 large beaten eggs

1. Preheat the air fryer to 350° fahrenheit. Spray a baking dish with Cooking spray. Take half of the chilies and arrange them in the baking dish. Sprinkle the chilies with half of the cheese and cover with the rest of chilies. In a medium bowl, combine milk, eggs, flour and pour the mixture over the chilies. Air fry for 25-minutes.
2. Remove the chilies from the air fryer pour tomato sauce over them and cook them for additional 10-minutes. Remove them from air fryer and top with remaining cheese.

Persian Mushrooms
Serves: 3
- Portobello large mushrooms 3-ounces of softened butter
- 1 cup parmesan cheese, grated A pinch of black pepper
- A pinch of sea salt
- 1 tablespoon parsley, fresh, chopped 2 cloves of garlic
- large shallots

1. Preheat your air fryer to 390° fahrenheit. Clean the mushrooms and remove the stems. Slice the shallots and garlic cloves.
2. Now, place the mushroom stems, garlic, shallots, parsley and softened butter into a blender.
3. Arrange the caps of the mushrooms in the air fryer basket.

4. Stuff the caps with the mixture and sprinkle tops with parmesan cheese. Cook for 20-minutes. Serve warm and enjoy!

Air Fried Chicken Cordon Bleu
Serves: 4
- skinless and boneless chicken breasts 4 slices of ham
- slices of swiss cheese
- tablespoons almond flour
- 1 cup of heavy whipping cream
- 1 teaspoon of chicken bouillon granules
- ½ cup dry white wine 5 tablespoons butter
- 1 teaspoon paprika

1. Preheat your air fryer to 390° fahrenheit. Pound the chicken breasts and put a slice of ham and swiss cheese on each breast. Fold over edges of the chicken; cover the filling and secure the edges with toothpicks. In a bowl, combine flour, and paprika. Coat chicken
with this mixture. Set the air fryer to cook the chicken for 15-minutes. In a large skillet, heat the butter, bouillon, and wine then reduce heat to low. Remove the chicken from air fryer and add it to the skillet. Allow the components to simmer for around 30- minutes. Serve warm and enjoy!

Chicken Noodles
Serves: 4
- chicken breasts
- 1 teaspoon rosemary
- 1 teaspoon allspices
- 1 teaspoon red pepper
- 1 teaspoon tomato paste 1 tablespoon butter
- cups chicken broth Sesame seeds for garnish
  For noodles:
- beaten eggs
- ½ teaspoon salt
- 2 cups almond flour

1. Preheat your air fryer to 350° fahrenheit. Coat the chicken with 1 tablespoon of butter, salt, and pepper. 2.Arrange the chicken breasts in the air fryer basket and cook for 20-minutes.
3. For the noodles, combine egg, salt, and flour to make a dough.
4. Put the dough on a floured surface knead it for a few minutes then cover it and set it aside for 30-minutes. 5.Roll the dough on a floured surface.
6. When the dough is thin, cut it into thin strips and dry for an hour.
7. Meanwhile, take the chicken out of the air fryer and place aside.
8. Boil the chicken broth and add the noodles, tomato paste and red pepper, cook for 5-minutes.
9. Add the spices and stir noodles. Add salt and pepper to taste.
10. Serve noodles with air fried chicken and garnish with sesame seeds. Serve hot and enjoy!

Mushroom & Herb Stuffed Pork Chops
Serves: 5
- thick pork chops
- mushrooms, chopped 1 pinch of herbs
- 1 tablespoon almond flour
- 1 tablespoon lemon juice Salt and black pepper to taste

1. Preheat your air fryer to 325°fahrenheit. Season both sides of meat with salt and pepper.
2.Arrange the chops in the air fryer and cook for 15-minutes at 350°fahrenheit.
3.Cook the mushrooms for 3- minutes in a pan over medium heat and stir in lemon juice. Add the flour and herbs to pan and stir.
4.Cook the mixture for 4-minutes, then set aside. Cut five pieces of foil for each chop.
5.On every piece of foil put a chop in the middle and cover it with mushroom mixture. Now, carefully fold the foil and seal around the chop.
6.Place chops back into air fryer and cook for an additional 30-minutes. Serve with salad.

Lemon And Cheese Rice

Serves: 4

- tablespoons of parmesan cheese, grated freshly 2 cups of white rice, boiled
- tablespoons of fresh lemon juice
- 2 teaspoons of fresh lemon zest, grated finely 4 tablespoons of fresh mint leaves, chopped
- Salt and black pepper, to taste 2 tablespoons of vegetable broth

1. Set the instant vortex on air fryer to 375 degrees f for 12 minutes. Place the rice in the Cooking tray and the vegetable broth, lemon juice, salt and black pepper. Insert the Cooking tray in the vortex when it displays "add food".
2.Remove from the vortex when Cooking time is complete.
3.Fold in the lemon zest and parmesan cheese. Cook again in the vortex for about 3 minutes and serve garnished with mint.

Quinoa Pilaf

Serves: 8

- 1 cup of almonds, sliced
- ½ cup of dried cherries
- cups of quinoa, rinsed and drained 2 tablespoons of butter
- 2 tablespoons of chicken broth
- ½ cup of water
- 2 celery stalks, chopped finely 1 cup of onions, chopped

1. Set the instant vortex on air fryer to 375 degrees f for 15 minutes. Put butter in a pan and add celery, garlic, and onions. Sauté for about 3 minutes and stir in the remaining . Transfer this mixture into the Cooking tray. Insert the Cooking tray in the vortex when it displays "add food". Remove from the vortex when cooking time is complete. Serve warm.

Gram Lentil Curry

Serves: 4

- tablespoons of water
- 1½ teaspoons of salt
- 1½ teaspoons of cumin seeds 3 medium tomatoes, chopped
- 1½ cups of green gram lentils whole, boiled 1 tablespoon of garlic, minced
- 1½ tablespoons of lemon juice 1½ tablespoons of ginger, minced 1½ tablespoons of oil
- 2 medium onions, diced Cilantro, to garnish

1. Set the instant vortex on roast to 375 degrees f for 12 minutes. Put oil in a pan and add cumin seeds, garlic, and onions.
2.Sauté for about 3 minutes and stir in the tomato, lentils, water and spices.
3. Transfer this mixture into the Cooking dish and place on the Cooking tray.
4. Insert the Cooking tray in the vortex when it displays "add food".
5. Remove from the vortex when cooking time is complete.
6. Squeeze in the lime juice and serve garnished with cilantro.

Tuna Patties

Serves: 4

- 1 teaspoon of garlic powder
- ½ teaspoon of onion powder Pinch of salt and pepper
- cans of tuna packed in water 1 ½ tablespoons of mayo
- 1 teaspoon of dried dill
- ½ lemon, juiced
- 1 ½ tablespoons of almond flour

1. Set the instant vortex on air fryer to 390 degrees f for 12 minutes.
2.Combine the tuna with all other and form 4 equal sized patties.
3.Place the tuna patties on the Cooking tray.
4.Insert the Cooking tray in the vortex when it displays "add food".
5.Flip the patties when it displays "turn food". Remove from the oven when cooking time is complete. Serve with ketchup.

Spinach Lentil

Serves: 3

- ½ cup of water
- ½ tablespoon of oil
- ½ inch ginger, finely chopped 1 tomato, chopped
- 1 cup of spinach, chopped
- ¼ teaspoon of cumin seeds
- garlic cloves, finely chopped
- ½ teaspoon of salt
- ½ cup of split pigeon pea, washed

1. Set the instant vortex on air fryer to 375 degrees f for 8 minutes.
2. Sauté garlic, ginger, and cumin seeds in the olive oil in a pan for about 1 minute.
3. Stir in the tomato paste, water, lentils, and salt. Sauté for about 3 minutes and add spinach.
4. Transfer this mixture into the Cooking dish and place on the Cooking tray.
5. Insert the Cooking tray in the vortex when it displays "add food".
6. Remove from the vortex when cooking time is complete. Serve warm.

Confetti Rice

Serves: 4

- ¼ cup of vegetable broth
- ¼ cup of lemon juice
- 1 small onion, chopped
- 1 cup of lengthy grain white rice, boiled 3 cups of

- frozen peas, thawed
- cloves garlic, minced
- 1 tablespoon of cumin powder
- ½ teaspoon of salt
- ½ teaspoon of black pepper 3 tablespoons of butter

1. Set the instant vortex on roast to 375 degrees f for 12 minutes.
2. Put butter in a pan and add onions. Sauté for about 3 minutes and stir in rest of the.
3. Sauté for about 3 minutes and add spinach.
4. Transfer this mixture into the Cooking dish and place on the Cooking tray. Insert the Cooking tray. Serve warm.

Chili Lime Tilapia

Serves: 2
- 1 lb. Of tilapia fillets
- 1 cup of panko crumbs
- ½ cup of flour
- Salt and black pepper, to taste 2 eggs
- 1 tablespoon of chili powder Juice of 1 lime

1. Set the instant vortex on air fryer to 375 degrees f for 8 minutes.
2. Mix panko crumbs with salt, chili powder, and black pepper in a plate.
3. Put the flour in another plate and whisk eggs in a bowl.
4. Dredge the tilapia fillets in the flour, then dip in the whisked eggs.
5. Rub with the panko mixture and place on the Cooking tray.
6. Insert the Cooking tray in the vortex when it displays "add food".
7. Flip the fillets when it displays "turn food". Remove from the vortex when Cooking time is complete.
Serve drizzled with lime juice.

Asian Salad

Serves: 4
- tsp sesame oil
- tbsp rice vinegar 1 tbsp soy sauce
- 1 tbsp water
- ½ tsp red pepper
- 1 cup sesame seeds 8 oz chicken
- 1 tbsp flour
- 1 egg white
- cups lettuce
- 2 cups coleslaw mix 1 cup peas
- 1 cup canned mandarin oranges
- ¼ cup sliced almonds

1. Boil chicken.
2. Mix all
3. Then mix in chicken.
4. Cook it for 20 mins in air fryer.
5. Spray oil on it.
6. Again, cook for 5 min.

Parmesan Pasta

Serves: 6
- tbsp pine nuts
- ¾ cup fresh basil leaves 2 garlic cloves
- 1 tbsp lemon juice
- oz uncooked pasta- 1 ½ cups water 1 cup skim milk - 1 tsp salt

- 2 cups fresh broccoli florets
- 1 cup chopped zucchini
- ½ cup frozen peas - 4 oz parmesan cheese

1. Combine 2 tbsp of the roasted pine nuts with the basil, garlic and lemon juice in the bowl and grind it and set aside.
2. Add water and milk in the dry pasta; add the salt and the broccoli, zucchini and peas.
3. Cook the mixture in air fryer 13-16 minutes until the liquid is mostly absorbed (pasta and veggies will be cooked).
4. Remove from heat and stir in almost all the shredded parmesan and nuts mixture.
5. Cover the pan with a lid for 2-3 minutes until the cheese is melted and then stir until well combined and cheesy.

Cheese Stuffed Chicken

Serves: 4
- oz cream cheese
- 2 tbsp low Fat mayonnaise 2 oz cheddar cheese
- 1 tbsp diced pimientos
- A pinch of garlic powder A pinch of onion powder 6 oz chicken breasts
- tsp all-purpose flour
- 2 tsp cajun seasoning 1 egg white, beaten 2/3 cup breadcrumbs 2 tsp canola oil

1. Preheat the oven to 400.
2. Line a baking sheet with parchment paper and set aside.
3. In a mixing bowl, combine the mayo, cheddar, pimientos, flour, eggs, cajun and a sprinkle of garlic powder and onion powder and mix.
4. Place the chicken breasts on a cutting board. Using a sharp knife, slice the breasts from the side.
5. Spread cheese mixture on it.
6. Press it in breadcrumbs.
7. Place the stuffed breasts in parchment paper and spray oil.
8. Bake for 40 mins in air fryer.

Hummus And Feta Omelet

Serves: 1
- 1 large egg
- large egg whites 1 tsp water
- Salt and pepper to taste 1 tbsp light butter
- 0.5 oz feta cheese
- 1 tbsp fresh, thinly sliced basil
- 2 tbsp diced tomatoes 3

1. In a mixing bowl, combine the agg, egg whites, water, salt and pepper and whisk together.
2. Add the butter. Make sure the butter coats the bottom of baking dish as it melts. Once the butter is melted, add the egg mixture to the baking dish and cook in air fryer for 5 mins.
3. Drop small amounts of hummus in the center of the omelet. Sprinkle feta over it and cook for 5 mins in air fryer.
4. When cooked, sprinkle the sliced basil and diced tomatoes over the top of the omelet and serve.

Stuffed Strawberries

Serves: 16
- 1 lb. Fresh strawberries 4 oz cream cheese
- ¼ cup powdered Sugar
- ¼ tsp vanilla extract
- 1 full-sized low-Fat graham cracker

1. Cut tops off strawberries.
2. Remove interior of each strawberry.

3.Cook it for 5 mins in air fryer.
4.Take a bowl, add cheese, Sugar, vanilla and mix it in mixer.
5.Add this mixture inside strawberries.
6.Then coat the strawberries with crackers.
7.Enjoy

Beef Cheese Mini Puffs

Serves: 24

- oz raw beef 3 tbsp onion
- 1 clove garlic
- ¾ cup white whole wheat flour
- ¾ tsp baking powder 1/8 tsp salt
- 1/8 tsp crushed red pepper flakes
- ¾ cup skim milk 1 large egg
- oz reduced Fat sharp cheddar cheese

1.Preheat the oven to 350. Lightly mist a 24-count mini muffin tin with Cooking spray
2.Add ground beef in baking dish, spray with oil, and cook in fryer.
3.When cooked, add the hamburger seasoning, chopped onion, and garlic and cook in fryer.
4.In a large bowl, stir together flour, baking powder, salt and crushed red pepper. Add the milk and egg and whisk together to thoroughly combine. Add the ground beef mixture, cheese and stir until combined.
5.Divide the batter evenly amongst the prepared mini muffin tin cups.
6.Bake in the fryer for 18-20 minutes until golden.

Chicken Chili

Serves: 8

- 1 tbsp canola oil
- cups yellow onion, 2 tbsp chili powder 1 tbsp minced garlic 2 tbsp ground cumin 1 tbsp oregano
- oz beans
- cups chicken broth
- cups skinless chicken breast
- 14.5 oz diced tomatoes
- 1/3 cup fresh cilantro 2 tbsp fresh lime juice
- ½ tsp salt
- ½ tsp pepper

1.Add the onions and chili powder, garlic and cumin and stir to coat the onions. Spray oil. Cook for 2 more minutes in fryer.
2.When cooked, add the oregano and beans, cook for 5 mins in fryer.
3.Add the broth and reduce the heat to medium-low. Simmer for 20 minutes, stirring occasionally.
4.When cooked, transfer this mixture to a blender and blend.
5.Then add the chicken and tomatoes and cook over medium-low for another 30 minutes in fryer.
6.Add the cilantro, lime juice, salt & pepper and stir to combine before serving.

Cornmeal & Potatoes

Serves: 4

- medium sweet potatoes 1 egg
- 1 tsp lemon juice 1/3 cup cornmeal 2 tsp flour
- 1/2 tsp onion powder 1/2 tsp garlic powder 1/4 tsp chili powder 1/4 tsp smoked paprika
- 1-pound cod fish, cut into 12 pieces 2 tbsp + 1 tsp light butter
- 1 tsp olive oil
- Salt and pepper

1.With a fork, poke holes in the sweet potatoes. Cook 10 minutes in air fryer.
2.In a shallow dish, whisk together the egg and lemon juice.
3.In a separate shallow dish, combine the cornmeal, flour, onion powder, garlic powder, chili powder, and smoked paprika.
4.Coat cod pieces with both mixtures.
5.Spray the fish pieces & cook 10 mins in fryer.
6.Once the sweet potatoes are cooked, cut them in half.
7.Place 1 tsp butter on each sweet potato half.
8.Serve 3 pieces cornmeal crusted cod with 1/2 of a sweet potato.
9.Sprinkle with salt and pepper to taste.

Nashville Hot Chicken In Air Fryer

Serves: 4

- Chicken with bones, 8 pieces – 4 pounds
- Vegetable oil – 2 tablespoons All-purpose flour – 2 cups Buttermilk – 1 cup
- Paprika – 2 tablespoons Onion powder – 1 teaspoon Garlic powder – 1 teaspoon
- Ground black pepper – 1 teaspoon Salt – 2 teaspoons

For Hot Sauce:

- Cayenne pepper – 1 tablespoon Vegetable oil - ¼ cup
- Salt – 1 teaspoon White bread – 4 slices
- Dill pickle – as required

1.Clean and wash chicken thoroughly, pat dry and keep ready aside.
2.In a bowl, whisk buttermilk and eggs.
3.Combine garlic powder, black pepper, paprika, onion powder, allpurpose flour and salt in a bowl.
4.Now dip the chicken in the egg and buttermilk and put in the second bowl marinade bowl and toss to get an even coating. Maybe you need to repeat the process twice for a better coat.
5.After that spray some vegetable oil and keep aside.
6.Before Cooking the chicken, pre-heat the fryer at 190 degrees celsius.
7.Brush vegetable oil on the fry basket before start Cooking .
8.Now place the coated chicken in the air fryer at 190 degrees celsius and set the timer for 20 minutes. Do not crowd the air fryer. It would be better if you can do the frying in 2 batches.
9.Keep the flipping the chicken intermittently for even frying.
10.Once the set timer elapsed, remove the chicken to plate and keep it there without covering.
11.Now start the second batch. Do the same process.
12.After 20 minutes, reduce the temperature to 170 degrees celsius and place the first batch of chicken over the second batch, which is already in the air fry basket.
13.Fry it again for another 7 minutes.
14.While the chicken is air frying, make the hot sauce.
15.In a bowl mix salt and cayenne pepper thoroughly.
16.In a small saucepan, heat some vegetable oil.
17.When the oil becomes hot add the spice mix and continue stirring to become smooth.
18.While serving, place the chicken over the white bread and spread the hot sauce over the chicken.
19.Use dill pickle to top it.
20.Serve hot.

Air Fryer Panko Breaded Chicken

Parmesan

Serves: 4

- Chicken breasts, skinless – 16 ounces Panko breadcrumbs – 1 cup
- Egg whites - ⅛ cup
- Parmesan cheese, shredded - ½ cup Mozzarella cheese, grated - ½ cup Marinara sauce - ¾ cup
- Salt - ½ teaspoon
- Ground pepper – 1 teaspoon
- Italian seasoning – 2 teaspoons Cooking spray – as required

1. Cut each chicken breasts into halves to make 4 breast pieces.
2. Wash and pat dry.
3. Place the chicken in a chopping board and pound to flatten.
4. Spritz the air fryer basket with cooking oil.
5. Set the temperature of air fryer to 200 degrees Celsius and preheat.
6. In a large bowl, mix cheese, panko breadcrumbs, and seasoning .
7. Put the egg white in a large bowl.
8. Dip the pounded chicken into the egg whites and dredge into breadcrumb mixture.
9. Now place the coated chicken into the air fryer basket and spray some Cooking oil.
10. Start cooking the chicken breasts for 7 minutes.
11. Dress on top of the chicken breasts with shredded mozzarella and marinara sauce.
12. Continue Cooking for another 3 minutes and remove for serving when the cheese starts to melt.

Air Fryer Rosemary Turkey

Serves: 6

- Turkey breast - 2½ pounds
- Fresh rosemary, chopped – 2 teaspoons Olive oil - ¼ cup
- Garlic, minced – 2 cloves Crushed pepper – 1 teaspoon Maple syrup - ¼ cup
- Ground mustard – 1 tablespoon
- Butter – 1 tablespoon - Salt - 1½ teaspoon

1. Combine thoroughly, minced garlic, olive oil, shredded rosemary, pepper and salt in medium bowl.
2. Rub the herb seasoning and oil all over the turkey breast loins.
3. Cover and refrigerate for at least 2 hours for better marinade effect.
4. Before Cooking , allow it to thaw for half an hour.
5. Spray some Cooking oil on the air fryer basket and place the turkey breast on it.
6. Set the temperature at 200 degrees celsius for 20 minutes.
7. Flip the turkey breast intermittently.
8. While Cooking in progress, melt a tablespoon of butter in a microwave oven.
9. Stir in mustard powder and maple syrup in the melted butter.
10. Pour the sauce mix over the turkey breast and continue Cooking for another 10 minutes.
11. After the Cooking is over, slice it for serving.

Air Fryer Italian Meatball

Serves: 6

- Ground beef – 2 pounds Eggs – 2
- Breadcrumbs - 1¼ cup
- Fresh parsley, chopped - ¼ cup Dried oregano – 1 teaspoon Parmigiano reggiano, grated - ¼ cup Light Cooking oil – 1 teaspoon
- Salt – to taste
- Pepper – as required
- Tomato sauce – for serving

1. In a mixing bowl put the meat and all except the Cooking oil.
2. Hands mix all the .
3. Once the mix blended thoroughly, make a small ball with your hand. The given quantity is enough to make 24 balls.
4. Spread a liner paper in the air fryer basket and lightly coat it with Cooking oil.
5. Place the bowls in the air fryer basket without overlapping one another.
6. Set the temperature to 200 degrees celsius and cook for 12-14 minutes until its side becomes brown.
7. Once the sides become brown, turn the balls and cook for another 5 minutes.
8. Serve hot along with tomato sauce.

Chicken Fried Rice In Air Fryer

Serves: 4

- Cooked cold white rice – 3 cups
- Chicken cooked & diced – 1 cup Carrots and peas, frozen – 1 cup Vegetable oil – 1 tablespoon Soy sauce – 1 tablespoon
- Onion - ½ cup
- Salt - ¼ teaspoon

1. In a large bowl, put the cooked cold rice.
2. Stir in soy sauce and vegetable oil.
3. Now add the frozen carrots and peas, diced chicken, diced onion, salt and combine.
4. Transfer the rice mixture into the mix.
5. Take a non-stick pan which you can comfortably place in the air fryer and transfer the complete rice mixture into the pan.
6. Place the pan in the air fryer.
7. Set the temperature at 180 degree celsius and timer for 20 minutes.
8. Remove the pan after the set time elapse.
9. Serve hot.

Air Fried Chicken Tikkas

Serves: 4

For Marinade:

- Chicken, bones cut into small bite size - 1¼ pounds Cherry tomatoes - ¼ pound
- Yogurt – 1 cup
- Ginger garlic paste (fresh) – 1 tablespoon Bell peppers, 1" cut size – 3
- Chili powder – 2 tablespoons Cumin powder – 2 tablespoons Turmeric powder – 1 tablespoon Coriander powder – 2 tablespoons Garam masala powder – 1 teaspoon Olive oil – 2 teaspoons
- Salt – to taste

For Garnishing:

- Lemon, cut into half
- 1 Coriander, fresh, chopped
- ⅓ cup Onion, nicely sliced
- 1 medium Mint leaves, fresh – few

1. In a large bowl mix all the marinade Ingredients and coat it thoroughly on the chicken pieces.

2.Cover the bowl and set aside for 2 hours minimum. If you can refrigerate overnight, it can give better marinade effect.
3.Thread the chicken in the skewers along with bell peppers and tomatoes alternately.
4.Preheat your air fryer at 200 degrees celsius.
5.Spread an aluminum liner on the air fryer basket and arrange the skewers on it.
6.Set the timer for 15 minutes and grill it.
7.Turn the skewer intermittently for an even grilling.
8.Once done, put into a plate and garnish with the given before serving.

Air Fryer Lamb Chops
Serves: 2
- Lamb chops – 4
- Oregano, fresh, coarsely chopped - ½ tablespoon Olive oil - 1½ tablespoons
- Black pepper, ground – 1 teaspoon Garlic – 1 clove
- Salt - ½ teaspoon

1.Set the air fryer temperature to 200 degrees celsius.
2.Spray olive on garlic clove and place it in the air fryer basket.
3.Bake it for 12 minutes.
4.Combine herbs with pepper, olive oil, and salt.
5.Rub half of the mix over the lamb chops and set aside for 3 minutes.
6.Remove the roasted garlic clove from the air fryer.
7.Set the temperature at 200 degrees celsius and preheat the air fryer.
8.Layer the lamb chops into the air fryer basket and cook for 5 minutes or until it becomes brown.
9.Do not roast the lambs altogether by overlapping one over the other. You can do the roasting in batches.
10.After finish roasting, squeeze the garlic into the herb sauce.
11.Add some more salt and pepper if required.
12.Serve the dish along with garlic sauce.

Side Dish Recipes

Air-Fried Okra
Serves: 4
- All-purpose flour (.25 cup) Cornmeal (1 cup)
- Large egg (1)
- Okra pods (.5 lb) Salt (as desired)

1.Set the Air Fryer to 400° Fahrenheit.
2.Whisk the egg in a shallow dish. Slice and stir in the okra.
3.Mix the cornmeal and flour in a gallon-size zipper plastic bag. Drop five slices of okra into the cornmeal mixture, zip the bag, and shake. Remove the breaded okra to a plate. Repeat with remaining okra slices.
4.Place half of the breaded slices into the fryer basket and mist using the cooking spray. Set the timer for four minutes. Shake the basket and mist okra with cooking oil spray again. Cook another four minutes. Shake the basket one last time and cook for another two minutes. Remove the okra from the basket and salt to your liking.
5.Repeat with the remaining okra slices.

Avocado & Bacon Fries
Serves: 2
- Egg (1)
- Almond flour (1 cup)
- Bacon – cooked – small bits (4 strips) Avocados (2 large)
- For Frying: Olive oil

1.Set the Air Fryer at 355° Fahrenheit.
2.Whisk the eggs in one container. Add the flour with the bacon in another.
3.Slice the avocado using lengthwise cuts. Dip into the eggs, then the flour mixture.
4.Drizzle oil in the fryer tray and cook for 10 minutes on each side or until they're the way you like them.

Battered Baby Ears Of Corn
Serves: 4
- Carom seeds (.5 tsp.) Almond flour (1 cup) Chili powder (.25 tsp.) Garlic powder (1 tsp.)
- Boiled baby ears of corn (4)
- Baking soda (1 pinch) Salt (to your liking)

1.Warm the Air Fryer to reach 350° Fahrenheit.
2.Whisk the flour, salt, garlic powder, baking soda, chili powder, and carom seeds. Pour a little water into a bowl to make a batter. Dip the boiled corn in the mixture and arrange it in a foil-lined fryer basket. Set the timer for 10 minutes.
3.Serve with your favorite entrée.

Breaded Avocado Fries
- Servings Provided: 2 :
- Large avocado (1)
- Breadcrumbs (.5 cup)
- Egg (1)
- Salt (.5 tsp.)

1.Warm the Air Fryer to reach 390° Fahrenheit.
2.Peel, remove the pit, and slice the avocado.
3.Prepare two shallow dishes, one with the breadcrumbs and salt, and one with a whisked egg.
4.Dip the avocado into the egg – then the breadcrumbs.
5.Add to the Air Fryer for ten minutes.
6.Serve as a side dish or an appetizer.

Brussels Sprouts
Serves: 4-5
- Olive oil (5 tbsp.)
- Fresh brussels sprouts (1 lb.)
- Kosher salt (.5 tsp.)

1.Prep the vegetables. Trim the stems and discard any damaged outer leaves. Cut into halves, rinse, and pat dry. Toss with the oil and salt.
2.Set the fryer temperature ahead of time to 390° Fahrenheit.
3.Toss the sprouts into the basket and air-fry for 15 minutes.
4.Shake the basket to ensure even browning.

Buffalo Cauliflower
Serves: 4
- Breadcrumbs (1 cup)
- Cauliflower florets (4 cups)
- Buffalo sauce (.25 cup)
- Melted butter (.25 cup)

1.Melt the butter in a microwaveable dish. Whisk in the buffalo sauce.
2.Dip the florets in the butter mixture. Use the stem as a handle, holding it over a cup and let the excess drip away.
3.Dredge the florets through the breadcrumbs. Drop them into the Air Fryer. Set the timer for 14 to 17 minutes at 350°

Fahrenheit. (The unit will not need to preheat since it is calculated into the time.)

4. Shake the basket several times during the cooking process. Serve alongside your favorite dip, making sure to eat it right away because the crunchiness goes away quickly.

Buttery Blossoming Onions

Serves: 4
- Small onions (4)
- Dollops of butter (4)
- Olive oil (1 tbsp.)

1. Preheat the Air Fryer to reach 350° Fahrenheit.
2. Peel the skin from the onion and remove the top and bottom to create flat ends.
3. Soak the onions in salted water for four (4) hours to remove its harshness.
4. Slice the onion as far down as you can without severing its body. Cut four times - making eight segments.
5. Toss the prepared onions into the fryer basket. Drizzle with oil, adding a dollop of butter to each one.
6. Cook in the fryer until the outside is dark (30 minutes).
7. Note: Four dollops equals about four (4) heaping tablespoons.

Charred Shishito Peppers Servings Provided: 4 :
Olive oil (1 tsp.)
Juiced lemon (1)
Shishito peppers (20) Sea salt (to taste)
1. Set the Air Fryer at 390° Fahrenheit.
2. Toss the peppers in with the oil and salt. Add them to the basket and air-fry for five minutes.

1. Serve on a platter with a squeeze of lemon.

Crispy Onion Rings Servings Provided: 2 :
Coconut flour (2 tbsp.)
Grated parmesan cheese (2 tbsp.) Egg (1)
Large onion (1 in ringlets) Garlic powder (1 pinch) Pepper and salt (as desired) Olive oil (.25 cup)
1. Whisk the flour, spices, and grated cheese.
2. Set the Air Fryer at 400° Fahrenheit.
3. Whisk the eggs in a separate mixing container and add the onion rings. Soak a minute or so, and dip into the flour mixture.
4. Place in the Air Fryer basket, setting the timer for 6 minutes per side.
5. Serve as a quick snack or favorite side dish.

Cumin Butternut Squash

Servings Provided: 4
:
Butternut squash (1 medium) Cumin seeds (2 tsp.)
Chili flakes (1 pinch)
Salt & black pepper (as desired) Coriander (1 bunch)
Pine nuts (.25 cup)
Olive oil (1 tbsp.) Greek yogurt (.66 cup)
1. Warm the Air Fryer temperature in advance to 380° Fahrenheit.
2. Cube the squash and toss using the spices and oil in a baking pan.
3. Add them to the Air Fryer for 20 minutes.
4. Toast the pine nuts. Serve with a portion of yogurt and garnish using a sprinkle of coriander.

Hasselback Potatoes

Serves: 4
- Potatoes (4)
- Olive oil (as needed)

1. Set the Air Fryer temperature at 356° Fahrenheit.
2. Peel the potatoes and slice in half, about 1/16-inches apart from the base. (You want to create a feathered effect by not cutting it all the way through.)
3. Gently brush the potatoes with oil. Position each one into the fryer for 15 minutes.
4. Brush again and air-fry for about 15 additional minutes until browned and well done.

Honey Roasted Carrots

Serves: 4
- Carrots - baby or regular (3 cups) Honey (1 tbsp.)
- Olive oil (1 tbsp.)
- Pepper and salt (as desired)

1. Heat the Air Fryer at 392° Fahrenheit. Dice the carrots into small chunks.
2. Combine the honey, oil, salt, pepper, and carrots in a mixing bowl, coating well.
3. Put the carrots into the Air Fryer and set the timer for 12 minutes.

Mediterranean Veggies

Serves: 4
- Large cucumber (1)
- Green pepper (1)
- Large parsnip (1)
- Cherry tomatoes (.25 cup) Medium carrot (1)
- Garlic puree (2 tbsp.) Honey (2 tbsp.) Olive oil (6 tbsp.) Mixed herbs (1 tsp.)
- Pepper and salt (as desired)

1. Warm the Air Fryer at 356° Fahrenheit.
2. Chop the cucumber and green pepper. Toss them into the Air
3. Fryer.
4. Peel and dice the carrot and parsnip, adding the whole cherry tomatoes. Drizzle with three tablespoons of oil. Set the timer for 15 minutes.
5. Mix the remainder of the fixings into an Air Fryer - safe baking dish.
6. Add the veggies to the marinade and shake well. Give it a sprinkle of pepper and salt and cook at 392° Fahrenheit for another five minutes.
7. Note: You can substitute different veggies, but don't use the cucumber
8. and cauliflower in the same dish. Together, they produce too much liquid.
9. For variety, serve with a portion of honey and sweet potatoes to the mixture.

Mushroom Melt

Serves: 10
- Button mushrooms (10)
- Italian dried mixed herbs Salt and pepper Mozzarella cheese Cheddar cheese
- Optional Topping: Dried dill

1. Rinse the mushrooms, remove the stems, and drain in a colander.
2. For the flavor, provide a pinch of chosen herbs, black pepper, salt, and olive oil.
3. Warm the Air Fryer to reach 356° Fahrenheit (3- 5 min.).
4. Arrange the mushrooms in the basket with the hollow section facing you. Sprinkle the cheese on top of each of the caps.
5. Place the mushrooms in the cooker for 7 to 8 minutes.

6.Serve hot with a drizzle of basil or other tasty herbs.

Potato Hay

Serves: 4
- Russet potatoes (2)
- Canola oil (1 tbsp.)
- Kosher salt and ground black pepper (as desired)

1.Preheat the Air Fryer to 360° Fahrenheit.
2.Slice the potatoes into spirals using the medium grating attachment on a spiralizer and kitchen shears after 4 or 5 rotations.
3.Soak the spirals in a bowl of water for 20 minutes. Drain and rinse
4.well. Pat potatoes dry with paper towels, removing as much moisture as possible.
5.Place the spirals in a large resealable plastic bag with the oil, salt, and pepper, tossing to coat.
6.Place half of the potato spirals in the fry basket and insert it into the Air Fryer. Set the timer for 5 minutes.
7.Increase temperature to 390° Fahrenheit. Pull out the fry basket and add the potato spirals using tongs. Return the bucket to the and continue cooking until golden brown for 10 to 12 minutes.
8.Reduce the temperature to 360° Fahrenheit and repeat with remaining potato spirals.

Semolina Veggie Cutlets

Serves: 2
- Milk (5 cups)
- Veggies of choice - ex. carrots, cauliflower, peas, green beans, etc. (1.5 cups total)
- Olive oil – for frying Semolina (1 cup)
- Salt and pepper (as desired)

1.Heat the milk in a saucepan (medium heat). When hot, add the vegetables, pepper, and salt. Set the timer for 3 minutes.
2.Mix in the semolina and air-fry for 10 minutes.
3.Prepare a baking sheet with a layer of parchment baking paper. Spread the mixture over the pan to chill in the fridge for a minimum of four hours.
4.Set the Air Fryer temperature to 350° Fahrenheit.
5.Remove the mixture from the fridge and slice into cutlets. Brush each one with oil and set the timer for 10 minutes.
6.Serve with a portion of hot sauce.

Smoked Cheese Asparagus

Serves: 4
- Asparagus (1 lb.)
- Shredded smoked gouda cheese (.25 cup) Italian seasoning (2 tbsp.)
- Parmesan cheese (.5 cup) Sea salt (.5 tsp.)
- Freshly cracked black pepper (.25 tsp.) Heavy cream (1 cup)

1.Set the Air Fryer temperature at 400° Fahrenheit.
2.Use a sharp knife to discard the ¼-inch portion each asparagus.
3.Whisk the heavy cream, Italian seasoning, and parmesan.

4. Arrange the asparagus in a shallow dish and cover with the mixture.
5.Place in the basket of the fryer. Set the timer for 6 minutes.
6.Serve with the asparagus a sprinkle of cheese, pepper, and salt.

Sour Cream Stuffed Mushrooms
Serves: 24
- Rashers of bacon/bacon with fat strips & meat (2 thinly sliced)
- Small carrot (1)
- Green pepper (half of 1) Grated cheese (1 cup) Sour cream (.5 cup)
- Mushrooms (24 medium-sized)

1.Dice the onion, carrots, bacon, and mushroom stalks.
2.Slowly cook the veggies and bacon bits in a saucepan until softened. Add the sour cream and cheese. Mix well.
3.Warm the Air Fryer for five minutes at 356° Fahrenheit. Air-fry for 8 minutes.

Sweet Potato Tots

Serves: 4 / 6 each
- Peeled sweet potatoes (2 small/14 oz. total) Potato starch (1 tbsp.)
- Garlic powder (.125 tsp.) Kosher salt (1.25 tsp. - divided) No-salt-added ketchup (.75 cup)

1.Set the Air Fryer to warm at 400° Fahrenheit.
2.Prepare a medium pot of water (high heat) and wait for it to boil. Add the potatoes and simmer until fork-tender (15 min.). Transfer them to a platter to cool (15 min.).
3.Grate the potatoes using the large holes of a box grater. Gently toss with garlic powder, potato starch, and one teaspoon of salt. Shape the mixture into about 24 (1-inch) tot-shaped cylinders.
4.Lightly coat the Air Fryer basket with a cooking oil spray. Place half of the tots (about 12) in a single layer in the fryer basket and spray with the cooking spray.
5.Cook until lightly browned, 12-14 minutes, turning the tots halfway through the cooking cycle. Remove from fryer basket and sprinkle with 1/8 teaspoon of salt. Repeat with the remaining tots.
6.Serve immediately with ketchup.

Thyme & Garlic Tomatoes

Serves: 4
- Clove of garlic (1) Roma tomatoes (4) Dried thyme (.5 tsp.)
- Freshly ground black pepper & salt (as desired) Olive oil (1 tbsp.)

1.Heat the Air Fryer at 390° Fahrenheit.
2.Mince the garlic clove. Slice the tomatoes and remove the pithy parts and seeds. Toss them into a mixing container along with the pepper, salt, thyme, garlic, and olive oil.
3.Arrange them in the Air Fryer with the cut side up. Set a timer for 15 minutes.
4.Cool for a few minutes. Add on top of poultry, fish, or pasta.

Addictive Zucchini Sticks

Serves: 4
- 1 small zucchinis (about ½ pound)
- ½ teaspoon garlic granules
- ¼ teaspoon sea salt
- ⅛ teaspoon freshly ground black pepper 2 teaspoons arrowroot (or cornstarch)
- tablespoons fish flour
- 1 tablespoon water
- Cooking oil spray (sunflower, safflower, or refined coconut)

1.Trim the ends off the zucchini and then cut into sticks about 2 inches long and ½ inch wide. You should end up with about 2 cups of sticks.
2.In a medium bowl, combine the zucchini sticks with the garlic, salt, pepper, arrowroot, and flour. Stir well. Add the water and stir again, using a rubber spatula if you have one.
3.Spray the air fryer basket with oil and add the zucchini sticks,
4.spreading them out as much as possible. Spray the zucchini with oil. Fry for 7 minutes.
5.Remove the basket, gently stir or shake so the zucchini cooks
6.evenly, and spray again with oil. Cook for another 7 minutes, or until tender, nicely browned, and crisp on the outside. Enjoy the sticks plain or with your preferred dipping sauce.

Tamari Roasted Eggplant

Serves: 4
- Cooking oil spray (sunflower, safflower, or refined coconut)
- 1 medium-size eggplant (1 pound), cut into ½-inch-thick slices 2½ tablespoons tamari or shoyu
- teaspoons garlic granules 2 teaspoons onion granules
- teaspoons oil (olive, sunflower, or safflower)

1. Spray the air fryer basket with oil and set aside.
2.Place the eggplant slices in a large bowl and sprinkle the tamari, garlic, onion, and oil on top. Stir well, coating the eggplant as evenly as possible.
3.Place the eggplant in a single (or at most, double) layer in the air fryer basket. You may need to do this recipe in batches, depending on the size of your air fryer. Set the bowl aside without discarding the liquid.
4.Roast for 5 minutes. Remove and place the eggplant in the bowl again.
5. Toss the eggplant slices to coat evenly with the remaining liquid mixture, and place back in the air fryer as before.
6. Roast for another 3 minutes. Remove the basket and flip the pieces over to ensure even Cooking .
7.Roast for another 5 minutes, or until the eggplant is nicely browned and very tender.

Balsamic Glazed Carrots

Serves: 3
- medium-size carrots (about ⅓ pound) 1 tablespoon orange juice
- 2 teaspoons balsamic vinegar
- 1 teaspoon Cooking oil (sunflower, avocado, or safflower) 1 teaspoon maple syrup
- ½ teaspoon dried rosemary
- ¼ teaspoon sea salt
- ¼ teaspoon lemon zest

1.Trim the ends and scrub the carrots; there's no need to peel them. Cut them into spears about 2 inches long and ½-inch thick.
2. Place the carrots in the 6-inch round, 2-inch deep baking pan. Add the orange juice, balsamic vinegar, oil, maple syrup, rosemary, salt, and zest. Stir well.
3.Roast for 4 minutes. Remove the pan and stir the mixture well.
4.Roast for 5 more minutes. Remove the pan, stir well, and cook for another 5 minutes.
5.Remove the pan and stir one last time. Cook for another 4 minutes, or until the carrots are bright orange, nicely glazed

(the mixture is glazed over the carrots, and no longer thin and liquid), and the carrots are fairly tender. Serve while hot.

Alethea's Kale Chips

Serves: 3
- cups lightly packed kale, de-stemmed and torn into 2-inch pieces 2 tablespoons apple cider vinegar
- 1 tablespoon nutritional yeast
- 1 tablespoon tamari or shoyu
- 1 tablespoon oil (olive, sunflower, or melted coconut) 2 large garlic cloves, minced or pressed

1.In a large bowl, combine the kale pieces with apple cider vinegar,
2.nutritional yeast, tamari, oil, and garlic, and stir well until evenly coated.
3.Place in an air fryer basket and fry for 5 minutes. Remove the air fryer basket and reserve any pieces done: they will be dried out and crisp (there probably won't be many at this point). Gently stir, and fry for another 3 minutes.
4.Remove any crisp, dry pieces and fry for another minute or more if needed to dry all of the kale.

Timeless Taro Chips

Serves: 2
- Cooking oil spray (coconut, sunflower, or safflower) 1 cup thinly sliced taro (see ingredient tip)
- Sea salt

1.Spray the air fryer basket with oil and set aside. Place the sliced taro in the air fryer basket, spreading the pieces out as much as possible, and spray with oil. Fry for about 4 minutes.
2.Remove the air fryer basket, shake (so that the chips cook evenly), and spray again with oil. Fry for another 4 minutes. If any chips are browned or crisp, remove them now.
3.Remove the air fryer basket, shake again, spray again, and sprinkle lightly with salt to taste. Fry for another 3 to 4 minutes. Remove all of the chips that are done, and cook any remaining underdone chips for another minute, or until crisp. Please note that they may crisp up a tiny bit more as they sit at room temperature for a few minutes,
4.but some may need extra time in the air fryer, as they don't always cook at the same rate. You'll get the hang of how to test for doneness after you make a few batches.

Garlic Lime Tortilla Chips

Serves: 3
- corn tortillas
- ½ teaspoon garlic granules
- ⅛ to ¼ teaspoon sea salt
- 2½ teaspoons fresh lime juice
- Cooking oil spray (coconut, sunflower, or safflower)

1.Cut the tortillas into quarters. Place in a medium bowl and toss gently with the garlic, salt to taste, and lime juice.
2.Spray the air fryer basket with the oil, add the chips, and fry for 3
3.minutes. Remove the air fryer basket, toss (so the chips cook evenly), and spray again with oil. Fry for another 2 minutes. Remove one last time, toss, spray with oil, and fry for 2 minutes, or until golden-browned and crisp. These may not all cook at the same

4.rate, so as you go, be sure to remove the ones that are done. Let sit at room
5.temperature for a few minutes to finish crisping up, and then enjoy.

Classic French Fries

Serves: 3

- medium potatoes, preferably yukon gold (but any kind will do) Cooking oil spray (sunflower, safflower, or refined coconut)
- 2 teaspoons oil (olive, sunflower, or melted coconut)
- ½ teaspoon garlic granules
- ¼ teaspoon plus ⅛ teaspoon sea salt
- ¼ teaspoon freshly ground black pepper
- ¼ teaspoon paprika
- Ketchup, hot sauce, or no-dairy ranch dressing, for serving

1.Scrub the potatoes and cut them into French fry shapes (about ¼- inch thick), in relatively uniform sizes. Spray the air fryer basket with oil and set aside.
2. In a medium bowl, toss the cut potato pieces with the oil, garlic,
3.salt, pepper, and paprika and stir very well (i use a rubber spatula). Place in an air fryer basket and fry for 8 minutes.
4.Remove the air fryer basket and shake (or gently stir) well. Fry for another 8 minutes. Remove one last time, stir or shake, and fry for another 6 minutes, or until tender and nicely browned. Enjoy plain or with ketchup, hot sauce, vegan ranch, or any other sauce that flips your fancy.

Cheesy French Fries With Shallots

Serves: 3

- Cooking oil spray (sunflower, safflower, or refined coconut)
- 1 large potato (russet or yukon gold), cut into ¼-inch-thick slices 1 teaspoon neutral-flavored oil (sunflower, safflower, or refined coconut)
- ¼ teaspoon sea salt
- ⅛ teaspoon freshly ground black pepper 1 large shallot, thinly sliced
- ½ cup plus 2 tablespoons prepared cheesy sauce
- tablespoons minced chives or sCal lions (optional)

1.spray the air fryer basket with oil. Set aside.
2.in a medium bowl, toss the potato slices with the oil, salt, and pepper. Place in the air fryer basket and fry for 6 minutes. Remove the air fryer basket, stir or shake (so that the slices cook evenly), and fry for another 4 minutes.
3.remove. Add the shallots, stir (or shake) again, and fry for another 5 minutes.
4.make the cheesy sauce according to the here. Set aside or keep warm on a very low heat burner.
5.remove the air fryer basket, stir or shake, and fry for a final 4 minutes, or until the fries and shallots are crisp and browned.

Berbere-Spiced Fries

Serves: 2

- 1 large (about ¾ pound) potato (preferably yukon gold, but any kind will do)
- Cooking oil spray (sunflower, safflower, or refined coconut)
- 1 tablespoon neutral-flavored Cooking oil (sunflower, safflower, or refined coconut)
- 1 teaspoon coconut Sugar 1 teaspoon garlic granules

- ½ teaspoon berbere
- ½ teaspoon sea salt
- ¼ teaspoon turmeric
- ¼ teaspoon paprika

1.Scrub the potato and cut it into french fry shapes (about ¼-inch
2.thick), in relatively uniform pieces. Spray the air fryer basket with oil and set aside.
3.In a medium bowl, toss the potato pieces with the oil, Sugar, garlic, barbered, salt, turmeric, and paprika and stir very well (i use a rubber spatula). Place in the air fryer basket and fry for 8 minutes.
4.Remove the air fryer basket and shake (or gently stir) well. Fry for another 8 minutes.
5.Remove one last time, stir or shake, and fry for another 3 to 5 minutes, or until tender and nicely browned. Enjoy while still hot or warm.

Potato Wedges

Serves: 4

- potatoes, cut into wedges
- 1 tablespoon olive oil
- Salt and black pepper to the taste 3 tablespoons sour cream
- 2 tablespoons sweet chili sauce

1.In a bowl, mix potato wedges with oil, salt and pepper, toss well, add to air fryer's basket and for 25 minutes boil at 360 degrees f, flipping them once.
2.Divide potato wedges on plates, drizzle sour cream and chili sauce all over and serve them as a side dish.

Mushroom Side Dish

Serves: 4

- button mushrooms, stems removed 1 tablespoon Italian seasoning
- Salt and black pepper to the taste
- tablespoons cheddar cheese, grated 1 tablespoon olive oil
- 2 tablespoons mozzarella, grated 1 tablespoon dill, chopped

1. In a bowl, mix mushrooms with Italian seasoning, salt, pepper, oil and dill and rub well.
2. Arrange mushrooms in your air fryer's basket, sprinkle mozzarella and cheddar in each and cook them at 360 degrees f for 8 minutes.
3. Divide them on plates and serve them as a side dish.

Corn With Lime And Cheese

Serves: 2

- corns on the cob, husks removed A drizzle of olive oil
- ½ cup feta cheese, grated
- 2 teaspoons sweet paprika Juice from 2 limes

1.Rub corn with oil and paprika, place in your air fryer and cook at 400 degrees f for 15 minutes, flipping once.
2.Divide corn on plates, sprinkle cheese on top, drizzle lime juice and serve as a side dish.

Hasselback Potatoes

Serves: 2

- potatoes, peeled and thinly sliced almost all the way

horizontally
- 2 tablespoons olive oil
- 1 teaspoon garlic, minced
- Salt and black pepper to the taste
- ½ teaspoon oregano, dried
- ½ teaspoon basil, dried
- ½ teaspoon sweet paprika

1.In a bowl, mix oil with garlic, salt, pepper, oregano, basil and paprika and whisk well.
2.Rub potatoes with this mix, place them in your air fryer's basket and fry them at 360 degrees f for 20 minutes. Divide them on plates and serve as a side dish.

Brussels Sprouts Side Dish

Serves: 4
- 1-pound Brussels sprouts, trimmed and halved Salt and black pepper to the taste
- teaspoons olive oil
- ½ teaspoon thyme, chopped
- ½ cup mayonnaise
- tablespoons roasted garlic, crushed

1.In your air fryer, mix Brussels sprouts with salt, pepper and oil, toss well and cook them at 390 degrees f for 15 minutes.
2.Meanwhile, in a bowl, mix thyme with mayo and garlic and whisk well.
3.Divide Brussels sprouts on plates, drizzle garlic sauce all over and serve as a side dish.

Creamy Air Fried Potato Side Dish

Serves: 2
- 1 big potato
- bacon strips, cooked and chopped 1 teaspoon olive oil
- 1/3 cup cheddar cheese, shredded
- 1 tablespoon green onions, chopped Salt and black pepper to the taste
- 1 tablespoon butter
- 2 tablespoons heavy cream

1.Rub potato with oil, season with salt and pepper, place in preheated air fryer and cook at 400 degrees f for 30 minutes.
2.Flip potato cook for 30 minutes more, transfer to a cutting board, cool it down, slice in half lengthwise and scoop pulp in a bowl.
3.Add bacon, cheese, butter, heavy cream, green onions, salt and pepper, stir well and stuff potato skins with this mix.
4.Return potatoes to your air fryer and for 20 minutes boil them at 400 degrees f
5.Serve after dividing.

Green Beans Side Dish

Serves: 4
- 1 and ½ pounds green beans, trimmed and steamed for 2 minutes Salt and black pepper to the taste
- ½ pound shallots, chopped
- ¼ cup almonds, toasted 2 tablespoons olive oil

1.In your air fryer's basket, mix green beans with salt, pepper, shallots, almonds and oil, toss well and cook at 400 degrees f for 25minutes.
2.Serve after dividing

Roasted Pumpkin

Serves: 4
- 1 and ½ pound pumpkin, deseeded, sliced and roughly chopped 3 garlic cloves, minced
- 1 tablespoon olive oil
- A pinch of sea salt
- A pinch of brown Sugar
- A pinch of nutmeg, ground A pinch of cinnamon powder

1.In your air fryer's basket, mix pumpkin with garlic, oil, salt, brown Sugar, cinnamon and nutmeg, stir and cover and for 12 minutes boil at 370 degrees f
2.Serve after dividing

Parmesan Mushrooms

Serves: 3
- button mushroom caps
- cream cracker slices, crumbled 1 egg white
- 2 tablespoons parmesan, grated 1 teaspoon italian seasoning
- A pinch of salt and black pepper
- 1 tablespoon butter, melted

1.In a bowl, mix crackers with egg white, parmesan, Italian seasoning, butter, salt and pepper, stir well and stuff mushrooms with this mix.
2.Arrange mushrooms in your air fryer's basket and cook them at 360 degrees f for 15 minutes.
3.Serve after dividing

Calories 124, Fat 4, Fiber 4, Carbs7, Protein 3

Garlic Potatoes

Serves: 6
- tablespoons parsley, chopped
- garlic cloves, minced
- ½ teaspoon basil, dried
- ½ teaspoon oregano, dried
- pounds red potatoes, halved 1 teaspoon thyme, dried
- 2 tablespoons olive oil
- Salt and black pepper to the taste 2 tablespoons butter
- 1/3 cup parmesan, grated

1.In a bowl, mix potato halves with parsley, garlic, basil, oregano, thyme, salt, pepper, oil and butter, toss well and transfer to your air fryer's basket.
2.Cover and for 20 minutes boil at 400 degrees f, flipping them once.
3.Sprinkle parmesan on top, divide potatoes on plates and serve as a side dish.

Eggplant Side Dish

Serves: 4
- baby eggplants, scooped in the center and pulp reserved Salt and black pepper to the taste
- A pinch of oregano, dried
- 1 green bell pepper, chopped 1 tablespoon tomato paste
- 1 bunch coriander, chopped

1.Using the pan, heat up over an average heat, add onion, stir and cook for 1 minute.

2.Add salt, pepper, eggplant pulp, oregano, green bell pepper, tomato paste, garlic power, coriander and tomato, stir, cook for 1-2 minutes more, take off heat and cool down.
3.Stuff eggplants with this mix, place them in your air fryer's basket and cook at 360 degrees f for 8 minutes.
4.Divide eggplants on plates and serve them as a side dish.

Mushrooms And Sour Cream
Serves: 6
- bacon strips, chopped 1 yellow onion, chopped
  - green bell pepper, chopped
- 24 mushrooms, stems removed
- 1 carrot, grated - ½ cup sour cream 1 cup cheddar cheese, grated
- Salt and black pepper to the taste
1.Over an average heat the pan, add bacon, onion, bell pepper and carrot, stir and cook for 1 minute.
2.Add salt, pepper and sour cream, stir cook for 1 minute more, take off heat and cool down.
3.Stuff mushrooms with this mix, sprinkle cheese on top and cook at 360 degrees f for 8 minutes.
4.Serve and enjoy!

Eggplant Fries
Serves: 4
- Cooking spray
  - eggplant, peeled and cut into medium fries 2 tablespoons milk
- 1 egg, whisked
  - cups panko breadcrumbs
- ½ cup Italian cheese, shredded Pepper and salt to taste
1.In a bowl, mix egg with milk, salt and pepper and whisk well.
2.In another bowl, mix panko with cheese and stir.
3.Dip eggplant fries in egg mix, then coat in panko mix, place them in your air fryer greased with Cooking spray and cook at 400 degrees f for 5 minutes.
4.Serve and enjoy!

Fried Tomatoes
Serves: 4
- green tomatoes, sliced
- Salt and black pepper to the taste
- ½ cup flour
- cup buttermilk
- cup panko breadcrumbs
- ½ tablespoon creole seasoning Cooking spray
1.Season tomato slices with salt and pepper.
2.Put flour in a bowl, buttermilk in another and panko crumbs and creole seasoning in a third one.
3.Dredge tomato slices in flour, then in buttermilk and panko breadcrumbs place them in your air fryer's basket greased with Cooking spray and cook them at 400 degrees f for 5 minutes.
4.Serve and enjoy!

Seafood Recipes (Part 7) Cumin Eggplant Mix
Serves: 4
- 1-pound eggplant, roughly cubed 1 cup cherry tomatoes, halved
  - red onion, chopped
- Salt and black pepper to the taste 2 tablespoons olive oil
- ½ teaspoon chili powder
- ½ teaspoon cumin, ground
- 1 tablespoon chives, chopped
1.Heat the air fryer with the oil at 350 degrees f, add the eggplants and the other , toss gently, and cook for 20 minutes.
2.Divide the mix between plates and serve as a side dish.

Garlic Kale
Serves: 4
- 1-pound kale leaves, torn 1 tablespoon avocado oil
  - teaspoon coriander, ground 1 teaspoon basil, dried
- 1 tablespoon balsamic vinegar
- garlic cloves, minced
- Salt and black pepper to the taste
1.In your air fryer, combine the kale with the oil and the other , toss well and cook them at 370 degrees f for 20 minutes.
2.Divide the mix between plates and serve as a side dish.

Green Beans Sauté
Serves: 4
- pounds green beans, trimmed and halved Salt and black pepper to the taste
- tablespoon balsamic vinegar
- 1 tablespoon dill, chopped 2 tablespoons olive oil
1.In your air fryer's basket, combine the green beans with the vinegar and the other , toss and cook at 350 degrees f for 20 minutes.
2.Divide between plates and serve as a side dish.

Herbed Tomatoes
Serves: 4
- 1-pound tomatoes, cut into wedges 2 tablespoons chives, chopped
- tablespoon oregano, chopped 1 tablespoon balsamic vinegar 1 teaspoon italian seasoning
- A pinch of salt and black pepper 2 tablespoons olive oil
1.In your air fryer's basket, combine the tomatoes with the chives,
2.vinegar and the other , toss and cook at 360 degrees f for 20 minutes.
3.Divide everything between plates and serve as a side dish.

Coriander Potatoes
Serves: 4
- 1-pound gold potatoes, peeled and cut into wedges Salt and black pepper to the taste
- tablespoon tomato sauce
- tablespoons coriander, chopped
- ½ teaspoon garlic powder 1 teaspoon chili powder 1 tablespoon olive oil
1.In a bowl, combine the potatoes with the tomato sauce and the other , toss, and transfer to the air fryer's basket.
2. Cook at 370 degrees f for 25 minutes, divide between plates and serve as a side dish.

Creamy Green Beans And Tomatoes

Serves: 4
- 1-pound green beans, trimmed and halved
- ½ pound cherry tomatoes, halved 2 tablespoons olive oil
    - teaspoon oregano, dried
- 1 teaspoon basil, dried
- Salt and black pepper to the taste 1 cup heavy cream
- ½ tablespoon cilantro, chopped

1.In your air fryer's pan, combine the green beans with the tomatoes and the other , toss and cook at 360 degrees f for 20 minutes.
2.Divide the mix between plates and serve.

Buttery Artichokes

Serves: 4
- artichokes, trimmed and halved 3 garlic cloves, minced
- tablespoon olive oil
- Salt and black pepper to the taste 4 tablespoons butter, melted
- ¼ teaspoon cumin, ground
- tablespoon lemon zest, grated

1.In a bowl, combine the artichokes with the oil, garlic and the other , toss well and transfer them to the air fryer's basket.
2.Cook for 20 minutes at 370 degrees f, divide between plates and serve as a side dish.

Sweet Potato And Eggplant Mix

Serves: 4
- sweet potatoes, peeled and cut into medium wedges 2 eggplants, roughly cubed
- tablespoon avocado oil
- Juice of 1 lemon
- garlic cloves, minced
- 1 teaspoon nutmeg, ground
- Salt and black pepper to the taste 1 tablespoon rosemary, chopped

1.In your air fryer, combine the potatoes with the eggplants and the other toss and cook at 370 degrees f for 20 minutes.
2.Divide the mix between plates and serve as a side dish.

Peppers And Tomatoes Mix

Serves: 4
- tablespoon olive oil
- red onion, sliced
- 1-pound cherry tomatoes, halved
- red bell pepper, cut into medium strips 1 green bell pepper, cut in medium strips 1 teaspoon chili powder
- teaspoon gram masala
- Salt and black pepper to the taste

1.In your air fryer, combine the tomatoes with the bell peppers and the other , toss and cook at 370 degrees f for 20 minutes.
2.Divide the mix between plates and serve as a side dish.

Chives Carrots And Onions

Serves: 4
- 1-pound baby carrots, peeled 2 red onions, sliced
- tablespoon lime zest, grated

- tablespoon balsamic vinegar 2 tablespoons chives, chopped

1.In your air fryer's basket, combine the carrots with the onions and the other , toss and cook at 320 degrees f for 20 minutes.
2.Divide between plates and serve as a side dish.

Cilantro Brussels Sprouts

Serves: 4
- pounds Brussels sprouts, trimmed and halved 1 tablespoon olive oil
- 2 tablespoons maple syrup
- tablespoon cilantro, chopped 1 tablespoon sweet paprika
- A pinch of salt and black pepper

1.In your air fryer's basket, combine the sprouts with the oil, maple syrup and the remaining , toss and cook at 360 degrees f for 25 minutes.
2.Divide between plates and serve as a side dish.

Garlic Beets

Serves: 4
- pounds beets, peeled and roughly cubed A pinch of salt and black pepper
- teaspoon chili powder 4 garlic cloves, minced 1 tablespoon olive oil

1.In your air fryer's basket, combine the beets with salt, pepper and
2.the other , toss and cook at 370 degrees f for 25 minutes.
3.Divide the beets between plates and serve as a side dish.

Ginger Mushrooms

Serves: 4
- tablespoons olive oil
- 2 tablespoons balsamic vinegar
- 2 pounds white mushrooms, halved 1 tablespoon ginger, grated
- A pinch of salt and black pepper 1 teaspoon cumin, ground

1.In your air fryer's basket, combine the mushrooms with the oil, vinegar and the other , toss and cook at 360 degrees f for 20 minutes.
2.Divide the mix between plates and serve.

Masala Potatoes

Serves: 4
- pounds gold potatoes, peeled and roughly cubed
    - tablespoon olive oil
    - 1 teaspoon garlic powder 1 teaspoon germ masala Juice of 1 lime
    - A pinch of salt and black pepper

1.In your air fryer's basket, combine the potatoes with the garam masala and the other , toss and cook at 370 degrees f for 20 minutes.
2.Divide the mix between plates and serve.

Lime Broccoli

Serves: 4
- tablespoon avocado oil
- 1-pound broccoli florets
- 1 tablespoon ginger, grated

- A pinch of salt and black pepper Juice of 1 lime

1.In your air fryer's basket, combine the broccoli with the oil and the other , toss and cook at 370 degrees f for 20 minutes.
2.Divide the mix between plates and serve.

Cajun Asparagus

Serves: 4

- teaspoon extra virgin olive oil 1 bunch asparagus, trimmed
- ½ tablespoon Cajun seasoning

1.In a bowl, mix the asparagus with the oil and Cajun seasoning; coat the asparagus well.
2.Put the asparagus in your air fryer and cook at 400 degrees f for 5
3.minutes.
4.Divide between plates and serve.

Squash Salad

Serves: 4

- butternut squash, cubed
- tablespoons balsamic vinegar 1 bunch cilantro, chopped
- Salt and black pepper to taste 1 tablespoon olive oil

1.Put the squash in your air fryer, and add the salt, pepper, and oil; toss well.
2.Cook at 400 degrees f for 12 minutes.
3.Transfer the squash to a bowl, add the vinegar and cilantro, and toss.
4.Serve and enjoy!

Creamy Squash Mix

Serves: 6

- big butternut squash, roughly cubed
- 1 cup sour cream
- Salt and black pepper to taste 1 tablespoon parsley, chopped A drizzle of olive oil

1.Put the squash in your air fryer, add the salt and pepper, and rub with the oil.
2.Cook at 400 degrees f for 12 minutes.
3.Transfer the squash to a bowl, and add the cream and the parsley.
4.Toss and serve.

Orange Carrots

Serves: 4

- 1½ pounds baby carrots 2 teaspoons orange zest
- tablespoons cider vinegar
- ½ cup orange juice
- A handful of parsley, chopped A drizzle of olive oil

1.Put the baby carrots in your air fryer's basket, add the orange zest and oil, and rub the carrots well.
2.Cook at 350 degrees f for 15 minutes.
3.Transfer the carrots to a bowl, and then add the vinegar, orange juice, and parsley.
4.Toss, serve, and enjoy!

Tomato Salad

Serves: 8

- red onion, sliced
- ounces feta cheese, crumbled Salt and black pepper to taste
- 1 pint mixed cherry tomatoes, halved 2 ounces pecans
- tablespoons olive oil

1.In your air fryer, mix the tomatoes with the salt, pepper, onions, and the oil.
2.Cook at 400 degrees f for 5 minutes.

3. Transfer to a bowl and add the pecans and the cheese.
4.Toss and serve.

Tomato And Green Beans Salad

Serves: 4

- 1-pound green beans, trimmed and halved 2 green onions, chopped
- ounces canned green chilies, chopped
- jalapeno pepper, chopped A drizzle of olive oil
- teaspoons chili powder 1 teaspoon garlic powder
- Salt and black pepper to taste
- cherry tomatoes, halved

1.Place all in a pan that fits your air fryer, and mix / toss.
2.Put the pan in the fryer and cook at 400 degrees f for 6 minutes.
3.Divide the mix between plates and serve hot.

Bell Peppers And Kale

Serves: 4

- red bell peppers, cut into strips
- 2 green bell peppers, cut into strips
- ½ pound kale leaves
- Salt and black pepper to taste
- 2 yellow onions, roughly chopped
- ¼ cup veggie stock
- tablespoons tomato sauce

1.Add all to a pan that fits your air fryer; mix well.
2.Place the pan in the fryer and cook at 360 degrees f for 15 minutes.
3.Divide between plates, serve, and enjoy!

Garlic Parsnips

Serves: 4

- 1-pound parsnips, cut into chunks 1 tablespoon olive oil
- garlic cloves, minced
- tablespoon balsamic vinegar Salt and black pepper to taste

1.Add all of the to a bowl and mix well.
2.Place them in the air fryer and cook at 380 degrees f for 15 minutes.
3.Divide between plates and serve.

Broccoli And Pomegranate

Serves: 4

- broccoli head, florets separated
- Salt and black pepper to taste
- 1 pomegranate, seeds separated A drizzle of olive oil

1.In a bowl, mix the broccoli with the salt, pepper, and oil; toss.
2.Put the florets in your air fryer and cook at 400 degrees f for 7 minutes.
3.Divide between plates, sprinkle the pomegranate seeds all over, and serve.

Bacon Cauliflower

Serves: 4

- cauliflower head, florets separated 1 tablespoon

olive oil
- Salt and black pepper to taste
- ½ cup bacon, cooked and chopped 2 tablespoons dill, chopped

1.Put the cauliflower in your air fryer and add the salt, pepper, and oil; toss well.
2.Cook at 400 degrees f for 12 minutes.
3.Divide the cauliflower between plates, sprinkle the bacon and the dill on top, and serve.

Paneer Cheese Balls

Serves: 6
- cup paneer, crumbled 1 cup cheese, grated
- 1 potato, boiled and mashed
- 1 onion, chopped finely
- 1 green chili, chopped finely 1 teaspoon red chili flakes Salt to taste
- tbsp coriander leaves, chopped finely
- ½ cup all-purpose flour
- ¾ cup of water Breadcrumbs as needed

1.Mix flour with water in a bowl and spread the breadcrumbs in a tray.
2.Add the rest of the to make the paneer mixture.
3.Make golf ball-sized balls out of this mixture.
4.Dip each ball in the flour liquid then coat with the breadcrumbs.
5.Place the cheese balls in the instant pot duo and spray it with Cooking spray.
6.Put on the air fryer lid and seal it.
7.Hit the "air fry button" and select 15 minutes of Cooking time, then press "start."
8.Once the instant pot duo beeps, remove its lid.
9.Serve.

Russet Potato Hay

Serves: 4
- russet potatoes
- tablespoon olive oil
- Salt and black pepper to taste

1. Pass the potatoes through a spiralizer to get potato spirals.
2.Soak these potato spirals in a bowl filled with water for about 20 minutes.
3.Drain and rinse the soaked potatoes then pat them dry.
4.Toss the potato spirals with salt, black pepper, and oil in a bowl.
5.Spread the seasoned potato spirals in the air fryer basket.
6.Set this air fryer basket in the instant pot duo.
7.Put on the air fryer lid and seal it.
8.Hit the "air fry button" and select 15 minutes of Cooking time, then press "start."
9.Toss the potato spiral when halfway cooked then resume Cooking .
10.once the instant pot duo beeps, remove its lid.
11.serve.

Onion Rings

Serves: 4
- 3/4 cup flour
- large yellow onion, sliced and rings separated
- ¼ tsp garlic powder
- ¼ tsp paprika
- 1 cup almond milk - 1 large egg 1/2 cup cornstarch
- 1 ½ teaspoons of baking powder 1 teaspoon salt
- 1 cup breadcrumbs

- Cooking spray

1.Whisk flour with baking powder, salt, and cornstarch in a bowl.

2. Coat the onion rings with this dry flour mixture and keep them aside.
3.Beat egg with milk in a bowl and dip the rings in this mixture.
4.Place the coated rings in the air fryer basket and set it inside the instant pot duo.
5.Spray the onion rings with Cooking oil. Put on the air fryer lid and seal it.
6.Hit the "air fry button" and select 10 minutes of Cooking time, then press "start." Flip the rings when cooked halfway through. Once the instant pot duo beeps, remove its lid. Serve.

Breaded Avocado Fries

Serves: 4
- 1/4 cup all-purpose flour
- 1/2 teaspoon ground black pepper 1/4 teaspoon salt
- egg
- 1 teaspoon water
- 1 ripe avocado, peeled, pitted and sliced 1/2 cup panko breadcrumbs
- Cooking spray

1.Whisk flour with salt and black pepper in one bowl.
2.Beat egg with water in another and spread the crumbs in a shallow tray.
3.First coat the avocado slices with the flour mixture then dip them into the egg.
4.Drop off the excess and coat the avocado with panko crumbs liberally.
5.Place all the coated slices in the air fryer basket and spray them with Cooking oil.
6.Set the air fryer basket inside the instant pot duo.
7.Put on the air fryer lid and seal it.
8.Hit the "air fry button" and select 7 minutes of Cooking time, then press "start."
9.Flip the fries after 4 minutes of Cooking and resume Cooking .
10.Once the instant pot duo beeps, remove its lid. Serve fresh.

Buffalo Chicken Strips

Serves:4
- 1/2 cup Greek yogurt 1/4 cup egg
- ½ tablespoon hot sauce 1 cup panko breadcrumbs
- 1 tablespoon sweet paprika
- 1 tablespoon garlic pepper seasoning 1 tablespoon cayenne pepper
- 1-pound chicken breasts, cut into strips

1.Mix greek yogurt with hot sauce and egg in a bowl.
2.Whisk breadcrumbs with garlic powder, cayenne pepper, and paprika in another bowl.
3.First, dip the chicken strips in the yogurt sauce then coat them with the crumb's mixture.
4.Place the coated strips in the air fryer basket and spray them with Cooking oil.
5.Set the air fryer basket inside the instant pot duo.
6.Put on the air fryer lid and seal it.
7. Hit the "air fry button" and select 16 minutes of Cooking time, then press "start."
8.Flip the chicken strips after 8 minutes of Cooking then resume air fearing.

9.Once the instant pot duo beeps, remove its lid.
10.Serve.

Sweet Potato Chips

Serves:2
- teaspoon avocado oil
- medium sweet potato, peeled and sliced 1/2 teaspoon creole seasoning

1.Toss the sweet potato with avocado oil and creole seasoning in a bowl.
2.Spread the potato slices in the air fryer basket and spray them with oil.
3.Set the air fryer basket in the instant pot duo.
4.Put on the air fryer lid and seal it.
5.Hit the "air fry button" and select 13 minutes of Cooking time, then press "start."
6.Toss the potato slices after 7 minutes of Cooking and resume air
7.frying.
8.Once the instant pot duo beeps, remove its lid.
9.Serve fresh.

Sweet Potato Tots

Serves:4

- sweet potatoes, peeled
- 1/2 teaspoon cajun seasoning Olive oil Cooking spray
- Sea salt to taste

1.Add sweet potatoes to boiling water in a pot and cook for 15 minutes until soft.
2.Drain the boiled sweet potatoes and allow them to cool down.
3.Grate the potatoes into a bowl and stir in cajun seasoning and salt.
4.Mix well and make small tater tots out of this mixture.
5.Place these tater tots in the air fryer basket and spray them with Cooking oil.
6.Set the air fryer basket in the instant pot duo.
7.Put on the air fryer lid and seal it.
8.Hit the "air fry button" and select 16 minutes of Cooking time, then press "start."
9.After 8 minutes, flip all the tots and spray them again with Cooking oil then resume Cooking .
10.Once the instant pot duo beeps, remove its lid.
11.Serve fresh.

Corn Nuts

Serves:6
- oz. Giant white corn
- tablespoons vegetable oil 1 1/2 teaspoons salt

1.Soak white corn in a bowl filled with water and leave it for 8 hours.
2.Drain the soaked corns and spread them in the air fryer basket.
3.Leave to dry for 20 minutes after patting them dry with a paper towel.
4.Add oil and salt on top of the corns and toss them well.
5.Set the air fryer basket in the instant pot.
6.Put on the air fryer lid and seal it.
7.Hit the "air fry button" and select 20 minutes of Cooking time, then press "start."
8.Shake the corns after every 5 minutes of Cooking , then resume the function.

9.Once the instant pot duo beeps, remove its lid.
10.Serve.

Tempura Vegetables

Serves: 4
- 1/2 cup all-purpose flour
- 1/2 teaspoon salt, divided, or more to taste 1/2 teaspoon ground black pepper
- eggs
- 2 tablespoons water
- cup panko breadcrumbs 2 teaspoons vegetable oil
- 1/2 cup whole green beans
- 1/2 cup asparagus spears
- 1/2 cup red onion rings
- 1/2 cup sweet pepper rings
- 1/2 cup avocado wedges
- 1/2 cup zucchini slices

1.Whisk flour with black pepper and salt in a shallow dish.
2.Beat eggs with water in a bowl and mix panko with oil in another tray.
3.Coat all the veggies with flour mixture first, then dip them in egg and finally in the panko mixture to a coat.
4.Shake off the excess and keep the coated veggies in separate plates.
5.Set half of the coated vegetables in a single layer in the air fryer basket.
6.Place the basket in the instant pot duo and spray them with Cooking oil.
7.Put on the air fryer lid and seal it.
8.Hit the "air fry button" and select 10 minutes of Cooking time, then press "start."
9.Once the instant pot duo beeps, remove its lid.
10.Transfer the fried veggies to the serving plates and cooking the remaining half using the same steps.
11.Serve.

Shrimp A La Bang Sauce

Serves: 6
- 1/2 cup mayonnaise
- 1/4 cup sweet chili sauce
- 1 tablespoon Sirach sauce
- 1/4 cup all-purpose flour
- 1 cup panko breadcrumbs
- 1-pound raw shrimp, peeled and deveined
- 1 head loose-leaf lettuce
- green onions, chopped, or to taste

1.Whisk mayonnaise with Sirach, chili sauce in a bowl until smooth.
2.Spread flour in one plate and panko in the other.
3.Place flour on a plate. Place panko on a separate plate.
4.First coat the shrimp with the flour, then dip in mayonnaise mixture and finally coat with the panko.
5.Arrange the shrimp in the air fryer basket in a single layer. (do not
6.overcrowd)
7.Set the air fryer basket in the instant pot duo.
8.Put on the air fryer lid and seal it.
9.Hit the "air fry button" and select 12 minutes of Cooking time, then press "start."
10.Once the instant pot duo beeps, remove its lid.
11.Air fry the remaining shrimp in the same way.
12.Garnish with lettuce and green onion.

13.Serve.

Zucchinis And Walnuts

Serves:4
- lb. Zucchinis; sliced
- ¼ cup chives; chopped.
- cup walnuts; chopped. 4 oz. Arugula leaves
- 1 tbsp. Olive oil
- Salt and white pepper to the taste

1.In a pan that fits the air fryer, combine all the except the arugula and walnuts, toss, put the pan in the machine and cook at 360°f for 20 minutes
2.Transfer this to a salad bowl, add the arugula and the walnuts, toss and serve as a side salad.

Coriander Artichokes

Serves: 4
- oz. Artichoke hearts 1 tbsp. Lemon juice
- tsp. Coriander, ground
- ½ tsp. Cumin seeds
- ½ tsp. Olive oil
- Salt and black pepper to taste.

1.In a pan that fits your air fryer, mix all the , toss, introduce the pan in the fryer and cook at 370°f for 15 minutes
2.Divide the mix between plates and serve as a side dish.

Tasty Eggplant Slices

Serves: 4
- eggplant, cut into 1/4-inch thick slices 1/4 tsp garlic powder
- tsp paprika
- 1/4 tsp onion powder

1.Add all into the mixing bowl and toss until well coated.
2.Spray the dehydrating tray with Cooking spray and place in instant pot duo crisp air fryer basket.
3.Arrange eggplant slices on the dehydrating tray.
4.Place air fryer basket into the pot.
5.Seal the pot with air fryer lid, select dehydrate mode and cook at 145 f for 4 hours.
6.Serve or store.

Baba Ghanoush

Serves: 6
- eggplant, pierce with a fork
- tbsp sesame seeds 2 tbsp sesame oil
- tsp lemon juice
- 1/2 tsp ground cumin 1 garlic clove, minced 1/2 onion, chopped
- tsp sea salt

1.Pour 1 cup of water into the inner pot of instant pot duo crisp. Place steamer rack in the pot.
2. Place eggplant on top of the steamer rack.
3.Seal the pot with pressure Cooking lid and cook on high pressure for 8 minutes.
4.Once done, release pressure using a quick release. Remove lid.
5.Remove eggplant from pot and clean the pot. Peel and slice cooked eggplant.
6.Add oil into the pot and set a pot on sauté mode.

7.Add onion and eggplant and sauté for 3-5 minutes.
8.Add remaining and stir everything well to combine.
9.Turn off the instant pot. Blend eggplant mixture using blender until smooth.
10.Serve and enjoy.

Healthy Beet Hummus

Serves: 16
- cup chickpeas 1/3 cup
- water 1/4 cup
- olive oil 1/4 cup
- fresh lemon juice 3 beets,
- peeled and diced 2 garlic cloves,
- peeled 1/4 cup sunflower seeds 1 1/2 tsp kosher salt

1.Add beets, chickpeas, 1 tsp salt, 3 cups water, garlic, and sunflower seeds into the instant pot.
2.Seal pot with lid and cook on manual high pressure for 40 minutes.
3. Strain beet, chickpeas, garlic, and sunflower seeds and place in a food processor and lemon juice and remaining salt and process until smooth.
4.Add oil and 1/3 cup water and process until smooth.
5.Serve and enjoy.

Chicken Jalapeno Popper Dip

Serves: 10
- lb. Chicken breast, boneless 1/2 cup water
- 1/2 cup breadcrumbs 3/4 cup sour cream
- jalapeno pepper, sliced 8 oz cream cheese
- oz cheddar cheese

1.Add chicken, jalapeno, water, and cream cheese into the instant pot.
2.Seal pot with lid and cook on manual high pressure for 12 minutes.
3.Once done then release pressure using the quick-release method than open the lid.
4.Stir in cream and cheddar cheese.
5.Transfer instant pot mixture to the baking dish and top with breadcrumbs and broil for 2 minutes.
6.Serve and enjoy.

Roasted Eggplant

Serves:4
- large eggplant 2 tbsp. Olive oil
- ½ tsp. Garlic powder.
- ¼ tsp. Salt

1.Remove top and bottom from eggplant. Slice eggplant into ¼-inchthick round slices.
2.Brush slices with olive oil.
3.Sprinkle with salt and garlic powder
4.Place eggplant slices into the air fryer basket.
5.Adjust the temperature to 390 degrees f and set the timer for 15 minutes.
6.Serve immediately.

Spinach Dip

Serves: 8
- (8-oz. Package cream cheese, softened
- cup mayonnaise
- 1 cup parmesan cheese, grated
- 1 cup frozen spinach, thawed and squeezed 1/3 cup water chestnuts, drained and chopped

- ½ cup onion, minced
- ¼ teaspoon garlic powder Ground black pepper, as required

1. In a bowl, add all the and mix until well combined.
2. Transfer the mixture into a baking pan and spread in an even layer.
3. Press "power button" of air fry oven and turn the dial to select the
4. "air fry" mode.
5. Press the time button and again turn the dial to set the Cooking time to 35 minutes.
6. Now push the temp button and rotate the dial to set the temperature at 300 degrees f.
7. Press "start/pause" button to start.
8. When the unit beeps to show that it is preheated, open the lid.
9. Arrange pan over the "wire rack" and insert in the oven.
10. Stir the dip once halfway through.
11. Serve hot.

Spiced Cauliflower

Serves: 4

- cauliflower head, florets separated
- tbsp. Olive oil
- 1 tbsp. Butter; melted
- ¼ tsp. Cinnamon powder
- ¼ tsp. Cloves, ground
- ¼ tsp. Turmeric powder
- ½ tsp. Cumin, ground
- A pinch of salt and black pepper

1. Take a bowl and mix cauliflower florets with the rest of the and toss.

2. Put the cauliflower in your air fryer's basket and cook at 390°f for 15 minutes
3. Divide between plates and serve as a side dish.

Roasted Tomatoes

Serves: 4

- tomatoes; halved
- ½ cup parmesan; grated 1 tbsp. Basil; chopped.
- ½ tsp. Onion powder
- ½ tsp. Oregano; dried
- ½ tsp. Smoked paprika
- ½ tsp. Garlic powder Cooking spray

1. Take a bowl and mix all the except the Cooking spray and the parmesan.
2. Arrange the tomatoes in your air fryer's pan, sprinkle the parmesan on top and grease with Cooking spray
3. Cook at 370°f for 15 minutes, divide between plates and serve.

Roasted Red Pepper Hummus

Serves: 4

- cup chickpeas, dry and rinsed
- 2 tbsp olive oil
- 1/4 tsp cumin 2 garlic cloves
- 1/2 tbsp tahini
- tbsp fresh lemon juice 1/2 cup roasted red peppers 3 cups chicken broth
- 1/2 tsp salt

1. Add chickpeas and broth into the inner pot of instant pot duo crisp and stir well.
2. Seal the pot with pressure Cooking lid and cook on high for 40 minutes.
3. Once done, allow to release pressure naturally. Remove lid.
4. Drain chickpeas well and reserved half cup broth.
5. Transfer chickpeas, reserved broth, and remaining into the food processor and process until smooth.
6. Serve and enjoy.

Roasted Fennel

Serves: 4

- lb. Fennel; cut into small wedges
- tbsp. Olive oil
- tbsp. Sunflower seeds Juice of ½ lemon
- Salt and black pepper to taste.

1. Take a bowl and mix the fennel wedges with all the except the sunflower seeds, put them in your air fryer's basket and cook at 400°f for 15 minutes
2. Divide the fennel between plates, sprinkle the sunflower seeds on top and serve as a side dish.

Radishes And Sesame Seeds

Serves: 4

- 20 radishes; halved
- spring onions; chopped. 3 green onions; chopped. 2 tbsp. Olive oil
- tbsp. Olive oil
- tsp. Black sesame seeds Salt and black pepper to taste.

1. Take a bowl and mix all the and toss well.
2. Put the radishes in your air fryer's basket, cook at 400°f for 15 minutes, divide between plates and serve as a side dish

Herbed Radish Sauté

Serves: 4

- 2 bunches red radishes; halved 2 tbsp. Parsley; chopped.
- 2 tbsp. Balsamic vinegar
- tbsp. Olive oil
- Salt and black pepper to taste.

1. Take a bowl and mix the radishes with the remaining except the parsley, toss and put them in your air fryer's basket.
2. Cook at 400°f for 15 minutes, divide between plates, sprinkle the parsley on top and serve as a side dish

Sausage Mushroom Caps

Serves: 2

- ½ lb. Italian sausage
- 6 large Portobello mushroom caps
- ¼ cup grated parmesan cheese
- ¼ cup chopped onion
- 2 tbsp. Blanched finely ground almond flour
- 1 tsp. Minced fresh garlic

1. Use a spoon to hollow out each mushroom cap, reserving scrapings.
2. In a medium skillet over medium heat, brown the sausage about 10 minutes or until fully cooked and no pink remains. Drain and then add reserved

mushroom scrapings, onion, almond flour, parmesan and garlic.

3.Gently fold together and continue Cooking an additional minute, then remove from heat

4.Evenly spoon the mixture into mushroom caps and place the caps into a 6-inch round pan. Place pan into the air fryer basket

5.Adjust the temperature to 375 degrees f and set the timer for 8 minutes. When finished Cooking , the tops will be browned and bubbling. Serve warm.

Spanakopita Minis

Serves: 8

- Olive oil, extra virgin (1 tablespoon)
- Water (2 tablespoons) Egg white, large (1 piece)
- Salt, kosher (1/4 teaspoon)
- Feta cheese, crumbled (1 ounce) Oregano, dried (1 teaspoon)
- Phyllo dough, frozen, thawed (4 sheets)
- Baby spinach leaves (10 ounces)
- Cottage cheese, 1% low Fat (1/4 cup)
- Parmesan cheese, grated finely (2 tablespoons)
- Lemon zest, freshly grated (1 teaspoon)
- Black pepper, freshly ground (1/4 teaspoon) Cayenne pepper (1/8 teaspoon)
- Cooking spray

1.Boil the spinach in a pot of water; once wilted, drain, cool, and patdry.

2.Add to a bowl filled with egg white, feta cheese, cottage cheese, parmesan cheese, black pepper, cayenne pepper, oregano, lemon zest, and salt; mix well.

3.Brush the phyllo sheets with a little oil before stacking. Cut into 16 equal-sized strips.

4.Add filling (1 tablespoon) onto one of each strip's end before folding the entire phyllo sheet into a triangular packet.

5.Mist Cooking spray onto the air fryer basket. Top with the packets, then mist again with Cooking spray.

6.Cook for twelve minutes at 375 degrees Fahrenheit.

Greek Feta Fries Overload

Serves: 2

- Potatoes, russet/yukon gold, 7-ounce, scrubbed, dried (2 pieces)
- Salt, kosher (1/4 teaspoon)
- Black pepper, freshly ground (1/4 teaspoon) Plum tomatoes, seeded, diced (1/4 cup) Lemon zest, freshly grated (2 teaspoons) Onion powder (1/4 teaspoon)
- Chicken breast, rotisserie, skinless, shredded (2 ounces) Parsley, flat leaf, fresh, chopped (1/2 tablespoon) Oregano, fresh, chopped (1/2 tablespoon)
- Cooking spray
- Olive oil, extra virgin (1 tablespoon) Oregano, dried (1/2 teaspoon) Garlic powder (1/4 teaspoon) Paprika (1/4 teaspoon)
- Feta cheese, grated finely (2 ounces) Tzatziki, prepared (1/4 cup)
- Red onion, chopped (2 tablespoons)

1.Set the air fryer at 380 degrees Fahrenheit to preheat.

2.Slice the potatoes into quarter inch-thick fries. Add to a bowl filled with salt, pepper, onion powder, dried oregano, garlic powder, paprika, and zest, then toss until well-coated.

3.Cook potato fries in the air fryer for fifteen minutes. Serve topped with feta cheese, shredded chicken, tzatziki, diced plum tomatoes, chopped red onion, and fresh herbs.

SOUR CREAM MUSHROOMS

Serves: 24

- Bell pepper, orange, diced (1/2 piece) Cheddar cheese, shredded (1 cup) Carrot, small, diced (1 piece)
- Cheddar cheese, shredded (1 ½ tablespoons)
- Mushrooms, w/ stems & caps diced (24 pieces) Onion, diced (1/2 piece)
- Bacon slices, diced (2 pieces) Sour cream (1/2 cup)

1.Sauté the onion, bacon, mushroom stems, carrot, and orange bell pepper. Once fully cooked, stir in sour cream and cheddar cheese (1 cup) and cook for two minutes Utes.

2.Set the air fryer at 350 degrees Fahrenheit to preheat.

3.Fill mushroom caps with prepared stuffing before topping with remaining cheddar cheese.

4.Cook in the air fryer for eight minutes utes or until cheese melts.

Riced Cauliflower Balls

Serves:2

- Cauliflower rice, frozen (2 ¼ cup) Egg, large, beaten (1 piece) Marinara, homemade (2 tablespoons)
- Cheese, parmesan/pecorino romano, grated (1 tablespoon)
- Chicken sausage, italian, w/ casing removed (1 link) Salt, kosher (1/4 teaspoon)
- Cheese, mozzarella, part skim, shredded (1/2 cup) Breadcrumbs (1/4 cup)
- Cooking spray

1.Cook the sausage on medium-high until cooked through and broken up. Stir in the marinara, salt, and cauliflower and cook for another six minutes utes over medium heat. Turn off heat before stirring in the mozzarella.

2.Spray the cooled cauliflower mixture with Cooking spray before molding into 6 balls. Dip each ball in the beaten egg before coating with breadcrumbs. Load in the air fryer, coat with Cooking spray, and cook for four to five minutes utes on each side at 400 degrees fahrenheit.

All-Crisp Sweet Potato Skins

Serves: 6

- SCal lions, sliced thinly (2 pieces)
- Cooking spray, olive oil
- Black beans, Fat free, re-fried (1 cup)
- Salt, kosher (1/4 teaspoon)
- Cheese, cheddar, reduced Fat, shredded (3/4 cup)
- Sweet potatoes, small (6 pieces)
- Taco seasoning (1/2 tablespoon)
- Black pepper, freshly ground (1/4 teaspoon) Salsa (3/4 cup)
- Cilantro, chopped (1 tablespoon)

1.Set the air fryer at 370 degrees fahrenheit to preheat.

2.Cover the sweet potatoes in parchment and cook in the air fryer for thirty minutes utes. Let cool.

3.Mix the taco seasoning and black beans.
4.Halve the cooled sweet potatoes and remove most of the flesh. Spray the skins with Cooking spray, sprinkle with pepper and salt, and air-fry for two to three minutes utes.
5.Fill each skin with black beans, salsa (1 tablespoon), and cheese (1 tablespoon). Return to the air fryer and cook for two minutes utes.
6.Serve topped with cilantro and sCal lions.

CREAMY CAULIFLOWER DIP

Serves: 10
- Green onions, chopped (4 pieces) Olive oil, extra virgin (2 tablespoons) Worcestershire sauce (1 teaspoon) Mayonnaise (3/4 cup)
- Parmesan cheese, shredded (1 ½ cups)
- Cauliflower head (1 piece)
- Cream cheese, softened (8 ounces) Sour cream (1/2 cup)
- Garlic cloves (2 pieces)

1.Break the cauliflower into florets after washing and patting dry. Toss with olive oil until evenly coated.
2.Place florets in the air fryer and cook for twenty minutes utes at 390 degrees fahrenheit, turning halfway.
3.Transfer the roasted florets into the blender and process with the sour cream, cream cheese, parmesan cheese (1 cup), mayonnaise, green onions, garlic, and worcestershire sauce.
4.Pour the blended cauliflower mixture into a bake dish (7x7-inch) and top with the remaining parmesan cheese. Cook in the air fryer for ten to fifteen minutes utes at 360 degrees fahrenheit.

Chicken Bacon Bites

Serves: 4
- Bacon slices, cut into 1/3-portions (6 pieces) Chili powder (1/2 tablespoon)
- Chicken breast, sliced into one-inch chunks (1 pound)
- Brown Sugar (1/3 cup) Cayenne pepper (1/8 teaspoon)

1.Stick a bacon piece onto a chicken piece, then roll to secure,
2.finishing by piercing with a toothpick. Repeat with the remaining bacon and chicken pieces.
3.Mix the brown Sugar, cayenne pepper, and chili powder and season the chicken bacon bites.
4.Cook in the air fryer for fifteen minutes utes at 390 degrees f.

Vegetarian Recipes

Tasty Hasselback Potatoes

Serves:4
- potatoes wash and dry 1 tbsp. Dried thyme
- tbsp. Dried rosemary 1 tbsp. Dried parsley
- ½ cup butter, melted Pepper
- Salt

1.Place potato in hassel back slicer and slice potato using a sharp knife.
2.In a small bowl, mix melted butter, thyme, rosemary, parsley, pepper, and salt.
3.Rub melted butter mixture over potatoes and arrange potatoes on air fryer
4.oven tray.

5.Bake potatoes at 350 f for 25 minutes.

Honey Sriracha Brussels Sprouts

Serves:4
- ½ lb. Brussels sprouts, cut stems then cut each in half
- 1 tbsp. Olive oil
- ½ tsp salt

For Sauce:
- tbsp. Sriracha sauce 1 tbsp. Vinegar
- tbsp. Lemon juice - 2 tsp Sugar
- 1 tbsp. Honey - 1 tsp garlic, minced
- ½ tsp olive oil

1.Add all sauce into the small saucepan and heat over low heat for 2-3 minutes or until thickened.
2.Remove saucepan from heat and set aside.
3.Add brussels sprouts, oil, and salt in a zip-lock bag and shake well.
4.Transfer brussels sprouts on air fryer oven tray and air fry at 390 f for 15 minutes. Shake halfway through.
5.Transfer brussels sprouts to the mixing bowl. Drizzle with sauce and toss until well coated.

Roasted Carrots

Serves: 6
- lbs. Carrots, peeled, slice in half again slice half 2 ½ tbsp. Dried parsley
- tsp dried oregano 1 tsp dried thyme 3 tbsp. Olive oil Pepper
- Salt

1.Add carrots in a mixing bowl. Add remaining on top of carrots and toss well.
2.Arrange carrots on air fryer oven pan and roast at 400 f for 10 minutes.
3.After 10 minutes turn carrots slices to the other side and roast for 10 minutes more

Roasted Parmesan Broccoli

Serves:4

- lb. Broccoli florets
- ¼ cup parmesan cheese, grated 1 tbsp. Garlic, minced
- tbsp. Olive oil Pepper
- Salt

1.Add broccoli florets into the mixing bowl.
2.Add cheese, garlic, oil, pepper, and salt on top of broccoli florets and toss well.
3.Arrange broccoli florets on air fryer oven pan and bake at 350 f for 4 minutes.
4.Turn broccoli florets to other side and cook for 2 minutes more.

Simple Baked Potatoes

Serves: 4
- 4 potatoes, scrubbed and washed
- ¾ tsp garlic powder
- ½ tsp italian seasoning
- ½ tbsp. Butter, melted
- ½ tsp sea salt

1. Prick potatoes using a fork.
2. Rub potatoes with melted butter and sprinkle with garlic powder, italian seasoning, and sea salt.
3. Arrange potatoes on instant vortex air fryer oven drip pan and bake at 400 f for 40 minutes.

Parmesan Green Bean

Serves: 6
- lb. Fresh green beans
- ½ cup flour
- eggs, lightly beaten
- ¾ tbsp. Garlic powder
- ½ cup parmesan cheese, grated 1 cup breadcrumbs
  1. In a shallow dish, add flour.
  2. In a second shallow dish add eggs.
  3. In a third shallow dish, mix breadcrumbs, garlic powder, and cheese.
  4. Coat beans with flour then coat with eggs and finally coat with breadcrumbs.
  5. Arrange coated beans on instant vortex air fryer pan and air fry at 390 f for 5 minutes.

Roasted Asparagus

Serves: 4
- lb. Asparagus cut the ends 1 tsp olive oil
- Pepper
- Salt

1. Arrange asparagus on instant vortex air fryer oven pan. Drizzle with olive oil and season with pepper and salt.
2. Place pan in instant vortex air fryer oven and bake asparagus at 370 f for 7-9 minutes. Turn asparagus halfway through.

Healthy Air Fryer Veggies

Serves:4
- cup carrots, sliced
- cup cauliflower, cut into florets 1 cup broccoli florets
- 1 tbsp. Olive oil
- Pepper Salt

1. Add all vegetables in a mixing bowl. Drizzle with olive oil and season with pepper and salt. Toss well.
2. Add vegetables to the rotisserie basket and air fry at 380 f for 18 minutes.

Baked Sweet Potatoes

Serves: 4
- sweet potatoes, scrubbed and washed
- ½ tbsp. Butter, melted
- ½ tsp sea salt
  1. Prick sweet potatoes using a fork.
  2. Rub sweet potatoes with melted butter and season with salt.
  3. Arrange sweet potatoes on instant vortex air fryer drip pan and bake at 400 f for 40 minutes.

HERBED ROASTED CARROTS

Serves: 4
- 1-pound heirloom carrots, peeled
- tablespoons fresh thyme, chopped finely
- tablespoon fresh tarragon leaves, chopped finely 2 teaspoons olive oil

- Salt and ground black pepper, as required
1. Place the carrots, herbs, oil, salt and black pepper in a bowl and toss to coat well
2. Arrange the greased "inner basket" in air fryer and press "preheat".
3. Select "start/cancel" to begin preheating.
4. When the unit beeps to show that it is preheated, arrange the carrots in "inner basket".
5. Insert the "inner basket" and select "root vegetables".
6. Set the temperature to 400 degrees f for 10 minutes.
7. Select "start/cancel" to begin Cooking.
8. Shake the carrots once halfway through.

Glazed Carrots

Serves: 4
- cups carrots, peeled and cut into large chunks
- 1 tablespoon olive oil 1 tablespoon honey
- tablespoon fresh thyme, finely chopped Salt and ground black pepper, as required
1. In a bowl, place all and toss to coat well.
2. Place the carrot mixture into a greased baking pan.
3. Arrange the "inner basket" in air fryer and press "preheat".

4. Select "start/cancel" to begin preheating.
5. When the unit beeps to show that it is preheated, arrange the baking pan in "inner basket".
6. Insert the "inner basket" and select "air fry".
7. Set the temperature to 390 degrees f for 12 minutes.
8. Select "start/cancel" to begin Cooking.
9. Select "start/cancel" to stop Cooking.

Buttery Roasted Potatoes

Serves: 4
- 1½ pounds of small new potatoes, halved
- tablespoons butter, melted
- ¼ teaspoon dried thyme
- ¼ teaspoon dried rosemary
- ½ teaspoon garlic powder
- Salt and ground black pepper, as required
1. In a large bowl, add all the and toss to coat well.
2. Arrange the greased "inner basket" in air fryer and press "preheat".
3. Select "start/cancel" to begin preheating.
4. When the unit beeps to show that it is preheated, arrange the potatoes in "inner basket".
5. Insert the "inner basket" and select "French fries".
6. Set the temperature to 380 degrees f for 20 minutes.
7. Select "start/cancel" to begin Cooking.
8. Shake the potatoes once halfway through.

Parmesan Brussels Sprout

Serves: 3
- 1-pound brussels sprouts, trimmed and halved - 1 tablespoon balsamic
- vinegar
- tablespoon extra-virgin olive oil
- Salt and ground black pepper, as required
- ¼ cup whole-wheat breadcrumbs
- ¼ cup parmesan cheese, shredded
1. Arrange the greased "inner basket" in air fryer and press "preheat".
1. Select "start/cancel" to begin preheating.

2.When the unit beeps to show that it is preheated, arrange the brussels in "inner basket".

3.Insert the "inner basket" and select "air fry".

4.Set the temperature to 400 degrees f for 10 minutes.

5.Select "start/cancel" to begin Cooking .

6.After 5 minutes, flip the brussel sprouts and sprinkle with breadcrumbs, followed by the cheese. Select "start/cancel" to stop Cooking .

CHEESY SPINACH

Serves: 3

- (10-ounce) package frozen spinach, thawed - ½ cup onion, chopped 2 teaspoons garlic, minced
- ounces cream cheese, chopped
- ½ teaspoon ground nutmeg
- Salt and ground black pepper, as required
- ¼ cup parmesan cheese, shredded

1.In a bowl, mix well spinach, onion, garlic, cream cheese, nutmeg, salt, and black pepper.

2.Place spinach mixture into a baking pan.

3.Arrange the "inner basket" in air fryer and press "preheat".

4.Select "start/cancel" to begin preheating.

5.When the unit beeps to show that it is preheated, arrange the baking pan in "inner basket".

6.Insert the "inner basket" and select "air fry".

7.Set the temperature to 350 degrees f for 10 minutes.

8.Select "start/cancel" to begin Cooking.

9.Now, set the temperature to 400 degrees f for 5 minutes.

Roasted Corn With Butter And Lime

Serves: 4

- corns
- tablespoon parsley, chopped 1 teaspoon lime juice
- tablespoon butter
- ½ teaspoon pepper
- ¼ teaspoon salt

1.Preheat air fryer to 400 degrees f

2.Remove husk and transfer corns into the air fryer

3.Cook for 20 minutes

4.After 5 minutes shake fryer basket

5.Once done, rub butter

6.Sprinkle parsley, salt, and pepper

7.Drizzle with lime juice on top

Cauliflower Rice

Serves: 3

- carrots, diced
- ½ cup onion, diced
- 2 tablespoons soy sauce 1 teaspoon turmeric
- ½ block firm tofu, crumbled
- cups, riced cauliflower
- 2 tablespoons Sodium soy sauce, reduced
- ½ cup broccoli, finely chopped 1 tablespoon rice vinegar
- ½ cup peas, frozen
- 2 garlic cloves, minced
- and ½ teaspoon sesame oil, toasted 1 tablespoon ginger, minced
- ½ cup, frozen peas
- tablespoon rice vinegar

1.Preheat your air fryer to 370 degrees f

2.Take a large bowl and add tofu alongside remaining tofu

3.Stir well to combine

4.Set in the air fryer to cook for 10 minutes

5.Take another bowl and add remaining

6.Stir them well

7.Transfer into the air fryer and cook 10 minutes more

Sweet Potato Cauliflower Patties

Serves: 1

- cups cauliflower florets
- 2 tablespoons arrowroot powder 1 teaspoon garlic, minced
- large sweet potato, peeled and chopped
- ¼ cup flaxseed, grounded 1 cup cilantro, packed
- ¼ teaspoon cumin
- tablespoons ranch seasoning mix
- ¼ cup sunflower seeds
- ½ teaspoon chili powder 1 cup cilantro, packed
- green onion, chopped
- Salt and pepper
- Any dipping sauce, for serving

1.Preheat your air fryer to 400 degrees f

2.Add sweet potato, cauliflower, onion, garlic, and sizzle into your food processor

3.Blend until smooth

4.Mold the mixture into patties and place onto a greased baking sheet

5.Place into your freezer for 10 minutes

6.Then transfer into your air fryer

7.Cook for 20 minutes and flip after 10 minutes

Corn With Lime And Cheese

Serves: 2

- corns
- 2 tablespoons sweet paprika 2 limes juice
- Olive oil

1.Rub your corn with oil and paprika

2.Arrange in your air fryer basket

3.Cook them for 15 minutes at 400 degrees f

4.Flip once during cook

5.Drizzle with lime juice

Breaded Mushrooms

Serves:2

- ½ pound button mushrooms 1 cup almond meal
- flax-egg
- cup almond flour
- ounces cashew cheese Salt and pepper

1.Preheat your air fryer to 360 degrees f

2.Take a shallow bowl and toss almond meal with cheese into it

3.Whisk egg in one bowl and spread flour in another

4.Wash mushrooms then pat dry

5.Coat every mushroom with flour

6.Dip each of them in the egg first then in breadcrumb

7.Spray with Cooking oil and place back in the air fryer

8.Air fry these mushrooms for 7 minutes in your air fryer

9.Toss the mushrooms after 3 minutes

10.Once cooked serve warm

Sweet Potato Fries

Serves: 2

- sweet potatoes
- 2 tablespoons olive oil
- ½ teaspoon curry powder
- ¼ teaspoon ginger powder
- ¼ cup ketchup
- 2 tablespoons egg-free mayonnaise
- ½ teaspoon cumin, grounded
- ¼ teaspoon coriander, grounded
- ¼ teaspoon cinnamon powder Salt and black pepper

1.Put the sweet potato, coriander, curry powder, oil, salt, and pepper into your air fryer basket
2.Mix them
3.Cook for 20 minutes at 370 degrees f
4.Flip once
5.Take a bowl and add cinnamon, ginger, cumin, ketchup, and mayo
6.Whisk them well
7.Serve with ketchup mixture

Creamy Potato

Serves: 2

- big potato
- tablespoon almond butter
- 1 tablespoon green onions, chopped 1 teaspoon olive oil
- tablespoons cashew cream 1/3 cup cashew cheese
- Salt and black pepper

1.Preheat your air fryer to 400 degrees f
2.Rub your corn with oil and paprika and season with salt and pepper
3.Cook for 30 minutes and flip the potato
4.Then cook for 30 minutes more
5.Take a cutting board and transfer them, slice them lengthwise
6.Take a bowl and add cheese, bacon, heavy cream, green onion, butter, salt, and pepper into it
7. Stir well and stuff potato skin with this mixture
8.Place potato in the air fryer and cook for 20 minutes more

Eggplant Fries

Serves:4

- eggplant, peeled and sliced 1 flax-egg
- ½ cup cashew cheese
- tablespoons almond milk 2 cups almond meal Cooking spray
- Black pepper
- Salt

1.Take a bowl and add egg, salt, and pepper into it
2.Whisk it well
3.Take another bowl, mix cheese and panko, then stir
4.Dip eggplant fries in the egg mixture, coat in panko mix
5.Grease the air fryer basket with Cooking spray
6. Place the eggplant fries in it
7.Cook for 5 minutes at 400 degrees

Crispy And Salty Tofu

Serves: 4

- ¼ cup chickpea flour
- ¼ cup arrowroot 1 teaspoon salt
- teaspoon garlic powder
- ½ teaspoon black pepper
- pack (15 ounces) tofu, firm Cooking spray as needed

1.Preheat your air fryer 392 degrees f
2.Take a medium-sized bowl and add flour, arrowroot, salt, garlic, pepper, and stir well
3.Cut tofu into cubes, transfer cubes into the flour mix
4.Toss well
5.Spray tofu with oil and transfer to air fryer Cooking basket
6.Spray oil on top and cook for 8 minutes
7.Shake and toss well, fry for 7 minutes more

The Easy Paneer Pizza

Serves: 4

- Cooking oil spray as needed 1 flour tortilla, sprouted
- ¼ cup vegan pizza sauce
- ½ cup vegan cheese
- Vegan-friendly topping of your choice

1.Preheat your air fryer 347 degrees f
2.Spray your air fryer Cooking basket with oil, add tortilla to your air fryer basket and pour the sauce in the center
3.Evenly distribute your topping on top alongside vegan cheese
4.Bake for 9 minutes
5.Serve and enjoy!

Cauliflower Sauce And Pasta

Serves: 4

- cups cauliflower florets Cooking oil as needed
- medium onion, chopped
- ounces pasta of your choice Fresh chives for garnish
- ½ cup cashew pieces 1 and ½ cups of water
- tablespoon nutritional yeast 2 large garlic cloves, peeled
- tablespoons fresh lemon juice
- 1 and ½ teaspoon salt
- ¼ teaspoon fresh ground black pepper

1.Preheat your air fryer 392 degrees f
2.Add cauliflower to your air fryer basket and spray oil on top, add onion
3.Roast for 8 minutes and stir, roast for 10 minutes more
4.Cook the pasta according to package instructions
5.Take a blender and add roasted cauliflower and onions alongside cashews, water, yeast, garlic, lemon, garlic, salt, pepper and blend well
6.Serve pasta with the sauce on top and a garnish of minced chives and sCal lions
7.Serve and enjoy!

Tamarind Glazed Sweet Potatoes

Serves: 4

- garnet sweet potatoes, peeled and diced 1/3 teaspoon white pepper
- A few drops liquid stevia
- tablespoon butter, melted 2 teaspoons tamarind paste

- ½ teaspoon turmeric powder
- and ½ tablespoons lime juice A pinch of the ground allspice

1. Preheat your air fryer to 395 degrees f
2. Take a mixing bowl and add all into it
3. Mix them until sweet potatoes are well coated
4. Cook for 12 minutes
5. Pause the air fryer and toss again
6. Increase the temperature to 390 degrees f
7. Cook for 10 minutes more
8. Serve warm and enjoy!

Lemon Lentils And Fried Onion
Serves: 4
- cups of water
- Cooking oil spray as needed
- medium onion, peeled and cut into ¼ inch thick rings Salt as needed
- ½ cup kale stems removed
- large garlic cloves, pressed
- tablespoons fresh lemon juice 2 teaspoons nutritional yeast
- teaspoon salt
- 1 teaspoon lemon zest
- ¾ teaspoon fresh pepper

1. Preheat your air fryer to 392 degrees f
2. Take a large-sized pot and bring lentils to boil over medium-high heat
3. Lower heat to low and simmer for 30 minutes, making sure to stir after every 5 minutes
4. Once they are cooked, take your air fryer basket and spray with
5. Cooking oil, add onion rings and sprinkle salt
6. Fry for 5 minutes, shaking basket and fry for 5 minutes more
7. Remove the basket and spray with oil, cook for 5 minutes more until crispy and browned
8. Add kale to the lentils and stir, add sliced greens
9. Stir in garlic, lemon juice, yeast, salt, pepper, and stir well
10. Top with crispy onion rings and serve
11. Enjoy!

The Daily Bean Dish
Serves: 4
- can (15 ounces) pinto beans, drained
- ¼ cup tomato sauce
- tablespoons nutritional yeast 2 large garlic cloves, minced
- ½ teaspoon dried oregano
- ½ teaspoon cumin
- ¼ teaspoon salt
- 1/8 teaspoon ground black pepper
- Cooking oil spray as needed

1. Preheat your air fryer to 392 degrees f
2. Take a medium bowl and add beans, tomato sauce, yeast, garlic, oregano, cumin, salt, pepper and mix well
3. Take your baking pan and add oil, pour bean mixture
4. Transfer to air fryer and bake for 4 minutes until cooked thoroughly with a slightly golden crust on top
5. Serve and enjoy!

Fine 10 Minute Chimichanga
Serves: 4

- whole-grain tortilla
- ½ cup vegan refried beans
- ¼ cup grated vegan cheese Cooking oil spray as needed
- ½ cup fresh salsa
- cups romaine lettuce, chopped Guacamole
- Chopped cilantro

1. Preheat your air fryer to 392 degrees f
2. Lay tortilla on flat surface and place beans on center, top with cheese and wrap bottom up over filling, fold insides
3. Roll all up and enclose beans inside
4. Spray air fryer Cooking basket with oil and place wrap inside the basket, fry for 5 minutes, spray on top and cook for 2-3 minutes more
5. Transfer to a plate and serve with salsa, lettuce, and guacamole
6. Enjoy!

The Great Taquito
Serves: 4
- 8 corn tortillas
- Cooking oil spray as needed
- (15 ounces) can vegan refried beans 1 cup shredded vegan cheese Guacamole
- Cashew cheese Vegan sour cream Fresh salsa

1. Preheat your air fryer to 392 degrees f
2. Warm your tortilla and run them underwater for a second, transfer to air fryer Cooking basket and cook for 1 minute
3. Remove to the flat surface and place equal amounts of beans at the
4. center of each tortilla, top with vegan cheese
5. Roll tortilla sides up over filling, place seam side down in air fryer
6. Spray oil on top and cook for 7 minutes until golden brown
7. Serve and enjoy!

Basil Tomatoes
Serves: 2
- 4 tomatoes, halved
- Olive oil Cooking spray
- Salt and ground black pepper, as required 1 tablespoon fresh basil, chopped

1. Drizzle cut sides of the tomato halves with Cooking spray evenly.
2. Sprinkle with salt, black pepper and basil.
3. Press "power button" of air fry oven and turn the dial to select the "air fry" mode.
4. Press the time button and again turn the dial to set the Cooking time to 10 minutes.
5. Now push the temp button and rotate the dial to set the temperature at 320 degrees f.
6. Press "start/pause" button to start.
7. When the unit beeps to show that it is preheated, open the lid.
8. Arrange the tomatoes in "air fry basket" and insert in the oven.
9. Serve warm.

Pesto Tomatoes
Serves: 4
- large heirloom tomatoes cut into ½ inch thick

slices. 1 cup pesto
- oz. Feta cheese cut into ½ inch thick slices.
- ½ cup red onions, sliced thinly
- tablespoon olive oil

1.Spread some pesto on each slice of tomato.
2.Top each tomato slice with a feta slice and onion and drizzle with oil.
3.Press "power button" of air fry oven and turn the dial to select the "air fry" mode.
4.Press the time button and again turn the dial to set the Cooking time to 14 minutes.
5.Now push the temp button and rotate the dial to set the temperature at 390 degrees f.
6.Press "start/pause" button to start.
7.When the unit beeps to show that it is preheated, open the lid.
8.Arrange the tomatoes in greased "air fry basket" and insert in the oven.
9.Serve warm.

Stuffed Tomatoes
Serves: 2
- large tomatoes
- ½ cup broccoli, chopped finely
- ½ cup cheddar cheese, shredded
- Salt and ground black pepper, as required 1 tablespoon unsalted butter, melted
- ½ teaspoon dried thyme, crushed

1.Carefully, cut the top of each tomato and scoop out pulp and seeds.
2.In a bowl, mix chopped broccoli, cheese, salt and black pepper.
3.Stuff each tomato with broccoli mixture evenly.
4.Press "power button" of air fry oven and turn the dial to select the "air fry" mode.
5.Press the time button and again turn the dial to set the Cooking time to 15 minutes.
6.Now push the temp button and rotate the dial to set the temperature at 355 degrees f.
7.Press "start/pause" button to start.
8.When the unit beeps to show that it is preheated, open the lid.
9.Arrange the tomatoes in greased "air fry basket" and insert in the oven.
10.Serve warm with the garnishing of thyme.

Parmesan Asparagus
Serves: 3
- lb. Fresh asparagus, trimmed
- tablespoon parmesan cheese, grated 1 tablespoon butter, melted
- 1 teaspoon garlic powder
- Salt and ground black pepper, as required

1.In a bowl, mix the asparagus, cheese, butter, garlic powder, salt, and black pepper.
2.Press "power button" of air fry oven and turn the dial to select the "air fry" mode.
3.Press the time button and again turn the dial to set the Cooking time
4.to 10 minutes.
5.Now push the temp button and rotate the dial to set the temperature at 400 degrees f.
6.Press "start/pause" button to start.

7.When the unit beeps to show that it is preheated, open the lid.
8.Arrange the veggie mixture in greased "air fry basket" and insert in the oven.
9.Serve hot.

Almond Asparagus
Serves: 3
- lb. Asparagus
- tablespoons olive oil
- tablespoons balsamic vinegar
- Salt and ground black pepper, as required 1/3 cup almonds, sliced

1.In a bowl, mix the asparagus, oil, vinegar, salt, and black pepper.
2.Press "power button" of air fry oven and turn the dial to select the
3."air fry" mode.
4.Press the time button and again turn the dial to set the Cooking time to 6minutes.
5.Now push the temp button and rotate the dial to set the temperature at 400 degrees f.
6.Press "start/pause" button to start.
7.When the unit beeps to show that it is preheated, open the lid.
8.Arrange the veggie mixture in greased "air fry basket" and insert in the oven.
9.Serve hot.

Spicy Butternut Squash
Serves: 4
- medium butternut squash, peeled, seeded and cut into chunk 2 teaspoons cumin seeds
- 1/8 teaspoon garlic powder
- 1/8 teaspoon chili flakes, crushed
- Salt and ground black pepper, as required 1 tablespoon olive oil
- tablespoons pine nuts
- tablespoons fresh cilantro, chopped

1.In a bowl, mix the squash, spices, and oil.
2.Press "power button" of air fry oven and turn the dial to select the "air fry" mode.
3.Press the time button and again turn the dial to set the Cooking time to 20 minutes.
4.Now push the temp button and rotate the dial to set the temperature at 375 degrees f.
5.Press "start/pause" button to start.
6.When the unit beeps to show that it is preheated, open the lid.
7.Arrange the squash chunks in greased "air fry basket" and insert in the oven.
8.Serve hot with the garnishing of pine nuts and cilantro.

Caramelized Baby Carrots
Serves: 4
- ½ cup butter, melted
- ½ cup brown Sugar
- lb. Bag baby carrots

1.In a bowl, mix the butter, brown Sugar and carrots.
2.Press "power button" of air fry oven and turn the dial to select the "air fry" mode.
3.Press the time button and again turn the dial to set the Cooking time to 15 minutes.

4.Now push the temp button and rotate the dial to set the temperature
5.at 400 degrees f.
6.Press "start/pause" button to start.
7.When the unit beeps to show that it is preheated, open the lid.
8.Arrange the carrots in greased "air fry basket" and insert in the oven.
9.Serve warm.

Broccoli With Cauliflower

Serves: 4

- 1½ cups broccoli, cut into 1-inch pieces
- 1½ cups cauliflower, cut into 1-inch pieces 1 tablespoon olive oil
- Salt, as required

1.In a bowl, add the vegetables, oil, and salt and toss to coat well.
2.Press "power button" of air fry oven and turn the dial to select the "air fry" mode.
3.Press the time button and again turn the dial to set the Cooking time to 20 minutes.
4.Now push the temp button and rotate the dial to set the temperature
5.at 375 degrees f.
6.Press "start/pause" button to start.
7.When the unit beeps to show that it is preheated, open the lid.
8.Arrange the veggie mixture in greased "air fry basket" and insert in the oven.
9.Serve hot.

Cauliflower In Buffalo Sauce

Serves: 4

- large head cauliflower, cut into bite-size florets 1 tablespoon olive oil
- teaspoons garlic powder
- Salt and ground black pepper, as required
- **1** tablespoon butter, melted 2/3 cup warm buffalo sauce

1.In a large bowl, add cauliflower florets, olive oil, garlic powder,
2.salt and pepper and toss to coat.
3.Press "power button" of air fry oven and turn the dial to select the "air fry" mode.
4.Press the time button and again turn the dial to set the Cooking time to 12 minutes.
5.Now push the temp button and rotate the dial to set the temperature at 375 degrees f.
6.Press "start/pause" button to start.
7.When the unit beeps to show that it is preheated, open the lid.
8.Arrange the cauliflower florets in "air fry basket" and insert in the oven.
9.After 7 minutes of Cooking , coat the cauliflower florets with buffalo sauce.
10.Serve hot.

Curried Cauliflower

Serves: 4

- tablespoons golden raisins
- ½ head cauliflower, cored and cut into 1-inch pieces
- ½ cup olive oil, divided
- ½ tablespoon curry powder Salt, to taste

- 2 tablespoons pine nuts, toasted

1.Soak the raisins in boiling water and set aside.

2. In a bowl, mix the cauliflower, oil, curry powder and salt.
3.Press "power button" of air fry oven and turn the dial to select the "air fry" mode.
4.Press the time button and again turn the dial to set the Cooking time
5.to 10 minutes.
6.Now push the temp button and rotate the dial to set the temperature at 390 degrees f.
7.Press "start/pause" button to start.
8.When the unit beeps to show that it is preheated, open the lid.
9.Arrange the cauliflower florets in "air fry basket" and insert in the oven.
10.Drain the golden raisins into a strainer.
11.In a bowl, add cauliflower, raisins and pine nuts and toss to coat.
12.Serve immediately.

Lemony Green Beans

Serves: 4

- lb. Green beans, trimmed 1 tablespoon butter, melted
- tablespoon fresh lemon juice
- ¼ teaspoon garlic powder
- Salt and ground black pepper, as required
- ½ teaspoon lemon zest, grated

1.In a large bowl, add all the except the lemon zest and toss to coat well.
2.Press "power button" of air fry oven and turn the dial to select the "air fry" mode.
3.Press the time button and again turn the dial to set the Cooking time to 12 minutes.
4.Now push the temp button and rotate the dial to set the temperature at 400 degrees f.
5.Press "start/pause" button to start.
6.When the unit beeps to show that it is preheated, open the lid.
7.Arrange the green beans in "air fry basket" and insert in the oven.
8.Serve warm with the garnishing of lemon zest.

Parm Asparagus

Serves: 3

- 1-pound asparagus, trimmed
- tablespoon parmesan cheese, grated 1 tablespoon butter, melted
- teaspoon garlic powder
- Salt and pepper to taste

1.Take a bowl and add asparagus, cheese, butter, garlic powder, salt, and pepper
2.Press "power button" on your air fryer and select "air fry" mode
3.Press the time button and set time to 10 minutes
4.Push temp button and set temp to 400 degrees f
5.Press the "start/pause" button and start the device
6.Once the appliance beeps to indicated that it is pre-heated, arrange the vegetable mixture in air fryer Cooking basket, let them cook
7.Once done, serve warm and enjoy!

Spiced Up Butternut Squash

Serves: 4

- 1 medium butternut squash, peeled, seeded and cut into chunks
- 1/8 teaspoons cumin seeds
- 1/8 teaspoon garlic powder
- 1/8 teaspoon chili flakes, crushed Salt and pepper to taste
- 1/8 tablespoon pine nuts
- 1/8 tablespoons fresh cilantro

1.Take a bowl and add squash, spices, and oil
2.Press "power button" on your air fryer and select "air fry" mode
3.Press the time button and set time to 20 minutes
4.Push temp button and set temp to 375 degrees f
5.Press the "start/pause" button and start the device
6.Arrange squash chunks into your air fryer Cooking basket and push into oven
7.Let it cook until done, serve with a sprinkle of cilantro and pine nuts
8.Enjoy!

Hearty Caramelized Baby Carrots

Serves: 4

- ½ cup butter, melted
- ½ cup brown Sugar
- A 1-pound bag of baby carrots

1.Take a bowl and mix in brown Sugar, butter, and carrots
2.Press "power button" on your air fryer and select "air fry" mode
3.Press the time button and set time to 15 minutes
4.Push temp button and set temp to 400 degrees f
5.Press the "start/pause" button and start the device
6.Arrange carrots int the Cooking basket (greased), let it cook until the timer runs out
7.Serve and enjoy!

Sweet Potatoes And Broccoli

Serves: 4

- 2 medium sweet potatoes, peeled and cut into 1-inch cubes
- 1 head broccoli, cut into 1-inch florets
- 2 tablespoons vegetable oil Salt and pepper to taste

1.Take a large-sized bowl and add all listed
2.Toss them well to coat them
3.Press "power button" on your air fryer and select "air roast" mode
4.Press the time button and set time to 20 minutes
5.Push temp button and set temp to 415 degrees f
6.Press the "start/pause" button and start the device
7.Arrange prepared carrots to Cooking basket (greased)
8.Push it in and let it cook until the timer runs out
9.Take a large-sized bowl and add remaining butter, zucchini, basil, salt, and pepper, mix well
10.After the first 5 minutes of Cooking , pour the zucchini mixture into the Cooking basket alongside carrots.

Cauliflower And Broccoli Dish

Serves: 4

- and ½ cups broccoli, cut into 1-inch pieces
- and ½ cups cauliflower, cut into 1-inch pieces 1 tablespoon olive oil

- Salt as needed

1.Take a bowl and add vegetables, oil, and salt. Toss well and coat them well
2.Press "power button" on your air fryer and select "air fry" mode
3.Press the time button and set time to 20 minutes
4.Push temp button and set temp to 375 degrees f
5.Press the "start/pause" button and start the device
6.Arrange the vegetable mixture into your air fryer basket and push it into the oven, let it cook until the timer runs out
7.Serve and enjoy!

Hearty Lemon Green Beans

Serves: 4

- 1-pound green beans, trimmed 1 tablespoon butter, melted
- 1 tablespoon fresh lemon juice
- ¼ teaspoon garlic powder Salt and pepper to taste
- ½ teaspoon lemon zest, grated

1.Take a large-sized bowl and add all listed , except lemon zest
2.Toss and coat well
3.Press "power button" on your air fryer and select "air fry" mode
4.Press the time button and set time to 12 minutes
5.Push temp button and set temp to 400 degrees f
6.Press the "start/pause" button and start the device
7.Arrange the green beans into air fryer basket and push into the oven, let it cook until the timer runs out
8.Serve warm with a garnish with lemon zest!

Green Beans With Okra

Serves: 2

- 10 ounces frozen cut okra
- 10 ounces frozen green beans
- ¼ cup nutritional yeast
- **3** tablespoons balsamic vinegar Salt and pepper to taste

1.Take a bowl and add okra, green beans, nutritional yeast, vinegar, salt, pepper and toss the mixture well, make sure everything is coated well
2.Press "power button" on your air fryer and select "air fry" mode
3.Press the time button and set time to 20 minutes
4.Push temp button and set temp to 400 degrees f
5.Press the "start/pause" button and start the device
6. Grease the air fryer basket well and arrange okra mixture in the basket
7.Put the basket in the oven and let it cook, until it is done
8.Enjoy!

Glazed Mushrooms

Serves: 4

- ½ cup low-Sodium soy sauce 2 teaspoons honey
- tablespoons balsamic vinegar
- 2 teaspoons chinese five-spice powder
- ½ teaspoon ground ginger
- 20 ounces fresh cremini mushrooms, halved

1.Take a bowl and add soy sauce, honey, garlic, vinegar, five-spice powder, ground ginger and mix well
2.Arrange mushroom mixture in a greased-up baking pan in a single layer
3.Press "power button" on your air fryer and select "air fry" mode
4.Press the time button and set time to 15 minutes
5.Push temp button and set temp to 350 degrees f
6.Press the "start/pause" button and start the device
7.Arrange the pan over a wire rack and insert in the oven, let it cook for 10 minutes, add vinegar mixture on top
8.Stir well, let it cook until done
9.Serve and enjoy!

Herbed Bell Pepper

Serves: 4

- 1 and ½ pounds bell pepper, seeded and cubed
- ½ teaspoon dried thyme, crushed
- ½ teaspoon dried savory, crushed Salt and pepper to taste
- teaspoons butter, melted
1.Take a bowl and add bell pepper herbs, salt, pepper and toss well
2.Press "power button" on your air fryer and select "air fry" mode
3.Press the time button and set time to 8 minutes
4.Push temp button and set temp to 360 degrees f
5.Press the "start/pause" button and start the device
6.Arrange bell pepper in the air fryer basket and push it in the oven
7.Drizzle with butter, let it cook until done
8.Serve and enjoy!

Stuffed Pumpkin

Serves: 2

- parsnip, diced
- carrot, diced
- ½ pumpkin, little
- 1 sweet potato, diced
1.Scrape out the seeds from the pumpkin; integrate the sweet potato, parsnip, carrot, and the egg in a bowl.
2.Fill up your pumpkin with this vegetable mix.
3.Pre-heat your air fryer to 350 degrees f.
4.Keep your packed pumpkin in the fryer's basket.
5.Cook for 25 minutes up until tender.

VEGAN FRIED RAVIOLI

Serves: 4

- teaspoon of garlic powder
- 11/ oz. Vegan ravioli
- ½ cup marinara
- Pinch of pepper and salt
- teaspoons of nutritional yeast flakes
- ½ cup breadcrumbs
- teaspoon oregano, dried 1 teaspoon basil, dried
- ¼ cup of aquafaba liquid from a can of chickpeas
1.Combine the nutritional yeast flakes, breadcrumbs, garlic powder, basil, oregano, pepper, and salt on a plate.
2.Keep the aquafaba in a bowl. Now dip your ravioli

into the aquafaba. Get rid of the excess liquid.
3.Dig up in the bread crumb mix.
4.Keep the ravioli in your fryer basket. Apply Cooking spray and cook for 6 minutes.
5.Flip and cook for another 4 minutes.
6.Take them out and serve with the marinara for dipping.

Veggie Tian

Serves: 4

- ¼ teaspoon salt
- ¼ cup parmesan cheese, grated
- ½ cup mozzarella cheese, shredded
- ½ onion, peeled and diced 1 tablespoon olive oil
- 1 cup of water
- 2 cloves of garlic, minced
- 2 zucchini, cut into half-inch slices
- 1 yellow squash, cut into half-inch pieces 1 russet potato, cut into half-inch slices
- 2 roma tomatoes, cut into half-inch slices 1/8 teaspoon black pepper
1.Include garlic, onion and oil to your pot and cook for 5 minutes.
2. Secure the onion and garlic. Keep in a pan.
3.Clean the inside of your pot and keep them back in it.
4.Add trivet and water to your pot. Arrange the zucchini, squash, potato, and tomato around the edge of the pan.
5.Cover the pan's top with a paper towel and foil.
6.Lower it into the pot; close the lid and cook for 30 minutes.
7.Release the pressure when done and open the cover. Secure.
8.Sprinkle mozzarella, parmesan cheese, pepper, and salt.

Maple Cinnamon Roasted Squash

Serves: 4

- tablespoon olive oil 2 tbsp maple syrup
- pounds. Butternut squash, peeled and cut into 2-inch cubes
- ½ tsp cinnamon powder
- ½ tsp salt
- 2 pinches cayenne pepper
1.Place the leaking pan at the bottom of the air fryer and pre-heat the oven at roast mode at 400 f for 2 to 3 minutes.
2.Add all the to a medium bowl and blend well till the squash pieces seem well coated with the spices. 3.Transfer to the rotisserie basket and close the lid to seal.
4.Attach the rotisserie basket to the lever in the oven and close the door.
5.Set the timer for 10 minutes, and press start. Cook till golden brown and tender.
6.When all set, move the squash to serving bowls and serve right away.

Easy Air Fried Okra

Serves: 4

- tsp olive oil
- ½ pound. Okra, ends trimmed and pods sliced Salt and black pepper to taste
1.Insert the leaking pan at the bottom of the air fryer and preheat the oven at air fryer mode at 400 f for 2 to 3 minutes. Add all the to a medium bowl and blend well. Transfer the okras to the rotisserie basket and close the cover to seal. Attach the

2.rotisserie basket to the lever in the oven and close the door. Set the timer for 10 minutes, and press start. Cook up until golden brown and tender. When prepared, move the okras to serving bowls and serve immediately.

Fried Chickpeas
Serves: 4

- teaspoon garlic, granulated 1 teaspoon of smoked paprika
- can chickpeas, rinsed and drained 1 tablespoon olive oil
- tablespoon of dietary yeast

1. Spread the chickpeas on paper towels.
2.Cover using a 2nd paper towel later on to dry for half an hour.
3.Preheat your air fryer to 355 degrees f.
4.Unite the dietary yeast, chickpeas, smoked paprika, olive oil, salt, and garlic in a mid-sized bowl.
5. Cover well by tossing.
6.Now add your chickpeas to the fryer.
7.Cook for 1g minutes until crispy.
8.Shake them in 4-minute intervals.

Air Fryer Lemon Tofu
Serves: 4

- 1 teaspoon of lemon zest
- 2 tablespoons organic Sugar
- ½ cup of water
- 1 tablespoon tamari
- 1 oz * tofu, drained pipes and pushed, extra-firm
- 1-½ tablespoons of arrowroot powder or cornstarch 1/3 cup of lemon juice

1.Cube the tofu.
2.Keep in a plastic storage bag.
3.Consist of the tamari.
4. Seal the bag and shake till the tofu is well coated with the tamari.
5.Now add the tablespoon cornstarch to this bag. Shake well.
6.Tofu must be nicely covered.
7.Set aside to marinade.
8.Add all your sauce on the other hand to a bowl.
9.Mix well and reserved.
10.Keep your tofu in the fryer and cook for 10 minutes.
11.Include them to a frying pan over high heat.
12.Stir the sauce and pour this over your tofu.
13.Now stir till the sauce thickens.
14.Serve with the steamed vegetables and rice.

Vegan Beignets
Serves: 24

- 2 tablespoons of coconut oil, melted 3 cups white flour
- 2 teaspoons of vanilla
- 1 teaspoon corn starch
- 1 cup sweetener baking blend 3 tablespoons of baking blend 1 cup coconut milk, full Fat
- 1-½ teaspoons of baking yeast
- 3 tablespoons of aquafaba

1.Include the corn starch and baking blend to your blender. Blend.
2.Heat your coconut milk, and after that add to the mix with the yeast and Sugar. Set aside.

3.Now mix in the aquafaba, coconut oil, vanilla and flour.
4.Knead the dough and keep in your mixing bowl.
5.Sprinkle a little flour on your cutting board.
6.Make a rectangle from the dough. Produce 24 squares.
7.Pre-heat your fryer to 390 degrees f and cook one side for 3 minutes.
8.Flip and cook for 2 more minutes.
9.Sprinkle your powdered baking blend liberally. Preheat the oven to 350 degrees f.
10.Keep the beignets on a baking sheet covering parchment paper.
11.Bake for 15 minutes. Sprinkle the baking blend liberally.

Seitan Riblets
Serves: 4

- teaspoon salt
- ¼ cup barbecue sauce
- ¾ cup of water
- ¼ cup of dietary yeast 1 cup of wheat gluten
- teaspoon of onion powder
- 1 teaspoon mushroom powder
- ½ teaspoon garlic powder

1.Include the wheat gluten, mushroom powder, dietary yeast, garlic powder, salt, and onion powder to the food processor.
2.Mix well.
3.Drizzle water and run the processor for 4 minutes.
4.Take out the dough and knead on your cutting board.
5.Produce a square or circle to fit the air fryer basket.
6.Place the seitan pieces in the fryer and cook for 8 minutes at 370 degrees f.
7.Flip and cook for 6 more minutes.
8.Cut into chunks or piece for sandwiches.

Vegetable & Coconut Curry Rice Bowl
Serves: 6

- 1 oz. Coconut milk
- 1 oz. Chickpeas, rinsed and drained pipes 1-½ tablespoons of Sugar
- tablespoon ginger, grated
- teaspoon curry powder
- 2/3 cup wild rice, rinsed and drained 1 cup of water
- 1 cup onion, sliced
- ¾ teaspoon salt 1 cup carrots
- 1 cup yellow or red bell pepper, sliced
- 1 can water chestnuts, sliced and drained 1 cup purple or red cabbage, sliced

1.Combine the curry powder, water, rice, and ¾ teaspoon of salt in your pot.
2.Close the cover and cook for 15 minutes.
3.Release pressure naturally.
4.Open the cover and stir the other in.
5.Now boil for 5 minutes. Stir sometimes.

Spinach Lasagna Rolls
Serves:4

- ½ teaspoon salt
- cooked lasagna noodles 1-¼ cups of pasta sauce 15 oz. Ricotta cheese

- ½ cup parmesan cheese
- cup of water
- 4 cloves of garlic, minced 1 cup spinach, chopped
- ¼ teaspoon of black pepper

1. Put water into your pot.
2. Integrate the ricotta, ¼ cup parmesan, spinach, garlic, pepper, and salt in a bowl.
3. Mix well.
4. Spread ¼ cup pasta sauce at the bottom of your pan. Now lay the prepared lasagna noodles flat and spread out the ricotta filling on top of your noodles.
5. Roll the lasagna noodle lengthwise then spread the remaining sauce portion over the rolls.
6. Keep parmesan cheese on top.
7. Close the lid of your pot and cook for 12 minutes. Release pressure and open.

Honey Roasted Brussels Sprouts

Serves: 4
- 1 tbsp honey
- 5 tbsp olive oil 1 ½ lbs.
- Brussels sprouts, cut in half
- Salt and black pepper to taste

1. Insert the leaking pan at the bottom of the air fryer and pre-heat the oven at roast mode at 400 f for 2 to 3 minutes.
2. Include all the to a medium bowl and blend well until the vegetables appear well coated with the seasoning.
3. Transfer to the rotisserie basket and close the cover to seal.
4. Attach the rotisserie basket to the lever in the oven and close the door.
5. Set the timer for 10 minutes, and press start.
6. Cook till golden brown and tender.
7. When ready, transfer the brussels sprouts to serving bowls and serve right away.

Sweet Grilled Green Beans

Serves: 4
- 1 tablespoon honey
- 1 lb. Green beans
- 1 tablespoon olive oil

1. Place the dripping pan at the bottom of the air fryer and preheat the oven at air fry mode at 400 f for 2 to 3 minutes.
2. In a medium bowl, mix the green beans, honey, and olive oil.
3. Put the green beans into the rotisserie basket and near to seal.
4. Connect the rotisserie basket to the lever in the oven and close the door.
5. Set the timer for 8 minutes and press start.
6. Cook up until golden brown and tender.
7. When ready, move the green beans to serving bowls and serve immediately.

Best Ever Jalapeño Poppers

Serves: 4
- 12-18 whole fresh jalapeño
- cup nonfat refried beans
- cup shredded monterey jack or extra-sharp cheddar cheese 1 sCal lion, sliced

- 1 teaspoon salt, divided 1/4 cup all-purpose flour 2 large eggs
- 1/2 cup fine cornmeal
- Olive oil or canola oil Cooking spray

1. Start by slicing each jalapeño lengthwise on one side. Place the jalapeños side by side in a microwave safe bowl and microwave them until they are slightly soft; usually around 5 minutes.
2. While your jalapeños cook; mix refried beans, sCal lions, 1/2 teaspoon salt, and cheese in a bowl.
3. Once your jalapeños are softened you can scoop out the seeds and add one tablespoon of your refried bean mixture (it can be a little less if the pepper is smaller.) Press the jalapeño closed around the filling.
4. Beat your eggs in a small bowl and place your flour in a separate bowl. In a third bowl mix your cornmeal and the remaining salt.
5. Roll each pepper in the flour, then dip it in the egg, and finally roll it in the cornmeal to coat the entire pepper.
6. Place the peppers on a flat surface and coat them with a Cooking spray; olive oil Cooking spray is suggested.
7. Pour into the oven rack/basket. Place the rack on the middle-shelf of the cosori air fryer oven. Set temperature to 400°f and set time to 5 minutes. Select start/stop to begin. Turn each pepper, and then cook for another 5 minutes; serve hot.

Bell Peppercorn Wrapped In Tortilla

Serves: 4
- 1 small red bell pepper, chopped 1 small yellow onion, diced
- 1 tablespoon water
- 2 cobs grilled corn kernels 4 large tortillas
- 4 pieces commercial vegan nuggets, chopped Mixed greens for garnish

1. Preheat the cosori air fryer oven to 400°f.
2. In a skillet heated over medium heat, water sauté the vegan nuggets together with the onions, bell peppers, and corn kernels. Set aside.
3. Place filling inside the corn tortillas.
4. Pour the tortillas into the oven rack/basket. Place the rack on the middle-shelf of the cosori air fryer oven. Set temperature to 400°f and set time to 15 minutes until the tortilla wraps are crispy.
5. Serve with mix greens on top.

Brown Rice, Spinach And Tofu Frittata

Serves: 4
- ½ cup baby spinach, chopped
- ½ cup kale, chopped
- ½ onion, chopped
- ½ teaspoon turmeric
- 1 ¾ cups brown rice, cooked
- 1 flax egg (1 tablespoon flaxseed meal + 3 tablespoon cold water) 1 package firm tofu
- 1 tablespoon olive oil
- 1 yellow pepper, chopped 2 tablespoons soy sauce
- teaspoons arrowroot powder
- teaspoons dijon mustard 2/3 cup almond milk
- big mushrooms, chopped

- 3 tablespoons nutritional yeast 4 cloves garlic, crushed
- 4 spring onions, chopped
- A handful of basil leaves, chopped

1. Preheat the cosori air fryer oven to 375°f. Grease a plan that will fit inside the cosori air fryer oven.
2. Prepare the frittata crust by mixing the brown rice and flax egg. Press the rice onto the baking dish until you form a crust. Brush with a little oil and cook for 10 minutes.
3. Meanwhile, heat olive oil in a skillet over medium flame and sauté the garlic and onions for 2 minutes.
4. Add the pepper and mushroom and continue stirring for 3 minutes.
5. Stir in the kale, spinach, spring onions, and basil. Remove from the pan and set aside.
6. In a food processor, pulse together the tofu, mustard, turmeric, soy sauce, nutritional yeast, vegan milk and arrowroot powder. Pour in a mixing bowl and stir in the sautéed vegetables.
7. Pour the vegan frittata mixture over the rice crust and cook in the cosori air fryer oven for 40 minutes.

Brussels Sprouts With Balsamic Oil

Serves: 4
- ¼ teaspoon salt
- 1 tablespoon balsamic vinegar 2 cups brussels sprouts, halved Tablespoons olive oil

1. Preheat the cosori air fryer oven for 5 minutes.
2. Mix all in a bowl until the zucchini fries are well coated.
3. Place in the cosori air fryer oven basket.
4. Close and cook for 15 minutes for 350°f.

Cheesy Cauliflower Fritters

Serves: 8
- ½ c. Chopped parsley
- 1 c. Italian breadcrumbs
- 1/3 c. Shredded mozzarella cheese
- 1/3 c. Shredded sharp cheddar cheese 1 egg
- **2** minced garlic cloves 3 chopped sCal lions 1 head of cauliflower

1. Cut cauliflower up into florets. Wash well and pat dry. Place into a
2. food processor and pulse 20-30 seconds till it looks like rice.
3. Place cauliflower rice in a bowl and mix with pepper, salt, egg, cheeses, breadcrumbs, garlic, and sCal lions.
4. With hands, form 15 patties of the mixture. Add more breadcrumbs if needed.
5. With olive oil, spritz patties, and place into your cosori air fryer oven basket in a single layer. Set temperature to 390°f, and set time to 7 minutes, flipping after 7 minutes.

Buttered Carrot-Zucchini With Mayo

Serves: 4
- 1 tablespoon grated onion
- 2 tablespoons butter, melted 1/2-pound carrots, sliced
- 1-1/2 zucchinis, sliced 1/4 cup water
- 1/4 cup mayonnaise
- 1/4 teaspoon prepared horseradish 1/4 teaspoon salt

- 1/4 teaspoon ground black pepper
- 1/4 cup italian breadcrumbs

1. Lightly grease baking pan of air fryer with Cooking spray. Add carrots. For 8 minutes, cook on 360°f. Add zucchini and continue Cooking for another 5 minutes.
2. Meanwhile, in a bowl whisk well pepper, salt, horseradish, onion, mayonnaise, and water.
3. Pour into pan of veggies. Toss well to coat.
4. In a small bowl mix melted butter and breadcrumbs. Sprinkle over veggies.
5. Pour into the oven rack/basket. Place the rack on the middle-shelf of the cosori air fryer oven.
6. Set temperature to 490°f and set time to 10 minutes until tops are lightly browned.
7. Serve and enjoy.

Cheddar, Squash And Zucchini Casserole

Serves: 4
- 1 egg
- 5 saltine crackers, or as needed, crushed 2 tablespoons breadcrumbs
- 1/2-pound yellow squash,
- sliced 1/2-pound zucchini, sliced
- 1/2 cup shredded cheddar cheese 1-1/2 teaspoons white Sugar
- 1/2 teaspoon salt
- 1/4 onion, diced
- 1/4 cup biscuit baking mix
- 1/4 cup butter

1. Lightly grease baking pan of air fryer with Cooking spray. Add onion, zucchini, and yellow squash. Cover pan with foil and for 15 minutes, cook on 360° f or until tender.
2. Stir in salt, Sugar, egg, butter, baking mix, and cheddar cheese. Mix well. Fold in crushed crackers. Top with breadcrumbs.
3. Cook for 15 minutes at 390° f until tops are lightly browned.
4. Serve and enjoy.

Zucchini Parmesan Chips

Serves: 10
- ½ tsp. Paprika
- ½ c. Grated parmesan cheese
- ½ c. Italian breadcrumbs 1 lightly beaten egg
- 2 thinly sliced zucchinis

1. Use a very sharp knife or mandolin slicer to slice zucchini as thinly as you can. Pat off extra moisture.
1. Beat egg with a pinch of pepper and salt and a bit of water.
2. Combine paprika, cheese, and breadcrumbs in a bowl.
3. Dip slices of zucchini into the egg mixture and then into breadcrumb mixture. Press gently to coat.
4. With olive oil Cooking spray, mist coated zucchini slices. Place into your cosori air fryer oven basket in a single layer. Set temperature to 350°f and set time to 8 minutes.
5. Sprinkle with salt and serve with salsa.

Jalapeño Cheese Balls

Serves: 12
- 4 ounces cream cheese
- ⅓ cup shredded mozzarella cheese
- ⅓ cup shredded cheddar cheese 2 jalapeños,

finely chopped
- ½ cup breadcrumbs 2 eggs
- ½ cup all-purpose flour Salt
- Pepper Cooking oil

1.In a medium bowl, combine the cream cheese, mozzarella, cheddar, and jalapeños. Mix well.
2.Form the cheese mixture into balls about an inch thick. Using a small ice cream scoop works well.
3.Arrange the cheese balls on a sheet pan and place in the freezer for 15 minutes. This will help the cheese balls maintain their shape while frying.
4.Spray the cosori air fryer oven basket with Cooking oil. Place the breadcrumbs in a small bowl. In another small bowl, beat the eggs. In a third small bowl, combine the flour with salt and pepper to taste, and mix well. Remove the cheese balls from the freezer. Dip the cheese balls in the flour, then the eggs, and then the breadcrumbs.
5.Place the cheese balls in the air fryer. Spray with Cooking oil. Cook for 8 minutes.
6.Open the cosori air fryer oven and flip the cheese balls.
7.I recommend flipping them instead of shaking so the balls maintain their form. Cook an additional 4 minutes. Cool before serving.

Crispy Roasted Broccoli

Serves: 2
- ¼ tsp. Masala
- ½ tsp. Red chili powder
- ½ tsp. Salt
- ¼ tsp. Turmeric powder 1 tbsp. Chickpea flour 2 tbsp. Yogurt
- 1-pound broccoli

1.Cut broccoli up into florets. Soak in a bowl of water with 2 teaspoons of salt for at least half an hour to remove impurities.
2.Take out broccoli florets from water and let drain. Wipe down thoroughly.
3.Mix all other to create a marinade.
4.Toss broccoli florets in the marinade. Cover and chill 15-30 minutes.
5. Preheat the air fryer oven to 390 degrees.
6.Place marinated broccoli florets into the fryer basket, set temperature to 350°f, and set time to 10 minutes.
7.Florets will be crispy when done.

Vegan Recipes

Carrot Mix

Serves: 4

- Coconut milk (2 cups)
- Steel-cut oats (.5 cup)
- Shredded carrots (1 cup)
- Agave nectar (.5 tsp.)
- Ground cardamom (1 tsp.)
- Saffron (1 pinch)

1.Lightly spritz the Air Fryer pan using a cooking oil spray.
2.Warm the fryer to reach 365° Fahrenheit.
3.When it's hot, whisk and add the fixings (omit the saffron).
4.Set the timer for 15 minutes.

5.After the timer buzzes, portion into the serving dishes with a sprinkle of saffron.

Chinese Breakfast Bowls

Serves:: 4
- Firm tofu (12 oz.)

- Maple syrup (3 tbsp.) Coconut aminos (.25 cup) Sesame oil (2 tbsp.)
- Lime juice (2 tbsp.)
- Fresh romanesco (1 lb.) Carrots (3)
- Red bell pepper (1)
- Cooked red quinoa (2 cups)

1.Warm the Air Fryer at 370° Fahrenheit.
2.Cube the tofu and roughly chop the romanesco, carrots, and bell pepper.
3.Combine the juice, aminos, maple syrup, and oil with the tofu cubes in a mixing container.
4.Toss everything into the Air Fryer for 15 minutes. Shake the basket often.
5.Add the peppers, quinoa, spinach, carrots, and romanesco into serving dishes and enjoy.

Easy Breakfast Oats

Serves: 4
- Almond milk (2 cups)
- Steel-cut oats (1 cup)
- Water (2 cups)
- Dried cherries (.33 cup)
- Cocoa powder (2 tbsp.)
- Stevia (.25 cup)
- Almond extract (.5 tsp.)
- The Sauce: Water (2 tbsp.)
- Cherries (1.5 cups)
- Almond extract (.25 tsp.)

1.Warm the fryer to reach 360° Fahrenheit.
2.Stir the first set of into the pan of the Air Fryer. Set the timer for 15 minutes.
3.In a small pot, whisk the sauce fixings. Simmer for 10 minutes.
4.Portion into serving bowls with a drizzle of the cherry sauce.

Pumpkin Oatmeal

- Water (1.5 cups)
- Pumpkin puree (.5 cup)
- Stevia (3 tbsp.)
- Pumpkin pie spice (1 tsp.)
- Steel-cut oats (.5 cup)

1.Set the Air Fryer at 360° Fahrenheit to preheat.
2.Toss in and mix the fixings into the pan of the Air Fryer.
3.Set the timer for 20 minutes.
4.When the time has elapsed, portion the oatmeal into bowls and serve.

Carrot & Potato Mix

Serves: 6
- Potatoes (2)
- Carrots (3 lb.)
- Yellow onion (1)
- Dried thyme (1 tsp.)
- Black pepper and salt (to your liking)
- Curry powder (2 tsp.)

- Coconut milk (3 tbsp.)
- Vegan cheese (3 tbsp.) Parsley (1 tbsp.)

1. Cube/chop the parsley, carrots, and onions. Crumble the vegan cheese.
2. Warm the Air Fryer to reach 365° Fahrenheit.
3. Once it's heated, toss in the veggies, thyme, curry powder, salt, and pepper. Set the timer and air-fry for 16 minutes.
4. Stir in the milk and cheese.
5. Portion and serve.

Curried Cauliflower Florets With Nuts & Raisins

Serves: 4
- Golden raisins (.25 cup)
- Cauliflower (1 head)
- Pine nuts (.25 cup)
- Boiling water (1 cup)
- Olive oil (.5 cup)
- Curry powder (1 tbsp.)
- Salt (.25 tsp.)

1. Slice the cauliflower into small florets.
2. Dump the raisins into the cup of boiling water to plump.
3. Set the Air Fryer temperature at 350° Fahrenheit.
4. Toast the nuts in the fryer with the oil for about one minute.
5. Toss the florets with the salt and curry powder in another mixing bowl. Toss into the Air Fryer.
6. Cook for ten minutes. Drain and toss all of the fixings well before serving.

Falafel - Gluten-Free

Serves: 4
- Brined lupini beans (1 cup)
- Thawed - frozen broccoli (1.5 cups)
- Tahini (.25 cup)
- Lemon juice (2 tbsp.)
- Dried parsley (1 tbsp.)
- Cumin (2 tsp.)
- Ground chia seeds (2 tbsp.)
- Garlic powder (.5 tsp.)
- Onion powder (.25 tsp.)
- Allspice (.25 tsp.)

1. Before you begin, soak the lupini beans in hot water (30-60 min.) and drain them.
2. Warm the fryer to 350° Fahrenheit.
3. Chop the broccoli and beans using a food processor until they are in rice-like pieces. Transfer this mixture to a medium-sized mixing container.
4. Add the lemon juice, tahini, and seasoning to the mixture and stir until combined.
5. Stir in the ground chia seeds. Wait for the mixture to sit for about 5 minutes, so the chia can absorb some liquid to make a thick dough form.
6. Shape the dough mixture into 12 patties, and then flattened them to be about 2 inches across and a little less than ½-inch thick.
7. Arrange the patties in a single layer in the Air Fryer and air-fry for 14-15 minutes, depending on how crunchy you like them.
8. Serve while warm.
9. To Reheat: Air-fry for 8 minutes at 350° Fahrenheit.

Roasted Asian Broccoli

Serves: 4 sides
- Broccoli (1 lb.)
- Peanut oil (1.5 tbsp.)
- Garlic (1 tbsp.) Salt
- Reduced sodium soy sauce (2 tbsp.) Honey (or agave (2 tsp.)
- Sriracha (2 tsp.) Rice vinegar (1 tsp.)
- Roasted salted peanuts (.33 cup)
- Optional: Fresh lime juice

1. Warm the Air Fryer to reach 400° Fahrenheit.
2. Mince the garlic. Slice the broccoli into florets.
3. Toss the broccoli, peanut oil, garlic, and sea salt until well covered.
4. Arrange the broccoli in the Air Fryer's wire basket, trying to leave a little bit of space between each of the florets.
5. Cook until golden brown and crispy (15-20 min.), stirring halfway.
6. Mix the honey, soy sauce, sriracha, and rice vinegar in a small, microwave-safe bowl.
7. Once well mixed, microwave the mixture for 10-15 seconds until the honey is melted and evenly incorporated.
8. Toss the broccoli into a bowl and add in the soy sauce mixture.
9. Toss to coat and season to taste with a pinch more salt, if needed. Stir in the peanuts and squeeze a drizzle of lime on top as desired.

Yellow Squash - Carrots & Zucchini

Serves: 4
- Carrots (.5 lb.)
- Olive oil (6 tsp. - divided)
- Lime (1 sliced into wedges)
- Zucchini (1 lb. sliced into .75-inch semi-circles)
- Yellow squash (1 lb.)
- Tarragon leaves (1 tbsp.)
- White pepper (.5 tsp.) Sea salt (1 tsp.)

1. Set the Air Fryer at 400° Fahrenheit.
2. Trim the stem and roots from the squash and zucchini.
3. Dice and add the carrots into a bowl with two teaspoons of oil.
4. Toss the carrots into the fryer basket. Prepare for 5 minutes.
5. Mix in the zucchini, oil, salt, and pepper in the bowl.
6. When the carrots are done, fold in the mixture. Cook 30 minutes.
7. Stir the mixture occasionally. Chop the tarragon and garnish using and lime wedges.

Mexican Casserole

Serves: 4 sides
- Olive oil (1 tbsp.) Garlic (4 cloves)
- Onion (1 yellow)
- Cilantro (2 tbsp.) Red chili (1 small)
- Ground cumin (2 tsp.) Coriander seeds (1 tsp.) Sweet paprika (1 tsp.)
- Black pepper and salt (as desired) Sweet potatoes (1 lb.)
- Lime juice (half of 1 lime) Green beans (10 oz.) Tomatoes (2 cups)

- Parsley (1 tbsp.)

1. Set the Air Fryer at 365º Fahrenheit.
2. Mince or chop the garlic, onions, red chili, tomatoes, parsley, and cilantro. Cube the sweet potatoes.
3. Spritz a pan to fit inside of the Air Fryer using a bit of cooking oil spray.
4. Mix and add all of the fixings (omitting the parsley for now).
5. Set the timer for 15 minutes. Add parsley to the casserole and serve.

Rice & Endive Casserole
Serves: 4
- Olive oil (1 tbsp.)
- Scallions (2)
- Garlic (3 cloves) Fresh ginger (1 tbsp.) Chili sauce (1 tsp.)
- White/brown rice (.5 cup)
- Veggie stock (1 cup) Endives (3)
- Black pepper and salt (1 pinch)

1. Chop/grate the garlic, scallions, trimmed endives, and ginger.
2. Lightly grease a pan that will fit in the Air Fryer using a spritz of oil.
3. Mix all of the fixings in the fryer and set the timer for 20 minutes.
4. When it's ready, divide into plates and serve.

Baby Ears Of Corn
Serves: 4
- Carom seeds (.5 tsp.)
- Almond flour (1 cup)
- Chili powder (.25 tsp.)
- Garlic powder (1 tsp.)
- Boiled baby ears of corn (4)
- Baking soda (1 pinch) Salt (to your liking)

1. Warm the Air Fryer (350º Fahrenheit).
2. Whisk the flour, salt, carom seeds, baking soda, garlic powder, and chili powder.
3. Pour in a little water to make a batter. Dip the boiled corn in the mixture.
4. Place the corn in a foil-lined fryer basket. Air-fry 10 minutes.
5. Serve with a sprinkle of salt if desired.

Crunchy Black-Eyed Peas
Serves: 6
- Black-eyed peas (15 oz. can)
- Salt (.25 tsp.)
- Chipotle chili powder (.125 tsp.)
- Black pepper (.125 tsp.)
- Chili powder (.5 tsp.)

1. Use cold tap water to rinse the beans. Set aside for now.
2. Set the Air Fryer temperature at 360º Fahrenheit.
3. Whisk the spices and add the peas.
4. Add to the fryer basket and air-fry for 10 minutes.

Easy Tofu
Serves: 4
- Sesame oil (2 tbsp.)
- Cornstarch (1 tbsp.)
- Tofu (1 block/1-inch cubes)
- Rice vinegar (1 tsp.)
- Tamari/Coconut Aminos/keto-friendly substitute for soy sauce (2 tbsp.)

1. Warm up the fryer ahead of time to 370º Fahrenheit.
2. Combine the oil, vinegar, tofu, and tamari/aminos. Toss well and set aside.
3. Toss the cornstarch in a dish and cover the tofu.
4. Place it in the Air Fryer basket for 20 minutes. Toss the tofu a couple of times during the air-fry cycle.

Lemony Green Beans
Serves: 4
- Lemon (1)
- Green beans (1 lb.)
- Extra-virgin olive oil (.25 tsp.)
- Black pepper & sea salt (as desired)

1. Set the Air Fryer temperature setting at 400º Fahrenheit.
2. Pour the beans into the fryer basket, and spritz using the lemon juice, oil, salt, and pepper.
3. Air-fry for 12 minutes. Serve immediately.

Tawa Vegetables
Serves: 4
- Potato (.25 cup)
- Okra (.25 cup) Taro root (.25 cup) Eggplant (.25 cup)
- Garam masala (2 tsp.) Red chili powder (1 tsp.) Amchur powder (1 tsp.) Salt (as desired)
- For Brushing: Olive oil

1. Set the Air Fryer at 390º Fahrenheit.
2. Slice the taro root and potatoes into fries and soak them in salted water for ten minutes.
3. Slice the eggplant and okra into four sections.
4. Rinse the potatoes and taro root; pat dry. Combine with the spices, okra, and eggplant.
5. Brush the pan with the oil and air-fry for 10 minutes. Lower the heat setting to 355º Fahrenheit and cook 15 additional minutes.
6. Enjoy them any way you choose.

Apple Chips
Serves: 2
- Apple (1 large thinly sliced)
- Cinnamon (1 tsp.)
- Salt (1 pinch)
- Avocado/olive oil spray (1 tsp.)

1. Warm the Air Fryer to 350º Fahrenheit.
2. Use a mandolin or sharp knife to slice the apples.
3. Toss them into a container with the salt and cinnamon. Toss well. Lightly spritz with oil as needed.
4. Arrange them in the fryer basket - not touching.
5. Set the timer for 8 to 10 minutes. Flatten them a couple of times while cooking.
6. Remove the batch and repeat until the rest of the slices are air-fried.

Blueberry Smoothie
Serves: 1
- Coconut/almond milk (1 cup)
- Blueberries (.25 cup)

- Vanilla extract (1 tsp.)
- MCT Oil/more coconut oil (1 tsp.)
- Optional: Protein powder/your choice (30 grams)

1 Toss each of the fixings into a blender.
2 Mix well and serve in a chilled glass.

Clean & Green Smoothie
Serves: 1
- Filtered water (1 cup)
- Avocado (half of 1)
- MCT oil (1 tbsp.)
- Organic cucumber (half of 1)
- Dark leafy greens (1 large handful)
- Dandelion (1 – 2 leaves)
- Parsley (2 tbsp.)
- Hemp seeds (2 tbsp.)
- Lemon juice (1 lemon)
- Turmeric powder (.25 tsp.)

1.Toss each of the components into a high-speed blender.
2.Pulse the smoothie about one minute. Serve and enjoy immediately.

Frozen Berry Shake
Serves: 1
- Frozen mixed berries (.5 cup)
- Creamed coconut milk (.33 cup)
- MCT/Virgin coconut oil (1 tbsp.)
- Water/unsweetened almond milk (.5 cup) Optional: Stevia extract (3-5 drops)

1.Cream the coconut milk by placing the can in the fridge overnight. The next day, open and spoon out the solidified coconut milk and discard the liquids. Don't shake before opening the can. (One 400 gram container yields about 200 grams of coconut cream.)
2.Place the creamed coconut milk, berries, water/almond milk, MCT oil, and stevia (if using) and ice into a blender. Pulse until smooth.

Green Avocado Pudding
Serves: 3
- Pitted avocado (1)
- Almond milk (5 tbsp.)
- Stevia (3 tsp.)
- Vanilla extract (.25 tsp.)
- Salt (.25 tsp.)
- Cocoa powder (1 tbsp.)

1.Set the Air Fryer at 360° Fahrenheit.
2.Peel and mash the avocad. Mix it with the milk, salt, vanilla extract, and stevia. Stir in the cocoa powder.
3.Cook the pudding in the Air Fryer for three minutes.
4.Chill and serve.

Ketogenic Air Fried Specialties
Air Bread & Egg Butter
Serves: 19
- Eggs (3)
- Baking powder (1 tsp.)
- Sea salt (.25 tsp.)

- Almond flour (1 cup)
- Unchilled butter (.25 cup)

1 Set the Air Fryer at 350° Fahrenheit.
2 Whisk the eggs with a hand mixer. Mix in the rest of the fixings to make a dough. Knead the dough and cover using a tea towel for about ten minutes.
3 Air-fry the bread 15 minutes. Remove the bread and let it cool down on a wooden board.
4 Slice and serve with your favorite meal or as it is with butter (below).

For The Butter:
Serves: 4
- Eggs (4)
- Salt (1 tsp.)
- Butter (4 tbsp.)

1 Prepare the Air Fryer basket using a layer of foil and add the eggs.
2 Air-fry the eggs at 320° Fahrenheit for 17 minutes. Transfer to an ice- cold water bath to chill.
3 Peel and chop the eggs and combine with the rest of the fixings. Enjoy with your Air Fried Bread.

Asparagus Omelet
Serves: Eggs (3)
- Pepper & salt (1 pinch each)
- Steamed asparagus tips (5)
- Warm water (2 tbsp.)
- Parmesan cheese (1 tbsp.)

1.Set the Air Fryer temperature setting to 320° Fahrenheit.
2.Whisk the eggs, water, pepper, salt, and cheese.
3.Spritz a skillet with cooking oil spray and steam the asparagus.
4.Add to the fryer basket. Pour in the egg mixture.
5.Fry for 5 minutes and serve.

Bacon Egg & Cheese Roll-Ups
Serves: 4
- Unsalted butter (2 tbsp.)
- Chopped onion (.25 cup)
- Almond flour (1 cup)
- Medium green bell pepper (half of 1)
- Large eggs (6)
- Shredded sharp cheddar cheese (1 cup)
- Sugar-free bacon (12 slices)
- For Dipping: Mild salsa (.5 cup)

1 Prepare a skillet using the medium heat temperature setting to melt butter.
2 Discard the seeds and dice the peppers and onion. Toss them into the pan and sauté for three minutes.
3 Whisk the eggs in another small mixing bowl, and pour into the pan. Scramble the eggs with the onions and peppers about five minutes or until fluffy and fully cooked. Take it away from the heat and set aside.
4 Heat the Air Fryer to reach 350° Fahrenheit.
5 Arrange three slices of bacon side by side. You can overlap them about 1/4-inch. Divide the eggs in a pile (on the side that's the closest to you). Garnish the top of the eggs with a portion of cheese.
6 Roll the bacon tightly around the eggs. Hold them together using a toothpick or skewer if necessary. Arrange each of the rolls into the Air Fryer basket.

7 Air-fry them for 15 minutes. Turn the rolls halfway through the cooking time.
8 The bacon will be browned and crispy when done.
9 Serve immediately with salsa for dipping. It's great for brunch!

Brunch Ham Hash

Serves: 3
- Parmesan cheese (5 oz.)
- Ham (10 oz.) Onion (half of 1) Butter (1 tbsp.)
- Egg (1)
- Paprika (1 tsp.)
- Freshly ground black pepper (1 tsp.) Also Needed: 3 ramekins

1 Set the Air Fryer at 350° Fahrenheit.
2 Peel and dice the onion. Slice the ham into small strips and shred the parmesan cheese.
3 Lastly, whisk the egg, salt, pepper, and paprika; and add to the remainder of the fixings.
4 Sprinkle with pepper, paprika, and salt. Pour into the ramekins and
sprinkle with the parmesan. Arrange the ramekins in the Air Fryer for 10 minutes.
5 When ready, remove from the fryer, and scramble.

Dark Chocolate Avocado Muffins

Serves: 7
- Almond flour (1 cup) Baking soda (.5 tsp.)
- Apple cider vinegar (1 tsp.)
- Egg (1)
- Butter (4 tbsp.)
- Stevia powder (3 scoops) Pitted avocado (.5 cup) Melted dark chocolate (1 oz.)

1 Set the Air Fryer temperature at 355° Fahrenheit.
2 Whisk the almond flour, baking soda, vinegar, stevia powder, and melted chocolate.
3 Whisk the egg in another container and add to the mixture along with the butter.
4 Peel, cube, and mash the avocado and add. Mix using a hand mixer to make the flour mixture smooth. Pour into muffin forms (½ full).
5 Set the timer for 9 minutes.
6 Lower the heat (340° Fahrenheit) and air-fry three additional minutes.
7 Chill before serving for the best results.

Eggs - Ham & Spinach

Serves: 4
- Sliced ham (7 oz.)
- Spinach (2.25 cups)
- Cream milk (4 tsp.)
- Olive oil (1 tbsp.)
- Large eggs (4)
- Salt and pepper (to your liking)
- Also Needed:
- Ramekins (4)

1 Set the Air Fryer temperature to 356° Fahrenheit. Spray the ramekins.
2 Warm up the oil in a skillet (med. heat) and saute the spinach until wilted. Drain.
3 Divide the spinach and rest of the fixings in each of the ramekins.
4 Sprinkle with salt and pepper. Bake until set (20 min.).
5 Serve when they are to your liking.

Pumpkin Pie French Toast

Serves: 4
- Water (.25 cup)
- Large eggs (2)
- Pumpkin puree (.25 cup) Pumpkin pie spices (.25 tsp.) Butter (.25 cup)
- Low-carb bread (4 slices)

1 Warm up the fryer to reach 340°Fahrenheit before fry time.
2 Whisk the eggs, water, pie spice, and pumpkin puree.
3 Once it's smooth, dip the bread into the mixture.
4 Arrange each slice in the fryer and set the timer for 10 minutes.
5 Serve with a portion of butter.

Scrambled Pancake Hash

Serves: 7
- Coconut flour (1 cup)
- Ground ginger (1 tsp.)
- Salt (1 tsp.)
- Baking soda (1 tsp.)
- Apple cider vinegar (1 tbsp.) Heavy cream (.25 cup)
- Egg (1) - Butter (5 tbsp.)

1 Heat the Air Fryer to 400° Fahrenheit.
2 Whisk the baking soda, flour, ginger, and salt in a mixing container.
3 In another mixing container, add the egg, butter, and cream. Blend well using a hand mixer.
4 Combine the fixings and mix until smooth.
5 Carefully pour the mixture into the fryer basket tray and cook for four (4) minutes.
6 Remove and scramble the hash. Air-fry for another five minutes.
7 Transfer to a serving platter.

Thai Omelet

Serves: 4
- Fish sauce (2 tbsp.)
- Eggs (4)
- White pepper powder (2 tbsp.)
- Shallot (1)
- Garlic (2 cloves)
- Lime juice (half of 1 lime)
- Sausage (.5 cup)
- Green onion (1)
- Fresh spinach (1 handful)
- For the Pan: Olive oil or keto-friendly option (as needed) For the Garnish: Cilantro

1 Warm the fryer to reach 340° Fahrenheit.
2 Mince the shallots, garlic, and green onions. Finely chop the sausage.
3 Heat the oil in a skillet. Whisk the eggs in a large mixing container. Mix in with the pepper and fish sauce.
4 Whisk well and add the remainder of the fixings until combined.
5 Pour into the pan and place it into the Air Fryer Basket.
6 Air-fry for 10 minutes.
7 Garnish with the cilantro and serve.

Tofu Egg Muffins

Serves: 4
- Small tofu chunk (1 cut in cubes)

- Large eggs (3)
- Sesame oil (.25 tsp.)
- Ground cumin (.25 tsp.)
- Ground coriander (.25 tsp.)
- Black pepper (.25 tsp.)
- Soy sauce substitute - ex: Keto-friendly is liquid aminos (.5 tsp.) Spring onion (1 handful)
- Coriander (1 handful)
- Also Needed: 4 muffin molds

1 Set the Air Fryer at 392º Fahrenheit (5 min.).
2 Chop the coriander and onion. Combine all of the fixings (omit the tofu for now). Whisk well.
3 Break the tofu into equal portions in the mold. Pour the mixture over each one.
4 Place in the Air Fryer for 10 minutes and serve.

Turkey "Sausage" Patties

Serves: 6
- Large garlic clove (1)
- Small onion (1)
- Olive oil (1 tsp.)
- Pepper and salt (to your liking)
- Chopped chives (1 tbsp.)
- Paprika (.75 tsp.)
- Nutmeg (1 pinch) Fennel seeds (1 tsp.) Vinegar (1 tbsp.)
- Lean ground turkey (1 lb.)

1 Heat the Air Fryer to reach 375º Fahrenheit.
2 Mince the onion and garlic.
3 Pour half of the oil with the garlic and onion into the Air Fryer. Cook for 1 minute; add the seeds and place them on a platter.
4 Combine the paprika, nutmeg, pepper, salt, chives, onion, turkey, and
vinegar. Mix well and shape into patties.
5 Add the remainder of the oil and air fry the patties for three minutes.
6 Serve the substitute "sausage" patties on keto-friendly buns.

Bacon-Wrapped Chicken

Serves: 3
- Breast of chicken (1)
- Unsmoked bacon (6 strips)
- Soft garlic cheese (1 tbsp.)

1 Slice the chicken into six pieces.
2 Spread the garlic cheese over each bacon strip. Add a piece of chicken to each one. Roll and secure with a toothpick.
3 Prepare the Air Fryer and let it warm up for about 3 minutes. Arrange the wraps in the fryer basket. Air-fry for about 15 minutes.

Beef Roll-Ups

Serves: 4
- Pesto (3 tbsp.)
- Beef flank steak (2 lb.)
- Fresh baby spinach (.75 cup)
- Roasted red bell peppers (3 oz.) Provolone cheese (6 slices)
- Sea salt and black pepper (as desired)

1 Set the Air Fryer in advance to 400º Fahrenheit.
2 Slice the steak open, but not all the way through. Spread the pesto over the steak.

3 Layer and add the peppers, cheese, and spinach (¾ of the way into the meat). Dust it using a sprinkle of pepper and salt.
4 Roll the wraps and securely close each one using toothpicks to hold it together.
5 Set the timer for 14 minutes – turning the roll-ups about halfway through the frying cycle.
6 When the cycle is completed, wait for about 10 minutes before slicing to serve.

Chicken Hash

Serves: 3
- Salt (1 pinch)
- Back pepper (1 tsp.) Chicken fillet (7 oz.)
- Cauliflower (6 oz. or 1 medium) Yellow onion (half of 1)
- Green pepper (1)
- Water (1 tbsp.)
- Butter (3 tbsp.)
- Cream (1 tbsp.)

1 Warm the Air Fryer to reach 380º Fahrenheit.
2 Dice the onion. Chop the green peppers and cauliflower. Toss into a blender to make rice. Chop the chicken into chunks. Sprinkle using pepper and salt.
3 Prepare the veggies and combine the fixings.
4 Add them to the fryer basket and cook until done (6-7 min.).
5 Serve anytime for lunch or a snack.

Dragon Shrimp

Serves: 2
- Almond flour (.25 cup)
- Ginger (1 pinch)
- Chopped onions (1 cup)
- Shrimp (.5 lb.)
- Eggs (2)
- Soya sauce (.5 cup)
- Olive oil (2 tbsp.)

1 Heat the Air Fryer to reach 390º Fahrenheit.
2 Boil the shrimp for about five minutes.
3 Make a paste from the mixture of mashed onions and ginger.
4 Whisk the eggs and add with the rest of the fixings.
5 Add the shrimp to the mixture and air-fry for 10 minutes.
6 Serve with a dish of keto-friendly mayo.

Fish Nuggets

Serves: 4
- Cod fillet (1 lb.)
- Eggs (3)
- Olive oil (4 tbsp.) Almond flour (1 cup)
- Gluten-free breadcrumbs (1 cup) Salt (1 tsp.)

1 Preset the temperature of the Air Fryer at 390º Fahrenheit.
2 Slice the cod into nuggets.
3 Prepare three bowls. Beat the eggs in one. Combine the salt, oil, and breadcrumbs in another. Sift the almond flour into the third one.
4 Cover each of the nuggets with the flour, dip in the eggs, and the breadcrumbs.
5 Arrange the breaded nuggets into the basket and set the timer for 20
minutes.

Roast Beef For Sandwiches

Serves: 6
- Oregano (.5 tsp.)
- Garlic powder (.5 tsp.)
- Dried thyme (1 tsp.)
- Olive oil (1 tbsp.)
- Round roast (2 lb.)

1 Warm the Air Fryer to reach 330° Fahrenheit.
2 Combine the spices. Brush the oil over the beef and rub in the spice mixture.
3 Arrange the roast in a baking dish. Place it in the fryer for 30 minutes. Flip it over and continue frying another 25 minutes.
4 Wait for a few minutes before slicing.
5 Serve on your choice of keto-friendly bread for a delicious sandwich or serve with a favorite side dish.

Turkey & Avocado Burrito

Serves: 2
- Eggs (4)
- Pepper & Salt (as desired) Salsa (4 tbsp.)
- Sliced avocado (.5 cup)
- Cooked turkey breast (8 slices)
- Grated mozzarella cheese (.25 cup)
- Sliced red bell pepper (half of 1)
- Tortillas (2)

1 Preheat the Air Fryer at 390° Fahrenheit for 5 minutes, and spray the fryer tray with a spritz of cooking oil spray.
2 Whisk the eggs, pepper, and salt. Add the eggs to a skillet. When done, add the eggs to the tortillas.
3 Prepare the burrito beginning with a layer of turkey, avocado, peppers, cheese, and salsa. Roll it up slowly.
4 Spray the fryer and arrange the burritos in the basket. Prepare for 5 minutes.
5 Serve warm.

Chicken Strips

Serves: 4
- Paprika (1 tsp.)
- Chicken fillets (1 lb.)
- Cream (1 tbsp.)
- Pepper and salt (.5 tsp.)

1 Slice the chicken into fillet strips. Sprinkle using pepper and salt.
2 Set the Air Fryer at 365° Fahrenheit.
3 Arrange the strips in the basket and air-fry for 6 minutes.
4 Flip the strips and cook another 5 minutes.
5 Garnish using the cream and paprika. Serve warm.

Creamy Salmon

Serves: 2
- Chopped dill (1 tbsp.)
- Salt (1 pinch)
- Olive oil (1 tbsp.)
- Sour cream (3 tbsp.)
- Plain yogurt (1.76 oz.)
- Salmon (.75 lb./6 pieces)

1 Heat the Air Fryer and wait for it to reach 285° Fahrenheit.
2 Shake the salt over the salmon and add them to the fryer basket with the olive oil to air-fry for 10 minutes.
3 Whisk the yogurt, salt, and dill.

4 Serve the salmon with the sauce with your favorite sides.

Shrimp Scampi

Serves: 4
Lemon juice (1 tbsp.) Butter (4 tbsp.) Minced garlic (1 tbsp.)
Dried chives (1 tsp.) or Chopped chives (1 tbsp.) Red pepper flakes (2 tsp.)
Dried (1 tsp.) or Minced basil leaves (1 tbsp.) plus more for sprinkling Chicken stock or white wine (2 tbsp.)
Defrosted shrimp (1 lb. or about 21-25 count) Also Needed: 6x3 metal pan and silicone mitts

1. Heat the Air Fryer at 330° Fahrenheit. Also, warm the skillet.
2. Add the pepper flakes, garlic, and butter into the hot pan and sauté for about 2 minutes. Stir once to infuse the garlic.
3. Open the Air Fryer and add the shrimp. Air-fry for 5 minutes, stirring once.
4. Remove the pan using oven mitts. The shrimp will continue cooking, but let it sit on the countertop to cool.
5. Stir well and dust with a layer of freshly chopped basil leaves to serve.

Stuffed Pork Chops

Serves: 3
- Salt and pepper (as desired)
- Thick-cut pork chops (3)
- Mushrooms (7)
- Lemon juice (1 tbsp.)
- Almond flour (1 tbsp.)

1 Heat the Air Fryer to reach 350° Fahrenheit.
2 Sprinkle the chops using pepper and salt.
3 Arrange the pork chops in the Air Fryer. Set the timer for 15 minutes.
4 Chop and sauté the mushrooms for 3 minutes and spritz with lemon juice.
5 Toss in the flour and herbs. Continue to sauté for about 4 minutes and set aside.
6 Prepare five sheets of foil for the chops. Arrange the chops on the foil and add some of the mushroom fixings.
7 Carefully fold the foil to seal in the chop and juices.
8 Add the chops in the fryer for 30 minutes.
9 Serve with a side salad.

Tandoori Chicken

Serves: 4
- Greek yogurt (.25 cup)
- Chicken tenders (1 lb.)
- Fresh ginger (1 tbsp.) Garlic (1 tbsp.)
- Cilantro or parsley (.25 cup)
- Salt (1 tsp.)
- Cayenne pepper (.5-1 tsp.) Turmeric (1 tsp.)
- Garam masala (1 tsp.)
- Sweet smoked paprika (1 tsp.)

1 Cut each of the chicken tenders into halves. Mince the ginger and garlic.
2 Use a glass mixing container to mix each of the fixings except for the basting oil, lemon juice, and two tablespoons of the cilantro.
3 Set the timer for 25 minutes. At that time, turn on your Air Fryer to preheat to 350° Fahrenheit for 5 minutes.
4 After about 30 minutes, carefully lay the tandoori chicken in a single

layer on the rack of the basket of the Air Fryer.

5 Baste the chicken using a silicone brush using the ghee or oil on one side. Air-fry for 10 minutes.

6 Remove the chicken and flip it over. Baste the other side. Cook for another 5 minutes. Using a meat thermometer, check to see if the internal temperature has reached 165° Fahrenheit. Do not skip this step.

7 Transfer it to a large bowl or platter. Spritz with the lemon juice and toss. Sprinkle with cilantro.

Whole Chicken: Rotisserie Style

Serves:4
- Olive oil (2 tsp. or as needed)
- Whole chicken (6-7 lb.)
- Seasoned salt (1 tbsp.)

1 Preheat the fryer at 350° Fahrenheit.

2 Clean and dry the chicken and coat with oil. Season with the salt.

3 Arrange the chicken in the Air Fryer – skin-side down.

4 Cook for 30 minutes. Flip the chicken over and air-fry for another 30 minutes.

5 Wait for ten minutes before slicing

6 Serve any way you like it.

7 Note: Under 6 lb. for a 3.7-quart Air Fryer

Butter Cake

Serves: 8
- Butter (1 cup)
- Liquid stevia (.25 cup)
- Pure vanilla extract (1 tbsp.) Almond flour (3 cups)
- Egg yolks (6) + Whole egg (1 large) Salt (.25 tsp.)
- Also Needed: 9-inch springform pan

1 Warm the Air Fryer to reach 350° Fahrenheit.

2 Combine the stevia and butter using an electric hand mixer until creamy.

3 Gradually, mix in the yolks and vanilla.

4 Add to the pan, spreading the batter smoothly using a spatula.

5 Put the batter in the refrigerator and wait for about 15 minutes before cooking.

6 Whisk an egg and brush the cake. Air-fry for 35 minutes.

Delicious Blackberry Pie

Serves:8
- Egg (1 large)
- Unsalted butter (2 tbsp.)
- Stevia (1 scoop)
- Baking powder (1 tbsp.)
- Almond flour (1 cup)
- Blackberries (.5 cup)
- Also Needed: Parchment paper

1 Warm the Air Fryer to reach 350° Fahrenheit.

2 Whisk the egg, butter, stevia, and baking powder.

3 Reserve 1 teaspoon of the flour and add the rest to the mixture. Knead until smooth – not sticky.

4 Cover the fryer basket using a layer of baking paper and add the dough. Flatten into a pie crust and add the berries. Sprinkle with the rest of the almond flour on top.

5 Air-fry until it's golden or about 20 minutes. Chill before slicing to serve.

Easy Cheesecake

Serves:6

- Butter (6 tbsp.)
- Almonds (.5 cup)
- Stevia 1 tbsp.)
- Vanilla extract (.5 tsp.) Cream cheese (1 cup) Eggs (2)
- Swerve (2 tbsp.)
- Lemon zest (1 tsp.) Cinnamon (.25 tsp.)
- Also Needed: Parchment paper

1 Combine the butter, vanilla, stevia, and sliced almonds.

2 Cover the Air Fryer tray with the paper and add the cheesecake crust.

3 Combine the cinnamon, swerve, lemon zest, and cream cheese.

4 Use a hand mixer to prepare the eggs until soft and fluffy. Pour the cream cheese mixture over the almond crust.

5 Set the Air Fryer at 310° Fahrenheit. Cook for 16 minutes. When it's done, chill for at least two hours.

6 Then, slice and serve.

Keto Chocolate Chip Cookies

Serves:5
- Dark chocolate chips (2 tbsp.)
- Egg (1)
- Salted butter (3 tbsp.)
- Crushed macadamia nuts (3 tbsp.) Almond flour (1 cup)
- Vanilla extract (.5 tsp.) Stevia (1 tsp.)
- Baking powder (.25 tsp.)
- Salt (.25 tsp.)

1 Whisk the eggs and mix in with the flour and butter.

2 Stir in the rest of the fixings and knead the dough.

3 Make five balls for the cookie dough.

4 Heat the Air Fryer at 360° Fahrenheit.

5 Arrange the cookies in the fryer and flatten (lightly) and set the timer for 15 minutes.

6 Cool slightly and enjoy.

Lemon Cake

Serves:16
- Sea salt (1 pinch)
- Warmed butter (2 cups)
- Liquid stevia (.25 cup)
- Large eggs (4)
- Baking powder (2 tbsp.)
- Almond flour (2 cups)
- Untreated & grated lemon rind (1)

1 Heat the Air Fryer at 320° Fahrenheit.

2 Use a sheet of parchment baking paper to line a baking tray or use a coating of butter.

3 Warm the two cups of butter with the salt and stevia.

4 Zest the lemon and combine with the eggs, mixing until consistent and creamy.

5 Sift in the baking powder and flour. Empty the batter into the baking pan.

6 Air-fry for 35 minutes.

Rolled Cookies

Serves:8
- Vanilla extract (1 tbsp.)
- Liquid stevia (4 tbsp.)
- Unchilled butter (1.5 cups)

- Large eggs (4)
- Almond flour (4 cups)
- Baking powder (2 tbsp.) Salt (1 tsp.)

1 Cream the stevia and butter in a deep mixing dish.

2 Whisk and fold in the eggs and vanilla.

3 Stir in the baking powder, flour, and salt. Mix well and cover the batter container, and place it in the refrigerator for two hours to chill.

4 Warm the Air Fryer to reach 390⁰ Fahrenheit.

5 Roll the dough until flat using a floured cutting board or another flat surface. Use a cookie cutter to make the cookie shapes.

6 Arrange the cookies in the fryer basket to cook for 10 minutes or until
browned.

7 Cool And Store.

Poultry Recipes

BBQ Chicken – Gluten-Free
Serves:4
- Boneless – skinless chicken breast (2 large)
- Seasoned flour/Gluten-free seasoned flour (.5 cup) Barbecue sauce (1 cup)
- Olive oil cooking spray

1.Heat the Air Fryer to 390º Fahrenheit.
2.Chop the chicken into bite-size chunks and place in a mixing bowl. Coat with the seasoned flour.
3.Lightly spritz the basket of the Air Fryer with olive oil cooking spray
4.and evenly pour the chicken into the cooker.
5.Set the timer for 8 minutes.
6.Open the Air Fryer, coat with olive oil spray, and flip the chicken as needed.
7.Air-fry the chicken for eight more minutes.
8.Be sure its internal reading is at least 165º Fahrenheit.
9.Place the chicken into a dish and add the sauce to cover. Line the Air Fryer with a sheet of foil or add the chicken back to the fryer and cook for another 3 minutes until the sauce is warmed and the chicken is a bit more crispy and coated. Serve.

Buffalo Chicken Wings
Serves:2-3
- Chicken wings (5 – trombo. 14 oz.)
- Salt & black pepper (as desired) Cayenne pepper (2 tsp. or to taste) Red hot sauce (2 tbsp.)
- Melted butter (1 tbsp.)
- Optional: Garlic powder (.5 tsp.)

1.Heat the Air Fryer temperature to reach 356º Fahrenheit.
2. Slice the wings into three sections (end tip, middle joint, and drumstick). Pat each one thoroughly dry using a paper towel.
3.Combine the pepper, salt, garlic powder, and cayenne pepper on a platter. Lightly cover the wings with the powder.
4.Arrange the chicken onto the wire rack and bake for 15 minutes, turning once at 7 minutes.
5.Combine the hot sauce with the melted butter in a dish to garnish the baked chicken when it is time to be served.

Chicken Breast Tenderloins
Serves:4
- Butter/vegetable oil (2 tbsp.)
- Breadcrumbs (3.33 tbsp.)
- Egg (1)
- Chicken tenderloins (8)

1.Heat the Air Fryer temperature to 356º Fahrenheit.
2.Combine the breadcrumbs and oil – stirring until the mixture crumbles.
3.Whisk the egg and dredge the chicken through the egg, shaking off the excess.
4.Dip each piece of chicken into the crumbs and evenly coat.
5.Set the timer for 12 minutes.

Chicken Curry
Serves:4
- Chicken breast (1 lb.) Olive oil (1 tsp.) Onion (1)
- Garlic (2 tsp.)

- Lemongrass (1 tbsp.) Chicken stock (.5 cup)
- Apple cider vinegar (1 tbsp.) Coconut milk (.5 cup)
- Curry paste (2 tbsp.)

1.Warm the fryer to reach 365º Fahrenheit.
2.Dice the chicken into cubes. Peel and dice the onion and combine in the Air Fryer basket. Cook for five minutes.
3.Remove the basket and add the rest of the fixings. Mix well and air- fry for ten more minutes.
4.Serve for a quick and easy meal.

Chicken Fillet Strips
Serves:4
- Chicken fillets (1 lb.)
- Paprika (1 tsp.)
- Heavy cream (1 tbsp.)
- Salt & pepper (.5 tsp.) Butter (as needed)

1.Heat the Air Fryer at 365º Fahrenheit.
2.Slice the fillets into strips and dust with salt and pepper.
3.Add a light coating of butter to the basket.
4.Arrange the strips in the basket and air-fry for six minutes.
5.Flip the strips and continue frying for another five minutes.
6.When done, garnish with the cream and paprika. Serve warm.

Chicken Kabobs
Serves: 2
- Chicken breasts (2) Mushrooms (6)
- Bell peppers (3 various colors)
- Honey (.33 cup) Soy sauce (.33 cup)
- Salt and pepper (to your liking) Sesame seeds

1.Set the temperature of the fryer to 338º Fahrenheit.
2.Slice the mushrooms in half. Dice the peppers and chicken.
3.Coat the chicken with a couple of squirts of oil and a pinch of pepper and salt.
4.Mix the soy and honey. Toss in a few sesame seeds and stir.
5.Arrange the peppers, chicken, and mushroom bits onto a skewer.
6.Cover the kabobs with the sauce and arrange them in the basket of the Air Fryer.
7.Air-fry for 15-20 minutes and serve.

Chicken Pot Pie
Serves:4
- Chicken tenders (6)
- Potatoes (2)
- Condensed cream of celery soup (1.5 cups) Heavy cream (.75 cup)
- Thyme (1 sprig)
- Dried bay leaf (1 whole) Refrigerated buttermilk biscuits (5) Milk (1 tbsp.)
- Egg yolk (1)

1.Set the Air Fryer at 320º Fahrenheit.
2.Peel and dice the potatoes. Combine all of the fixings in a skillet except for the milk, egg yolk, and biscuits. Bring it to a boil using the medium-heat temperature setting.
3.Empty the mixture into the baking tin. Cover with a sheet of aluminum foil. Prepare a sling using a length of foil to

make a handle. Place the pan into the fry basket using the sling and cook for 15 minutes.

4.After the pie completes the cycle, prepare an egg wash using the milk and egg yolk.

5.Arrange the biscuits onto the baking pan and brush using the egg wash mixture. Set the timer for an additional ten minutes (300° Fahrenheit).

6.Serve when the biscuits are golden brown.

Crispy Chicken Sliders
Serves:6
- Tyson Crispy Chicken Strips (1 pkg.)
- Sweet Hawaiian Rolls (1 pkg.)
- Optional: Spinach leaves Tomatoes Honey mustard

1.Place the six chicken strips in the Air Fryer basket with a coating of olive oil spray. Cook at 390° Fahrenheit for 8 minutes.

2.Slice the rolls in half and top them with honey mustard, spinach, and tomatoes or other toppings of your choice.

3.Slice the chicken strips into chunks and place them on the rolls.

Fried Chicken Thighs
Serves: 2
- Chicken thighs – no skin (2)
- Fresh parsley (3 sprigs) Garlic powder – for dusting Lemon (half if 1)
- Fresh rosemary (1-2 sprigs)
- Chili flakes – salt & black pepper (as desired)

1.Rinse the thighs and drain between a few paper towels.

2.Clean the rosemary sprigs and remove the stems. Mince the parsley.

3.Combine the parsley, chili flakes, salt, pepper, garlic powder, rosemary leaves, and lemon juice. Add the thighs and marinate overnight in the fridge.

4.Warm the Air Fryer at 356° Fahrenheit. Air-fry for 12 minutes.

Garlic Herb Turkey Breast
Serves: 6
- Turkey breast (2 lb.)
- Freshly ground black pepper & Kosher salt Melted butter (4 tbsp.)
- Garlic (3 cloves)
- Thyme (1 tsp.)
- Rosemary (1 tsp.)

1.Warm the Air Fryer to reach 375° Fahrenheit.

2.Pat the turkey breast dry and season both sides with salt and pepper.

3.Mince the garlic and chop the rosemary and thyme.

4.In a small bowl, combine the melted butter, garlic, thyme, and rosemary. Brush using butter all over turkey breast.

5.Place in the Air Fryer basket, skin side up, and cook for 40 minutes

6.or until internal temperature reaches 160° Fahrenheit, flipping halfway through.

7.Wait for five minutes before slicing.

Mustard-Glazed Turkey Breast

Serves: 6
- Olive oil (2 tsp.)
- Whole turkey breast (5 lb.) Salt (1 tsp.)

- Dried thyme (1 tsp.) Butter (1 tsp.)
- Freshly cracked black pepper (.5 tsp.) Smoked paprika (.5 tsp.)
- Dried sage (.5 tsp.) Maple syrup (.25 tsp.) Dijon mustard (2 tbsp.)

1.Warm the fryer to 350° Fahrenheit.

2.Prepare the turkey with a spritz of olive oil.

3.Mix the sage, salt, thyme, pepper, and paprika as a rub. Use it as a coating for the turkey.

4.Arrange the breast in the fryer basket and set the timer for 25 minutes. Rotate it on its side and fry another 12 minutes. It's done when it reaches 165° Fahrenheit – internal temperature.

5.In the meantime, whisk the butter, syrup, and mustard in a saucepan. Turn the breast again and brush using the glaze. Give it a final five minutes until crispy.

6.Cover using a foil tent for five minutes, slice, and serve.

Parmesan Chicken
Serves:4
- Chicken breast (2 – about 8 oz. each)
- Seasoned breadcrumbs (6 tbsp.)
- Grated parmesan cheese (2 tbsp.)
- Olive oil/melted butter (1 tbsp.)
- Reduced-fat mozzarella cheese (6 tbsp.)
- Marinara sauce (.5 cup)

1.Set the Air Fryer at 360° Fahrenheit for 3 minutes.

2.Slice the chicken breasts into halves, then into four thin cutlets.

3.Combine the parmesan cheese and breadcrumbs in a bowl.

4.Melt the butter in another dish.

5.Lightly brush the butter onto the chicken, then dip into the breadcrumb mixture.

6.When the Air Fryer is ready, arrange two pieces in the basket and spray the top with a bit of cooking oil.

7. Fry for 6 minutes; turn and top each with one tablespoon of the sauce, and 1.5 tablespoons of shredded mozzarella cheese.

8.Cook until the cheese is melted (3 min.).

9.Set aside and keep warm, repeat with the remaining two pieces.

Philly Chicken Cheese Steak Stromboli
Serves: 2-4
- Vegetable oil (1 tsp.) Onion (half of 1)
- Chicken breasts (2/total of 1 lb.) Worcestershire sauce (1 tbsp.)
- Pizza dough (14 oz. pkg. – homemade or store-bought) Freshly cracked black pepper & salt
- Cheese Whiz or your favorite cheese sauce (.5 cup) Grated Cheddar cheese (1.5 cups)

1.Warm the Cheese Whiz in the microwave.

2.Set the temperature to 400° Fahrenheit in the Air Fryer.

3.Place the onion in the fryer for eight minutes – shaking gently halfway through the cycle. Thinly slice and add the chicken and Worcestershire sauce, salt, and pepper – tossing evenly. Air fry for another eight minutes – stirring several times. Remove and let the mixture cool.

4.Lightly flour a flat surface and press out the dough into a rectangle of 11x13 (the long side facing you). Sprinkle half of the cheddar over the dough. Leave a one-inch border – topping it off with the onion/chicken mixture.

5. Drizzle the warmed cheese sauce over the top, finishing with the rest of the cheddar cheese.

6. Roll the tromboli toward the empty corner (away from you). Keep the filling tight and tuck in the ends. Arrange it seam side down and shape in a "U" to fit into the basket. Slice four slits in the top with the tip of a knife.

7. Lightly brush the top with a little oil. Set the temperature to 370° Fahrenheit.

8. Spray the basket and add the stromboli. Fry for 12 minutes – turning about halfway through the cooking process.

9. Use a serving platter and invert the tasty treat from the basket. Arrange it on a cutting board and cut into three-inch segments. Serve with ketchup for dipping.

Chicken Tenders

Serves: 4
- 1lb. Chicken tenders 1 egg, lightly beaten
- 3/4 cup pecans, crushed
- ¼ cup ground mustard
- ½ tsp paprika
- tsp garlic powder
- ¼ tsp onion powder 1/4 tsp pepper
- 1 tsp salt

1. Spray air fryer basket with cooking spray.
2. Add chicken into the large bowl. Season with paprika, pepper, garlic powder, onion powder, and salt. Add mustard mix well.
3. In a separate bowl, add egg and whisk well.
4. In a shallow bowl, add crushed pecans.
5. Dip chicken into the egg then coats with pecans and place into the air fryer basket.
6. Cook at 350 f for 12 minutes.
7. Serve and enjoy.

CHICKEN COCONUT MEATBALLS

Servings: 4
- 1lb. Ground chicken 1 ½ tsp sriracha
- 1/2 tbsp soy sauce 1/2 tbsp hoisin sauce
- ¼ cup shredded coconut 1 tsp sesame oil
- ½ cup fresh cilantro, chopped
- 1 green onions, 1 chopped Pepper
- Salt

1. Spray air fryer basket with cooking spray.
2. Add all into the large bowl and mix until well combined.
3. Make small balls from meat mixture and place into the air fryer basket.
4. Cook at 350 f for 10 minutes. Turn halfway through.
5. Serve and enjoy.

Cheese Herb Chicken Wings

Servings: 4
- 2lbs. Chicken wings
- 1 tsp herb de provence
- ½ cup parmesan cheese, grated 1 tsp paprika
- Salt

1. Preheat the air fryer to 350 f.

2. In a small bowl, mix cheese, herb de provence, paprika, and salt.
3. Spray air fryer basket with cooking spray.

4. Toss chicken wings with cheese mixture and place into the air fryer basket and cook for 15 minutes. Turn halfway through.
5. Serve and enjoy.

Delicious Chicken Tenderloins

Serves: 6
- egg, lightly beaten
- ¼ cup heavy whipping cream 8 oz chicken breast tenderloins 1 cup almond flour
- ¼ tsp garlic powder
- ¼ tsp onion powder 1 tsp pepper
- tsp salt

1. Whisk egg, with garlic powder, onion powder, cream, pepper, and salt in a bowl.
2. In a shallow dish, add the almond flour.
3. Dip chicken in egg mixture then coats with almond flour mixture.
4. Spray air fryer basket with cooking spray.
5. Place chicken into the air fryer basket and cook at 450 f for 15 minutes.
6. Serve and enjoy.

GARLIC HERB CHICKEN BREASTS

Serves: 5
- 2lbs. Chicken breasts, skinless and boneless
- 2garlic cloves, minced
- ¼ cup yogurt
- ¼ cup mayonnaise
- 2 tsp garlic herb seasoning 1/2 tsp onion powder
- ¼ tsp salt

1. Preheat the air fryer to 380 f.
2. In a small bowl, mix mayonnaise, seasoning, onion powder, garlic, and yogurt.
3. Brush chicken with mayo mixture and season with salt.
4. Spray air fryer basket with cooking spray.
5. Place chicken into the air fryer basket and cook for 15 minutes.
6. Serve and enjoy.

Tasty Caribbean Chicken

Serves: 8
- 3lbs. Chicken thigh, skinless and boneless 1 tbsp coriander powder
- 3 tbsp coconut oil, melted
- ½ tsp ground nutmeg
- ½ tsp ground ginger 1 tbsp cayenne
- 1 tbsp cinnamon
- Pepper and salt

1. In a small bowl, mix all spices and rub all over the chicken.
2. Spray air fryer basket with cooking spray.
3. Place chicken into the air fryer basket and cook at 390 f for 10 minutes.
4. Serve and enjoy.

CHICKEN KABAB

Servings: 3
- lb. Ground chicken
- tbsp fresh lemon juice
- ¼ cup almond flour
- green onion, chopped 1 egg, lightly beaten

- 1/3 cup fresh parsley, chopped 3 garlic cloves
- oz onion, chopped
- ¼ tsp turmeric powder
- ½ tsp pepper

1.Add all into the food processor and process until well combined.
2.Transfer chicken mixture to the bowl and place in the refrigerator for 1 hour.
3.Divide mixture into the 6 equal portions and roll around the soaked wooden skewers.
4. Spray air fryer basket with cooking spray.
5.Place skewers into the air fryer basket and cooks at 400 f for 6 minutes.
6.Serve and enjoy.

Mediterranean Chicken
Servings: 6
- lbs. Whole chicken, cut into pieces 2 tsp ground sumac
- 2 garlic cloves, minced 2 lemons, sliced
- 2 tbsp olive oil 1 tsp lemon zest 2 tsp kosher salt

1.Rub chicken with oil, sumac, lemon zest, and salt. Place in the refrigerator for 2-3 hours.
2.Add lemon sliced into the air fryer basket top with marinated chicken.
3.Cook at 350 for 35 minutes.
4.Serve and enjoy.

Asian Chicken Wings
Servings: 2
- chicken wings
- 3/4 tbsp chinese spice 1 tbsp soy sauce
- tsp mixed spice Pepper
- Salt

1.Add chicken wings into the bowl. Add remaining and toss to coat.
2.Transfer chicken wings into the air fryer basket.
3.Cook at 350 f for 15 minutes.
4.Turn chicken to another side and cook for 15 minutes more.
5.Serve and enjoy.

Delicious Chicken Fajitas
Servings: 4
- chicken breasts
- onion, sliced
- bell pepper, sliced
- 1 1/2 tbsp fajita seasoning 2 tbsp olive oil
- 3/4 cup cheddar cheese, shredded
  1.Preheat the air fryer at 380 f.
  2.Coat chicken with oil and rub with seasoning.
  3.Place chicken into the air fryer baking dish and top with bell peppers and onion.
  4.Cook for 15 minutes.
  5.Top with shredded cheese and cook for 1-2 minutes until cheese is melted.
  6.Serve and enjoy.

Juicy & Spicy Chicken Wings
Servings: 4
- lbs. Chicken wings 12 oz hot sauce
- tsp worcestershire sauce
- tsp tabasco

- tbsp butter, melted
  1.Spray air fryer basket with Cooking spray.
  2.Add chicken wings into the air fryer basket and cook at 380 f for 25 minutes. Shake basket after every 5 minutes.
  3.Meanwhile, in a bowl, mix hot sauce, worcestershire sauce, and butter. Set aside.
  4.Add chicken wings into the sauce and toss well.
  5.Serve and enjoy.

Indian Chicken Tenders
Servings: 4
- 1lb. Chicken tenders, cut in half
- ¼ cup parsley, chopped
- 1/2 tbsp garlic, minced
- 1/2 tbsp ginger, minced
- ¼ cup yogurt 3/4 tsp paprika
- 1 tsp garam masala 1 tsp turmeric
- 1/2 tsp cayenne pepper 1 tsp salt

1.Preheat the air fryer to 350 f.
2.Add all into the large bowl and mix well. Place in refrigerator for 30 minutes.
3.Spray air fryer basket with Cooking spray.
4.Add marinated chicken into the air fryer basket and cook for 10 minutes.
5.Turn chicken to another side and cook for 5 minutes more.
6.Serve and enjoy.

Dijon Turkey Drumstick
Servings: 2
- 4 turkey drumsticks
- 1/3 tsp paprika
- 1/3 cup sherry wine
- 1/3 cup coconut milk
- 1/2 tbsp ginger, minced
- 2 tbsp dijon mustard Pepper
- Salt

1.Add all Ingredients into the large bowl and stir to coat. Place in refrigerator for 2 hours.
2.Spray air fryer basket with cooking spray.
3.Place marinated turkey drumsticks into the air fryer basket and cook at 380 f for 28 minutes. Turn halfway through.
4. Serve and enjoy.

Curried Drumsticks
Servings: 2
- 2 turkey drumsticks
- 1/3 cup coconut milk
- 1/2 tbsp ginger, minced
- 1/4 tsp cayenne pepper
- 1/4 tbsp red curry paste
- 1/4 tsp pepper
- 1/4 tsp kosher salt

1.Add all into the bowl and stir to coat. Place in refrigerator for overnight.
2.Spray air fryer basket with cooking spray.
3.Place marinated drumsticks into the air fryer basket and cook at 390 f for 22 minutes.
4.Serve and enjoy.

Korean Chicken Tenders

Servings: 3

- 12 oz chicken tenders, skinless and boneless
- 2 tbsp green onion, chopped 3 garlic cloves, chopped
- 2 tsp sesame seeds, toasted
- **1** tbsp ginger, grated
- 1/4 cup sesame oil
- 1/2 cup soy sauce
- 1/4 tsp pepper

1. Slide chicken tenders onto the skewers.
2. In a large bowl, mix green onion, garlic, sesame seeds, ginger, sesame oil, soy sauce, and pepper.
3. Add chicken skewers into the bowl and coat well with marinade.
4. Place in refrigerator for overnight.
5. Preheat the air fryer to 390 f.
6. Place marinated chicken skewers into the air fryer basket and cook for 10 minutes.

Air Fried Chicken With Coconut & Turmeric

Servings: 3

- 1½ oz. Coconut milk
- 3 tsp. Ginger, grated
- 4 tsp. Ground turmeric
- ½ tsp. Sea salt
- 3 chicken legs (skin removed)

1. Combine the coconut milk, ginger, turmeric and salt.
2. Make a few slits on the chicken meat.
3. Marinate the chicken in the mixture for 4 hours.
4. Keep inside the refrigerator.
5. Preheat air fryer at 375 degrees f.
6. Cook for 10 minutes.
7. Flip and cook for another 10 to 12 minutes.

Chicken Parmesan

Servings: 4

- 1 egg
- 1 tsp. Garlic powder 1 tsp. Italian herbs
- 8 breast-meat chicken tenders
- ½ cup parmesan cheese
- 1 cup panko breadcrumbs

1. Beat the egg in a bowl.
2. Add the garlic powder and italian herbs.
3. Soak the chicken strips in this mixture.
4. In a different bowl, mix the parmesan and breadcrumbs.
5. Coat the chicken tenders with the parmesan mixture.
6. Cover the air fryer base with foil.
7. Preheat at 400 degrees f for 3 minutes.
8. Put the chicken tenders inside the basket.
9. Cook for 6 minutes.
10. Serve while warm.

Crunchy Curry Chicken Strips

Servings: 4

- 12 oz. Chicken breast, cut into strips Salt and pepper to taste
- 1 egg, beaten
- ¼ cup whole wheat flour
- ½ cup panko breadcrumbs
- ¼ cup curry powder

1. Season the chicken strips with the salt and pepper.
2. Dip each of the chicken strips into the flour, then into the egg.
3. In a bowl, mix the curry powder and breadcrumbs.
4. Coat each of the chicken strips with the curry powder mixture.
5. Cook in the air fryer at 350 degrees f for 10 minutes.
6. Flip and cook for another 5 minutes.

Chicken Pie

Servings: 8 to 10

- 2 chicken thighs (boneless, sliced into cubes)
- 1 tsp. Reduced Sodium soy sauce
- 1 onion, diced
- 1 carrot, diced
- 2 potatoes, diced
- 1 cup mushrooms
- 1 tsp. Garlic powder 1 tsp. Flour ½ cup milk
- **2** hard-boiled eggs, sliced in half 2 sheets puff pastry

1. Season the chicken cubes with the low Sodium soy sauce.
2. In a pan over low heat, sauté the onions, carrots and potatoes.
3. Add the chicken cubes and mushrooms.
4. Season with the garlic powder.
5. Add the flour and milk.
6. Mix well.
7. Lay the pastry sheet on the tray of the air fryer.
8. Poke it with holes using a fork.
9. Arrange the eggs on top of the pastry sheet.
10. Pour in the chicken mixture on top of the eggs.
11. Top with the second pastry sheet.
12. Press a little.
13. Air fry at 360 degrees f for 6 minutes.
14. Slice into several portions and serve.

Buttermilk Chicken

Servings: 6 to 8

- 30 oz. Chicken thighs (skinless)
- 1 ½ tsp. salt
- 2 tsp. Black pepper
- 1 ½ tbsp. Garlic powder
- 2 cups buttermilk
- 2 cups all-purpose flour
- 1 tsp. Paprika powder
- 1 tbsp. Baking powder

1. Season the chicken with the salt, pepper and garlic powder.
2. Coat the chicken with the buttermilk.
3. Marinate in the refrigerator covered for 6 hours.
4. Preheat the air fryer at 360 degrees f.
5. In another bowl, mix the all-purpose flour, paprika powder and baking powder.
6. Dredge the chicken in this mixture.
7. Cook in the air fryer for 8 minutes.
8. Flip the chicken and cook for another 10 minutes.
9. Drain in paper towels before serving.

Lemon Chili Chicken Wings

Servings: 4

- 8 chicken wings
- Sea salt and pepper to taste 1 tbsp. Lemon juice
- 1 tbsp. Chili paste
- 2 tbsp. Cornstarch

- ½ tsp. Baking powder
1. Rub the chicken wings with a little salt and pepper.
2. Combine the lemon juice and chili paste.
3. Soak the chicken wings in the chili mixture.
4. Cover with foil and refrigerate for 4 hours.
5. Preheat your air fryer to 360 degrees f.
6. Coat the chicken wings with a mix of the cornstarch and baking powder.
7. Air fry for 12 minutes.
8. Flip and cook for another 6 minutes.

Lemon Garlic Rosemary Chicken
Servings: 2
- 4 chicken thighs (skin removed) Sea salt and pepper to taste
- 1 tbsp. Lemon juice
- 3 tsp. Dried rosemary
- 3 cloves garlic, crushed and minced
- 1 tsp. Olive oil

1. Season the chicken thighs with the sea salt, pepper, lemon juice, and dried rosemary.
2. Marinate for 1 hour.
3. Meanwhile, sauté the crushed garlic in the olive oil.
4. Cook the chicken thighs in the air fryer at 400 degrees for 6 minutes.
5. Flip the chicken and cook for another 6 minutes.
6. Pour the garlic oil on top of the chicken before serving.

Fried Whole Chicken
Servings: 4
- 1 whole chicken
- 2 tbsp or spray of oil of choice
- 1 tsp garlic powder
- 1 tsp onion powder
- 1 tsp paprika
- 1 tsp italian seasoning
- 2 tbsp montreal steak seasoning (or salt and pepper to taste)
- 1.4 cup chicken broth
1. Truss and wash the chicken.
2. Mix the seasoning and rub a little amount on the chicken.
3. Pour the broth inside the instant pot duo crisp air fryer.
4. Place the chicken in the air fryer basket.
5. Select the option air fry and close the air fryer lid and cook for 25 minutes.
6. Spray or rub the top of the chicken with oil and rub it with half of the seasoning.
7. Close the air fryer lid and air fry again at 400°f for 10 minutes.
8. Flip the chicken, spray it with oil, and rub with the remaining seasoning.
9. Again, air fry it for another ten minutes.
10. Allow the chicken to rest for 10 minutes.

Barbecue Air Fried Chicken
Servings: 10
- 1 teaspoon liquid smoke
- 2 cloves fresh garlic smashed 1/2 cup apple cider vinegar
- 3 pounds chuck roast well-marbled with intramuscular Fat 1 tablespoon kosher salt

- 1 tablespoon freshly ground black pepper 2 teaspoons garlic powder
- 1.5 cups barbecue sauce
- 1/4 cup light brown Sugar + more for sprinkling
- tablespoons honey optional and in place of 2 tbl Sugar
1. Add meat to the instant pot duo crisp air fryer basket, spreading out the meat.
2. Select the option air fry.
3. Close the air fryer lid and cook at 300 degrees f for 8 minutes. Pause the air fryer and flip meat over after 4 minutes.
4. Remove the lid and baste with more barbecue sauce and sprinkle with a little brown Sugar.
5. Again, close the air fryer lid and set the temperature at 400°f for 9 minutes. Watch meat though the lid and flip it over after 5 minutes.

Boneless Air Fryer Turkey Breasts
Servings: 4
- 3 lb. Boneless breast
- ¼ cup mayonnaise
- 2 tsp poultry seasoning
- 1 tsp salt
- ½ tsp garlic powder
- ¼ tsp black pepper
1. Choose the air fry option on the instant pot duo crisp air fryer. Set the temperature to 360°f and push start. The preheating will start.
2. Season your boneless turkey breast with mayonnaise, poultry
3. seasoning, salt, garlic powder, and black pepper.
4. Once preheated, air fry the turkey breasts on 360°f for 1 hour, turning every 15 minutes or until internal temperature has reached a temperature of 165°f.

Bbq Chicken Breasts
Servings: 4
- 4 boneless skinless chicken breasts about 6 oz each
- 1-2 tbsp bbq seasoning
1. Cover both sides of chicken breast with the bbq seasoning. Cover and marinate the in the refrigerator for 45 minutes.
2. Choose the air fry option and set the temperature to 400°f. Push
3. start and let it preheat for 5 minutes.
4. Upon preheating, place the chicken breast in the instant pot duo crisp air fryer basket, making sure they do not overlap. Spray with oil.
5. Cook for 13-14 minutes, flipping halfway.
6. Remove chicken when the chicken reaches an internal temperature of 160°f. Place on a plate and allow to rest for 5 minutes before slicing.

Juicy Turkey Burgers
Servings: 8
- 1 lb. Ground turkey 85% lean / 15% Fat
- ¼ cup unsweetened apple sauce
- ½ onion grated
- 1 tbsp ranch seasoning
- 2 tsp worcestershire sauce 1 tsp minced garlic
- ¼ cup plain breadcrumbs
- Salt and pepper to taste

1. Combine the onion, ground turkey, unsweetened apple sauce, minced garlic, breadcrumbs, ranch seasoning, worchester sauce, and salt and pepper. Mix them with your hands until well combined. Form 4 equally sized hamburger patties with them.
2. Place these burgers in the refrigerator for about 30 minutes to have them firm up a bit.
3. While preparing for Cooking, select the air fry option. Set the temperature of 360°f and the cook time as required. Press start to
4. begin preheating.
5. Once the preheating temperature is reached, place the burgers on the tray in the air fryer basket, making sure they don't overlap or touch. Cook on for 15 minutes, flipping halfway through.

Turkey Legs

Servings: 2

- 2 large turkey legs
- 1 1/2 tsp smoked paprika
- 1 tsp brown Sugar
- 1 tsp season salt
- ½ tsp garlic powder
- Oil for spraying avocado, canola, etc.

1. Mix the smoked paprika, brown Sugar, seasoned salt, garlic powder thoroughly.
2. Wash and pat dry the turkey legs.
3. Rub the made seasoning mixture all over the turkey legs making sure to get under the skin also.
4. While preparing for Cooking, select the air fry option. Press start to begin preheating.
5. Once the preheating temperature is reached, place the turkey legs on the tray in the instant pot duo crisp air fryer basket. Lightly spray them with oil.
6. Air fry the turkey legs on 400°f for 20 minutes. Then, open the air fryer lid and flip the turkey legs and lightly spray with oil. Close
7. the instant pot duo crisp air fryer lid and cook for 20 more minutes.
8. Remove and enjoy.

Zingy & Nutty Chicken Wings

Servings: 4

- 1 tablespoon fish sauce
- 1 tablespoon fresh lemon juice
- 1 teaspoon Sugar
- 12 chicken middle wings, cut into half
- 2 fresh lemongrass stalks, chopped finely
- ¼ cup unsalted cashews, crushed

1. In a bowl, mix fish sauce, lime juice and Sugar.
2. Add wings ad coat with mixture generously. Refrigerate to marinate for about 1-2 hours.
3. Preheat the air fryer oven to 355 degrees f.
4. In the air fryer oven pan, place lemongrass stalks. Cook for about 2-3 minutes. Remove the cashew mixture from air fryer and transfer into a bowl. Now, set the air fryer oven to 390 degrees f.
5. Place the chicken wings in air fryer pan. Cook for about 13-15 minutes further.
6. Transfer the wings into serving plates. Sprinkle with cashew mixture and serve.

Honey And Wine Chicken Breasts

Servings: 4

- 2 chicken breasts, rinsed and halved 1 tablespoon melted butter
- 1/2 teaspoon freshly ground pepper, or to taste 3/4 teaspoon sea salt, or to taste
- 1 teaspoon paprika
- 1 teaspoon dried rosemary
- **2** tablespoons dry white wine
- 1 tablespoon honey

1. Firstly, pat the chicken breasts dry. Lightly coat them with the melted butter.
2. Then, add the remaining .
3. Transfer them to the air fryer basket; bake about 15 minutes at 330 degrees f°
4. Serve warm and enjoy!

Chicken Fillets, Brie & Ham

Servings: 4

- 2 large chicken fillets Freshly ground black pepper
- 4 small slices of brie (or your cheese of choice)
- 1 tbsp. Freshly chopped chives 4 slices cured ham

1. Slice the fillets into four and make incisions as you would for a hamburger bun. Leave a little "hinge" uncut at the back. Season the inside and pop some brie and chives in there. Close them and wrap them each in a slice of ham. Brush with oil and pop them into the basket.
2. Heat your fryer to 350° f. Pour into the oven rack/basket. Place the rack on the middle-shelf of the air fryer oven.
3. Set temperature to 400°f and set time to 15 minutes. Roast the little parcels until they look tasty (15 min)

Bbq Chicken Recipe From Greece

Servings: 4

- 1 (8 ounce) container Fat-free plain yogurt 2 tablespoons fresh lemon juice
- 2 teaspoons dried oregano
- 1-pound skinless, boneless chicken breast halves - cut into 1-inch pieces
- 1 large red onion, cut into wedges
- 1/2 teaspoon lemon zest 1/2 teaspoon salt
- large green bell pepper, cut into 1 1/2-inch pieces
- 1/3 cup crumbled feta cheese with basil and sun-dried tomatoes 1/4 teaspoon ground black pepper

1. 1/4 teaspoon crushed dried rosemary
In a shallow dish, mix well rosemary, pepper, salt, oregano, lemon juice, lemon zest, feta cheese, and yogurt. Add chicken and toss
2. well to coat. Marinate in the ref for 3 hours.
3. Thread bell pepper, onion, and chicken pieces in skewers. Place on skewer rack.
4. For 12 minutes, cook on 360°f. Halfway through Cooking time, turnover skewers. If needed, cook in batches.
5. Serve and enjoy.

Cheesy Chicken In Leek-Tomato Sauce

Servings: 4

- 2 large-sized chicken breasts, cut in half lengthwise
- Salt and ground black pepper, to taste
- 4 ounces cheddar cheese, cut into sticks 1 tablespoon sesame oil
- 1 cup leeks, chopped
- 2 cloves garlic, minced

- 2/3 cup roasted vegetable stock 2/3 cup tomato puree
- 1teaspoon dried rosemary
- 1teaspoon dried thyme

1.Firstly, season chicken breasts with the salt and black pepper; place a piece of cheddar cheese in the middle. Then, tie it using a kitchen string; drizzle with sesame oil and reserve.
2.Add the leeks and garlic to the oven safe bowl.
3.Cook in the air fryer oven at 390 degrees f for 5 minutes or until tender.
4.Add the reserved chicken. Throw in the other and cook for 12 to 13 minutes more or until the chicken is done. Enjoy.

Oven Fried Chicken Wings

Servings: 3
- 1½ lbs. Chicken wings
- 1/3 c. Grated parmesan cheese 1/3 c. Breadcrumbs
- 1/8 tsp. Garlic powder 1/8 tsp. Onion powder
- ¼ c. Melted butter
- Salt and black pepper to taste Cooking spray

1.In a baking sheet, spray with Cooking spray.
2.A large bowl mix parmesan cheese, garlic powder, onion powder, black pepper, breadcrumbs and salt. Stir to combine well.
3.Dip chicken wings one at a time into melted butter and then into bread mixture until thoroughly covered. Arrange wings in single layer on the baking sheet.
4.Place on 1-inch rack and cook on high power (350 degrees f) for 10 minutes. Flip wings over and cook for another 10-12 minutes until no longer pink in center and juices run clear. Remove promptly from nuwave oven and serve.

Garlic Ginger Chicken Wings

Servings: 4
- 2pounds chicken wings
- 1 tbsp. Vegetable oil
- A pinch of salt and black pepper
- 1 tbsp. Frank's red-hot sauce 1/3 c. Flour

For Glaze
3 garlic cloves, minced
1 tbsp. Asian chili pepper sauce
¼ c. Rice wine vinegar 1 tbsp. Minced ginger
¼ c. Light brown Sugar 1½ tbsp. Soy sauce

1.In a large mixing bowl, combine frank's red-hot sauce, vegetable oil, salt and pepper. Add chicken wings and toss to coat thoroughly.
2.Place coated wings in large zip lock bag. Add flour, seal bag and shake until wings are coated with flour.
3.Place wings on the 4-inch rack and cook on high power (350 degrees f) for 10 minutes. Turn wings over and cook for an additional 8 minutes.
4.Meanwhile, in a large bowl, whisk together all for glaze. Place wings in glaze and toss to coat evenly. Place wings back on the 4-inch rack and cook on high power for an additional 5 minutes.
5.Remove from oven then serve.

Apple-Stuffed Chicken Breast

Servings: 2
- 2chicken breasts
- 1large apple
- 1/4cup cheddar cheese, shredded 2 tbsp panko

breadcrumbs
- 2tbsp. Chopped pecans, 2 tbsp. Light brown Sugar 1 tsp. Cinnamon
- 1tsp. Curry powder

1.In a large bowl, add chopped apple, cheese, breadcrumbs, pecans, brown Sugar, cinnamon, and curry powder. Stir to combine well.
2.Pound chicken breasts between waxed paper sheets till thick.
3.Spread half the apple mixture on every chicken breast. Roll the chicken up and secure with toothpicks.
4.Place chicken on the 4-inch rack and cook on high power for 12 minutes. Flip over and cook for another 10-12 minutes.
5.Serve hot.

Air Fried Turkey Breast

Servings: 6
- 23/4 pounds turkey breast
- 2tablespoons unsalted butter
- 1tablespoon chopped fresh rosemary 1 teaspoon chopped fresh chives
- 1teaspoon minced fresh garlic 1/4 teaspoon black pepper
- 1/2teaspoon salt

1. Preheat your air fryer toast oven to 350° f.
2.In a bowl, mix chives, rosemary, garlic, salt and pepper until well combined. Cut in butter and mash until well blended.
3.Rub the turkey breast with the herbed butter and then add to the air
4.fryer toast oven basket; fry for 20 minutes. Turn the turkey breast and cook for another 20 minutes.
5.Transfer the cooked turkey onto an aluminum foil and wrap; let rest for at least 10 minutes and then slice it up. Serve warm.

Healthy Turkey Lettuce Wraps

Servings: 4
- 250g ground turkey
- 1/2 small onion, finely chopped 1 garlic clove, minced
- 2tablespoons extra virgin olive oil 1 head lettuce
- teaspoon cumin
- 1/2tablespoon fresh ginger, sliced 2 tablespoons apple cider vinegar
- 2tablespoons freshly chopped cilantro 1 teaspoon freshly ground black pepper 1 teaspoon sea salt

1.Sauté garlic and onion in extra virgin olive oil until fragrant and translucent in your air fryer toast oven pan at 350 degrees f.
2.Add turkey and cook well for 5-8 minutes or until done to desire.
3.Add in the remaining and continue Cooking for 5 minutes more.
4.To serve, spoon a spoonful of turkey mixture onto a lettuce leaf and wrap. Enjoy!

Duo Crisp Chicken Wings

Servings: 6
- 12chicken wings
- 1/2 cup chicken broth
- Salt and black pepper to taste
- 1/4 cup melted butter

1. Set a metal rack in the instant pot duo crisp and pour broth into it.
2. Place the wings on the metal rack then put on its pressure-Cooking lid.
3. Hit the "pressure button" and select 8 minutes of Cooking time, then press "start."
4. Once the instant pot duo beeps, do a quick release and remove its
5. lid.
6. Transfer the pressure-cooked wings to a plate.
7. Empty the pot and set an air fryer basket in the instant pot duo
8. Toss the wings with butter and seasoning.
9. Spread the seasoned wings in the air fryer basket.
10. Put on the air fryer lid, hit the air fryer button, and then set the time to 10 minutes.10. Remove the lid and serve.
11. Enjoy!

Italian Whole Chicken

Servings: 4
- 1whole chicken
- 2tablespoon or spray of oil of choice
- 1teaspoon garlic powder 1 teaspoon onion powder 1teaspoon paprika
- 1teaspoon italian seasoning
- 2tablespoon montreal steak seasoning
- 1.5cup chicken broth

1. Whisk all the seasoning in a bowl and rub it on the chicken.
2. Set a metal rack in the instant pot duo crisp and pour broth into it.
3. Place the chicken on the metal rack then put on its pressure- Cooking lid.
4. Hit the "pressure button" and select 25 minutes of Cooking time, then press "start."
5. Once the instant pot duo beeps, do a natural release and remove its lid.
6. Transfer the pressure-cooked chicken to a plate.
7. Empty the pot and set an air fryer basket in the instant pot duo.
8. Toss the chicken pieces with oil to coat well.
9. Spread the seasoned chicken in the air fryer basket.
10. Put on the air fryer lid, hit the air fryer button, and then set the time to 10 minutes.
11. Remove the lid and serve. Enjoy!

Chicken Pot Pie

Servings: 6
- 2tbsp olive oil
- 1-pound chicken breast cubed 1 tbsp garlic powder
- 1tbsp thyme
- 1tbsp pepper
- 1cup chicken broth
- 12oz. Bag frozen mixed vegetables 4 large potatoes cubed
- 10oz. Can cream of chicken soup
- 1cup heavy cream 1 pie crust
- 1egg
- 1tbsp water

1. Hit sauté on the instant pot duo crispy and add chicken and olive oil.
2. Sauté chicken for 5 minutes then stirs in spices.

3. Pour in the broth along with vegetables and cream of chicken soup
4. Put on the pressure-Cooking lid and seal it.
5. Hit the "pressure button" and select 10 minutes of Cooking time, then press "start."
6. Once the instant pot duo beeps, do a quick release and remove its lid.
7. Remove the lid and stir in cream.
8. Hit sauté and cook for 2 minutes.
9. Enjoy!

Ranch Chicken Wings

Servings: 6
- 12chicken wings
- 1tablespoon olive oil 1 cup chicken broth 1/4 cup butter
- 1/2 cup red hot sauce
- 1/4 teaspoon worcestershire sauce 1 tablespoon white vinegar
- 1/4 teaspoon cayenne pepper
- 1/8 teaspoon garlic powder Seasoned salt to taste Ranch dressing for dipping Celery for garnish

1. Set the air fryer basket in the instant pot duo and pour the broth in it.
2. Spread the chicken wings in the basket and put on the pressure- Cooking lid.
3. Hit the "pressure button" and select 10 minutes of Cooking time, then press "start."
4. Meanwhile, prepare the sauce and add butter, vinegar, cayenne pepper, garlic powder, worcestershire sauce, and hot sauce in a small saucepan.
5. Stir cook this sauce for 5 minutes on medium heat until it thickens.
6. Once the instant pot duo beeps, do a quick release and remove its lid.
7. Remove the wings and empty the instant pot duo.
8. Toss the wings with oil, salt, and black pepper.
9. Set the air fryer basket in the instant pot duo and arrange the wings in it.
10. Put on the air fryer lid and seal it.
11. Hit the "air fryer button" and select 20 minutes of Cooking time, then press "start."
12. Once the instant pot duo beeps, remove its lid.
13. Serve.

Chicken Mac And Cheese

Servings: 6
- 2 1/2 cup macaroni
- 2cup chicken stock
- 1cup cooked chicken, shredded 1 1/4 cup heavy cream
- 8tablespoon butter
- 22/3 cups cheddar cheese, shredded 1/3 cup parmesan cheese, shredded 1 bag ritz crackers
- 1/4 teaspoon garlic powder Salt and pepper to taste

1. Add chicken stock, heavy cream, chicken, 4 tablespoon butter, and macaroni to the instant pot duo.
2. Put on the pressure-Cooking lid and seal it.
3. Hit the "pressure button" and select 4 minutes of Cooking time, then press "start."
4. Crush the crackers and mix them well with 4 tablespoons melted butter.
5. Once the instant pot duo beeps, do a quick release and remove its lid.

6. Put on the air fryer lid and seal it.
7. Hit the "air fryer button" and select 5 minutes of Cooking time, then press "start."
8. Once the instant pot duo beeps, remove its lid.
9. Serve.

Broccoli Chicken Casserole

Servings: 6

- 11/2 lbs. Chicken, cubed
- 2teaspoon chopped garlic 2 tablespoon butter
- 11/2 cups chicken broth 1 1/2 cups long-grain rice
- 1(10.75 oz) can cream of chicken soup
- 2cups broccoli florets
- 1cup crushed ritz cracker 2 tablespoon melted butter
- 2cups shredded cheddar cheese

1. Add 1 cup water to the instant pot dup and place a basket in it.
2. Place the broccoli in the basket evenly.
3. Put on the pressure-Cooking lid and seal it.
4. Hit the "pressure button" and select 1 minute of Cooking time, then press "start."
5. Once the instant pot duo beeps, do a quick release and remove its lid.
6. Remove the broccoli and empty the instant pot duo.
7. Hit the sauté button then add 2 tablespoon butter.
8. Toss in chicken and stir cook for 5 minutes, then add garlic and sauté for 30 seconds.
9. Stir in rice, chicken broth, and cream of chicken soup.
10. Put on the pressure-Cooking lid and seal it.
11. Hit the "pressure button" and select 12 minutes of Cooking time, then press "start."
12. Once the instant pot duo beeps, do a quick release and remove its lid.
13. Add cheese and broccoli, then mix well gently.
14. Toss the cracker with 2 tablespoon butter in a bowl and spread over the chicken in the pot.
15. Put on the air fryer lid and seal it.
16. Hit the "air fryer button" and select 4 minutes of Cooking time, then press "start."
17. Once the instant pot duo beeps, remove its lid.
18. Serve.

Chicken Tikka Kebab

Servings: 4

- 1lb. Chicken thighs boneless skinless, cubed 1 tablespoon oil
- 1/2 cup red onion, cubed
- 1/2 cup green bell pepper, cubed 1/2 cup red bell pepper, cubed Lime wedges to garnish
- Onion rounds to garnish

For Marinade:

- ½ cup yogurt greek
- 3/4 tablespoon ginger, grated 3/4 tablespoon garlic, minced 1 tablespoon lime juice
- 2teaspoon red chili powder mild 1/2 teaspoon ground turmeric
- 1teaspoon garam masala
- 1teaspoon coriander powder
- 1/2 tablespoon dried fenugreek leaves 1 teaspoon salt

1. Prepare the marinade by mixing yogurt with all its in a bowl.

2. Fold in chicken, then mix well to coat and refrigerate for 8 hours.
3. Add bell pepper, onions, and oil to the marinade and mix well.
4. Thread the chicken, peppers, and onions on the skewers.
5. Set the air fryer basket in the instant pot duo.
6. Put on the air fryer lid and seal it.
7. Hit the "air fry button" and select 10 minutes of Cooking time, then press "start."
8. Once the instant pot duo beeps and removes its lid.
9. Serve.

Creamy Chicken Thighs

Servings: 6

- 1tablespoon olive oil
- 6chicken thighs, bone-in, skin-on Salt
- Freshly ground black pepper 2 cloves garlic, minced
- 1tablespoon fresh thyme leaves
- 1teaspoon crushed red pepper flakes 3/4 cup low-Sodium chicken broth 1/2 cup heavy cream
- 1/2 cup sun-dried tomatoes, chopped 1/4 cup parmesan, grated
- Freshly torn basil, for serving

1. Hit sauté on the instant pot duo crisp and add oil to heat.
2. Stir in chicken, salt, and black then sear for 5 minutes per side.
3. Add broth, cream, parmesan, and tomatoes.
4. Put on the air fryer lid and seal it.
5. Hit the "bake button" and select 20 minutes of Cooking time, then press "start."
6. Once the instant pot duo beeps, remove its lid.
7. Garnish with basil and serve.

Chicken In Coconut Sauce Recipe

Servings: 6

- Sweet paprika-2 tsp.
- Coconut milk 1/4 cup
- Red pepper flakes-1 tsp.
- Olive oil-1 tbsp.
- Chopped green onions-2 tbsp.
- Chicken breasts-3 ½ lbs.
- Chicken stock-1 cup
- Salt and black pepper to the taste Chopped yellow onion -1 ¼ cups Lime juice-1 tbsp.

1. Start by heating a dish that accommodates your air fryer with the oil to over medium-high-warmth, include onions; blend and cook for 4 minutes.
2. Add stock, coconut milk, pepper drops, paprika, lime squeeze, salt and pepper and blend well.
3. Include chicken to the skillet, include increasingly salt and pepper;
4. hurl well.
5. Introduce chicken in your air fryer and cook at 360 °f, for 12 minutes.
6. Share chicken and sauce among plates and serve.

Sticky Marinated Duck Breasts Recipe

Servings: 2

- Minced garlic cloves; -2 Soy sauce 1/4 cup Butter-1 tbsp.
- Duck breasts 2
- Salt and black pepper to the taste Sherry wine 1/4 cup

Tarragon springs 6 White wine-1 cup

1.Mix duck bosoms with white wine, soy sauce, garlic, tarragon, salt and pepper in a bowl; hurl well and refrigerate for 1 day.

2.Transfer duck bosoms to your preheated air fryer at 350 °f and cook for 10 minutes; flipping midway.

3.On the other hand; pour the marinade in a skillet, and warmth up to

4.over medium warmth, include margarine and sherry; mix, bring to a stew, cook for 5 minutes and remove the warmth.

5.Share duck bosoms on plates; spread the sauce all finished and serve.

Chicken Breasts With Passion Fruit Sauce

Servings: 4
- Passion fruits; halved, de-seeded and pulp reserved-4
- Maple syrup-2 oz.
- Whiskey-1 tbsp. Chicken breasts 4 Anise-2-star
- Chopped chives; -1 bunch
- Salt and black pepper to the taste

1.Start by warming a skillet with the enthusiasm natural product mash to over medium warmth, incorporate bourbon, star anise, maple syrup, and chives; mix well, stew for 5-6 minutes and remove the heat.

2.Season chicken with salt and pepper; put in a preheated air fryer and cook at 360 °f, for 10 minutes; flipping most of the way during Cooking .

3.Share chicken on plates, heat the sauce a bit, and spread it over chicken and serve.

Turkey With Mushrooms And Peas Casserole

Servings: 4
- Chopped yellow onion 1
- Salt and black pepper to the taste Chopped celery stalk 1
- Skinless, boneless turkey breasts-2 lbs. Peas 1/2 cup
- Cream of mushrooms soup-1 cup Chicken stock-1 cup
- Bread cubes-1 cup

  1.Mix turkey with salt, pepper, onion, celery, peas, and stock in a dish that accommodates your air fryer

  2.Introduce blend in your air fryer and cook at 360 °f, for 15 minutes.

  3.Include bread solid shapes and cream of mushroom soup; mix, hurl and cook at 360 °f, for 5 minutes more.

  4.Share the supper among plates and serve hot.

Chicken And Creamy Vegetable Mix Recipe

Servings: 6
- Chicken stock-29 oz.
- Whipping cream-2 cups
- Chicken pieces; boneless and skinless-40 oz. Butter; melted-3 tbsp.
- Chopped yellow onion; -1/2 cup Red peppers; chopped-3/4 cup Bay leaf 1
- Chopped mushrooms; -8 oz. Asparagus; trimmed-17 oz. Chopped thyme; chopped-3 tsp. Salt and black pepper to the taste

1.Start by heating a container with the spread over medium warmth, incorporate onion and peppers; mix appropriately and cook for 3 minutes.

2.Include stock, cove leaf, salt, and pepper bring to a bubble and stew for 10 minutes.

3.Add asparagus, mushrooms, chicken, cream, thyme, salt and pepper to the taste and consolidate appropriately,

4.Introduce the stock in your air fryer and cook at 360 °f, for 15

5.minutes.

6.Share chicken and veggie blend among plates and serve.

Duck Breasts With Red Wine And Orange Sauce Recipe

Servings: 4
- Cups chicken stock 2
- Orange juice-2 cups Pumpkin pie spice2 tsp. Olive oil-2 tbsp.
- Duck breasts; skin on and halved-2 Red wine-4 cups
- Butter-2 tbsp. Honey 1/2 cup
- Sherry vinegar-2 tbsp.

1.Start by warming a skillet with the squeezed orange over medium warmth, include nectar; mix appropriately and cook for 10

2.minutes.

3.Include wine, vinegar, stock, pie zest, and margarine and blend well; cook for 10 minutes more and expel from warmth.

4.Season duck bosoms with salt and pepper, rub with olive oil,

5.Place duck bosom in the preheated air fryer at 370 °f and cook for 7 minutes on each side.

6.Divide duck bosoms on plates.

7.Drizzle wine and squeezed orange all finished and serve immediately.

Tasty Turkey Burgers Recipe

Servings: 4
- Turkey meat - 1 lb.; ground
- Shallot - 1; minced A drizzle of olive oil
- Small jalapeno pepper - 1; minced Lime juice - 2 tsp.
- Lime zest – 1; grated Cumin - 1 tsp.; ground Sweet paprika - 1 tsp.
- Salt and black pepper to the taste Guacamole for serving

1.Mix turkey meat with salt, pepper, cumin, paprika, shallot, jalapeno, lime juice and zest in a clean bowl.

2.Stir gently and shape burgers from this mix.

3.Drizzle the oil over the burgers.

4.Move to the preheated air fryer and cook them at a temperature of 370 °f for 8 minutes on each side.

5.Divide into different

6.Serve with guacamole as toppings.

Special Coconut Creamy Chicken

Servings: 4

- Big chicken legs 4
- Salt and black pepper to the taste Grated ginger; -2 tbsp.
- Coconut cream-4 tbsp. Turmeric powder-5 tsp.

1.Mix the cream with turmeric, ginger, salt, and pepper, in a bowl; whisk and include chicken pieces, hurl them well and put aside for 2 hours.

2. Move chicken to your preheated air fryer, cook at 370 °f, for 25 minutes;

3.Share meal between plates and present with a side serving of mixed greens.

Duck With Cherries Recipe

Servings: 4

- Duck breasts; boneless, skin on and scored-4 Ginger; grated-1 tbsp.
- Rhubarb; sliced-2 cups
- Salt and black pepper to the taste Ground cumin-1 tsp.
- Minced garlic-1 tsp. Pitted cherries-2 cups Sugar 1/2 cup Ground clove 1/2 tsp. Honey 1/4 cup
- Chopped yellow onion 1/2 cup Cinnamon powder 1/2 tsp.
- Balsamic vinegar 1/3 cup Chopped sage leaves 4 Chopped
- Jalapeno 1

1.Start by spicing the duck bosom with salt and pepper, put in your air fryer preheated to 350 °f, and cook for 5 minutes on each side.

2.On the other hand; heat a dish to over medium warmth, include Sugar, nectar, vinegar, garlic, ginger, cumin, clove, cinnamon, sage, jalapeno, rhubarb, onion, and fruits; blend appropriately, at that point bring to a stew and cook for 10 minutes.

3.Add duck bosoms and hurl well, Share everything among plates and serve.

Quick And Easy Duck Breasts Recipe

Servings: 4

- Skinless and boneless-4 duck breasts Lemon juice-2 tbsp.
- Salt and black pepper to the taste
- Lemon pepper 1/2 tsp.
- Garlic heads; peeled, tops cut off and quartered-4 Olive oil-1 ½ tbsp.

1.Mix duck bosoms with garlic, lemon juice, salt, pepper, lemon pepper and olive oil in a bowl and hurl everything appropriately.

2.Move the duck and garlic to your air fryer and cook at 350 °f, for 15 minutes.

3.Share duck bosoms and garlic among plates and serve.

Duck And Tea Sauce Recipe

Servings: 2

Duck breast halves; boneless-2

Chopped shallot 3/4 cup

Salt and black pepper to the taste Chicken stock-2 ¼ cup

Orange juice-1 ½ cup Earl gray tea leaves-3 tsp.

Melted butter-3 tbsp. Honey-1 tbsp.

1.Season duck bosom parts with salt and pepper, move to your preheated air fryer and cook at 360 °f, for 10 minutes.

2.On the other hand; heat a skillet with the margarine to over medium warmth, include shallot; mix and cook for 2-3 minutes.

3.Include stock; mix and cook for one more moment.

4.Include squeezed orange, tea leaves, and nectar; mix, cook for 2-3 minutes more and strain into a bowl.

5.Share duck on plates; spread tea sauce all finished and serve.

Grilled Chicken And Radish Mix Recipe

Servings: 4

- Bone-in chicken things; -4
- Salt and black pepper to the taste Olive oil 1 tbsp.
- Carrots; cut into thin sticks 3 Chopped chives; -2 tbsp.
- Chicken stock-1 cup Sugar1 cup Radishes; halved-6

1.Start by heating a container that accommodates your air fryer over medium warmth, include stock, carrots, Sugar, and radishes; mix delicately,

2.Reduce warmth to medium, spread pot somewhat and permit to

3.stew for 20 minutes.

4.Coat the chicken with olive oil, season with salt and pepper, put in your air fryer and cook at 350 °f, for 4 minutes.

5.Introduce the chicken to radish blend and hurl appropriately

6. Introduce everything in your air fryer, cook for 4 minutes more,

7.Share among plates and serve.

Quick And Easy Creamy Chicken Casserole Recipe

Servings: 4

- Chopped spinach; -10 oz.
- Salt and black pepper to the taste Grated parmesan; -1/2 cup Butter-4 tbsp.
- Flour-3 tbsp.
- Heavy cream 1/2 cup Milk-1 ½ cups
- Chicken breasts; skinless, boneless and cubed-2 cup Breadcrumbs-1 cup

1.Heat a dish with the spread over medium warmth, include flour and mix well.

2.Add milk, substantial cream and parmesan; mix well, cook for 1-2 minutes more and remove the heat.

3.Spread chicken and spinach in a skillet that accommodates your air fryer.

4.Add salt and pepper and hurl.

5.Add cream blend and spread, sprinkle bread morsels on top,

6.Introduce the chicken into your air fryer and cook at 350 for 12 minutes.

7.Share chicken and spinach blend among plates and serve.

ROASTED DUCK BREASTS WITH ENDIVES RECIPE

Servings: 4

- Duck breasts 2 Sugar-1 tbsp.
- Salt and black pepper to the taste Olive oil-1 tbsp.
- Endives; julienned-6 Cranberries-2 tbsp. White wine-8 oz.
- Garlic; minced-1 tbsp.

1.Score duck bosoms and season them with salt and pepper, place in preheated air fryer and cook at 350 °f, for 20 minutes; flipping

2.them midway.

3.On the other hand; heat a skillet with the oil over medium warmth, include Sugar and endives; blend and cook for 2 minutes.

4.Include salt, pepper, wine, garlic, cream, and cranberries; blend and cook for 3 minutes.

5.Divide duck bosoms on plates; spread the endives sauce all finished and serve.

Red Thai Turkey Drumsticks In Coconut Milk

Servings: 2

- 1tablespoon red curry paste
- 1/2 teaspoon cayenne pepper
- 1½ tablespoons minced ginger 2 turkey drumsticks
- 1/4 cup coconut milk
- 1teaspoon kosher salt, or more to taste
- 1/3 teaspoon ground pepper, to more to taste

1.First of all, place turkey drumsticks with all in your refrigerator; let it marinate overnight.

2. Cook turkey drumsticks at 380 degrees f for 23 minutes; make sure to flip them over at half-time. Serve with the salad on the side.

Fried Turkey With Lemon And Herbs

Servings: 6

- 1½ tablespoons yellow mustard
- 1½ tablespoons herb seasoning blend 1/3 cup tamari sauce
- 1½ tablespoons olive oil
- 1/2lemon, juiced - 3 turkey drumsticks 1/3 cup pear or apple cider vinegar
- 2sprigs rosemary, chopped

1.Dump all into a mixing dish. Let it marinate overnight.

2.Set your air fryer to cook at 355 degrees f.

3.Season turkey drumsticks with salt and black pepper and roast them at 355 degrees f for 28 minutes. Cook one drumstick at a time.

4.Pause the machine after 14 minutes and flip turkey drumstick.

Chicken Sausage With Nestled Eggs

Servings:6

- 6eggs
- 2bell peppers, seeded and sliced 1 teaspoon dried oregano
- 1teaspoon hot paprika
- 1teaspoon freshly cracked black pepper 6 chicken sausages
- 1teaspoon sea salt
- 1/2 shallots, cut into wedges 1 teaspoon dried basil

1.Take four ramekins and divide chicken sausages, shallot, and bell pepper among those ramekins. Cook at 315 degrees f for about 12 minutes.

2.Now, crack an egg into each ramekin. Sprinkle the eggs with hot paprika, basil, oregano, salt, and cracked black pepper. Cook for 5 more minutes at 405 degrees f.

Parmesan Chicken Nuggets

Servings:4

- 1-pound chicken breast, ground 1 teaspoon hot paprika
- 2teaspoon sage, ground

- 1/3teaspoon powdered ginger 1/2 teaspoon dried thyme
- 1/3teaspoon ground black pepper, to taste 1 teaspoon kosher salt
- 2tablespoons melted butter
- 3eggs, beaten
- 1/2cup parmesan cheese, grated

1.In a mixing bowl, thoroughly combine ground chicken

2.with spices and an egg. After that, stir in the melted butter; mix to combine well.

3.Whisk the remaining eggs in a shallow bowl.

4.Form the mixture into chicken nugget shapes; now, coat them with the beaten eggs; then, dredge them in the grated parmesan cheese.

Cook in the preheated air fryer at 405 degrees f for 8 minutes.

Tangy And Buttery Chicken

Servings: 4

- ½ tablespoon Worcestershire sauce
- 1teaspoon finely grated orange zest 2 tablespoons melted butter
- ½teaspoon smoked paprika
- 4chicken drumsticks, rinsed and halved 1 teaspoon sea salt flakes
- 1tablespoon cider vinegar
- 1/2teaspoon mixed peppercorns, freshly cracked

1.Firstly, pat the chicken drumsticks dry. Coat them with the melted butter on all sides. Toss the chicken drumsticks with the other .

2.Transfer them to the air fryer Cooking basket and roast for about 13minutes at 345 degrees f.

Easy Turkey Kabobs

Servings: 8

- cup parmesan cheese, grated 1 ½ cups of water
- ounces ground turkey 2 small eggs, beaten
- 1teaspoon ground ginger
- 2½ tablespoons vegetable oil 1 cup chopped fresh parsley 2 tablespoons almond meal 3/4 teaspoon salt
- 1heaping teaspoon fresh rosemary, finely chopped 1/2 teaspoon ground allspice

1.Mix all of the above in a bowl. Knead the mixture with your hands.

2.Then, take small portions and gently roll them into balls.

3.Now, Preheat your air fryer to 380 degrees f. Air fry for 8 to 10 minutes in the air fryer basket. Serve on a serving platter with skewers and eat with your favorite dipping sauce.

Turkey Breasts With Greek Mustard Sauce

Servings: 4

- 1/2 teaspoon cumin powder
- 2pounds turkey breasts, quartered 2 cloves garlic, smashed
- ½ teaspoon hot paprika
- 2tablespoons melted butter 1 teaspoon fine sea salt
- Freshly cracked mixed peppercorns, to savor Fresh juice of 1 lemon
- For the mustard sauce:

- 1½ tablespoons mayonnaise 1 ½ cups greek yogurt
- 1/2 tablespoon yellow mustard

1. Grab a medium-sized mixing dish and combine the garlic and melted butter; rub this mixture evenly over the turkey's surface.

1. Add the cumin powder, followed by paprika, salt, peppercorns, and

2. lemon juice. Place in your refrigerator at least 55 minutes.

3. Set your air fryer to cook at 375 degrees f. Roast the turkey for 18 minutes, turning halfway through; roast in batches.

4. In the meantime, make the mustard sauce by mixing all for the sauce. Serve warm roasted turkey with the mustard sauce.

Country-Style Nutty Turkey Breast

Servings: 2

- 1½ tablespoons coconut aminos 1/2 tablespoon xanthan gum
- 2bay leaves
- 1/3cup dry sherry
- 1½ tablespoons chopped walnuts 1 teaspoon shallot powder
- 1-pound turkey breasts, sliced 1 teaspoon garlic powder
- 2teaspoons olive oil
- 1/2teaspoon onion salt
- 1/2teaspoon red pepper flakes, crushed 1 teaspoon ground black pepper

1. Begin by preheating your air fryer to 395 degrees f. Place all

2. ., minus chopped walnuts, in a mixing bowl and let them marinate at least 1 hour.

3. After that, cook the marinated turkey breast approximately 23 minutes or until heated through.

4. Pause the machine, scatter chopped walnuts over the top and air-fry an additional 5 minutes.

Bacon-Wrapped Turkey With Cheese

Servings: 12

- 1½ small-sized turkey breast, chop into 12 pieces 12 thin slices asiago cheese
- Paprika, to taste
- Fine sea salt and ground black pepper, to savor 12 rashers bacon

1. Lay out the bacon rashers; place 1 slice of asiago cheese on each bacon piece.

2. Top with turkey, season with paprika, salt, and pepper, and roll them up; secure with a cocktail stick.

3. Air-fry at 365 degrees f for 13 minutes.

Italian-Style Spicy Chicken Breasts

Servings: 4

- 2ounces asiago cheese, cut into sticks 1/3 cup tomato paste
- 1/2teaspoon garlic paste
- 2chicken breasts, cut in half lengthwise 1/2 cup green onions, chopped
- 1tablespoon chili sauce
- 1/2 cup roasted vegetable stock 1 tablespoon sesame oil
- 1teaspoon salt
- 2teaspoons unsweetened cocoa

- 1/2 teaspoon sweet paprika, or more to taste

1. Sprinkle chicken breasts with the salt and sweet paprika; drizzle with chili sauce. Now, place a stick of asiago cheese in the middle of each chicken breast.

2. Then, tie the whole thing using a kitchen string; give a drizzle of sesame oil.

3. Transfer the stuffed chicken to the Cooking basket. Add the other and toss to coat the chicken.

4. Afterward, cook for about 11 minutes at 395 degrees f. Serve the chicken on two serving plates, garnish with fresh or pickled salad and serve immediately.

Classic Chicken Nuggets

Servings: 4

- 1½ pounds chicken tenderloins, cut into small pieces 1/2 teaspoon garlic salt
- 1/2 teaspoon cayenne pepper
- 1/4 teaspoon black pepper, freshly cracked
- 4 tablespoons olive oil
- **2** scoops low-carb unflavored Protein powder 4 tablespoons parmesan cheese, freshly grated

1. Start by preheating your air fryer to 390 degrees f.

2. Season each piece of the chicken with garlic salt, cayenne pepper, and black pepper.

3. In a mixing bowl, thoroughly combine the olive oil with Protein powder and parmesan cheese. Dip each piece of chicken in the parmesan mixture.

4. Cook for 8 minutes, working in batches.

5. Later, if you want to warm the chicken nuggets, add them to the basket and cook for 1 minute more.

Thai Chicken With Bacon

Servings: 2

- 4 rashers smoked bacon
- 2chicken filets
- 1/2teaspoon coarse sea salt
- 1/4 teaspoon black pepper, preferably freshly ground 1 teaspoon garlic, minced
- 1(2-inch piece ginger, peeled and minced 1 teaspoon black mustard seeds
- 1teaspoon mild curry powder 1/2 cup coconut milk
- 1/2 cup parmesan cheese, grated

1. Start by preheating your air fryer to 400 degrees f. Add the smoked bacon and cook in the preheated air fryer for 5 to 7 minutes.

2. Reserve.

3. In a mixing bowl, place the chicken fillets, salt, black pepper, garlic, ginger, mustard seeds, curry powder, and milk. Let it marinate in your refrigerator about 30 minutes.

4. In another bowl, place the grated parmesan cheese.

5. Dredge the chicken fillets through the parmesan mixture and transfer them to the Cooking basket. Reduce the temperature to 380 degrees f and cook the chicken for 6 minutes.

6. Turn them over and cook for a further 6 minutes. Repeat the

7. process until you have run out of .

8. Serve with reserved bacon. Enjoy!

Thanksgiving Turkey With Mustard Gravy

Servings:6

- 2teaspoons butter, softened 1 teaspoon dried sage

- 2sprigs rosemary, chopped 1 teaspoon salt
- 1/4teaspoon freshly ground black pepper, or more to taste 1 whole turkey breast
- 2tablespoons turkey broth
- 2tablespoons whole-grain mustard 1 tablespoon butter

1.Start by preheating your air fryer to 360 degrees f.
2.To make the rub, combine 2 tablespoons of butter, sage, rosemary, salt, and pepper; mix well to combine and spread it evenly over the turkey breast's surface.
3.Roast for 20 minutes in an air fryer Cooking basket. Flip the turkey breast over and cook for a further 15 to 16 minutes. Now, flip it
4.back over and roast for 12 minutes more.
5.While the turkey is roasting, whisk the other in a saucepan. After that, spread the gravy all over the turkey breast.
6.Let the turkey rest for a few minutes before carving.

Spicy Coconut Chicken Wings
Servings: 4
- 16chicken drumettes (party wings)
- ¼ cup full-Fat coconut milk 1 tablespoon sriracha
- 1teaspoon onion powder
- 1teaspoon garlic powder Salt
- Freshly ground black pepper
- ⅓ cup shredded unsweetened coconut
- ½cup all-purpose flour Cooking oil spray
- 1cup mango, cut into ½-inch chunks
- ¼ cup fresh cilantro, chopped
- ½ cup red onion, chopped 2 garlic cloves, minced Juice of ½ lime

1.Place the drumettes in a resealable plastic bag.
2.In a small bowl, whisk the coconut milk and sriracha.
3.Drizzle the drumettes with the sriracha–coconut milk mixture. Season the drumettes with the onion powder, garlic powder, salt, and pepper. Seal the bag. Shake it thoroughly to combine the seasonings and coat the chicken. Marinate for at least 30 minutes, preferably overnight, in the refrigerator.
4.When the drumettes are almost done marinating, in a large bowl,
5.stir together the shredded coconut and flour.
6.Dip the drumettes into the coconut-flour mixture. Press the flour mixture onto the chicken with your hands.
7.Insert the crisper plate into the basket and the basket into the unit.
8.Preheat the unit by selecting air fry, setting the temperature to 400°f, and setting the time to 3 minutes. Select start/stop to begin.
9.Once the unit is preheated, spray the crisper plate and the basket with Cooking oil. Place the drumettes in the air fryer. It is okay to stack them. Spray the drumettes with Cooking oil, being sure to cover the bottom layer.
10.Select air fry, set the temperature to 400°f, and set the time to 20 minutes. Select start/stop to begin.
11.After 5 minutes, remove the basket and shake it to ensure all pieces
12.cook through. Reinsert the basket to resume Cooking . Remove and shake the basket every 5 minutes, twice more, until a food thermometer inserted into the drumettes registers 165°f.
13.When the Cooking is complete, let the chicken cool for 5 minutes.
14.While the chicken cooks and cools, make the salsa.

15.In a small bowl, combine the mango, cilantro, red onion, garlic, and lime juice. Mix well until fully combined. Serve with the wings.

Easy General Tso's Chicken
Servings:4
- 1tablespoon sesame oil 1 teaspoon minced garlic
- ½ teaspoon ground ginger 1 cup chicken broth
- 4tablespoons soy sauce, divided
- ½ teaspoon sriracha, plus more for serving 2 tablespoons hoisin sauce
- 4tablespoons cornstarch, divided
- 4boneless, skinless chicken breasts, cut into 1-inch pieces
- Olive oil spray
- 2medium sCal lions, sliced, green parts only Sesame seeds, for garnish

1.In a small saucepan over low heat, combine the sesame oil, garlic, and ginger and cook for 1 minute.
2.Add the chicken broth, 2 tablespoons of soy sauce, the sriracha, and hoisin. Whisk to combine.
3.Whisk in 2 tablespoons of cornstarch and continue Cooking over low heat until the sauce starts to thicken, about 5 minutes. Remove the pan from the heat, cover it, and set aside.
4.Insert the crisper plate into the basket and the basket into the unit. Preheat the unit by selecting bake, setting the temperature to 400°f, and setting the time to 3 minutes. Select start/stop to begin.
5.In a medium bowl, toss together the chicken, remaining 2 tablespoons of soy sauce, and remaining 2 tablespoons of cornstarch.
6.Once the unit is preheated, spray the crisper plate with olive oil. Place the chicken into the basket and spray it with olive oil.
7.Select bake, set the temperature to 400°f, and set the time to 9 minutes. Select start/stop to begin.
8.After 5 minutes, remove the basket, shake, and spray the chicken with more olive oil. Reinsert the basket to resume Cooking .
9.When the Cooking is complete, a food thermometer inserted into the chicken should register at least 165°f. Transfer the chicken to a large bowl and toss it with the sauce. Garnish with the sCal lions and sesame seeds and serve.

Italian Chicken Parmesan
Servings:4
- 2(4-ounce) boneless, skinless chicken breasts 2 egg whites, beaten
- 1cup italian breadcrumbs
- ½cup grated parmesan cheese 2 teaspoons italian seasoning Salt
- Freshly ground black pepper Cooking oil spray
- ¾cup marinara sauce
- ½cup shredded mozzarella cheese

1.With your knife blade parallel to the cutting board, cut the chicken breasts in half horizontally to create 4 thin cutlets. On a solid surface, pound the cutlets to flatten them. You can use your hands,
2.a rolling pin, a kitchen mallet, or a meat hammer.
3.Pour the egg whites into a bowl large enough to dip the chicken.

4.In another bowl large enough to dip a chicken cutlet in, stir together the breadcrumbs, parmesan cheese, and italian seasoning, and
5.season with salt and pepper.
6.Dip each cutlet into the egg whites and into the breadcrumb mixture to coat.
7.Insert the crisper plate into the basket and the basket into the unit. Preheat the unit by selecting air fry, setting the temperature to 375°f, and setting the time to 3 minutes. Select start/stop to begin.
8.Once the unit is preheated, spray the crisper plate with Cooking oil.
9.Working in batches, place 2 chicken cutlets into the basket. Spray the top of the chicken with Cooking oil.
10.Select air fry, set the temperature to 375°f, and set the time to 7
11.minutes. Select start/stop to begin.
12.When the Cooking is complete, repeat steps 6 and 7 with the remaining cutlets.
13.Top the chicken cutlets with the marinara sauce and shredded mozzarella cheese. If the chicken will fit into the basket without stacking, you can prepare all 4 at once. Otherwise, do these 2 cutlets at a time.
14.Select air fry, set the temperature to 375°f, and set the time to 3 minutes. Select start/stop to begin.
15.The Cooking is complete when the cheese is melted, and the chicken reaches an internal temperature of 165°f.
16.Cool for 5 minutes before serving.

Spicy Chicken Meatballs
Servings:4
- 1medium red onion, minced 2 garlic cloves, minced
- 1jalapeño pepper, minced
- 2teaspoons extra-virgin olive oil 3 tablespoons ground almonds
- 1egg
- 1teaspoon dried thyme
- 1-pound ground chicken breast Cooking oil spray

1.Insert the crisper plate into the basket and the basket into the unit. Preheat the unit by selecting bake, setting the temperature to 400°f, and setting the time to 3 minutes. Select start/stop to begin.
2.In a 6-by-2-inch round pan, combine the red onion, garlic, jalapeño,
3.and olive oil.
4.Once the unit is preheated, place the pan into the basket.
5.Select bake, set the temperature to 400°f, and set the time to 4 minutes. Select start/stop to begin.
6.When the Cooking is complete, the vegetables should be crisptender.
7.Transfer to a medium bowl.

8. Mix the almonds, egg, and thyme into the vegetable mixture. Add the chicken and mix until just combined. Form the chicken mixture into about 24 (1-inch) balls.
9.Insert the crisper plate into the basket and the basket into the unit.
10.Preheat the unit by selecting bake, setting the temperature to 400°f, and setting the time to 3 minutes. Select start/stop to begin.
11.Once the unit is preheated, spray the crisper plate with Cooking oil. Working in batches, place half the meatballs in a single layer, not touching, into the basket.
12.Select bake, set the temperature to 400°f, and set the time to 10 minutes. Select start/stop to begin.

13.When the Cooking is complete, a food
14.thermometer inserted into the meatballs should register at least 165°f.
15.Repeat steps 8 and 9 with the remaining meatballs. Serve warm.

Warm Chicken And Spinach Salad
Servings:4
- 3(5-ounce) boneless, skinless chicken breasts, cut into 1-inch cubes
- 5teaspoons extra-virgin olive oil
- ½ teaspoon dried thyme
- 1medium red onion, sliced 1 red bell pepper, sliced
- 1small zucchini, cut into strips
- 3tablespoons freshly squeezed lemon juice 6 cups fresh baby spinach leaves

1.Insert the crisper plate into the basket and the basket into the unit. Preheat the unit by selecting air roast, setting the temperature to 375°f, and setting the time to 3 minutes. Select start/stop to begin.
2.In a large bowl, combine the chicken, olive oil, and thyme. Toss to coat. Transfer to a medium metal bowl that fits into the basket.
3.Once the unit is preheated, place the bowl into the basket.
4.Select air roast, set the temperature to 375°f, and set the time to 20 minutes. Select start/stop to begin.
5.After 8 minutes, add the red onion, red bell pepper, and zucchini to the bowl. Resume Cooking . After about 6 minutes more, stir the chicken and vegetables. Resume Cooking .
6.When the Cooking is complete, a food thermometer inserted into the chicken should register at least 165°f. Remove the bowl from the unit and stir in the lemon juice.
7.Put the spinach in a serving bowl and top with the chicken mixture. Toss to combine and serve immediately.

Seafood Recipes

Air Fried Cod With Basil Vinaigrette
Servings:4
- ¼ cup olive oil
  3cod fillets
- A bunch of basil, torn
- Juice from 1 lemon, freshly squeezed Salt and pepper *to taste*

1.Preheat the air fryer for 5 minutes.
2.Season the cod fillets with salt and pepper to taste.
3.Place in the air fryer and cook for 15 minutes at 350of.
4.Meanwhile, mix the rest of the in a bowl and toss to combine.
5.Serve the air fried cod with the basil vinaigrette.

Almond Flour Coated Crispy Shrimps
Servings: 4
- ½ cup almond flour
- 1tablespoon yellow mustard
- 1-pound raw shrimps, peeled and deveined 3 tablespoons olive oil
- Salt and pepper to taste
  1.Place all in a ziploc bag and give a good shake.
  2.Place in the air fryer and cook for 10 minutes at 400of.

Apple Slaw Topped Alaskan Cod Filet

Servings: 3

- ¼ cup mayonnaise
- ½ red onion, diced
- 1½ pounds frozen alaskan cod
- 1box whole wheat panko breadcrumbs 1 granny smith apple, julienned
- 1tablespoon vegetable oil 1 teaspoon paprika
- 2cups napa cabbage, shredded Salt and pepper to taste

1.Preheat the air fryer to 390of.
2.Place the grill pan accessory in the air fryer.
3.Brush the fish with oil and dredge in the breadcrumbs.
4.Place the fish on the grill pan and cook for 15 minutes. Make sure to flip the fish halfway through the Cooking time.
5.Meanwhile, prepare the slaw by mixing the remaining in a bowl.
6.Serve the fish with the slaw.

Baked Cod Fillet Recipe From Thailand

Servings: 4

- ¼ cup coconut milk, freshly squeezed
- 1tablespoon lime juice, freshly squeezed
- 1-pound cod fillet, cut into bite-sized pieces Salt and pepper to taste

1.Preheat the air fryer for 5 minutes.
2.Place all in a baking dish that will fit in the air fryer.
3.Place in the air fryer.
4.Cook for 20 minutes at 325of.

Baked Scal Lops With Garlic Aioli

Servings: 4

- 1cup breadcrumbs
- 1/4 cup chopped parsley
- 16sea sCal lops, rinsed and drained 2 shallots, chopped
- 3pinches ground nutmeg 4 tablespoons olive oil
- 5cloves garlic, minced
- 5tablespoons butter, melted Salt and pepper to taste

1.Lightly grease baking pan of air fryer with Cooking spray.
2.Mix in shallots, garlic, melted butter, and sCal lops. Season with pepper, salt, and nutmeg.
3.In a small bowl, whisk well olive oil and breadcrumbs. Sprinkle
4.over sCal lops.
5.For 10 minutes, cook on 390of until tops are lightly browned.
6.Serve and enjoy with a sprinkle of parsley.

BASIL 'N LIME-CHILI CLAMS

Servings: 3

- ½ cup basil leaves
- ½ cup tomatoes, chopped
- 1tablespoon fresh lime juice 25 littleneck clams
- 4cloves of garlic, minced
- 6tablespoons unsalted butter Salt and pepper to taste

1. Preheat the air fryer to 390of.
   1.Place the grill pan accessory in the air fryer.

2.On a large foil, place all . Fold over the foil and close by crimping the edges.
3.Place on the grill pan and cook for 15 minutes.
4.Serve with bread.

Bass Filet In Coconut Sauce

Servings:4

- ¼ cup coconut milk
- ½ pound bass fillet
- 1tablespoon olive oil
- 2tablespoons jalapeno, chopped
- 2tablespoons lime juice, freshly squeezed 3 tablespoons parsley, chopped
- Salt and pepper to taste

1.Preheat the air fryer for 5 minutes
2.Season the bass with salt and pepper to taste
3.Brush the surface with olive oil.
4.Place in the air fryer and cook for 15 minutes at 350of.
5. Meanwhile, place in a saucepan, the coconut milk, lime juice, jalapeno and parsley.
6.Heat over medium flame.
7.Serve the fish with the coconut sauce.

Beer Battered Cod Filet

Servings: 2

- ½ cup all-purpose flour
- ¾ teaspoon baking powder 1 ¼ cup lager beer
- 2cod fillets
- 2eggs, beaten
- Salt and pepper to taste

1.Preheat the air fryer to 390of.
2.Pat the fish fillets dry then set aside.
3.In a bowl, combine the rest of the to create a batter.
4.Dip the fillets on the batter and place on the double layer rack.
5.Cook for 15 minutes.

Buttered Baked Cod With Wine

Servings: 2

- 1tablespoon butter
- 1tablespoon butter
- 2tablespoons dry white wine 1/2 pound thick-cut cod loin
- 1-1/2 teaspoons chopped fresh parsley
- 1-1/2 teaspoons chopped green onion 1/2 lemon, cut into wedges
- 1/4 sleeve buttery round crackers (such as ritz®), crushed 1/4 lemon, juiced

1.In a small bowl, melt butter in microwave. Whisk in crackers.
2.Lightly grease baking pan of air fryer with remaining butter. And melt for 2 minutes at 390of.
3.In a small bowl whisk well lemon juice, white wine, parsley, and
4.green onion.
5.Coat cod filets in melted butter. Pour dressing. Top with buttercracker mixture.
6.Cook for 10 minutes at 390of.
7.Serve and enjoy with a slice of lemon.

Buttered Garlic-Oregano On Clams

Servings: 4

¼ cup parmesan cheese, grated

¼ cup parsley, chopped 1 cup breadcrumbs
1teaspoon dried oregano 2 dozen clams, shucked
3cloves of garlic, minced
4tablespoons butter, melted

1.In a medium bowl, mix the breadcrumbs, parmesan cheese, parsley, oregano, and garlic. Stir in the melted butter.
2.Preheat the air fryer to 390of.
3.Place the baking dish accessory in the air fryer and place the clams.
4.Sprinkle the crumb mixture over the clams.
5. Cook for 5 minutes.

Cajun Spiced Lemon-Shrimp Kebabs
Servings: 2
- 1tsp cayenne
- 1tsp garlic powder 1 tsp kosher salt
- 1tsp onion powder 1 tsp oregano
- 1tsp paprika
- 12pcs xl shrimp
- 2lemons, sliced thinly crosswise 2 tbsp olive oil

1.In a bowl, mix all Ingredients except for sliced lemons. Marinate for 10 minutes.
2.Thread 3 shrimps per steel skewer.
3.Place in skewer rack.
4.Cook for 5 minutes at 390of.
5.Serve and enjoy with freshly squeezed lemon.

Panko-Crusted Tilapia
Servings: 3
- 2tsp. Italian seasoning
- 2tsp. Lemon pepper
- 1/3 c. Panko breadcrumbs 1/3 c. Egg whites
- 1/3 c. Almond flour 3 tilapia fillets Olive oil

1.Place panko, egg whites, and flour into separate bowls. Mix lemon pepper and italian seasoning in with breadcrumbs.
1.Pat tilapia fillets dry. Dredge in flour, then egg, breadcrumb mixture.
2.Add to the air fryer basket and spray lightly with olive oil.
3.Cook 10-11 minutes at 400 degrees, making sure to flip halfway through Cooking .

Coconut Shrimp
Servings: 3
- 1c. Almond flour
- 1c. Panko breadcrumbs 1 tbsp. Coconut flour
- 1c. Unsweetened, dried coconut
- 1egg white
- 12raw large shrimp

1.Put shrimp on paper towels to drain.
2.Mix coconut and panko breadcrumbs. Then mix in coconut flour and almond flour in a different bowl. Set to the side.
3.Dip shrimp into flour mixture, then into egg white, and then into coconut mixture.
4.Place into air fryer basket. Repeat with remaining shrimp.
5.Set temperature to 350°f and set time to 10 minutes. Turn halfway through Cooking process.

Scal Lops And Spring Veggies

Servings: 4
- ½ pound asparagus, ends trimmed, cut into 2-inch pieces 1 cup Sugar snap peas
- 1-pound sea sCal lops
- 1tablespoon lemon juice

- 1 teaspoons olive oil
- ½ teaspoon dried thyme Pinch salt
- Freshly ground black pepper

1.Place the asparagus and Sugar snap peas in the air fryer basket.
2.Cook for 2 to 3 minutes or until the vegetables are just starting to get tender.
3.Meanwhile, check the sCal lops for a small muscle attached to the
4.side, and pull it off and discard.
5.In a medium bowl, toss the sCal lops with the lemon juice, olive oil, thyme, salt, and pepper. Place into the air fryer oven basket on top of the vegetables.
6.Steam for 5 to 7 minutes, tossing the basket once during cooking time, until the sCal lops are just firm when tested with your finger and are opaque in the center, and the vegetables are tender. Serve immediately.

Air Fryer Salmon Patties
Servings: 4
- 1tbsp. Olive oil 1 tbsp. Ghee
- ¼ tsp. Salt
- 1/8 tsp. Pepper 1 egg
- 1c. Almond flour
- 1can wild alaskan pink salmon

1.Drain can of salmon into a bowl and keeps liquid. Discard skin and bones.
2.Add salt, pepper, and egg to salmon, mixing well with hands to incorporate. Make patties.
3.Dredge in flour and remaining egg. If it seems dry, spoon reserved salmon liquid from the can onto patties.
4.Pour the patties into the oven rack/basket. Place the rack on the
5.middle-shelf of the air fryer oven. Set temperature to 378°f and set time to 7 minutes. Cook 7 minutes till golden, making sure to flip once during cooking process.

Beer-Battered Fish And Chips
Servings: 4
- 2eggs
- 1cup malty beer, such as pabst blue ribbon 1 cup all-purpose flour
- ½ cup cornstarch
- 1teaspoon garlic powder Salt
- Pepper Cooking oil
- (4-ounce) cod fillets

1.In a medium bowl, beat the eggs with the beer. In another medium bowl, combine the flour and cornstarch, and season with the garlic powder and salt and pepper to taste.
2.Spray the air fryer basket with cooking oil.
3.Dip each cod fillet in the flour and cornstarch mixture and then in the egg and beer mixture. Dip the cod in the flour and cornstarch a second time.
4.2 place the cod in the air fryer oven. Do not stack. Cook in batches.
5.Spray with cooking oil. Cook for 8 minutes.
6.Open the air fryer oven and flip the cod. Cook for an additional 7 minutes.

7.Remove the cooked cod from the air fryer, repeat steps 4 and 5 for the remaining fillets.
8.Serve with prepared air fried frozen fries. Frozen fries will need to be
9.cooked for 18 to 20 minutes at 400°f.
10.Cool before serving.

AIR FRYER SALMON

Servings: 2
- ½ tsp. Salt
- ½ tsp. Garlic powder
- ½ tsp. Smoked paprika Salmon

1.Mix spices and sprinkle onto salmon.
2.Place seasoned salmon into the air fryer oven.
3.Pour into the oven rack/basket. Place the rack on the middle-shelf of the air fryer oven. Set temperature to 400°f and set time to 10 minutes.

Indian Fish Fingers

Servings: 4
- 1/2-pound fish fillet
- 1tablespoon finely chopped fresh mint leaves or any fresh herbs 1/3 cup breadcrumbs
- 1teaspoon ginger garlic paste or ginger and garlic powders 1 hot green chili finely chopped
- 1/2 teaspoon paprika
- Generous pinch of black pepper Salt to taste
- 3/4 tablespoons lemon juice
- 3/4 teaspoons garam masala powder 1/3 teaspoon rosemary
- 1egg

1.Start by removing any skin on the fish, washing, and patting dry. Cut the fish into fingers.
2.In a medium bowl mix all except for fish, mint, and breadcrumbs. Bury the fingers in the mixture and refrigerate for 30 minutes.
3.Remove from the bowl from the fridge and mix in mint leaves.
4.In a separate bowl beat the egg, pour breadcrumbs into a third bowl. Dip the fingers in the egg bowl then toss them in the breadcrumbs bowl.
5.Pour into the oven rack/basket. Place the rack on the middle-shelf of the air fryer oven. Set temperature to 360°f, and set time to 15 minutes, toss the fingers halfway through.

Quick Paella

Servings: 4
- 1(10-ounce) package frozen cooked rice, thawed
- (6-ounce) jar artichoke hearts, drained and chopped
- ¼ cup vegetable broth
- ½ teaspoon turmeric
- ½ teaspoon dried thyme
- cup frozen cooked small shrimp
- ½ cup frozen baby peas 1 tomato, diced

1.In a 6-by-6-by-2-inch pan, combine the rice, artichoke hearts, vegetable broth, turmeric, and thyme, and stir gently.
2.Place in the air fryer oven and bake for 8 to 9 minutes or until the rice is hot. Remove from the air fryer and gently stir in the shrimp, peas, and tomato. Cook for 5 to 8 minutes or until the shrimp and peas are hot and the paella is bubbling.

3-Ingredient Air Fryer Catfish

Servings: 4
- 1tbsp. Chopped parsley
- 1tbsp. Olive oil
- ¼ c. Seasoned fish fry 4 catfish fillets

1.Ensure your air fryer oven is preheated to 400 degrees.
2.Rinse off catfish fillets and pat dry.
3.Add fish fry seasoning to ziploc baggie, then catfish. Shake bag and ensure fish gets well coated.
4.Spray each fillet with olive oil.
5.Add fillets to air fryer basket.
6.Set temperature to 400°f and set time to 10 minutes.
7.Cook 10 minutes. Then flip and cook another 2-3 minutes.

Tuna Veggie Stir-Fry

Servings: 4
- 1tablespoon olive oil
- 1red bell pepper, chopped
- 1cup green beans, cut into 2-inch pieces 1 onion, sliced
- 2cloves garlic, sliced
- 2tablespoons low-Sodium soy sauce 1 tablespoon honey
- ½ pound fresh tuna, cubed

1.In a 6-inch metal bowl, combine the olive oil, pepper, green beans, onion, and garlic.
2.Pour into the oven rack/basket. Place the rack on the middle-shelf of the air fryer oven. Set temperature to 350°f, and set time to 4 to 6 minutes, stirring once, until crisp and tender. Add soy sauce, honey, and tuna, and stir. Cook for another 3 to 6 minutes, stirring once, until the tuna is cooked as desired. Tuna can be served rare or medium-rare, or you can cook it until well done.

BANG PANKO BREADED FRIED SHRIMP

Servings: 4
- 1tsp. Paprika
- Montreal chicken seasoning
- ¾ c. Panko breadcrumbs
- ½ c. Almond flour 1 egg white
- 1-pound raw shrimp (peeled and deveined) Bang bang sauce:
- ¼ c. Sweet chili sauce
- tbsp. Sriracha sauce 1/3 c. Plain greek yogurt

1.Ensure your air fryer oven is preheated to 400 degrees.
2.Season all shrimp with seasonings.
3.Add flour to one bowl, egg white in another, and breadcrumbs to a third.
4.Dip seasoned shrimp in flour, then egg whites, and then breadcrumbs.
5.Spray coated shrimp with olive oil and add to air fryer basket.
6.Set temperature to 400°f and set time to 4 minutes. Cook 4 minutes, flip, and cook an additional 4 minutes.
7.To make the sauce, mix all sauce until smooth.

Louisiana Shrimp Po Boy

Servings: 6
- 1tsp. Creole seasoning 8 slices of tomato Lettuce leaves

- ¼ c. Buttermilk
- ½ c. Louisiana fish fry
- 1-pound deveined shrimp remoulade sauce:
- 1chopped green onion 1 tsp. Hot sauce
- 1tsp. Dijon mustard
- ½ tsp. Creole seasoning
- 1tsp. Worcestershire sauce Juice of ½ a lemon
- ½ c. Vegan mayo

1.To make the sauce, combine all sauce until well incorporated. Chill while you cook shrimp.
2.Mix seasonings together and liberally season shrimp.
3.Add buttermilk to a bowl. Dip each shrimp into milk and place in a ziploc bag. Chill half an hour to marinate.
4.Add fish fry to a bowl. Take shrimp from marinating bag and dip into fish fry, then add to air fryer.
5.Ensure your air fryer is preheated to 400 degrees.
6.Spray shrimp with olive oil.
7.Pour into the oven rack/basket. Place the rack on the middle-shelf of the air fryer oven. Set temperature to 400°f and set time to 5 minutes. Cook 5 minutes, flip and then cook another 5 minutes. Assemble "keto" po boy by adding sauce to lettuce leaves, along with shrimp and tomato.

Old Bay Crab Cakes
Servings: 4
- Slices dried bread, crusts removed Small amount of milk
- 1tablespoon mayonnaise
- 1tablespoon worcestershire sauce 1 tablespoon baking powder
- 1tablespoon parsley flakes
- 1teaspoon old bay® seasoning 1/4 teaspoon salt
- 1egg
- 1-pound lump crabmeat

1.Crush your bread over a large bowl until it is broken down into small pieces. Add milk and stir until breadcrumbs are moistened. Mix in mayo and worcestershire sauce. Add remaining and mix well. Shape into 4 patties.
2.Pour into the oven rack/basket. Place the rack on the middle-shelf of the air fryer oven. Set temperature to 360°f, and set time to 20 minutes, flip halfway through.

Flavors Parmesan Shrimp
Servings: 3
- 1lb. Shrimp, peeled and deveined 1 tbsp olive oil
- 1/2 tsp onion powder 1/2 tsp basil
- 1/4 tsp oregano 1/2 tsp pepper
- 1/4 cup parmesan cheese, grated 3 garlic cloves, minced
  1.Add all into the large bowl and toss well.
  2.Line instant pot multi-level air fryer basket with aluminum foil.
  3.Add shrimp into the air fryer basket and place basket into the instant pot.
  4.Seal pot with air fryer lid and select air fry mode then set the temperature to 350 f and timer for 10 minutes.
  5.Serve and enjoy.

Bacon Wrap Shrimp
Servings: 2
- 8 shrimp, deveined
- 8 bacon slices

1.Place the dehydrating tray in a multi-level air fryer basket and place basket in the instant pot.
2.Wrap shrimp with bacon slices and place on dehydrating tray.
3.Seal pot with air fryer lid and select air fry mode then set the temperature to 390 f and timer for 7 minutes. Turn shrimp after 5 minutes.
4.Serve and enjoy.

Simple Garlic Lime Shrimp
Servings: 2
- 1cup shrimp
- 1garlic clove, minced 1 fresh lime juice Pepper
- Salt
1.Add all into the bowl and toss well.
2.Spray instant pot multi-level air fryer basket with Cooking spray.
3.Add shrimp into the air fryer basket and place basket into the instant pot.
4.Seal pot with air fryer lid and select air fry mode then set the temperature to 350 f and timer for 8 minutes. Turn shrimp halfway through.
5.Serve and enjoy.

Lemon Crab Patties
Servings: 4
- 1egg
- 12oz crabmeat
- 2green onion, chopped 1/4 cup mayonnaise
- cup almond flour
- **1**tsp old bay seasoning 1 tsp red pepper flakes 1 tbsp fresh lemon juice
1.Add half almond flour into the shallow bowl.
2.add remaining and mix until well combined.
3.Place the dehydrating tray in a multi-level air fryer basket and place basket in the instant pot.
4.Make patties and coat with remaining almond flour and place on dehydrating tray.
5.Seal pot with air fryer lid and select air fry mode then set the temperature to 400 f and timer for 10 minutes. Turn patties halfway through.
6.Serve and enjoy.

Cheese Crust Salmon
Servings: 2
- 2salmon fillets
- 2tbsp fresh parsley, chopped 1 garlic clove, minced
- 1/4 cup parmesan cheese, shredded 1/2 tsp mccormick's bbq seasoning 1/2 tsp paprika
- 1tbsp olive oil Pepper
- Salt
1.Add salmon, seasoning, and olive oil to the bowl and mix well.
2.Mix cheese, garlic, and parsley.
3.Sprinkle cheese mixture on top of salmon.
4.Place the dehydrating tray in a multi-level air fryer basket and place basket in the instant pot.
5.Place salmon fillets on dehydrating tray.
6.Seal pot with air fryer lid and select air fry mode then set the temperature to 400 f and timer for 10 minutes.
7.Serve and enjoy.

Lemon Butter Salmon
Servings: 2

- 2salmon fillets
- 1tsp olive oil
- 2tsp garlic, minced 2 tbsp butter
- 2tbsp fresh lemon juice 1/4 cup white wine Pepper
- Salt

1.Place the dehydrating tray in a multi-level air fryer basket and place basket in the instant pot.
2.Season salmon with pepper and salt and place on dehydrating tray.
3.Seal pot with air fryer lid and select air fry mode then set the temperature to 350 f and timer for 6 minutes.
4.Meanwhile, in a saucepan, add remaining and cook over low heat for 5 minutes.
5.Place cooked salmon fillets on serving dish and pour prepared sauce over salmon.
6.Serve and enjoy.

Tasty Spicy Shrimp

Servings: 2
- 1/2 lb. Shrimp, peeled and deveined
- 1/2 tsp old bay seasoning
- 1/4 tsp cayenne pepper
- 1tbsp olive oil
- 1/4 tsp paprika
- 1/8 tsp salt

1.Add all into the mixing bowl and toss well.
1.Spray instant pot multi-level air fryer basket with Cooking spray.
2.Add shrimp into the air fryer basket and place basket into the instant pot.
3.Seal pot with air fryer lid and select air fry mode then set the
4.temperature to 390 f and timer for 6 minutes.
5.Serve and enjoy.

Healthy Salmon Patties

Servings: 4
- 14oz can salmon, drained and remove bones 2 eggs, lightly beaten
- 1/2 cup almond flour 1/2 onion, minced 1/4 cup butter
- 1/2 tsp pepper
- 1avocado, diced
- 1tsp salt

1.Add all into the mixing bowl and mix until well combined.
2.Place the dehydrating tray in a multi-level air fryer basket and place basket in the instant pot.
3.Make patties from mixture and place on dehydrating tray.
4.Seal pot with air fryer lid and select air fry mode then set the temperature to 400 f and timer for 10 minutes. Turn patties halfway through.
5.Serve and enjoy.

Lemon Garlicky Shrimp

Servings: 4
- 1lb. Shrimp, peeled 1 tbsp olive oil
- 1lemon juice
- 1lemon zest
- 1/4 cup fresh parsley, chopped 4 garlic cloves, minced
- 1/4 tsp red pepper flakes 1/4 tsp sea salt

1.Add all except parsley and lemon juice into the mixing
1.bowl and toss well.
2.Spray instant pot multi-level air fryer basket with Cooking spray.
3.Add shrimp into the air fryer basket and place basket into the instant pot.
4.Seal pot with air fryer lid and select air fry mode then set the
5.temperature to 400 f and timer for 5 minutes.
6.Garnish shrimp with parsley and drizzle with lemon juice.
7.Serve and enjoy.

Spicy Prawns

Servings: 4
- 12king prawns
- 1/4 tsp black pepper 1 tsp chili powder
- 1tsp red chili flakes 1 tbsp vinegar
- 1tbsp ketchup
- 3tbsp mayonnaise 1/2 tsp sea salt

1.Add prawns, chili flakes, chili powder, black pepper, and salt to the bowl and toss well.
2.Spray instant pot multi-level air fryer basket with cooking spray.
3.Add shrimp into the air fryer basket and place basket into the instant pot.
4.Seal pot with air fryer lid and select air fry mode then set the temperature to 350 f and timer for 6 minutes. Stir halfway through.
5.In a small bowl, mix mayonnaise, ketchup, and vinegar.
6.Serve shrimp with mayo mixture.

Simple & Perfect Salmon

Servings: 2
- 2salmon fillets, remove any bones 2 tsp olive oil
- 2tsp paprika Pepper
- Salt

1. Coat salmon with oil and season with paprika, pepper, and salt.
2.Place the dehydrating tray in a multi-level air fryer basket and place basket in the instant pot.
3.Place salmon fillets on dehydrating tray.
4.Seal pot with air fryer lid and select air fry mode then set the temperature to 390 f and timer for 7 minutes.
5.Serve and enjoy.

Crispy Crust Ranch Fish Fillets

Servings: 2
- 2fish fillets
- 1/2packet ranch dressing mix 1/4 cup breadcrumbs
- 1egg, lightly beaten 1 1/4 tbsp olive oil

1.In a shallow dish mix together ranch dressing mix and breadcrumbs.
2.Add oil and mix until the mixture becomes crumbly.
3.Place the dehydrating tray in a multi-level air fryer basket and place basket in the instant pot.
4.Dip fish fillet in egg then coats with breadcrumb and place on dehydrating tray.
5.Seal pot with air fryer lid and select air fry mode then set the temperature to 350 f and timer for 12 minutes. Turn fish fillets halfway through.

6.Serve and enjoy.

Sweet Cod Fillets
Servings: 4
- 4cod fillets, boneless
- Salt and black pepper to taste 1 cup water
- 4tablespoons light soy sauce 1 tablespoon Sugar
- 3tablespoons olive oil + a drizzle
- 4ginger slices
- 3spring onions, chopped
- 2tablespoons coriander, chopped

1.Season the fish with salt and pepper, then drizzle some oil over it and rub well.
2.Put the fish in your air fryer and cook at 360 degrees f for 12 minutes.
3.Put the water in a pot and heat up over medium heat; add the soy sauce and Sugar, stir, bring to a simmer, and remove from the heat.
4.Heat a pan with the olive oil over medium heat; add the ginger and green onions, stir, cook for 2-3 minutes, and remove from the heat.
5.Divide the fish between plates and top with ginger, coriander, and green onions.
6.Drizzle the soy sauce mixture all over, serve, and enjoy!

Pecan Cod
Servings: 2
- 2black cod fillets, boneless 1 tablespoon olive oil
- Salt and black pepper to taste 2 leeks, sliced
- ½ cup pecans, chopped

1.In a bowl, mix the cod with the oil, salt, pepper, and the leeks; toss/coat well.
2.Transfer the cod to your air fryer and cook at 360 degrees f for 15 minutes.
3.Divide the fish and leeks between plates, sprinkle the pecans on top, and serve immediately.

Balsamic Cod
Servings: 2
- 2cod fillets, boneless
- 2tablespoons lemon juice Salt and black pepper to taste
- ½ teaspoon garlic powder
- ⅓cup water
- ⅓ cup balsamic vinegar 3 shallots, chopped
- 2tablespoons olive oil

1.In a bowl, toss the cod with the salt, pepper, lemon juice, garlic powder, water, vinegar, and oil; coat well.
2.Transfer the fish to your fryer's basket and cook at 360 degrees for 12 minutes, flipping them halfway.
3.Divide the fish between plates, sprinkle the shallots on top, and serve.

Garlic Salmon Fillets
Servings: 2
- 2salmon fillets, boneless Salt and black pepper to taste 3red chili peppers, chopped 2 tablespoons lemon juice
- 2tablespoon olive oil
- 2tablespoon garlic, minced

1.In a bowl, combine the , toss, and coat fish well.

2.Transfer everything to your air fryer and cook at 365 degrees f for 8 minutes, flipping the fish halfway.
3.Divide between plates and serve right away.

Shrimp And Veggie Mix
Servings: 4
- ½ cup red onion, chopped
- 1cup red bell pepper, chopped 1 cup celery, chopped
- 1-pound shrimp, peeled and deveined
- 1teaspoon worcestershire sauce Salt and black pepper to taste
- 1tablespoon butter, melted 1 teaspoon sweet paprika

1.Add all the to a bowl and mix well.
2.Transfer everything to your air fryer and cook 320 degrees f for 20 minutes, shaking halfway.
3.Divide between plates and serve.

White Fish With Peas And Basil
Servings: 4
- 4white fish fillets, boneless
- 2tablespoons cilantro, chopped 2 cups peas, cooked and drained 4 tablespoons veggie stock
- ½ teaspoon basil, dried
- ½ teaspoon sweet paprika 2 garlic cloves, minced Salt and pepper to taste

1.In a bowl, mix the fish with all except the peas; toss to coat the fish well.
2.Transfer everything to your air fryer and cook at 360 degrees f for 12 minutes.
3.Add the peas, toss, and divide everything between plates.
4.Serve and enjoy.

Cod And Chives
Servings: 4
- 4cod fillets, boneless
- Salt and black pepper to taste 3 teaspoons lime zest
- 2teaspoons lime juice
- 3tablespoons chives, chopped 6 tablespoons butter, melted
- 2 tablespoons olive oil

1.Season the fish with the salt and pepper, rub it with the oil, and then put it in your air fryer.
1.Cook at 360 degrees f for 10 minutes, flipping once.
2.Heat a pan with the butter over medium heat, and then add the chives, salt, pepper, lime juice, and zest, whisk; cook for 1-2 minutes.
3.Divide the fish between plates, drizzle the lime sauce all over, and
4.serve immediately.

Paprika Salmon Fillets
Servings: 4
- 4salmon fillets, boneless 1 tablespoon olive oil
- Salt and black pepper to taste 1 teaspoon cumin, ground
- 1teaspoon sweet paprika
- ½ teaspoon chili powder 1 teaspoon garlic powder Juice of 1 lime

1.In a bowl, mix the salmon with the other , rub / coat well, and transfer to your air fryer.
2.Cook at 350 degrees f for 6 minutes on each side.

3.Divide the fish between plates and serve right away with a side salad.

Thyme Tuna
Servings: 4
- ½ cup cilantro, chopped
- ⅓ cup olive oil
- 1small red onion, chopped
- 3tablespoons balsamic vinegar 2 tablespoons parsley, chopped 2 tablespoons basil, chopped
- 1jalapeno pepper, chopped 4 sushi tuna steaks
- Salt and black pepper to taste
- 1 teaspoon red pepper flakes 1 teaspoon thyme, chopped

3 garlic cloves, minced
    1.Place all except the fish into a bowl and stir well.
    2.Add the fish and toss, coating it well.
    3.Transfer everything to your air fryer and cook at 360 degrees f for 4 minutes on each side.
    4.Divide the fish between plates and serve.

Buttery Shrimp
Servings: 2
- 1tablespoon butter, melted A drizzle of olive oil
- 1-pound shrimp, peeled and deveined
- ¼ cup heavy cream
- 8ounces mushrooms, roughly sliced
- A pinch of red pepper flakes Salt and black pepper to taste 2 garlic cloves, minced
- ½ cup beef stock
- tablespoon parsley, chopped 1 tablespoon chives, chopped

1.Season the shrimp with salt and pepper and grease with the oil.
2.Place the shrimp in your air fryer, cook at 360 degrees f for 7 minutes, and divide between plates.
3.Heat a pan with the butter over medium heat, add the mushrooms, stir, and cook for 3-4 minutes.
4.Add all remaining ; stir and then cook for a few minutes more.
5.Drizzle the butter / garlic mixture over the shrimp and serve.

Maple Salmon
Servings: 2
- 2salmon fillets, boneless Salt and black pepper to taste 2tablespoons mustard
- 1tablespoon olive oil
- 1tablespoon maple syrup
    1.In a bowl, mix the mustard with the oil and the maple syrup; whisk well and brush the salmon with this mix.
    2.Place the salmon in your air fryer and cook it at 370 degrees f for 5
    3.minutes on each side.
    4.Serve immediately with a side salad.

Balsamic Orange Salmon
Servings: 4
- 4salmon fillets, boneless and cubed
- 2lemons, sliced
- ¼ cup balsamic vinegar
- ¼ cup orange juice

- A pinch of salt and black pepper
    1.In a pan that fits your air fryer, mix all except the fish; whisk.
    2.Heat the mixture over medium-high heat for 5 minutes and add the salmon.
    3.Toss gently and place the pan in the air fryer and cook at 360 degrees f for 10 minutes.
    4.Divide between plates and serve right away with a side salad.

Crunchy Pistachio Cod
Servings: 4
- 1cup pistachios, chopped 4 cod fillets, boneless
- ¼ cup lime juice
- 2tablespoons honey
- 1teaspoon parsley, chopped Salt and black pepper to taste 1 tablespoon mustard

1.Place all the except the fish into a bowl; whisk.
2. Spread the mixture over the fish fillets, put them in your air fryer, and cook at 350 degrees f for 10 minutes.
3.Divide the fish between plates and serve immediately with a side salad.

Roasted Parsley Cod
Servings: 4
- 3tablespoons parsley, chopped 4 medium cod filets, boneless
- ¼ cup butter, melted
- 2garlic cloves, minced
- 2tablespoons lemon juice 1 shallot, chopped
- Salt and black pepper to taste

1.In a bowl, mix all except the fish; whisk well.
2.Spread this mixture over the cod fillets.
3.Put them in your air fryer and cook at 390 degrees f for 10 minutes.
4.Divide the fish between plates and serve.

Salmon With Almonds
Servings: 4
- 2red onions, chopped 2 tablespoons olive oil
- 2small fennel bulbs, trimmed and sliced
- ¼ cup almonds, toasted and sliced Salt and black pepper to taste
- 4salmon fillets, boneless
- 5 teaspoons fennel seeds, toasted

1.Season the fish with salt and pepper, grease it with 1 tablespoon of the oil, and place in your air fryer's basket.
1.Cook at 350 degrees f for 5-6 minutes on each side and divide between plates.
2.Heat a pan with the remaining tablespoon of oil over mediumhigh heat; add the onions, stir, and sauté for 2 minutes.
3.Add the fennel bulbs and seeds, almonds, salt, and pepper, and
4.cook for 2-3 minutes more.
5.Spread the mixture over the fish and serve right away; enjoy!

Mediterranean Flounder
Servings: 5
- 1¾ pound salmon fillets
- ¼ tsp salt
- 1tsp smoked paprika

- 1tsp ground dried ginger
- ¼ cup pitted olives
- ¼ cup sundried tomatoes
- ¼ cup capers
- 1tbsp fresh chopped dill 1/3 cup keto pesto sauce
1.Preheat your air fryer to 400 degrees f and line your air fryer tray with a long piece of parchment paper.
2.Place the flounder filets on the parchment and sprinkle with the
3.salt, paprika, and ginger and rub the spices into the fish.
4.Top the fish with the remaining and then wrap the parchment paper around the fish filets, enclosing them completely.

5. Place the tray in the air fryer and bake for 12 minutes.
6.Remove from the air fryer, unwrap the parchment.

Tomato Parchment Cod
Servings: 5
- 1¾ pound cod fillets
- ¼ tsp salt
- 1tsp smoked paprika
- 1tsp ground dried ginger
- ¼ cup pitted olives
- ¼ cup sundried tomatoes
- ¼ cup capers
- 1tbsp fresh chopped dill 1/3 cup keto marinara
1.Preheat your air fryer to 400 degrees f and line your air fryer tray
2.with a long piece of parchment paper.
3.Place the cod filets on the parchment and sprinkle with the salt, paprika, ginger, and rub the fish's spices.
4.Top the fish with the remaining and then wrap the parchment paper around the fish filets, enclosing them completely.
5.Place the tray in the a. fryer and bake for 15 minutes.
6.Remove from the air fryer, unwrap the parchment and serve while hot!

Italian Style Flounder
Servings: 5
    1¾ pound salmon fillets
- ¼ tsp salt
- tsp italian seasoning 1 cup baby spinach
- ¼ cup sundried tomatoes 1 tbsp fresh chopped dill 1/3 cup keto pesto sauce
1.Preheat your air fryer to 400 degrees f and line your air fryer tray with a long piece of parchment paper.
2.Place the flounder filets on the parchment and sprinkle with the salt and italian seasoning and rub the fish's spices.
3.Top the fish with the remaining and then wrap the parchment paper around the fish filets, enclosing them completely.
4.Place the tray in the air fryer and bake for 20 minutes.
5.Remove from the air fryer, unwrap the parchment and serve while hot!

Lemon Parchment Salmon
Servings: 5
- 1¾ pound salmon fillets

- ¼ tsp salt
- ½ tsp ground black pepper 2 cups baby spinach
- lemon, sliced thinly
1.Preheat your air fryer to 400 degrees f and line your air fryer tray with a long piece of parchment paper.
1.Place the salmon filets on the parchment and sprinkle with the salt and pepper and rub the fish's spices.
2.Top the fish with the remaining and then wrap the parchment paper around the fish filets, enclosing them completely.
3.Place the tray in the air fryer and bake for 20 minutes.
4.Remove from the air fryer, unwrap the parchment and serve while hot!

Prosciutto Wrapped Ahi Ahi
Servings: 2
- 1-pound cod ahi ahi
- ¼ tsp salt
- ¼ tsp ground black pepper
- 2oz prosciutto de parma, very thinly sliced 2 tbsp olive oil
- 1tsp minced garlic 4 cups baby spinach 2 tsp lemon juice
1.Preheat your air fryer to 325 degrees f and line your air fryer tray
2.with foil.
3.Dry the cod fillets by patting with a paper towel the sprinkle with salt and pepper.
4.Wrap the filets in the prosciutto, enclosing them as fully as possible.
5.Place the wrapped filets on the prepared tray.
6.Place the tray in the air fryer and bake for 10 minutes.
7.Toss the spinach with the olive oil, garlic and lemon juice andremove the tray from the air fryer and place the spinach mix on the tray as well, around the wrapped cod.
8.Place in the air fryer and bake for another 10 minutes. The spinach should be nicely wilted and the fish 145 degrees f internally.
9.Serve hot!

Prosciutto Wrapped Tuna Bites
Servings: 2
- 1-pound tuna cut into 1" pieces
- ¼ tsp salt
- ¼ tsp ground black pepper
- 2oz prosciutto de parma, very thinly sliced 2 tbsp olive oil
- tsp minced garlic 4 cups baby spinach 2 tsp lemon juice
1.Preheat your air fryer to 325 degrees f and line your air fryer tray with foil.
2.Dry the tuna bites by patting with a paper towel the sprinkle with salt and pepper.
3.Wrap the bites in the prosciutto, enclosing them as fully as possible.
4.Place the wrapped bites on the prepared tray.
5.Toss the spinach with the olive oil, garlic and lemon juice and place on the tray as well, around the wrapped tuna.
6.Place in the air fryer and bake for 12 minutes. The spinach should be nicely wilted and the fish 145 degrees f internally.

7.Serve hot!

Garlicy And Crab Stuffed Mushrooms
Servings: 5
- 1-pound cremini mushrooms, stems and gills removed
- ¾ pound fresh crab meat
- ¾ cup cream cheese, softened 1/3 cup grated cheddar cheese
- ¼ cup sour cream
- tbsp minced garlic 1 tbsp mustard
- ½ tsp salt
- ¼ tsp ground black pepper
- ½ cup grated parmesan

1.Preheat your air fryer to 375 degrees f and line your air fryer tray with foil or parchment.
1.Place the mushroom caps on the tray and bake for 10 minutes in the air fryer. Remove from the air fryer and drain any excess water from the tray.
2.In a large mixing bowl, combine all the remaining except the parmesan cheese. Stir well to fully blend everything.
3.Stuff the mushroom caps with the crab mix and then sprinkle the parmesan over the mushrooms' top.
4.Return the tray to the air fryer and bake for another 10 minutes or until the mushrooms' tops are golden brown.
5.Remove from the air fryer and enjoy while hot.

Black Pepper Flounder
Servings: 4
- 1-pound flounder filets
- ¾ tsp black pepper
- ½ tsp salt
- ¼ tsp garlic powder 2 tbsp softened butter

1.Preheat your air fryer to 450 degrees f and line your air fryer tray with foil.
2.Place the flounder filets on the foil lined tray.
3.In a small bowl combine the remaining and mix well to make a cohesive butter.
4.Spread the seasoned butter over the fish filets.
5.Bake the filets in the preheated oven for 8 minutes until nicely browned.
6.Serve while hot.

Parmesan Butter Flounder
Servings: 4
- 1-pound salmon filets
- ½ cup fresh grated parmesan
- ¼ tsp black pepper
- ½ tsp salt
- ¼ tsp garlic powder 2 tbsp softened butter

1.Preheat your air fryer to 450 degrees f and line your air fryer tray with foil.
2.Place the flounder filets on the foil lined tray.
3.In a small bowl combine the remaining and mix well to make a cohesive butter.
4.Spread the seasoned butter over the fish filets.
5.Bake the filets in the preheated oven for 8 minutes until nicely browned.
6.Serve while hot.

Herbed Butter Flounder

Servings: 4
- 1-pound flounder filets
- ½ cup fresh grated parmesan
- ¼ tsp black pepper
- ½ tsp salt
- ¼ tsp garlic powder
- ½ tsp dried basil
- ½ tsp dried thyme
- 2tbsp softened butter

1.Preheat your air fryer to 450 degrees f and line your air fryer tray with foil.
2.Place the flounder filets on the foil lined tray.
3.In a small bowl combine the remaining and mix well to make a cohesive butter.
4.Spread the seasoned butter over the fish filets.
5.Bake the filets in the preheated oven for 8 minutes until nicely browned.
6.Serve while hot.

Garlic Butter Shrimp
Servings: 4
- 1-pound shrimp, cleaned completely 5 tbsp butter, melted
- ½ tsp ground black pepper
- ½ tsp salt
- ½ cup vegetable stock 2 tbsp lemon juice
- ¼ cup minced garlic 2 tbsp parsley

1.Preheat your air fryer to 350 degrees f and line the air fryer tray or baking pan with foil.
2.Place the shrimp, butter, pepper, salt, vegetable stock, and garlic in a large bowl and toss together well. Pour the mix onto the prepared tray or pan.
3.Bake for 12 minutes, stirring occasionally to flip the shrimp.
4.Divide on to plates and garnish with the lemon juice and garlic. Enjoy hot!

Cajun Butter Shrimp
Servings: 4
- 1-pound shrimp, cleaned completely 5 tbsp butter, melted
- ½ tsp ground black pepper
- ½ tsp salt
- tsp cajun seasoning
- ½ cup vegetable stock 2 tbsp lemon juice
- tbsp parsley

1.Preheat your air fryer to 350 degrees f and line the air fryer tray or baking pan with foil.
2.Place the shrimp, butter, pepper, salt, cajun seasoning and vegetable stock in a large bowl and toss together well. Pour the mix onto the prepared tray or pan.
3.Bake for 12 minutes, stirring occasionally to flip the shrimp.
4.Divide on to plates and garnish with the lemon juice and garlic. Enjoy hot!

Salmon & Eggs
Servings: 2
- 2eggs
- 1lb. Salmon, seasoned and cooked 1 cup celery, chopped
- 1onion, chopped

- tablespoon olive oil Salt and pepper to taste

1. Whisk the eggs in a bowl. Add celery, onion, salt, and pepper.
2. Add the oil to round baking tray and pour in egg mixture. Place in air fryer on 300°fahrenheit. Let it cook for 10-minutes. When done, serve with cooked salmon.

Sweet Asian Style Salmon

Servings: 4

- 2garlic cloves, minced 1 tbsp fresh ginger paste 2 tsp fresh orange zest
- ½ cup fresh orange juice
- ¼ cup soy sauce
- 3tbsp plain vinegar 1 tbsp olive oil
- Salt to taste
- 4(5 oz) salmon fillets

1. In a large bowl, mix all the except for the fish and place the sauce's fish. Spoon the sauce well on top and cover thebowl with a plastic wrap. Allow marinating at room temperature for 30 minutes.
2. After 30 minutes, insert the dripping pan in the bottom part of the air fryer and preheat the oven at bake mode at 400 f for 2 to 3 minutes.
3. Using tongs, remove the fish from the sauce, making sure to shake
4. off some marinade of the fish and place the Cooking tray. You can work in two batches.
5. Slide the tray onto the oven's top rack, close the oven, and set the timer for 12 minutes, flipping the fish after 6 minutes.
6. Once ready, transfer the fish to serving plates and serve warm with
7. steamed greens.

Zesty Ranch Fish Fillets

Servings: 4

- ¾ cup finely crushed cornflakes or panko breadcrumbs
- 3tbsp dry ranch-style dressing mix 1 tsp fresh lemon zest
- 2½ tbsp olive oil 2 eggs, beaten
- 4white fish fillets
- Lemon wedges to garnish

1. Insert the dripping pan in the bottom part of the air fryer and preheat the oven at air fry mode at 400 f for 2 to 3 minutes.
2. Mix the cornflakes, dressing mix, lemon zest, and oil on a shallow
3. plate and then pour the eggs on another.
4. Working in two batches, dip the fish into the egg, drip off excess egg, and coat well in the cornflake's mixture on both sides.
5. Place the fish on the Cooking tray and fix the tray on the middle rack of the oven. Close the oven and set the timer for 13 minutes and cook until the fish is golden brown and the fish flaky within.
6. Transfer to a serving plate and serve with the lemon wedges.

Easy Fish Sticks With Chili Ketchup Sauce

Servings: 4

- 8fish sticks, store bought
- ½ cup tomato ketchup 1 tbsp sriracha sauce
- 1tbsp chopped fresh parsley to garnish Sliced pickles for serving

1. Insert the dripping pan in the bottom part of the air fryer and
1. preheat the oven at air fry mode at 390 f for 2 to 3 minutes.
2. Arrange the fish sticks on the Cooking tray and fit onto the middle rack of the oven. Close and set the timer for 12 minutes and cook until the fish sticks are golden brown and crispy.
3. Meanwhile, in a small bowl, mix the tomato ketchup, sriracha
4. sauce, and parsley until well combined and set aside for serving.
5. When the fish is ready, transfer onto serving plates and serve warm with the sauce and pickles.

Basil Cod

Servings: 4

- 4cod fillets; boneless
- 2tbsp. Olive oil 1 tsp. Basil; dried
- 1tsp. Red pepper flakes
- ½tsp. Hot paprika
- Salt and black pepper to taste.

1. Take a bowl and mix the cod with all the other and toss.
2. Put the fish in your air fryer's basket and cook at 380°f for 15 minutes. Divide the cod between plates and serve

Lime Baked Salmon

Servings: 2

- 2(3-oz. Salmon fillets, skin removed
- ¼ cup sliced pickled jalapeños
- ½ medium lime, juiced 2 tbsp. Chopped cilantro
- 1tbsp. Salted butter; melted.
- ½ tsp. Finely minced garlic 1 tsp. Chili powder

1. Place salmon fillets into a 6-inch round baking pan. Brush each with butter and sprinkle with chili powder and garlic
2. Place jalapeño slices on top and around salmon. Pour half of the lime juice over the salmon and cover with foil. Place pan into the air fryer basket. Adjust the temperature to 370 degrees f and set the timer for 12 minutes
3. When fully cooked, salmon should flake easily with a fork and reach an internal temperature of at least 145 degrees f.
4. To serve, spritz with remaining lime juice and garnish with cilantro.

Sea Bass And Fennel

Servings: 2

- ¼ cup black olives, pitted and sliced 2 sea bass, fillets
- ¼ cup basil; chopped.
- 1fennel bulb; sliced Juice of 1 lemon
- 1tbsp. Olive oil
- A pinch of salt and black pepper

1. In a pan that fits the air fryer, combine all the .
2. Introduce the pan in the machine and cook at 380°f for 20 minutes, shaking the fryer halfway.
3. Divide between plates and serve

Snapper And Spring Onions

Servings: 4

- 4snapper fillets; boneless and skin scored 6 spring

- onions; chopped.
- Juice of ½ lemon 3 tbsp. Olive oil
- 2tbsp. Sweet paprika
- A pinch of salt and black pepper

1.Take a bowl and mix the paprika with the rest of the except the fish and whisk well
2.Rub the fish with this mix, place the fillets in your air fryer's basket and cook at 390°f for 7 minutes on each side.
3.Divide between plates and serve with a side salad.

Herbed Trout And Asparagus

Servings: 4
- 4trout fillets; boneless and skinless
- 1bunch asparagus; trimmed
- ¼ cup mixed chives and tarragon 2 tbsp. Ghee; melted
- tbsp. Olive oil
- 1tbsp. Lemon juice
- A pinch of salt and black pepper

1.Mix the asparagus with half of the oil, salt and pepper, put it in your air fryer's basket, cook at 380°f for 6 minutes and divide between plates
2.Take a bowl and mix the trout with salt, pepper, lemon juice, the rest of the oil and the herbs and toss,
3.Put the fillets in your air fryer's basket and cook at 380°f for 7 minutes on each side
4.Divide the fish next to the asparagus, drizzle the melted ghee all over and serve

Trout And Zucchinis

Servings: 4
- 3zucchinis, cut in medium chunks 4 trout fillets; boneless
- ¼ cup tomato sauce
- 1garlic clove; minced
- ½ cup cilantro; chopped. 1 tbsp. Lemon juice
- 2tbsp. Olive oil
- Salt and black pepper to taste.

1.In a pan that fits your air fryer, mix the fish with the other , toss, introduce in the fryer and cook at 380°f for 15 minutes.
2.Divide everything between plates and serve right away

Flounder Fillets

Servings: 4
- 4flounder fillets; boneless 1 cup parmesan; grated
- 2tbsp. Olive oil
- 4tbsp. Butter; melted
- A pinch of salt and black pepper

1.Take a bowl and mix the parmesan with salt, pepper, butter and the oil and stir well.
1.Arrange the fish in a pan that fits the air fryer, spread the parmesan mix all over, introduce in the fryer and cook at 400°f for 20 minutes
2.Divide between plates and serve with a side salad.

Japanese-Style Fried Prawns

Servings: 2
- 1pound of peeled and deveined prawns
- 1cup of rice flour
- 1cup of panko breadcrumbs 2 eggs
- 1teaspoon of ground ginger 1 tablespoon of paprika

- 1teaspoon of salt
- 1teaspoon of black pepper 1 teaspoon of garlic powder

1.Preheat your air fryer to 380 degrees fahrenheit.
2.Using a bowl, add the prawns, salt, black pepper, garlic powder, ground ginger and toss until it is properly mixed.
3.Then using another bowl, add the rice flour, paprika and mix it well. Pick a second bowl, add the eggs and beat it properly. Then using a third bowl, add the panko breadcrumbs.
4.Dredge the seasoned prawns into the flour, dip it into the egg wash, and then cover it with the panko breadcrumbs.
5.Grease your air fryer basket with a nonstick Cooking spray and add the prawns.
6.Cook it for 8 minutes or until it has a golden-brown color and repeat if necessary.
7.Serve and enjoy!

Great Air-Fried Soft-Shell Crab

Servings: 2
- 2soft-shell crabs 1 cup of flour
- 2beaten eggs
- 1cup of panko breadcrumbs 1 teaspoon of onion powder 1 teaspoon of garlic powder 1 teaspoon of salt
- 1teaspoon of black pepper

1.Preheat your air fryer to 360 degrees fahrenheit.
2.Use a bowl, add the flour, pick a second bowl, and add the eggs and mix properly. Then using a third bowl, mix the panko breadcrumbs and the seasonings properly.
3.Grease your air fryer basket with a nonstick Cooking spray and add the crabs inside.
4.Cook it inside your air fryer for 8 minutes or until it has a goldenbrown color.
5.After that, carefully remove it from your air fryer and allow it to cool off.
6.Serve and enjoy!

Stunning Air-Fried Clams

Servings: 2
- 1(10-ounce) can of whole baby clams, drained and shucked 2 beaten eggs
- 1cup of flour
- 1cup of panko breadcrumbs 1 teaspoon of salt
- 1teaspoon of black pepper 1 teaspoon of garlic powder
- 1teaspoon of onion powder 1 teaspoon of cayenne pepper
- 1tablespoon of dried oregano

1.Preheat your air fryer to 390 degrees fahrenheit.
1.Use a bowl, add the flour, pick a second bowl, and add the eggs and mix properly. Using a third bowl, add and mix the panko breadcrumbs, seasonings, and the herbs properly.
2.Dredge the clams in the flour, immerse it into the egg wash and
3.then cover it with the breadcrumb mixture.
4.Place the clams inside your air fryer and cook it for 2 minutes or until it has a golden-brown color, while being cautious of overCooking .
5.After that, carefully remove it from your air fryer and allow it to cool.
6.Serve and enjoy!

Tabasco Shrimp

Servings: 2

- ½ pound shrimp, peeled and deveined
- ½ teaspoon red pepper flakes
- ½ tablespoon olive oil
- ½ teaspoon tabasco sauce 1 tablespoon water
- ½ teaspoon dried oregano Salt and black pepper, to taste
- ¼ teaspoon dried parsley
- ¼ teaspoon smoked paprika

1.In a bowl, mix water, oil, tabasco sauce, shrimp, paprika, pepper, salt, parsley, oregano, and pepper flakes. Coat well.
2. Transfer shrimp to preheated air fryer at 370f and cook for 10 minutes. Shake once midway through.
3.Serve.

Buttered Shrimp Skewers

Servings: 2

- 8shrimps, peeled and deveined 4 cloves garlic, minced
- Salt and black pepper, to taste 8 green bell pepper slices
- 1tablespoon rosemary, chopped 1 tablespoon butter, melted

1.In a bowl, mix bell pepper slices, rosemary, pepper, salt, butter, garlic, and shrimp. Toss to coat and marinate for 10 minutes.
2.Arrange 2 bell pepper slices and 2 shrimp on a skewer. Repeat with the rest of the shrimp and bell pepper pieces.
3.Cook the skewers at 360f for 6 minutes.
4.Serve.

Asian Salmon

Servings: 2

- 2medium salmon fillets
- 6tablespoons light soy sauce 3 tablespoons mirin
- 1teaspoon water
- 6tablespoons honey

1.Mix soy sauce with water, honey, mirin, and whisk well. Add salmon, rub well and marinate in the refrigerator for 1 hour.
2.Cook at 360f for 15 minutes in the air-fryer. Flip once after 7 minutes.
3.Meanwhile, put the soy marinade in a pan, and bring to a simmer. Whisk on medium heat for 2 minutes.
4.Divide salmon on plates. Drizzle with the marinade and serve.

Shrimp And Crab Mix

Servings: 2

- ¼ cup yellow onion, chopped
- ½ cup green bell pepper, chopped
- ½ cup celery, chopped
- ½ cup shrimp, peeled and deveined
- ½ cup crabmeat, flaked
- ½ cup mayonnaise
- ½ teaspoon worcestershire sauce Salt and black pepper, to taste
- 1tablespoon breadcrumbs
- ½ tablespoon butter, melted
- ½ teaspoon sweet paprika

1.In a bowl, mix crab meat, shrimp, onion, bell pepper, celery, mayo, salt, pepper, and worcestershire sauce. Transfer to a pan.
1.Add melted butter, paprika, and breadcrumbs. Coat well and place
2.in the air fryer.
3.Cook at 320f for 25 minutes. Shake once at the halfway mark.
4.Serve.

Trout With Butter Sauce

Servings: 2

- 2trout fillets, boneless
- Salt and black pepper, to taste
- ½ teaspoons lemon zest, grated 1 ½ tablespoons chives, chopped 3 tablespoons butter
- 1tablespoon olive oil
- 1teaspoon lemon juice

1.Season trout with salt and pepper. Drizzle with oil and rub well.
2.Cook in the air fryer at 360f for 10 minutes. Flip once.
3.Meanwhile, heat a pan with the butter over medium heat. Add lemon juice, zest, chives, salt, and pepper. Whisk well and cook for 2 minutes, then remove from heat.
4.Divide fish fillets on plates. Drizzle with butter sauce and serve.

Crab Legs In Lemon Butter

Servings: 2

- 2tablespoons salted butter, melted and divided 1 ½ pounds crab legs
- ¼ teaspoon garlic powder Juice of ½ lemon

1.Drizzle 1 tablespoon butter over crab legs. Place crab legs into the air fryer basket.
1.Cook at 400f for 15 minutes. Flip the crab legs halfway through thecooking time.
2.Mix garlic powder, lemon juice, and remaining butter in a bowl.
3.Open crab legs and remove meat.
4.Dip in lemon butter and serve.

Lobster Tails

Servings: 2

- 2(6-ounce) lobster tails, halved
- 2tablespoons salted butter, melted
- ½ teaspoon old bay seasoning Juice of ½ lemon
- 1teaspoon dried parsley

1.Place two halved tails on a sheet of aluminum foil.
2.Drizzle with lemon juice, seasoning, and butter.
3.Seal the foil packets.
4.Place into the air fryer basket and cook at 375f for 12 minutes.
5.Sprinkle with dried parsley and serve.

Tuna Steak

Servings: 2

- 2(6-ounce) tuna steaks
- 1tablespoon coconut oil, melted
- ½ teaspoon garlic powder
- 2teaspoons white sesame seeds 2 teaspoons black sesame seeds

1. Brush each tuna steak with coconut oil and sprinkle with garlic powder.
2. In a bowl, mix sesame seeds and press each tuna steak into them. Coat well.
3. Place tuna steaks into the air fryer basket.
4. Cook at 400f for 8 minutes.
5. Flip steaks halfway through the Cooking time.
6. Serve.

Crab Cakes

Servings: 2

- 1(6-ounce) can lump crabmeat
- 2 tablespoons almond flour 1 egg
- 1 tablespoon full-Fat mayonnaise
- ½ teaspoon dijon mustard 1 teaspoon lemon juice
- ¼ bell pepper, seeded and chopped 2 tablespoons green onion
- ¼ teaspoon old bay seasoning
  1. Combine all in a bowl.
  2. Make 2 balls and flatten into patties.
  3. Place patties into the air fryer basket.
  4. Cook at 350f for 10 minutes.
  5. Flip patties halfway through the Cooking time.
  6. Serve.

Hot Prawns

Servings: 2

- 6 prawns
- ½ teaspoon chili powder 1 teaspoon chili flakes
- ¼ teaspoon black pepper
- ¼ teaspoon salt
1. preheat the air fryer to 350f.
2. in a bowl, add prawns and spices and mix well.
3. spray air fryer basket with Cooking spray, then cook for 8 minutes. Shake once.
5. serve.

Meat Recipes

Pork And Mixed Greens Salad

Servings: 4

- pounds pork tenderloin, cut into 1-inch slices 1 teaspoon olive oil
- teaspoon dried marjoram
- ⅛ teaspoon freshly ground black pepper 6 cups mixed salad greens
- red bell pepper, sliced
- 1 (8-ounce) package button mushrooms, sliced
- ⅓ cup low-Sodium low-Fat vinaigrette dressing

1. In a medium bowl, mix the pork slices and olive oil. Toss to coat.
2. Sprinkle with the marjoram and pepper and rub these into the pork.
3. Grill the pork in the air fryer, in batches, for about 4 to 6 minutes, or until the pork reaches at least 145°f on a meat thermometer.
4. Meanwhile, in a serving bowl, mix the salad greens, red bell pepper, and mushrooms. Toss gently.
5. When the pork is cooked, add the slices to the salad. drizzle with the vinaigrette and toss gently. Serve immediately.

Pork Satay

Servings: 4

- 1(1-pound) pork tenderloin, cut into 1½-inch cubes
- ¼ cup minced onion
- 2 garlic cloves, minced
- 1 jalapeño pepper, minced
- 2 tablespoons freshly squeezed lime juice 2 tablespoons coconut milk
- **2** tablespoons unsalted peanut butter 2 teaspoons curry powder

1. In a medium bowl, mix the pork, onion, garlic, jalapeño, lime juice,
2. coconut milk, peanut butter, and curry powder until well combined. Let stand for 10 minutes at room temperature.
3. With a slotted spoon, remove the pork from the marinade. Reserve the marinade.
4. Thread the pork onto about 8 bamboo or metal skewers. Grill for 9 to 14 minutes, brushing once with the reserved marinade, until the pork reaches at least 145°f on a meat thermometer. Discard any remaining marinade. Serve immediately.

Crispy Mustard Pork Tenderloin

Servings: 4

- 3 tablespoons low-Sodium grainy mustard 2 teaspoons olive oil
- ¼ teaspoon dry mustard powder
- (1-pound) pork tenderloin, silver skin and excess Fat trimmed and discarded
- 2 slices low-Sodium whole-wheat bread, crumbled
- ¼ cup ground walnuts
- 2 tablespoons cornstarch
  1. In a small bowl, stir together the mustard, olive oil, and mustard powder. Spread this mixture over the pork.
  2. On a plate, mix the breadcrumbs, walnuts, and cornstarch. Dip the mustard-coated pork into the crumb mixture to coat.
  3. Air-fry the pork for 12 to 16 minutes, or until it registers at least 145°f on a meat thermometer. Slice to serve.

Apple Pork Tenderloin

Servings: 4

- 1(1-pound) pork tenderloin, cut into 4 pieces 1 tablespoon apple butter
- 2 teaspoons olive oil
- 2 granny smith apples or jonagold apples, sliced 3 celery stalks, sliced
- onion, sliced
- ½ teaspoon dried marjoram
- ⅓ cup apple juice
  1. Rub each piece of pork with the apple butter and olive oil.
  2. In a medium metal bowl, mix the pork, apples, celery, onion, marjoram, and apple juice.
  3. Place the bowl into the air fryer and roast for 14 to 19 minutes, or until the pork reaches at least 145°f on a meat thermometer and the apples and vegetables are tender.
  4. Stir once during Cooking . Serve immediately.

Espresso-Grilled Pork Tenderloin

Servings: 4

- 1tablespoon packed brown Sugar 2 teaspoons espresso powder
- 1teaspoon ground paprika
- ½ teaspoon dried marjoram 1 tablespoon honey
- 1tablespoon freshly squeezed lemon juice
- 2teaspoons olive oil
- (1-pound) pork tenderloin

1.In a small bowl, mix the brown Sugar, espresso powder, paprika, and marjoram.

2.Stir in the honey, lemon juice, and olive oil until well mixed.

3.Spread the honey mixture over the pork and let stand for 10 minutes at room temperature.

4.Roast the tenderloin in the air fryer basket for 9 to 11 minutes, or until the pork registers at least 145°f on a meat thermometer. Slice the meat to serve.

Pork And Potatoes

Servings: 4
- 2cups creamer potatoes, rinsed and dried 2 teaspoons olive oil
- (1-pound) pork tenderloin, cut into 1-inch cubes 1 onion, chopped
- 1red bell pepper, chopped 2 garlic cloves, minced
- ½ teaspoon dried oregano
- 2tablespoons low-Sodium chicken broth

1.In a medium bowl, toss the potatoes and olive oil to coat.

2.Transfer the potatoes to the air fryer basket. Roast for 15 minutes.

3.In a medium metal bowl, mix the potatoes, pork, onion, red bell pepper, garlic, and oregano.

4.Drizzle with the chicken broth. Put the bowl in the air fryer basket.

5.Roast for about 10 minutes more, shaking the basket once during Cooking, until the pork reaches at least 145°f on a meat thermometer and the potatoes are tender. Serve immediately.

Pork And Fruit Kebabs

Servings: 4
- ⅓ cup apricot jam
- 2tablespoons freshly squeezed lemon juice 2 teaspoons olive oil
- ½ teaspoon dried tarragon
- 1(1-pound) pork tenderloin, cut into 1-inch cubes 4 plums, pitted and quartered
- 4small apricots, pitted and halved

1.In a large bowl, mix the jam, lemon juice, olive oil, and tarragon.

2.Add the pork and stir to coat. Let stand for 10 minutes at room temperature.

3.Alternating the items, thread the pork, plums, and apricots onto 4 metal skewers that fit into the air fryer. Brush with any remaining jam mixture. Discard any remaining marinade.

4.Grill the kebabs in the air fryer for 9 to 12 minutes, or until the pork reaches 145°f on a meat thermometer and the fruit is tender. Serve immediately.

Steak And Vegetable Kebabs

Servings: 4

- 2tablespoons balsamic vinegar 2 teaspoons olive oil
- ½ teaspoon dried marjoram
- ⅛ teaspoon freshly ground black pepper
- ¾ pound round steak, cut into 1-inch pieces 1 red bell pepper, sliced
- 16button mushrooms
- 1cup cherry tomatoes

1.In a medium bowl, stir together the balsamic vinegar, olive oil, marjoram, and black pepper.

2.Add the steak and stir to coat. Let stand for 10 minutes at room temperature.

3.Alternating items thread the beef, red bell pepper, mushrooms, and tomatoes onto 8 bamboo or metal skewers that fit in the air fryer.

4.Grill in the air fryer for 5 to 7 minutes, or until the beef is browned and reaches at least 145°f on a meat thermometer. Serve immediately.

Spicy Grilled Steak

Servings:4
- 2tablespoons low-Sodium salsa
- 1tablespoon minced chipotle pepper 1 tablespoon apple cider vinegar
- 1teaspoon ground cumin
- ⅛ teaspoon freshly ground black pepper
- ⅛ teaspoon red pepper flakes
- ¾ pound sirloin tip steak, cut into 4 pieces and gently pounded to about ⅓ inch thick

1.In a small bowl, thoroughly mix the salsa, chipotle pepper, cider vinegar, cumin, black pepper, and red pepper flakes. Rub this mixture into both sides of each steak piece. Let stand for 15 minutes at room temperature.

2.Grill the steaks in the air fryer, two at a time, for 6 to 9 minutes, or until they reach at least 145°f on a meat thermometer.

3.Remove the steaks to a clean plate and cover with aluminum foil to keep

4.warm. Repeat with the remaining steaks.

5.Slice the steaks thinly against the grain and serve.

Greek Vegetable Skillet

Servings:4
- ½ pound 96 percent lean ground beef 2 medium tomatoes, chopped
- 1onion, chopped
- 2garlic cloves, minced
- 2cups fresh baby spinach
- 2tablespoons freshly squeezed lemon juice
- ⅓ cup low-Sodium beef broth
- 2tablespoons crumbled low-Sodium feta cheese

1.In a 6-by-2-inch metal pan, crumble the beef. Cooking time: in the air fryer for 3 to 7 minutes, stirring once during Cooking, until browned. Drain off any Fat or liquid.

2.Add the tomatoes, onion, and garlic to the pan. Air-fry for 4 to 8 minutes more, or until the onion is tender.

3.Add the spinach, lemon juice, and beef broth. Air-fry for 2 to 4 minutes more, or until the spinach is wilted.

4.Sprinkle with the feta cheese and serve immediately.

Light Herbed Meatballs

Servings:24 meatballs
- 1medium onion, minced 2 garlic cloves, minced 1 teaspoon olive oil
- 1slice low-Sodium whole-wheat bread, crumbled
- 3tablespoons 1 percent milk 1 teaspoon dried marjoram
- 1teaspoon dried basil
- 1-pound 96 percent lean ground beef

1.In a 6-by-2-inch pan, combine the onion, garlic, and olive oil. Airfry for 2 to 4 minutes, or until the vegetables are crisp-tender.

2.Transfer the vegetables to a medium bowl, and add the breadcrumbs, milk, marjoram, and basil. Mix well.

3. Add the ground beef. With your hands, work the mixture gently but thoroughly until combined. Form the meat mixture into about 24 (1-inch) meatballs.

4.Bake the meatballs, in batches, in the air fryer basket for 12 to 17 minutes, or until they reach 160°f on a meat thermometer. Serve immediately.

(6 meatballs)

Beef And Broccoli

Servings:4
- 2tablespoons cornstarch
- ½ cup low-Sodium beef broth
- 1teaspoon low-Sodium soy sauce
- 12ounces sirloin strip steak, cut into 1-inch cubes 2½ cups broccoli florets
- 1onion, chopped
- 1cup sliced cremini mushrooms 1 tablespoon grated fresh ginger Brown rice, cooked (optional)

1.In a medium bowl, stir together the cornstarch, beef broth, and soy

2.sauce.

3.Add the beef and toss to coat. Let stand for 5 minutes at room temperature.

4.With a slotted spoon, transfer the beef from the broth mixture into a medium metal bowl. Reserve the broth.

5.Add the broccoli, onion, mushrooms, and ginger to the beef. Place

6.the bowl into the air fryer and cook for 12 to 15 minutes, or until the beef reaches at least 145°f on a meat thermometer and the vegetables are tender.

7.Add the reserved broth and cooked for 2 to 3 minutes more, or until the sauce boils.

8.Serve immediately over hot cooked brown rice, if desired.

Pork Chops

Servings:5
- 4slices of almond bread
- 5pork chops, bone-in, pastured ounces coconut flour
- 1teaspoon salt
- 3tablespoons parsley
- ½ teaspoon ground black pepper 1 tablespoon pork seasoning
- 2tablespoons olive oil
- 1/3 cup apple juice, unsweetened 1 egg, pastured

1.Switch on the air fryer, insert fryer basket, grease it with olive oil, then shut with its lid, set the fryer at 350 degrees f and preheat for 5 minutes.

2.Meanwhile, place bread slices in a food processor and pulse until mixture resembles crumbs.

3.Tip the breadcrumbs in a shallow dish, add parsley, ½ teaspoon salt, ¼ teaspoon ground black pepper and stir until mixed.

4.Place flour in another shallow dish, add remaining salt and black pepper, and pork seasoning and stir until mixed.

5.Crack the egg in a bowl, pour in apple juice and whisk until

6.combined.

7.Working on one pork chop at a time, first coat it into the flour mixture, then dip into egg and then evenly coat with breadcrumbs mixture.

8. Open the fryer, add coated pork chops in it in a single layer, close with its lid and cook for 10 minutes until nicely golden and cooked, flipping the pork chops halfway through the frying.

9.When air fryer beeps, open its lid, transfer pork chops onto a serving plate and serve.

Pork Belly

Servings:4
- 1-pound pork belly, pastured 6 cloves of garlic, peeled
- 1teaspoon ground black pepper
- 1teaspoon salt
- 2tablespoons soy sauce 2 bay leaves
- 3cups of water

1.Cut the pork belly evenly into three pieces, place them in an instant pot, and add remaining .

2.Switch on the instant pot, then shut it with lid and cook the pork belly for 15 minutes at high pressure.

3.When done, let the pressure release naturally for 10 minutes andthen do quick pressure release.

4.Rake out the pork by tongs and let it drain and dry for 10 minutes.

5.Then switch on the air fryer, insert fryer basket, grease it with olive oil, then shut with its lid, set the fryer at 400 degrees f and preheat

6.for 5 minutes.

7.While the air fryer preheats, cut each piece of the pork into two long slices.

8.Open the fryer, add pork slices in it, close with its lid and cook for 15 minutes until nicely golden and crispy, flipping the pork halfway through the frying.

9.When air fryer beeps, open its lid, transfer pork slices onto a serving plate.

Sirloin Steak

Servings:6

- 2 sirloin steaks, grass-fed
- 1 tablespoon olive oil
- 1 tablespoons steak seasoning

1.Switch on the air fryer, insert fryer basket, grease it with olive oil, then shut with its lid, set the fryer at 392 degrees f and preheat for 5 minutes.

2.Meanwhile, pat dries the steaks, brush with oil and then season well with steak seasoning until coated on both sides.

3.Open the fryer, add steaks in it, close with its lid and cook for 10 minutes until nicely golden and crispy, flipping the steaks halfway through the frying.
4.When air fryer beeps, open its lid, transfer steaks onto a serving plate.

Vietnamese Grilled Pork

Servings:6
- 1-pound sliced pork shoulder, pastured, Fat trimmed 2 tablespoons chopped parsley
- 1/4 cup crushed roasted peanuts

For The Marinade:
- 1/4 cup minced white onions 1 tablespoon minced garlic
- 1tablespoon lemongrass paste
- 1tablespoon erythritol sweetener 1/2 teaspoon ground black pepper 1 tablespoon fish sauce
- 2teaspoons soy sauce
- 2tablespoons olive oil

1.Place all the for the marinade in a bowl, stir well until combined and add it into a large plastic bag.
2.Cut the pork into ½-inch slices, cut each slice into 1-inches pieces, then add them into the plastic bag containing marinade, seal the bag, turn it upside down to coat the pork pieces with the marinade and marinate for a minimum of 1 hour.
3.Then switch on the air fryer, insert fryer basket, grease it with olive oil, then shut with its lid, set the fryer at 400 degrees f and preheat
4.for 5 minutes.
5.Open the fryer, add marinated pork in it in a single layer, close with its lid and cook for 10 minutes until nicely golden and cooked, flipping the pork halfway through the frying.
6.When air fryer beeps, open its lid, transfer pork onto a serving
7.plate, and keep warm.
8.Air fryer the remaining pork pieces in the same manner.

Meatloaf

Servings:4
- 1-pound ground beef, grass-fed 1 tablespoon minced garlic
- 1cup white onion, peeled and diced 1 tablespoon minced ginger
- 1/4 cup chopped cilantro 2 teaspoons garam masala
- 1teaspoon cayenne pepper 1 teaspoon salt
- 1/2 teaspoon ground cinnamon
- 1teaspoon turmeric powder 1/8 teaspoon ground cardamom 2 eggs, pastured

1.Switch on the air fryer, insert fryer basket, then shut with its lid, set the fryer at 360 degrees f and preheat for 5 minutes.
2.Meanwhile, place all the in a bowl, stir until well mixed, then take an 8-inches round pan, grease it with oil, add the beef mixture in it and spread it evenly.
3.Open the fryer, place the pan in it, close with its lid and cook for 15 minutes until the top is nicely golden and meatloaf is thoroughly cooked.
4.When air fryer beeps, open its lid, take out the pan, drain the excess fat, and take out the meatloaf.

5.Cut the meatloaf into four pieces.

Herbed Lamb Chops

Servings:6
1-pound lamb chops, pastured
For The Marinate:
- 2tablespoons lemon juice 1 teaspoon dried rosemary 1 teaspoon salt
- 1teaspoon dried thyme 1 teaspoon coriander
- 1teaspoon dried oregano 2 tablespoons olive oil

1.Prepare the marinade and for this, place all its in a bowl and whisk until combined.
2.Pour the marinade in a large plastic bag, add lamb chops in it, seal the bag, turn it upside down to coat lamb chops with the marinade, and let it marinate in the refrigerator minimum of 1 hour.
3.Then switch on the air fryer, insert fryer basket, grease it with olive oil, then shut with its lid, set the fryer at 390 degrees f and preheat
4.for 5 minutes.
5.Meanwhile,
6.Open the fryer, add marinated lamb chops in it, close with its lid and cook for 8 minutes until nicely golden and cooked, turning the lamb chops halfway through the frying.
7.When air fryer beeps, open its lid, transfer lamb chops onto a serving plate.

Spicy Lamb Sirloin Steak

Servings:
- 1-pound lamb sirloin steaks, pastured, boneless
For The Marinade:
- ½ of white onion, peeled
- 1teaspoon ground fennel 5 cloves of garlic, peeled 4 slices of ginger
- 1teaspoon salt
- 1/2 teaspoon ground cardamom 1 teaspoon garam masala
- 1teaspoon ground cinnamon 1 teaspoon cayenne pepper

1.Place all the for the marinade in a food processor and then pulse until well blended.
2.Make cuts in the lamb chops by using a knife, then place them in a large bowl and add prepared marinade in it.
3.Mix well until lamb chops are coated with the marinade and let
4.them marinate in the refrigerator for a minimum of 30 minutes.
5.Then switch on the air fryer, insert fryer basket, grease it with olive oil, then shut with its lid, set the fryer at 330 degrees f and preheat
6.for 5 minutes.
7.Open the fryer, add lamb chops in it, close with its lid and cook for 15 minutes until nicely golden and cooked, flipping the steaks halfway through the frying.
8.When air fryer beeps, open its lid, transfer lamb steaks onto a serving plate and serve.

Garlic Rosemary Lamb Chops

Servings:4
- 4lamb chops, pastured
- 1teaspoon ground black pepper 2 teaspoons minced garlic

- ½ teaspoon salt
- 2teaspoons olive oil
- 4 cloves of garlic, peeled 4 rosemary sprigs

1.Take the fryer pan, place lamb chops in it, season the top with ½
2.teaspoon black pepper and ¾ teaspoon salt, then drizzle evenly with oil and spread with 1 teaspoon minced garlic.
3.Add garlic cloves and rosemary and then let the lamb chops marinate in the pan into the refrigerator for a minimum of 1 hour.
4.Then switch on the air fryer, insert fryer pan, then shut with its lid,
5.set the fryer at 360 degrees f and cook for 6 minutes.
6.Flip the lamb chops, season them with remaining salt and black pepper, add remaining minced garlic and continue Cooking for 6 minutes or until lamb chops are cooked.
7.When air fryer beeps, open its lid, transfer lamb chops onto a serving plate and serve.

Double Cheeseburger

Servings: 1
- 2beef patties, pastured
- 1/8 teaspoon onion powder
- 2slices of mozzarella cheese, low Fat 1/8 teaspoon ground black pepper
- 1/8 teaspoon salt

1.Switch on the air fryer, insert fryer basket, grease it with olive oil, then shut with its lid, set the fryer at 370 degrees f and preheat for 5 minutes.
2.Meanwhile, season the patties well with onion powder, black pepper, and salt.
3.Open the fryer, add beef patties in it, close with its lid and cook for 4 minutes until nicely golden and cooked, flipping the patties halfway through the frying.
4.Then top the patties with a cheese slice and continue Cooking for 1 minute or until cheese melts.

Steak Bites With Mushrooms

Servings:3
- 1-pound sirloin steaks, grass-fed 1/2 teaspoon garlic powder
- 8ounces mushrooms, halved
- ¾ teaspoon ground black pepper 1 teaspoon worcestershire sauce 1 teaspoon salt
- 2tablespoons olive oil
- 1teaspoon minced parsley

1.Switch on the air fryer, insert fryer basket, grease it with olive oil, then shut with its lid, set the fryer at 400 degrees f and preheat for 5 minutes.
2.Meanwhile, cut the steaks into 1-inch pieces, then add them in a bowl, add remaining except for parsley and toss until well coated.
3.Open the fryer, add steaks and mushrooms in it in a single layer, close with its lid and cook for 10 to 18 minutes or until steaks and mushrooms are cooked to desired doneness, stirring and shaking
4.the basket halfway through the frying.
5.When air fryer beeps, open its lid, transfer steaks and mushrooms onto a serving plate and keep warm.
6.Cook remaining steaks and mushroom in the same manner, then garnish with parsley and serve.

Easy Rib Eye Steak

Servings:4
- 2lbs. Rib eye steak
- 1tablespoon olive oil
- 1tablespoon steak rub*

1.Set the temperature of air fryer to 400 degrees f. Grease an air fryer basket.
2.Coat the steak with oil and then, generously rub with steak rub.
3.Place steak into the prepared air fryer basket.
4.Air fry for about 14 minutes, flipping once halfway through.
5.Remove from air fryer and place the steak onto a cutting board for about 10 minutes before slicing.
6.Cut the steak into desired size slices and transfer onto serving plates.

Buttered Striploin Steak

Servings:2
- (7-ounces) striploin steak
- 1½ tablespoons butter, softened
- Salt and ground black pepper, as required

1.Coat each steak evenly with butter and then, season with salt and black pepper.
2.Set the temperature of air fryer to 392 degrees f. Grease an air fryer basket.
3.Arrange steaks into the prepared air fryer basket.
4.Air fry for about 8-12 minutes.
5.Remove from air fryer and transfer the steaks onto serving plates.
6.Serve hot.

Crispy Sirloin Steak

Servings:2
1 cup white flour
2 eggs
1 cup panko breadcrumbs 1 teaspoon garlic powder 1 teaspoon onion powder
Salt and ground black pepper, as required
2 (6-ounces) sirloin steaks, pounded
1.In a shallow bowl, place the flour.
2. Crack the eggs in a second bowl and beat well.
3.In a third bowl, mix the panko and spices.
4.Coat each steak with the white flour, then dip into beaten eggs and finally, coat with panko mixture.
5.Set the temperature of air fryer to 360 degrees f. Grease an air fryer basket.
6.Arrange steaks into the prepared air fryer basket.
7.Air fry for about 10 minutes.
8.Remove from air fryer and transfer the steaks onto the serving plates.
9.Serve immediately.

Spiced & Herbed Skirt Steak

Servings: 3
- 3garlic cloves, minced
- 1cup fresh parsley leaves, finely chopped
- 3tablespoons fresh oregano, finely chopped
- 3tablespoons fresh mint leaves, finely chopped 1 tablespoon ground cumin
- 2teaspoons smoked paprika 1 teaspoon cayenne pepper
- 1teaspoon red pepper flakes, crushed Salt and ground black pepper, as required
- ¾ cup olive oil

- 3tablespoons red wine vinegar 2 (8-ounces) skirt steaks

1. In a bowl, mix the garlic, herbs, spices, oil, and vinegar.
2. In a resalable bag, place ¼ cup of the herb mixture and steaks.
3. Seal the bag and shake to coat well.
4. Refrigerate for about 24 hours.
5. Reserve the remaining herb mixture in refrigerator.
6. Take out the steaks from fridge and place at room temperature for about 30 minutes.
7. Set the temperature of air fryer to 390 degrees f. Grease an air fryer
8. basket.
9. Arrange steaks into the prepared air fryer basket.
10. Air fry for about 8-10 minutes.
11. Remove from air fryer and place the steaks onto a cutting board for about 10 minutes before slicing.
12. Cut each steak into desired size slices and transfer onto serving platter.
13. Top with reserved herb mixture and serve.

Steak With Bell Peppers

Servings: 4

- 1teaspoon dried oregano, crushed 1 teaspoon onion powder
- 1teaspoon garlic powder
- 1teaspoon red chili powder 1 teaspoon paprika
- Salt, to taste
- 1¼ pounds beef steak, cut into thin strips 2 green bell peppers, seeded and cubed
- red bell pepper, seeded and cubed 1 red onion, sliced
- 2tablespoons olive oil

1. In a large bowl, mix the oregano and spices.
2. Add the beef strips, bell peppers, onion, and oil. Mix until well combined.
3. Set the temperature of air fryer to 390 degrees f. Grease an air fryer basket.
4. Arrange steak strips mixture into the prepared air fryer basket in 2
5. batches.
6. Air fry for about 10-11 minutes or until done completely.
7. Remove from air fryer and transfer the steak mixture onto serving plates.
8. Serve immediately.

Buttered Filet Mignon

Servings: 4

- 2(6-ounces) filet mignon steaks 1 tablespoon butter, softened
- Salt and ground black pepper, as required

1. Coat each steak evenly with butter and then, season with salt and black pepper.
2. Set the temperature of air fryer to 390 degrees f. Grease an air fryer basket.
3. Arrange steaks into the prepared air fryer basket.
4. Air fry for about 14 minutes, flipping once halfway through.
5. Remove from the air fryer and transfer onto serving plates. Serve hot.

Bacon Wrapped Filet Mignon

Servings: 2

- 2bacon slices
- 2(6-ounces) filet mignon steaks
- Salt and ground black pepper, as required 1 teaspoon avocado oil

1. Wrap 1 bacon slice around each mignon steak and secure with a toothpick.
2. Season the steak evenly with salt and black pepper.
3. Then, coat each steak with avocado oil.
4. Set the temperature of air fryer to 375 degrees f. Grease an air fryer basket.
5. Arrange steaks into the prepared air fryer basket.
6. Air fry for about 15 minutes, flipping once halfway through.
7. Remove from air fryer and transfer the steaks onto serving plates.
8. Serve hot.

Beef Short Ribs

Servings: 8

- 4pounds bone-in beef short ribs 1/3 cup sCal lions, chopped
- 1tablespoon fresh ginger, finely grated
- 1cup low-Sodium soy sauce
- ½ cup rice vinegar
- 1tablespoon sriracha
- 2tablespoons brown Sugar
- 1teaspoon ground black pepper

1. In a resealable bag, put the ribs and all the above
2. Seal the bag and shake to coat well.
3. Refrigerate overnight.
4. Set the temperature of air fryer to 380 degrees f. Grease an air fryer basket.
5. Take out the short ribs from resealable bag and arrange into the prepared air fryer basket in 2 batches in a single layer.
6. Air fry for about 8 minutes, flipping once halfway through.
7. Remove from air fryer and transfer onto a serving platter.
8. Serve hot.

Herbed Beef Roast

Servings: 5

- 2pounds beef roast
- 1tablespoon olive oil
- 1teaspoon dried rosemary, crushed
- 1teaspoon dried thyme, crushed Salt, as required

1. In a bowl, mix the oil, herbs, and salt.
2. Generously coat the roast with herb mixture.
3. Set the temperature of air fryer to 360 degrees f. Grease an air fryer basket.
4. Arrange roast into the prepared air fryer basket.
5. Air fry for about 45 minutes.
6. Remove from air fryer and transfer the roast onto a platter.
7. With a piece of foil, cover the roast for about 10 minutes before slicing.
8. Cut the roast into desired size slices and serve.

Beef Roast

Servings: 6

- 2½ pounds beef eye of round roast, trimmed

- 2tablespoons olive oil
- ½ teaspoon onion powder
- ½ teaspoon garlic powder
- ½ teaspoon cayenne pepper
- ½ teaspoon ground black pepper Salt, to taste

1.In a bowl, mix the oil, and spices.
2.Generously coat the roast with spice mixture.
3.Set the temperature of air fryer to 360 degrees f. Grease an air fryer basket.
4.Arrange roast into the prepared air fryer basket.
5.Air fry for about 50 minutes.
6.Remove from air fryer and transfer the roast onto a platter.
7.With a piece of foil, cover the roast for about 10 minutes before slicing.
8.Cut the roast into desired size slices and serve.

Beef Tips With Onion

Servings:2
- 1-pound top round beef, cut into 1½-inch cubes
- ½ yellow onion, chopped
- 2tablespoons worcestershire sauce 1 tablespoon avocado oil
- 1teaspoon onion powder
- 1teaspoon garlic powder
- Salt and ground black pepper, as required

1.In a bowl, mix the beef tips, onion, worcestershire sauce, oil, and spices.
2.Set the temperature of air fryer to 360 degrees f. Grease an air fryer basket.
3.Arrange beef mixture into the prepared air fryer basket.
4.Air fry for about 8-10 minutes.
5.Remove from air fryer and transfer the steak mixture onto serving plates.
6.Serve hot.

Buttered Rib Eye Steak

Servings:2
- ½ cup unsalted butter, softened
- 2tablespoons fresh parsley, chopped 2 teaspoons garlic, minced
- 1teaspoon worcestershire sauce Salt, as required
- 2(8-ounces) rib eye steak Ground black pepper, as required
- 1 tablespoon olive oil

1.In a bowl, add the butter, parsley, garlic, worcestershire sauce, and salt. Mix until well combined.
2.Place the butter mixture onto a parchment paper and roll into a log.
3.Refrigerate until using.
4.Coat the steak evenly with oil and then, sprinkle with salt and black pepper.
5.Set the temperature of air fryer to 400 degrees f. Grease an air fryer basket.
6.Arrange steaks into the prepared air fryer basket.
7.Air fry for about 14 minutes, flipping once halfway through.
8.Remove from air fryer and place the steaks onto a platter for about 5 minutes.
9.Cut each steak into desired size slices and divide onto serving plates.
10.Now, cut the butter log into slices.
11.Top each steak with butter slices and serve.

Beef Jerky

Servings: 3
- ½ cup dark brown Sugar
- ½ cup soy sauce
- ¼ cup worcestershire sauce
- 1tablespoon chili pepper sauce
- 1tablespoon hickory liquid smoke 1 teaspoon garlic powder
- 1teaspoon onion powder 1 teaspoon cayenne pepper
- ½ teaspoon smoked paprika
- ½ teaspoon ground black pepper
- 1-pound bottom round beef, cut into thin strips

1.In a large bowl, mix the brown Sugar, all sauces, liquid smoke, and spices.
2.Add the beef strips and generously coat with marinade.
3.Cover the bowl and marinate overnight.
4.Set the temperature of air fryer to 180 degrees f. Lightly, grease an air fryer basket.
5. Remove the beef strips from fridge and with paper towels, pat them dry.
6.Arrange half of the beef strips in the bottom of prepared air fryer basket in a single layer.
7.Now, arrange a Cooking rack over the strips.
8.Place the remaining beef strips on top of the rack in a single layer.
9.Air fry for about 1 hour.
10.Remove from air fryer and arrange the strips onto a paper towel-lined baking sheet to cool completely before serving.

Meatloaf Slider Wraps

Servings: 6
- 1-poundground beef, grass-fed
- ½ cup almond flour
- ¼ cup coconut flour
- ½ tablespoon minced garlic
- ¼ cup chopped white onion 1 teaspoon italian seasoning
- ½ teaspoon sea salt
- ½ teaspoon dried tarragon
- ½ teaspoon ground black pepper 1 tablespoon worcestershire sauce
- ¼ cup ketchup
- 2 eggs, pastured, beaten

1.Place all the in a bowl, stir well, then shape the mixture into 2-inch diameter and 1-inch thick patties and refrigerate them
2.for 10 minutes.
3.Meanwhile, switch on the air fryer, insert fryer basket, grease it with olive oil, then shut with its lid, set the fryer at 360 degrees f and preheat for 10 minutes.
4.Open the fryer, add patties in it in a single layer, close with its lid and cook for 10 minutes until nicely golden and cooked, flipping the patties halfway through the frying.
5.When air fryer beeps, open its lid and transfer patties to a plate.
6.Wrap each patty in lettuce and serve.

Pork Belly

Servings: 4

- 1-pound pork belly, pastured 6 cloves of garlic, peeled
- 1teaspoon ground black pepper
- 1teaspoon salt
- 2tablespoons soy sauce 2 bay leaves
- 3cups of water

1.Cut the pork belly evenly into three pieces, place them in an instant pot, and add remaining
2.Switch on the instant pot, then shut it with lid and cook the pork
3.belly for 15 minutes at high pressure.
4.When done, let the pressure release naturally for 10 minutes and then do quick pressure release.
5.Rake out the pork by tongs and let it drain and dry for 10 minutes.
6.Then switch on the air fryer, insert fryer basket, grease it with olive oil, then shut with its lid, set the fryer at 400 degrees f and preheat
7.for 5 minutes.
8.While the air fryer preheats, cut each piece of the pork into two long slices.
9.Open the fryer, add pork slices in it, close with its lid and cook for
10.minutes until nicely golden and crispy, flipping the pork halfway through the frying.
11.When air fryer beeps, open its lid, transfer pork slices onto a serving plate and serve.

Sirloin Steak
Servings: 6

- 2sirloin steaks, grass-fed
- 1tablespoon olive oil
- 2tablespoons steak seasoning
  1.Switch on the air fryer, insert fryer basket, grease it with olive oil, then shut with its lid, set the fryer at 392 degrees f and preheat for 5 minutes.
  2.Meanwhile, pat dries the steaks, brush with oil and then season well with steak seasoning until coated on both sides.
  3.Open the fryer, add steaks in it, close with its lid and cook for 10 minutes until nicely golden and crispy, flipping the steaks halfway through the frying.
  4.When air fryer beeps, open its lid, transfer steaks onto a serving plate and serve.

Vietnamese Grilled Pork
Servings:6

- 1-pound sliced pork shoulder, pastured, Fat trimmed 2 tablespoons chopped parsley
- 1/4 cup crushed roasted peanuts

For The Marinade

- 1/4 cup minced white onions 1 tablespoon minced garlic
- 1tablespoon lemongrass paste
- 1tablespoon erythritol sweetener 1/2 teaspoon ground black pepper 1 tablespoon fish sauce
- **2**teaspoons soy sauce 2 tablespoons olive oil

1.Place all the for the marinade in a bowl, stir well until combined and add it into a large plastic bag.
2.Cut the pork into ½-inch slices, cut each slice into 1-inches pieces, then add them into the plastic bag containing marinade, seal the
3.bag, turn it upside down to coat the pork pieces with the

marinade and marinate for a minimum of 1 hour.
4.Then switch on the air fryer, insert fryer basket, grease it with olive
5.oil, then shut with its lid, set the fryer at 400 degrees f and preheat for 5 minutes.
6.Open the fryer, add marinated pork in it in a single layer, close with its lid and cook for 10 minutes until nicely golden and cooked, flipping the pork halfway through the frying.
7.When air fryer beeps, open its lid, transfer pork onto a serving plate, and keep warm.
8.Air fryer the remaining pork pieces in the same manner and then serve.

Meatloaf
Servings:4

- 1-poundground beef, grass-fed 1 tablespoon minced garlic
- 1cup white onion, peeled and diced 1 tablespoon minced ginger
- 1/4 cup chopped cilantro 2 teaspoons garam masala
- 1teaspoon cayenne pepper 1 teaspoon salt
- 1/2 teaspoon ground cinnamon
- 1 teaspoon turmeric powder
- 1/8 teaspoon ground cardamom 2 eggs, pastured
  1.Switch on the air fryer, insert fryer basket, then shut with its lid, set
  2.the fryer at 360 degrees f and preheat for 5 minutes.
  3.Meanwhile, place all the in a bowl, stir until well mixed, then take an 8-inches round pan, grease it with oil, add the beef mixture in it and spread it evenly.
  4.Open the fryer, place the pan in it, close with its lid and cook for 15
  5.minutes until the top is nicely golden and meatloaf is thoroughly cooked.
  6.When air fryer beeps, open its lid, take out the pan, drain the excess fat, and take out the meatloaf.
  7. Cut the meatloaf into four pieces and serve.

Herbed Lamb Chops
Servings: 6

- 1-pound lamb chops, pastured

For The Marinate:

- 2tablespoons lemon juice 1 teaspoon dried rosemary 1 teaspoon salt
- 1teaspoon dried thyme 1 teaspoon coriander
- 1teaspoon dried oregano
- 2tablespoons olive oil
  1.Prepare the marinade and for this, place all its in a bowl and whisk until combined.
  2.Pour the marinade in a large plastic bag, add lamb chops in it, seal the bag, then turn it upside down to coat lamb chops with the marinade and let it marinate in the refrigerator for a minimum of 1 hour.
  3.Then switch on the air fryer, insert fryer basket, grease it with olive oil, then shut with its lid, set the fryer at 390 degrees f and preheat for 5 minutes.
  4.Meanwhile, open the fryer, add marinated lamb chops in it, close with its lid and cook for 8 minutes until nicely golden and cooked, turning the lamb chops halfway through the frying.

5.When air fryer beeps, open its lid, transfer lamb chops onto a serving plate and serve.

Garlic Rosemary Lamb Chops

Servings:4
- 4lamb chops, pastured
- 1teaspoon ground black pepper 2 teaspoons minced garlic
- ½ teaspoon salt
- 2teaspoons olive oil
- 4cloves of garlic, peeled 4 rosemary sprigs

1.Take the fryer pan, place lamb chops in it, season the top with ½ teaspoon black pepper and ¾ teaspoon salt, then drizzle evenly with oil and spread with 1 teaspoon minced garlic.

2.Add garlic cloves and rosemary and then let the lamb chops marinate in the pan into the refrigerator for a minimum of 1 hour.

3.Then switch on the air fryer, insert fryer pan, then shut with its lid, set the fryer at 360 degrees f and cook for 6 minutes.

4.Flip the lamb chops, season them with remaining salt and black

5.pepper, add remaining minced garlic and continue Cooking for 6 minutes or until lamb chops are cooked.

6.When air fryer beeps, open its lid, transfer lamb chops onto a serving plate and serve.

Double Cheeseburger

Servings:1
- 2beef patties, pastured
- 1/8 teaspoon onion powder
- 2slices of mozzarella cheese, low Fat 1/8 teaspoon ground black pepper
- 1/8 teaspoon salt

1.Switch on the air fryer, insert fryer basket, grease it with olive oil, then shut with its lid, set the fryer at 370 degrees f and preheat for 5 minutes.

2.Meanwhile, season the patties well with onion powder, black pepper, and salt.

3.Open the fryer, add beef patties in it, close with its lid and cook for 12 minutes until nicely golden and cooked, flipping the patties halfway through the frying.

4.Then top the patties with a cheese slice and continue Cooking for 1 minute or until cheese melts.

5.Serve straight away.

Pork Olive Salad

Servings: 4
- 2tablespoons olive oil 1garlic clove, crushed
- ¼ pound boneless pork, diced 2 teaspoons balsamic vinegar **Salad:**
- 1handful black olives, chopped 9-ounce feta cheese, crumbled 4 large tomatoes, chopped
- 1cucumber, chopped
- 1bunch of parsley, chopped

1.In a mixing bowl, add balsamic vinegar, garlic, and olive oil. Combine the to mix well with each other.

2.Add and toss in pork cube. Marinate for 30 minutes in the refrigerator.

3.Take skewers and thread pork cubes grease a baking pan with some

4.Cooking spray. Place skewers over the pan.

5.Place instant vortex over the kitchen platform. Arrange to drip pan in the lower position. Press "air fry," set the timer to 20 minutes,

6.and set the temperature to 360°f. Instant vortex will start preheating.

7.When instant vortex is pre-heated, it will display "add food" on its screen. Open the door and take out the middle roasting tray.

8.Place the pan over the tray and push it back; close door and Cooking will start. Midway, it will display "turn food" on its screen; flip skewers and close door.

9.Open the door after the Cooking cycle is over.

In a mixing bowl, add salad . Combine the to mix well with each other. Serve pork cubes with salad on the side.

Bbq Meatballs

Servings: 4
- ½ cup chopped white onions 2garlic cloves, minced
- egg, beaten
- 1-poundground beef
- ½ cup breadcrumbs
- teaspoon your favorite steak seasoning Ground black pepper and salt to taste
- ¼ cup shredded monterey jack cheese 1 teaspoon worcestershire sauce
- ½ cup bbq sauce

1. In a mixing bowl, add beef, breadcrumbs, onions, garlic, egg, cheese, worcestershire sauce, steak seasoning, salt, and black pepper. Combine the to mix well with each other.

2.Prepare meatballs from it.

3.Grease a baking pan with some Cooking spray. Place meatballs over the pan and brush with the bbq sauce.

4.Place instant vortex over the kitchen platform. Arrange to drip pan in the lower position. Press "air fry," set the timer to 15 minutes,

5.and set the temperature to 370°f. Instant vortex will start preheating.

6.When instant vortex is pre-heated, it will display "add food" on its screen. Open the door and take out the middle roasting tray.

7.Place the pan over the tray and push it back; close door and Cooking will start. Midway, it will display "turn food" on its screen; flip meatballs and close door.

8.Open the door after the Cooking cycle is over; serve warm.

Cold Soba With Beef And Cucumber

Servings: 4

Soba
- 8ounces soba noodles 1 tablespoon sesame oil Steak and dressing
- ¾ cup rice vinegar
- 1tablespoon asian sesame oil 3 garlic cloves, minced
- 1jalapeño pepper, seeded and minced
- ½ teaspoon salt
- 1-pound flank steak, about 1 inch thick
- tablespoons fresh lime juice (from 2 limes

Salad
- 1large seedless cucumber, halved lengthwise and thinly sliced 1 ripe mango, halved and thinly sliced
  - cup chopped fresh basil leaves 1 cup chopped fresh mint leaves
- ½ cup unsalted roasted cashews, chopped

- 1carrot, halved lengthwise and thinly sliced 1 teaspoon sesame seeds
- 1sCal lion, chopped

1.Bring a medium saucepan of water to a boil. Add the soba and cook for about 3 to 5 minutes until it is al dente-soft with just a little firmness left. Drain, rinse with cold water, and transfer to a medium serving bowl. Toss with the sesame oil, cover with plastic wrap,

2.and refrigerate for at least 2 hours or overnight.

3.Combine the rice vinegar, sesame oil, garlic, jalapeño, and salt in a shallow baking dish. Add the steak, turning to coat. Cover with plastic wrap and refrigerate for at least 2 hours or overnight.

4.Insert the grill grate and close the hood. Select grill, set temperature to high, and set time to 5 minutes. Select start/stop to begin preheating. Remove the steak from the marinade and reserve the marinade in a small saucepan. Grill the steak for about 5 minutes

5.for medium-rare. It should have grill marks and feel firm to the touch. Let the steak rest on a cutting board for about 5 minutes.

6.Bring the marinade to a boil, cook for 1 minute, then remove from

7.the heat. Pour into a small bowl, stir in the lime juice, and refrigerate the dressing to cool while preparing the salad.

8.Seedless cucumbers are available in supermarkets, but you can easily remove the seeds from the standard variety: after peeling, cut the cucumber in half lengthwise. Use a teaspoon to scoop out the middle core of seeds.

9.Add the dressing to the soba noodles and toss thoroughly. Add the cucumber, mango, basil, and mint and toss gently to combine.

10.Thinly slice the steak across the grain and arrange over the noodles. Sprinkle the cashews and chopped sCal lion over the top. Serve immediately.

Beef Ribeye Steak

Servings: 4
- 4(8-ounce ribeye steaks)
- 1tablespoon mccormick grill mates montreal steak seasoning Salt
- Pepper

1.Insert the grill grate and close the hood. Select grill, set temperature to high, and set time to 10 minutes. Select start/stop to begin preheating. Season the steaks with the steak seasoning and salt and pepper to taste. Place 2 steaks in the grill grate.

2.Cook for 4 minutes. Open the hood and flip the steaks.

3.Cook for an additional 4 to 5 minutes. Check for doneness to determine how much additional cook time is need. Remove the cooked steaks from the grill, then repeat steps for the remaining 2 steaks. Cool before serving.

Chili-Espresso Marinated Steak

Servings: 3
- ½ teaspoon garlic powder
- 1½ pounds beef flank steak
- 1teaspoon instant espresso powder 2 tablespoons olive oil
- 2teaspoons chili powder Salt and pepper to taste

1.Insert the grill grate and close the hood. Select grill, set temperature to high, and set time to 40 minutes. Select start/stop to begin preheating.

2.Make the dry rub by mixing the chili powder, salt, pepper, espresso powder, and garlic powder.

3.Rub all over the steak and brush with oil.

4.Place on the grill grate and cook for 40 minutes.

5.Halfway through the Cooking time, flip the beef to cook evenly.

Cumin-Paprika Rubbed Beef Brisket

Servings: 12
- ¼ teaspoon cayenne pepper 1 ½ tablespoons paprika
- 1teaspoon garlic powder 1 teaspoon ground cumin 1 teaspoon onion powder 2 teaspoons dry mustard
- 2teaspoons ground black pepper 2 teaspoons salt
- 5pounds brisket roast 5 tablespoons olive oil

1.Place all in a ziploc bag and marinate in the fridge for at least 2 hours.

2.Remove the grill grate from the unit. Select bake, set the temperature to 350°f, and set the time to 30 minutes. Select start/stop to begin preheating and cook for 2 hours at 350°f.

Beef With Pesto

Servings:4
- 4cups penne pasta, uncooked
- 10oz. Fresh baby spinach, chopped 4 beef (6 oz. Tenderloin steaks
- 1/2 teaspoon salt 1/2 teaspoon pepper
- 4cups grape tomatoes, halved 1/2 cup chopped walnuts
- 2/3 cup pesto
- 1/2 cup crumbled feta cheese

1.At first, prepared the pasta as per the given instructions on the pack.

2.Drain and rinse, then keep this pasta aside.

3.Now season the tenderloin steaks with salt and pepper.

4.Prepare and preheat the ninja foodi grill on a high-temperature setting.

5.Once it is preheated, open the lid and place the steaks on the grill.

6.Cover the ninja foodi grill's lid and let it grill on the "grilling mode" for 7 minutes.

7.Flip the steaks and continue grilling for another 7 minutes

8.Toss the pasta with spinach, tomatoes, walnuts, and pesto in a bowl.

9.Slice the grilled steak and top the salad with the steak.

10.Garnish with cheese.

11.Enjoy.

Sweet Chipotle Ribs

Servings:6
3lbs. Baby back ribs

Sauce/Glaze:
- 1bottle (11.2 oz. Beer
- 1tablespoon dijon mustard 1 cup barbecue sauce
- 1/3 cup honey
- 2teaspoon ground chipotle pepper 1 ½ cups

- ketchup
- ½ small onion, chopped 1/4 teaspoon pepper
- 1/8 cup worcestershire sauce
- 1tablespoon chipotle in adobo sauce, chopped
- ½ teaspoon salt
- ½ teaspoon garlic powder

1.First, wrap the ribs in a large foil and keep it aside.
2.Prepare and preheat the ninja foodi grill on roasting mode with medium temperature setting.
3.Once it is preheated, open the lid and place the wrapped ribs on the grill.
4.Cover the ninja foodi grill's lid and let it roast for 1 ½ hour.
5.Take the rest of the in a saucepan and cook for 45 minutes on a simmer.
6.brush the grilled ribs with the prepared sauce generously.
7.Place the ribs back into the grill and continue grilling for 10 minutes per side.
8.Serve.

Steak With Salsa Verde

Servings:4
- 2cups salsa verde
- 2beef flank steak, diced 1/2 teaspoon salt
- 1/2 teaspoon pepper
- 1cup fresh cilantro leaves 2 ripe avocados, diced
- 2medium tomatoes, seeded and diced

1.First, rub the steak with salt and pepper to season well.
2.Prepare and preheat the ninja foodi grill on a high-temperature setting.
3.Once it is preheated, open the lid and place the bread slices in the grill.
4.Cover the ninja foodi grill's lid and let it grill on the "grilling mode" for 9 minutes.
5.Flip and grill for another 9 minutes until al dente.
6.During this time, blend salsa with cilantro in a blender jug.
7.Slice the steak and serve with salsa, tomato, and avocado.

Pork With Salsa

Servings: 6
- 2lbs. Pork tenderloin, ¾ inch slices 1/4 cup lime juice
- 2tablespoons olive oil 2 garlic cloves, minced
- 1-1/2 teaspoons ground cumin 1-1/2 teaspoons dried oregano 1/2 teaspoon pepper

Salsa:
- 1jalapeno pepper, seeded and chopped 1 teaspoon Sugar
- 1/3 cup chopped red onion
- 2tablespoons chopped fresh mint 2 tablespoons lime juice
- 4cups pears, chopped peeled 1 tablespoon lime zest, grated 1/2 teaspoon pepper

1.Season the pork with lime juice, cumin, oregano, oil, garlic, and
2.pepper in a suitable bowl.
3.Cover to refrigerate for overnight margination.
4.Prepare and preheat the ninja foodi grill on a high-temperature setting.
5.Once it is preheated, open the lid and place the pork in the grill.

6.Cover the ninja foodi grill's lid and let it grill on the "grilling mode" for 6 minutes.
7.Flip the pork and continue grilling for another 6 minutes until al dente.
8.Mix the pear salsa into a separate bowl.
9.Serve the sliced pork with pear salsa.

Steak & Bread Salad

Servings: 4
- 1tablespoon mustard
- 2teaspoons packed brown Sugar 1/2 teaspoon salt
- 1/2 teaspoon pepper
- 1cup ranch salad dressing
- 1beef top sirloin steak, diced 2 teaspoons chili powder
- 3large tomatoes, diced 2 cups bread, cubed
- 2tablespoons olive oil
- 2tablespoons horseradish, finely grated 1 cucumber, chopped
- 1red onion, thinly sliced

1.First mix the chili powder with salt, pepper, and brown Sugar in a bowl
2.Sauté the bread cubes with oil in a skillet for 10 minutes until golden.
3.Take a small bowl and mix horseradish with mustard and salad dressing.
4.Prepare and preheat the ninja foodi grill on high-temperature setting.
5.Once it is preheated, open the lid and place the steaks in the grill.
6.Cover the ninja foodi grill's lid and let it grill on the "grilling mode" for 4 minutes.
7.Flip the steak and continue grilling for another 4 minutes.
8.Toss the sautéed bread cubes with rest of the and dressing mix in a salad bowl.
9.Slice the grilled steak and serve on top of the salad.
10.Enjoy.

Raspberry Pork Chops

Servings: 2
- ½chipotle in adobo sauce, chopped
- ¼ cup raspberry preserves, seedless 1/4 teaspoon salt
- 2bone-in pork loin chops

1.Take a small pan and mix preserves with chipotle pepper sauce on medium heat.
2.Keep ¼ cup of this sauce aside and rub the remaining over the pork.
3.Sprinkle salt over the pork and mix well.
4.Prepare and preheat the ninja foodi grill on high-temperature setting.
5.Once it is preheated, open the lid and place 2 pork chops in the grill.
6.Cover the ninja foodi grill's lid and grill them on the "grilling mode" for 5 minutes per side.
7.Serve with the reserved sauce.
8.Enjoy.

Cashew Pork Mix

Servings: 4
- 1-pound pork tenderloin, thinly cut into strips 1 egg, whisked
- 1green onion, chopped 1 red bell pepper, sliced 1/3

cup cashews
- 1tablespoon ginger, grated
- 3garlic cloves, minced
- 1 tablespoon olive oil
- 2 tablespoons coconut amines
- A pinch of salt and black pepper
1.Heat a pan that fits your air fryer with the oil over medium-high heat, add the pork and brown for 3 minutes.
2.Add the rest of the except the egg, toss and cook for 1 minute more.
3.Add the egg, toss, put the pan in the fryer and cook at 380 degrees f for 15 minutes, shaking the fryer halfway.
4.Divide everything into bowls and serve.

Pork And Ginger Sauce

Servings: 4
- 1-pound pork tenderloin, cut into strips 1 garlic clove, minced
- A pinch of salt and black pepper 1 tablespoon ginger, grated
- 3tablespoons coconut amines
- 2tablespoons coconut oil, melted
1.Heat a pan that fits the air fryer with the oil over medium-high heat, add the meat and brown for 3 minutes.
2.Add the rest of the , cook for 2 minutes more, put the pan in the fryer and cook at 380 degrees f for 30 minutes
3.Divide between plates and serve with a side salad.

Beef And Spinach Mix

Servings: 4
- 1and ½ pounds beef meat, cubed Salt and black pepper to the taste 2 cup baby spinach
- 3tablespoons olive oil
- 1tablespoon sweet paprika
- ¼ cup beef stock
1.A pan that fits your air fryer mix all the except the spinach, toss, introduce the pan the fryer and cook at 390 degrees f for 20 minutes.
2.Add the spinach, cook for 5 minutes more, divide everything between plates and serve.

Beef Salad

Servings: 4
- 1-pound beef, cubed
- ¼ cup coconut amines
- 1tablespoon coconut oil, melted 6 ounces iceberg lettuce, shredded 2 tablespoons cilantro, chopped
- 2tablespoons chives, chopped 1 zucchini, shredded
- ½ green cabbage head, shredded
- 2tablespoons almonds, sliced 1 tablespoon sesame seeds
- ½ tablespoon white vinegar
- A pinch of salt and black pepper
1.Heat a pan that fits the air fryer with the oil over medium-high heat, add the meat and brown for 5 minutes.

2.Add the aminos, zucchini, cabbage, salt and pepper, toss, put the
3.pan in the fryer and cook at 370 degrees f for 20 minutes.
4.Cool the mix down, transfer to a salad bowl, add the rest of the , toss well and serve.

Coconut Beef And Broccoli Mix

Servings: 4
- 1-pound beef, cubed
- 1broccoli head, florets separated 2 tablespoons olive oil
- 1teaspoon coconut aminos 1 teaspoon stevia
- 1/3 cup balsamic vinegar 2 garlic cloves, minced
1.In a pan that fits your air fryer, mix the beef with the rest of the , toss, put the pan in the fryer and cook at 390 degrees for 225 minutes.
2.Divide into bowls and serve hot.

Creamy Beef

Servings: 2
- 1-pound beef, cut into strips
- tablespoons coconut oil, melted
- A pinch of salt and black pepper 1 shallot, chopped
- 2 garlic cloves, minced
- white mushrooms, sliced 1 tablespoon coconut aminos 1 tablespoon mustard
- cup beef stock - ¼ cup coconut cream
- ¼ cup parsley, chopped
1.Heat a pan that fits your air fryer with the oil over medium-high heat, add the meat and brown for 2 minutes.
2.Add the garlic, shallots, mushrooms, salt and pepper, and cook for 3 minutes more.
3.Add the remaining except the parsley, toss, put the pan in the fryer and cook at 390 degrees f for 20 minutes.
4.Divide the mix into bowls and serve with parsley sprinkled on top.

Beef And Radishes
Preparation time: 5 minutes Cooking time: 15 minutes
Servings: 2
2 cups corned beef, cooked and shredded
2 garlic cloves, minced
1-pound radishes, quartered 2 spring onions, chopped
A pinch of salt and black pepper

1.In a pan that fits your air fryer, mix the beef with the rest of the , toss, put the pan in the fryer and cook at 390 degrees for 15 minutes.
2.Divide everything into bowls and serve.

Beef And Fennel Pan

Servings: 4
- 2tablespoons olive oil
- 1-pound beef, cut into strips 1 fennel bulb, sliced
- Salt and black pepper to the taste 1 teaspoon sweet paprika
- ¼ cup tomato sauce
1.Heat a pan that fits the air fryer with the oil over medium-high heat, add the beef and brown for 5 minutes.
2.Add the rest of the , toss, put the pan in the machine and cook at 380 degrees f for 15 minutes.
3.Divide the mix between plates and serve.

Beef And Napa Cabbage Mix

Servings: 4

- 2pounds beef, cubed
- ½ pound bacon, chopped 2 shallots, chopped
- 1napa cabbage, shredded 2 garlic cloves, minced
- Apinch of salt and black pepper
- 2tablespoons olive oil 1 teaspoon thyme, dried 1 cup beef stock

  1. Heat a pan that fits the air fryer with the oil over medium-high heat, add the beef and brown for 3 minutes.

  2.Add the bacon, shallots and garlic and cook for 2 minutes more.

  3.Add the rest of the , toss, put the pan in the air fryer and cook at 390 degrees f for 20 minutes.

  4.Divide between plates and serve.

Beef Meatloaf

Servings: 4

- 1-pound beef meat, ground 3 tablespoons almond meal Cooking spray
- 1egg, whisked
- Salt and black pepper to the taste 1 tablespoon parsley, chopped
- 1tablespoon oregano, chopped 1 yellow onion, chopped

  1.In a bowl, mix all the except the Cooking spray, stir well and put in a loaf pan that fits the air fryer.

  2.Put the pan in the fryer and cook at 390 degrees f for 25 minutes.

  3.Slice and serve hot.

Ground Beef And Chilies

Servings:4

- 1-pound beef, ground
- A pinch of salt and black pepper
- A drizzle of olive oil
- 2spring onions, chopped 3 red chilies, chopped
- 1cup beef stock
- 6garlic cloves, minced
- 1green bell pepper, chopped
- 8ounces canned tomatoes, chopped 2 tablespoons chili powder

1.Heat a pan that fits your air fryer with the oil over medium-high heat, add the beef and brown for 3 minutes.

2.Add the rest of the , toss, put the pan in the fryer and cook at 380 degrees f for 16 minutes.

3.Divide into bowls and serve.

Beef Steaks And Mushrooms

Servings: 4

- 4beef steaks
- 1tablespoon olive oil
- A pinch of salt and black pepper 2 tablespoons ghee, melted
- 2garlic cloves, minced
- 5cups wild mushrooms, sliced 1 tablespoon parsley, chopped

1.Heat a pan that fits the air fryer with the oil over medium-high heat, add the steaks and sear them for 2 minutes on each side.

2.Add the rest of the , toss, transfer the pan to your air fryer and cook at 380 degrees f for 20 minutes.

3.Divide between plates and serve.

Adobo Beef

Servings: 4

- 1-pound beef roast, trimmed
- ½ teaspoon oregano, dried
- ¼ teaspoon garlic powder
- A pinch of salt and black pepper
- ½ teaspoon turmeric powder 1 tablespoon olive oil

1.In a bowl, mix the roast with the rest of the , and rub well.

2.Put the roast in the air fryer's basket and cook at 390 degrees f for30 minutes.

3.Slice the roast, divide it between plates and serve with a side salad.

Beef Meatballs And Sauce

Servings: 4

- 2tablespoons olive oil
- 2spring onions, chopped 1 egg, whisked
- 2tablespoons rosemary, chopped 2 pounds beef, ground
- 1garlic clove, minced
- A pinch of salt and black pepper
- 24 ounces canned tomatoes, crushed

1. In a bowl, mix the beef with all the except the oil and the tomatoes, stir well and shape medium meatballs out of this

2.mix.

3.Heat a pan that fits the air fryer with the oil over medium-high heat, add the meatballs and cook for 2 minutes on each side.

4.Add the tomatoes, toss, put the pan in the fryer and cook at 370 degrees f for 20 minutes.

5.Divide into bowls and serve.

Beef And Avocado Pan

Servings: 4

- 4flank steaks
- 1garlic clove, minced 1/3 cup beef stock
- 2avocados, peeled, pitted and sliced 1 teaspoon chili flakes
- ½ cup basil, chopped
- 2spring onions, chopped 2 teaspoons olive oil
- A pinch of salt and black pepper

  1.Heat a pan that fits the air fryer with the oil over medium-high heat, add the steaks and cook for 2 minutes on each side.

  2.Add the rest of the except the avocados, put the pan in the air fryer and cook at 380 degrees f for 15 minutes.

  3.Add the avocado slices, cook for 5 minutes more, divide everything between plates and serve.

Crispy Fried Pork Chops The Southern Way

Servings: 4

- ½ cup all-purpose flour
- ½ cup low Fat buttermilk
- ½ teaspoon black pepper
- ½ teaspoon tabasco sauce Teaspoon paprika
- 3bone-in pork chops

1.Place the buttermilk and hot sauce in a ziploc bag and add the pork chops. Allow to marinate for at least an hour in the fridge.

2.In a bowl, combine the flour, paprika, and black pepper.
3.Remove pork from the ziploc bag and dredge in the flour mixture.
4.Preheat the air fryer oven to 390°f.
5.Spray the pork chops with Cooking oil.
6.Pour into the oven rack/basket. Place the rack on the middle-shelf of the air fryer oven. Set temperature to 390°f and set time to 25 minutes.

Cilantro-Mint Pork Bbq Thai Style
Servings: 3
- 1minced hot chili
- 1minced shallot
- 1-pound ground pork
- 2tablespoons fish sauce
- tablespoons lime juice
- tablespoons basil
- Tablespoons chopped mint
- tablespoons cilantro

1.In a shallow dish, mix well all with hands. Form into 1- inch ovals.
2.Thread ovals in skewers. Place on skewer rack in air fryer.
3.For 15 minutes, cook on 360°f. Halfway through Cooking time, turnover skewers. If needed, cook in batches.
4.Serve and enjoy.

Tuscan Pork Chops
Servings: 4
- 1/4 cup all-purpose flour 1 teaspoon salt
- 3/4 teaspoons seasoned pepper
- 4(1-inch-thick) boneless pork chops 1 tablespoon olive oil
- to 4 garlic cloves
- 1/3 cup balsamic vinegar 1/3 cup chicken broth
- 3plum tomatoes, seeded and diced Tablespoons capers

1.Combine flour, salt, and pepper
2.Press pork chops into flour mixture on both sides until evenly covered.
3.Cook in your air fryer oven at 360 degrees for 14 minutes, flipping
4.halfway through.
5.While the pork chops cook, warm olive oil in a medium skillet.
6.Add garlic and sauté for 1 minute; then mix in vinegar and chicken broth.
7.Add capers and tomatoes and turn to high heat.
8.Bring the sauce to a boil, stirring regularly, then add pork chops, Cooking for one minute.
9.Remove from heat and cover for about 5 minutes to allow the pork to absorb some of the sauce; serve hot.

Italian Parmesan Breaded Pork Chops
Servings: 5
- 5(3½- to 5-ounce) pork chops (bone-in or boneless) 1 teaspoon italian seasoning
- Seasoning salt
- Pepper
- ¼ cup all-purpose flour
- 2tablespoons italian breadcrumbs
- 3tablespoons finely grated parmesan cheese Cooking oil

1.Season the pork chops with the italian seasoning and seasoning salt and pepper to taste.
2.Sprinkle the flour on both sides of the pork chops, then coat both sides with the breadcrumbs and parmesan cheese.
3.Place the pork chops in the air fryer basket. Stacking them is okay.
4.Spray the pork chops with Cooking oil. Set temperature to 390°f and cook for 6 minutes.
5.Open the air fryer and flip the pork chops. Cook for an additional 6 minutes.
6.Cool before serving. Instead of seasoning salt, you can use either chicken or pork rub for additional flavor. You can find these rubs in the spice aisle of the grocery store.

Crispy Roast Garlic-Salt Pork
Servings: 4
- 1teaspoon chinese five spice powder 1 teaspoon white pepper
- 2pounds pork belly
- 2teaspoons garlic salt

1.Preheat the air fryer oven to 390°f.
2.Mix all the spices in a bowl to create the dry rub.
3.Score the pork belly's skin with a knife and season the entire pork with the spice rub.
4.Place in the air fryer basket and cook for 40 to 45 minutes until the skin is crispy.
5.Chop before serving.

Crispy Breaded Pork Chops
Servings: 8
- 1/8 tsp. Pepper
- ¼ tsp. Chili powder
- ½ tsp. Onion powder
- ½ tsp. Garlic powder 1 ¼ tsp. Sweet paprika
- 2tbsp. Grated parmesan cheese
- 1/3 c. Crushed cornflake crumbs
- ½ c. Panko breadcrumbs 1 beaten egg
- 6center-cut boneless pork chops

1.Ensure that your air fryer is preheated to 400 degrees. Spray the basket with olive oil.
2.With ½ teaspoon salt and pepper, season both sides of pork chops.
3.Combine ¾ teaspoon salt with pepper, chili powder, onion powder, garlic powder, paprika, cornflake crumbs, panko breadcrumbs and parmesan cheese.
4.Beat egg in another bowl.
5.Dip pork chops into the egg and then crumb mixture.
6.Add pork chops to air fryer and spritz with olive oil.
7.Pour into the oven rack/basket. Place the rack on the middle-shelf of the air fryer oven. Set temperature to 400°f and set time to 12
8.minutes. Cook 12 minutes, making sure to flip over halfway through Cooking process.
9.Only add 3 chops in at a time and repeat the process with remaining pork chops.

Ginger, Garlic And Pork Dumplings
Servings: 8
- ¼ teaspoon crushed red pepper
- ½ teaspoon Sugar
- 1tablespoon chopped fresh ginger 1 tablespoon chopped garlic

- 1teaspoon canola oil
- 1teaspoon toasted sesame oil 18 dumpling wrappers
- 2tablespoons rice vinegar 2 teaspoons soy sauce
- 4cups bok choy, chopped
- 4ounces ground pork

1.Heat oil in a skillet and sauté the ginger and garlic until fragrant. Stir in the ground pork and cook for 5 minutes.
2.Stir in the bok choy and crushed red pepper. Season with salt and
3.pepper to taste. Allow to cool.
4.Place the meat mixture in the middle of the dumpling wrappers. Fold the wrappers to seal the meat mixture in.
5.Place the bok choy in the grill pan.
6.Cook the dumplings in the air fryer at 330°f for 15 minutes.
7.Meanwhile, prepare the dipping sauce by combining the remaining in a bowl.

Caramelized Pork Shoulder

Servings: 8
- 1/3 cup soy sauce
- 2tablespoons Sugar
- 1tablespoon honey
- 2- pound pork shoulder, cut into 1½-inch thick slices

1.In a bowl, mix all except pork.
2.Add pork and coat with marinade generously.
3.Cover and refrigerate o marinate for about 2-8 hours.
4.Preheat the air fryer oven to 335 degrees f.
5.Place the pork in an air fryer basket.
6.Cook for about 10 minutes.
7.Now, set the air fryer oven to 390 degrees f. Cook for about 10 Minutes

Curry Pork Roast In Coconut Sauce

Servings: 6
- ½ teaspoon curry powder
- ½ teaspoon ground turmeric powder 1 can unsweetened coconut milk
- 1tablespoons Sugar
- 2tablespoons fish sauce
- 2tablespoons soy sauce 3 pounds pork shoulder Salt and pepper to taste

1.Place all in bowl and allow the meat to marinate in the fridge for at least 2 hours.
2.Preheat the air fryer to 390°f.
3.Place the grill pan accessory in the air fryer.
4.Grill the meat for 20 minutes making sure to flip the pork every 10 minutes for even grilling and cook in batches.
5.Meanwhile, pour the marinade in a saucepan and allow to simmer for 10 minutes until the sauce thickens.
6.Baste the pork with the sauce before serving.

Garlic Butter Pork Chops

Servings: 4
- 2tsp. Parsley
- 2tsp. Grated garlic cloves 1 tbsp. Coconut oil
- 1tbsp. Coconut butter 4 pork chops

1.Ensure your air fryer oven is preheated to 350 degrees.
2.Mix butter, coconut oil, and all seasoning together. Then rub seasoning mixture over all sides of pork chops. Place in foil, seal, and chill for 1 hour.

3.Remove pork chops from foil and place into air fryer.
4.Pour into the oven rack/basket. Place the rack on the middle-shelf of the air fryer oven. Set temperature to 350°f and set time to 7 minutes. Cook 7 minutes on one side and 8 minutes on the other.
5.Drizzle with olive oil and serve alongside a green salad.

Fried Pork With Sweet And Sour Glaze

Servings: 4
- ¼ cup rice wine vinegar
- ¼ teaspoon chinese five spice powder 1 cup potato starch
- 1green onion, chopped
- 2large eggs, beaten
- 2pounds pork chops cut into chunks
- 2tablespoons cornstarch + 3 tablespoons water 5 tablespoons brown Sugar
- Salt and pepper to taste

1.Preheat the air fryer oven to 390°f.
2.Season pork chops with salt and pepper to taste.
3.Dip the pork chops in egg. Set aside.
4.In a bowl, combine the potato starch and chinese five spice powder.
5.Dredge the pork chops in the flour mixture.
6.Place in the double layer rack and cook for 30 minutes.
7.Meanwhile, place the vinegar and brown Sugar in a saucepan. Season with salt and pepper to taste. Stir in the cornstarch slurry and allow to simmer until thick.
8.Serve the pork chops with the sauce and garnish with green onions.

Oregano-Paprika On Breaded Pork

Servings: 4
- ¼ cup water
- ¼ teaspoon dry mustard
- ½ teaspoon black pepper
- ½ teaspoon cayenne pepper
- ½ teaspoon garlic powder
- ½ teaspoon salt
- 1cup panko breadcrumbs 1 egg, beaten
- 2teaspoons oregano
- 4lean pork chops
- 4teaspoons paprika

1.Preheat the air fryer oven to 390°f.
2.Pat dry the pork chops.
3.In a mixing bowl, combine the egg and water. Then set aside.
4.In another bowl, combine the rest of the .
5.Dip the pork chops in the egg mixture and dredge in the flour mixture.
6.Place in the air fryer basket and cook for 25 to 30 minutes until golden.

Pork Neck With Salad

Servings: 2
For Pork:
- tablespoon soy sauce 1 tablespoon fish sauce
- ½ tablespoon oyster sauce
- ½ pound pork neck
- For Salad:
- ripe tomato, sliced tickly 8-10 thai shallots, sliced
- 1sCal lion, chopped

- 1bunch fresh basil leaves
- 1bunch fresh cilantro leaves
- For Dressing:
- 3tablespoons fish sauce 2 tablespoons olive oil
- 1teaspoon apple cider vinegar 1 tablespoon palm Sugar
- 2bird eye chilies
- 1tablespoon garlic, minced

1.For pork in a bowl, mix all except pork.
2.Add pork neck and coat with marinade evenly. Refrigerate for about 2-3 hours.
3.Preheat the air fryer oven to 340 degrees f.
4.Place the pork neck onto a grill pan. Cook for about 12 minutes.
5.Meanwhile in a large salad bowl, mix all salad .
6.In a bowl, add all dressing and beat till well combined.
7.Remove pork neck from air fryer and cut into desired slices.
8.Place pork slices over salad.

Cajun Pork Steaks

Servings: 6
- 4-6pork steaks Bbq sauce:
- Cajun seasoning 1 tbsp. Vinegar
- 1tsp. Low-Sodium soy sauce
- ½ c. Brown Sugar
- ½ c. Vegan ketchup

1.Ensure your air fryer oven is preheated to 290 degrees.
2. Sprinkle pork steaks with cajun seasoning.
3.Combine remaining and brush onto steaks. Add coated steaks to air fryer.
4.Pour into the oven rack/basket. Place the rack on the middle-shelf
of the air fryer oven. Set temperature to 290°f and set time to 20 minutes. Cook 15-20 minutes till just browned.

Seasoned Beef Roast

Servings: 8
- 2½ pounds beef roast 1 tablespoon olive oil
- 2tablespoons montreal steak seasoning

1.With kitchen twines, tie the roast into a compact shape.
2.Brush the roast with oil and then rub with seasoning.
3.Arrange the beef roast onto a greased baking pan.
4.Arrange the baking pan in the center of instant omni plus toaster oven.
5.Select "air fry" and then adjust the temperature to 360 degrees f.
6.Set the timer for 45 minutes and press "start".
7.When the display shows "turn food" do nothing.
8.When cooking time is complete, remove the baking pan from toaster oven.
9.Place the steak onto a cutting board for about 10-15 minutes before slicing.
10.With a sharp knife, cut the steak into desired size slices and serve.

Lemony Flank Steak

Servings: 6

- 2pounds flank steak
- 3tablespoons fresh lemon juice 2 tablespoons olive oil
- 3garlic cloves, minced
- 1teaspoon red chili powder
- Salt and ground black pepper, as required

1.In a large bowl, add all the except for steak and mix well.
2.Add the flank steak and coat with the marinade generously.
3.Refrigerate to marinate for 24 hours, flipping occasionally.
4.Arrange the steak onto a greased sheet pan.
5.Arrange the baking pan in the top portion of instant omni plus toaster oven.
6.Select "broil" and set the timer for 12 minutes and press "start".
7.When the display shows "turn food" flip the steak.
8.When Cooking time is complete, remove the air baking pan from toaster oven.
9.Place the roast onto a cutting board for about 10-15 minutes before slicing.
10.With a sharp knife, cut the roast into desired size slices and serve.

Seasoned Flank Steak

Servings:6
- 2pounds flank steak
- 3tablespoons taco seasoning rub

1.Rub the steak with taco seasoning evenly.
2.Place the steak onto a greased baking pan.
3.Arrange the drip pan in the bottom of instant omni plus toaster oven.
4.Place the baking pan over the drip pan.
5.Select "bake" and then adjust the temperature to 425 degrees f.
6.Set the timer for 30 minutes and press "start".
7.When the display shows "turn food" do nothing.
8.When Cooking time is complete, remove the baking pan from toaster oven.
9.Place the steak onto a cutting board for about 10-15 minutes before slicing.
10.Wuth a sharp knife, cut the steak into desired size slices and serve.

Glazed Skirt Steak

Servings: 4
- 1¼ pounds skirt steak
- ½ cup low-Sodium soy sauce
- ¼ cup white wine
- 3-4 tablespoons fresh lemon juice 2 tablespoons sesame oil
- 3tablespoons maple syrup
- tablespoon red pepper flakes, crushed 2 garlic cloves, minced

1.In a large resealable bag, place all the except for the sCal lions.
2.Seal the bag and shake to mix well.
3.Refrigerate for up to 2 hours.
4. Remove the steak from bag and set aside at room temperature for 20 minutes before Cooking .
5.Place the skirt steak onto a greased baking pan.
6.Arrange the drip pan in the bottom of instant omni plus toaster oven.
7.Place the baking pan over the drip pan.

8.Select "bake" and then adjust the temperature to 400 degrees f.

9.Set the timer for 10 minutes and press "start".

10.When the display shows "turn food" do nothing.

11.When Cooking time is complete, remove the baking pan from toaster oven.

12.Place the steak onto a cutting board for about 10-15 minutes before slicing.

13.With a sharp knife, cut the steak into desired size slices and serve.

Simple Filet Mignon

Servings: 2

- 2 (6-ounces) filet mignon
- 1tablespoon olive oil
- Salt and ground black pepper, as required

1.Coat both sides of filet with oil and then, season with salt and black pepper.

2.Place the filets onto a greased air fryer basket.

3.Arrange the air fryer basket in the center of instant omni plus toaster oven.

4.Select "air fry" and then adjust the temperature to 390 degrees f.

5.Set the timer for 14 minutes and press "start".

6.When the display shows "turn food" flip the filets.

7.When Cooking time is complete, remove the air fryer basket from toaster oven.

1. Serve hot.

Crusted Rack Of Lamb

Servings: 6

- 1¾ pounds rack of lamb
- Salt and ground black pepper, as required 1 egg
- tablespoon seasoned breadcrumbs 3 ounces pistachios, chopped finely

1.Season the rack of lamb with salt and black pepper evenly and then, drizzle with Cooking spray.

2.In a shallow dish, beat the egg.

3.In another shallow dish mix together breadcrumbs and pistachios.

4.Dip the rack of lamb in egg and then coat with the pistachio mixture.

5.Place the rack of lamb into a greased air fryer basket.

6.Arrange the air fryer basket in the center of instant omni plus toaster oven.

7.Select "air fry" and then adjust the temperature to 220 degrees f.

8.Set the timer for 35 minutes and press "start".

9.When the display shows "turn food" do nothing.

10.After 30 minutes of Cooking, adjust the temperature to 390 degrees f.

11.When cooking time is complete, remove the air fryer basket from toaster oven.

12.Place the rack onto a cutting board for about 5 minutes.

13. Cut the rack into individual chops and serve hot.

Sweet & Sour Lamb Chops

Servings: 3

- 3(8-ounce) lamb shoulder chops
- Salt and ground black pepper, as required
- ¼ cup brown Sugar
- 2tablespoons fresh lemon juice

1.Season the lamb chops with salt and black pepper generously.

2.In a baking pan, place the chops and sprinkle with Sugar, followed by the lime juice.

3.Arrange the drip pan in the bottom of instant omni plus toaster oven.

4.Place the baking pan over the drip pan.

5.Select "bake" and then adjust the temperature to 376 degrees f.

6.Set the timer for 40 minutes and press "start".

7.When the display shows "turn food" flip the chops.

8.When Cooking time is complete, remove the baking pan from toaster oven.

9.Serve hot.

Leg Of Lamb

Servings: 10

- ¼ cup olive oil
- 4garlic cloves, chopped
- ¼ cup fresh rosemary
- 3tablespoons dijon mustard 2 tablespoons maple syrup
- Salt and ground black pepper, as required
- 1(4-pound) leg of lamb

1.In a food processor, add the oil, garlic, herbs, mustard, honey, salt and black pepper and pulse until smooth.

2.Place the leg of lamb and marinade into a glass baking dish and mix well

3.With plastic wrap, cover the baking dish and refrigerate to marinate for 6-8 hours.

4.Arrange a wire rack in a baking pan.

5.Arrange the leg of lamb into the prepared baking pan.

6.Arrange the drip pan in the bottom of instant omni plus toaster oven.

7.Place the baking pan over the drip pan.

8.Select "bake" and then adjust the temperature to 420 degrees f.

9.Set the timer for 20 minutes and press "start".

10.after 20 minutes, set the temperature to 320 degrees f for 1 hour and 20 minutes.

11.when Cooking time is complete, remove the baking pan from toaster oven.

12.place the leg of lamb onto a cutting board.

13.with a piece of foil, cover the leg of lamb for about 10 minutes before slicing.

14.with a sharp knife, cut the leg of lamb into desired size slices and serve.

Dessert Recipe

Air Fried Plantains

Servings: 4

- Avocado or sunflower oil (2 tsp.)
- Ripened/almost brown – plantains (2) Optional: Salt (.125 tsp.)

1.Warm up the Air Fryer to 400° Fahrenheit.

2.Slice the plantains at an angle for a .5-inch thickness.

3.Mix the oil, salt, and plantains in a container – making sure you coat the surface thoroughly.

4.Set the timer for eight to ten minutes; shake after five minutes. If they are not done to your liking, add a minute or two more.

Air Fryer Beignets

Servings: 7

- All-purpose flour (.5 cup) White sugar (.25 cup) Water (.125 cup)
- Large egg (1 separated) Melted butter (1.5 tsp.) Baking powder (.5 tsp.) Vanilla extract (.5 tsp.) Salt (1 pinch)
- Confectioners' sugar (2 tbsp.)
- Also Needed: Silicone egg-bite mold

1.Warm the Air Fryer to reach 370° Fahrenheit. Spray the using a nonstick cooking spray.
2.Whisk the flour, sugar, water, egg yolk, butter, baking powder, vanilla extract, and salt together in a large mixing bowl. Stir to combine.
3. Using an electric hand mixer (medium speed), mix the egg white in a small bowl until soft peaks form. Fold into the
4.batter. Pour the mixture into the mold using a small hinged ice cream scoop.
5.Arrange the filled silicone mold in the basket of the Air Fryer.
6.Cook for 10 minutes. Remove mold from the basket carefully, pop the beignets out, and flip them over onto a parchment paper-lined round.
7.Place the parchment round with beignets back into the fryer basket. Cook for another 4 minutes.
8.Remove the beignets from the Air Fryer basket and dust with confectioners' sugar.
9.mold

Banana Smores

Servings: 4

- Bananas (4)
- Mini-peanut butter chips (3 tbsp.) Graham cracker cereal (3 tbsp.)
- Mini-semi-sweet chocolate chips (3 tbsp.)
  1.Heat the Air Fryer in advance to 400° Fahrenheit.
  2.Slice the un-peeled bananas lengthwise along the inside of the curve. Don't slice through the bottom of the peel. Open slightly - forming a pocket.
  3.Fill each pocket with chocolate chips, peanut butter chips, and marshmallows. Poke the cereal into the filling.
  4.Arrange the stuffed bananas in the fryer basket, keeping them upright with the filling facing up.
  5.Air-fry until the peel has blackened, and the chocolate and
  6.marshmallows have toasted (6 minutes).
  7.Cool for 1-2 minutes. Spoon out the filling to serve.

Blackberry & Apricot Crumble

Servings:6

- Fresh blackberries (5.5 oz.) Lemon juice (2 tbsp.) Fresh apricots (18 oz.) Sugar (.5 cup)
- Salt (1 pinch)
- Flour (1 cup)
- Cold butter (5 tbsp.)

1.Heat the Air Fryer to 390° Fahrenheit.
2.Lightly grease an 8-inch oven dish with a spritz of cooking oil.
3.Remove the stones, cut the apricots into cubes, and put them in a container.

4.Combine the lemon juice, blackberries, and two tablespoons of sugar with the apricots and mix. Place the fruit in the oven dish.
5.Combine the salt, remainder of the sugar, and flour in a mixing
6.container. Add one tablespoon of cold water and the butter, using your fingertips to make a crumbly mixture.
7.Crumble the mixture over the fruit, pressing them down.
8.Place the dish in the basket and slide it into the Air Fryer. Fry for 20 minutes. It is ready when it is cooked thoroughly, and the top is browned.

Blueberry Hand Pies

Servings: 8

- Refrigerated pie crust (14 oz.)
- Blueberries (1 cup) Castor sugar (2.5 tbsp.) Lemon juice (1 tsp.) Salt (1 pinch)
- Water
- Optional: Vanilla sugar

1.Heat the Air Fryer to reach 350° Fahrenheit.
2. Mix the sugar, lemon juice, salt, and blueberries in a medium mixing container.
3.Roll out the pie crusts and cut out six to eight 4-inch individual circles.
4.Scoop about one tablespoon of the blueberry filling in the center of each circle.
5.Moisten the edges of dough with a little water. Fold the dough over
6.the filling to form a half-moon shape.
7.Using a fork, gently crimp the edges of the crust together. Then slice three slits on the top of the hand pies.
8.Spray the hand pies with a spritz of cooking oil spray. Sprinkle with vanilla sugar if using.
9.Place three to four hand pies in a single layer inside the Air Fryer basket.
10.Cook the pies for 9-12 minutes or until golden brown. Let each of the hand pies cool for at least 10 minutes before serving.

Brownies

Servings: 2

- Granulated sugar (.5 cup) Cocoa powder (.33 cup) All-purpose flour (.25 cup) Baking powder (.25 tsp.) Pinch kosher salt
- Butter (.25 cup - melted and cooled slightly) Large egg (1)
- Also Needed: 6-inch round pan
  1.Prep the Air Fryer at 350° Fahrenheit.
  2.Grease the pan with a cooking oil spray. In a medium mixing bowl, whisk to combine the sugar, cocoa powder, flour, baking powder, and salt.
  3.In another mixing dish, whisk the melted butter and egg until combined. Add it all together and transfer the brownie batter to the prepared cake pan and smooth top.
  4.Air-fry for 16-18 minutes, and let them cool ten minutes before slicing.

Caramel Cream-Dipped Apple Fries

Servings:: 8-10

- Honey-crisp apples/your choice (3) Graham cracker crumbs (1 cup) Eggs (3)
- Flour (.5 cup)
- Sugar (.25 cup)

- Whipped cream cheese (8 oz.)
- Caramel sauce (.5 cup + more for garnish)

1. Peel and slice the apples into eight wedges. Toss the flour and apple slices together.
2. Prepare a dish with the eggs. Mix the sugar and crackers in
3. another bowl. Dip the apples in the eggs, and then the crumb mixture coating all sides. Arrange on a baking tray.
4. Set the fryer to 380° Fahrenheit. Brush or spray the bottom of the Air
5. Fryer with a spritz of oil.
6. Prepare in two batches using a single layer – spraying each batch lightly. Cook for 5 minutes and turn. Cook for another two minutes.
7. Make the cream dip by combining the caramel sauce and cream cheese.
8. Serve the hot apple fries with the caramel dip.

Cheesecake Egg Rolls
Servings: 15
- Unchilled cream cheese (2 - 16 oz. pkg.)
- Granulated sugar (.5 cup) Lemon juice (1 tbsp.) Vanilla extract (1 tsp.)
- Fig jam (1- 8.5 oz. jar)
- Refrigerated ready-made egg roll wrappers (15) Egg wash: 1 tablespoon water + 1 egg beaten Olive oil cooking spray
- Unsalted butter (2 tbsp. - melted) Sugar (.25 cup)
- Ground cinnamon (1 tsp.)

1. Use the mixing bowl of an electric mixer (with the whip attachment), combine the cream cheese, sugar, lemon juice, and vanilla extract. Mix well using medium speed for two minutes to combine. Remove the cheesecake filling and add it to a pastry bag or a zipper-top bag. Snip a corner.
2. Stir the jam, so it's easily scooped.
3. Prepare the egg roll wrapper with a pointed end toward you; in the center, pipe on approximately two tablespoons of cream cheese mixture. Add one tablespoon of jam. Use a pastry brush to coat the edges of the egg roll wrapper with egg wash. Fold the bottom corner over filling, roll snugly half- way to cover the filling. Fold in both sides and roll the wrap, making sure it's corner is well-sealed. Spray the egg rolls with olive oil cooking spray on both sides.
4. Warm the Air Fryer to 370° Fahrenheit for ten minutes. Set aside to cool while the fryer heats.
5. Place four or five egg rolls in the hot fryer basket. Air-fry for five to seven minutes, or until the egg rolls are golden brown on top.
6. Remove the rolls from the basket and cool.
7. Lightly brush the rolls with melted butter. Combine sugar and cinnamon in a small bowl and sprinkle over egg rolls. Serve warm or at room temperature. Store any leftovers in the fridge.

Cherry Pie
Serves: 8
- Cherry pie filling (21 oz. can)
- Milk (1 tbsp.)
- Refrigerated pie crusts (2) Egg yolk (1)

1. Warm the fryer at 310° Fahrenheit.
2. Poke holes into the crust after placing it in a pie plate. Allow the excess to hang over the edges. Place in the Air Fryer for five (5) minutes
3. Transfer the basket with the pie plate onto the countertop.

Fill it with the cherries. Remove the excess crust.
4. Cut the remaining crust into ¾-inch strips - placing weaving a lattice across the pie.
5. Make an egg wash with milk and egg. Brush the pie. Air-fry for 15 minutes. Serve with a scoop of ice cream.

Chocolate Cake
Servings: 4
- Unchilled butter (1 stick)
- Cocoa powder (.33 cup) Baking powder (1 tsp.) Baking soda (.5 tsp.) Eggs (3)
- Sour cream (.5 cup)
- Flour (1 cup)
- Sugar (.66 cup)
- Vanilla (2 tsp.)

1. Heat the Air Fryer to reach 320° Fahrenheit.
2. Mix the fixings using the low setting of an electric mixer.
3. Pour it into the basket and slide it into the Air Fryer.
4. Set the timer for 25 minutes. Once the timer buzzes, lightly push in the center to see if the cake is done. If it doesn't spring back when touched, air- fry for an additional 5 minutes. Cool the cake and frost with your favorite icing.

Cinnamon Rolls
Servings: 6
- Melted butter (2 tbsp. + more for brushing)
- Packed brown sugar (.33 cup) Ground cinnamon (.5 tsp.) Kosher salt
- All-purpose flour (as needed) Refrigerated Crescent rolls (8-oz. tube) The Glaze:
- Unchilled cream cheese (2 oz.)
- Powdered sugar (.5 cup)
- Whole milk (1 tbsp. + more if needed)

1 Set the Air Fryer at 350° Fahrenheit.
2 Make the rolls. Prepare the Air Fryer with a sheet of parchment baking paper and brush with butter.
3 In a medium mixing container, combine the butter, brown sugar, cinnamon, and a large pinch of salt until smooth and fluffy.
4 Lightly flour a countertop, and roll the crescent rolls in one piece. Pinch seams together and fold in half. Roll into a 9x7-inch rectangle.
5 Spread the prepared butter mixture over the dough, leaving a 1/4-inch border. Starting at a long edge, roll up the dough like a jelly roll, then cut crosswise into six pieces.
6 Arrange the pieces in the fryer, cut-side upward - spaced evenly. Air-fry until golden and cooked through
7 Make the glaze. Whisk the powdered sugar, cream cheese, and milk
together (adding milk by the teaspoonful, as needed for thinning the glaze.) Finish it off by adding glaze over the rolls and serve.

Donut Bread Pudding
Servings: 4
- Glazed donuts (6)
- Raw egg yolks (4) Whipping cream (1.5 cups) Sugar (.25 cups)
- Frozen sweet cherries (.75 cups)
- Cinnamon (1 tsp.)
- Semi-sweet chocolate baking chips (.5 cup) Raisins

(.5 cup)
1 Warm the Air Fryer at 310° Fahrenheit.
2 Toss the wet fixings in a container and add everything else.
3 Dump the mixture into a baking pan and cover it with foil. Place it into the basket and set the timer for one hour.
4 Chill the pudding thoroughly before serving.

Guilt-Free Paleo Pumpkin Muffins

Servings:12
- Pumpkin puree (1 cup) Gluten-free oats (2 cups) Honey (.0.5 cup)
- Medium eggs (2)
- Coconut butter (1 tsp.) Cocoa Nibs (1 tbsp.) Vanilla Essence (1 tbsp.) Nutmeg (1 tsp.)

1 Warm the Air Fryer to reach Toss each of the fixings into the blender and mix until smooth.
2 Place the muffin mix into little muffin cases, spreading it out over 12 separate ones.
3 Arrange it in the Air Fryer and set the timer for 15 minutes on 356° Fahrenheit.
4 Serve when cool.

Iced Strawberry Cupcakes

Servings: 10
- Butter (.5 cup +.5 cup)
- Caster sugar (.5 cup) Medium eggs (2) Vanilla essence (.5 tsp.) Self-rising flour (.5 cup) Icing sugar (.5 cup) Whipped cream (1 tbsp.)
- Pink food coloring (.5 tsp.)
- Fresh (blended) strawberries (.25 cup)

1 Heat the Air Fryer to reach 338° Fahrenheit.
2 Combine the butter and sugar in a large mixing bowl until it's creamy smooth. Break the eggs into the mix one at a time, along with the vanilla essence.
3 Blend in a small amount of flour at a time until all is thoroughly mixed.
4 Dump the mixture into greased ramekins, about 75% of the way full. Arrange them in the Air Fryer for eight minutes.
5 Make the Frosting: Cream the butter and slowly mix in the icing sugar until creamy. Pour in the food coloring, (blended) strawberries, and whipped cream—mix well.
6 Take them out and use a piping bag to make the swirl frosting for a tasty, fancy cupcake - every time.

Molten Lava Cakes

Servings: 4
- Self-rising flour (1.5 tbsp.)
- Baker's Sugar - not powdered (3.5 tbsp.) Unsalted Butter (3.5 oz.)
- Dark Chocolate (Pieces or Chopped- (3.5 oz.) Eggs (2)
- Also Needed: 4 Standard-sized oven-safe ramekins & microwave safe bowl

1 Warm the Air Fryer to 375° Fahrenheit.
2 Grease and flour the ramekins.
3 Melt the chocolate and butter in the microwave on level 7 (3 min.) stirring thoroughly.
4 Whisk the eggs and sugar until pale and frothy.
5 Mix the melted chocolate mixture into the egg mixture. Stir in flour. Use a spatula to combine everything.
6 Fill the ramekins about ¾ of the way to full with the cake. Set the timer for 10 minutes.
7 Remove from the Air Fryer and cool in ramekins for two minutes.

8 Carefully turn the ramekins upside down onto a serving plate, tapping the bottom with a butter knife to loosen edges. The cake should release from ramekin with little effort, and the center should appear dark/gooey.
9 Enjoy warm with a raspberry drizzle.

Smores

Servings: 4
- Whole graham crackers (4) Marshmallows (2)
- Chocolate - such as Hershey's (4 pieces)

1 Break the graham crackers in half to make eight squares. Cut marshmallows in half crosswise with a pair of scissors.
2 Place the marshmallows cut side down on four graham squares. Place
marshmallow side up in the Air Fryer basket and cook on 390° Fahrenheit for four to five minutes, or until golden.
3 Remove them from the fryer and place a piece Break all graham crackers in half to create eight squares. Cut marshmallows in half crosswise with a pair of scissors.
4 Place marshmallows cut side down on four graham squares. of chocolate and graham square on top of each toasted marshmallow and serve.

Yam & Marshmallow Hand Pies

Servings: 4
- Candied yams (16 oz. can)
- Crescent dough sheet/homemade crust (1) Cinnamon (.5 tsp.)
- Allspice (.25 tsp.)
- Salt (.25 tsp.)
- Marshmallow crème (2 tbsp.) Egg (1)
- The Maple Glaze:
- Confectioners' sugar (.5 cup) Maple syrup (.5 cup)

1 Warm the Air Fryer at 400° Fahrenheit.
2 Drain the syrup from the yams and combine with the cinnamon, salt, and allspice using a fork until thoroughy mixed.
3 Put the dough sheet onto a board and cut it into four equal segments.
4 Spoon the filling onto the squares and add a tablespoon of the crème.
5 Use a brush to spread thc egg over the dough's edges and place the remainder of the two pieces of dough on top of the pies.
6 Use a fork to crimp the edges and cut three slits in the top for venting.
7 Arrange in the Air Fryer for six minutes.
8 Prepare the glaze using the sugar and syrup in a small dish— slowly adding the syrup—until the sugar dissolves.
9 To serve, drizzle the glaze over the warm pies and enjoy

Fiesta Pastries

Servings: 8
- ½ of apple, peeled, cored and chopped
- 1teaspoon fresh orange zest, grated finely
- 7.05-ounce prepared frozen puff pastry, cut into 16 squares
- ½ tablespoon white Sugar
- ½ teaspoon ground cinnamon
  1.Preheat the air fryer to 390 o f and grease an air fryer basket.
  2.Mix all in a bowl except puff pastry.
  3.Arrange about 1 teaspoon of this mixture in the center of each square.

4. Fold each square into a triangle and slightly press the edges with a fork.
5. Arrange the pastries in the air fryer basket and cook for about 10 minutes.
6. Dish out and serve immediately.

Classic Buttermilk Biscuits

Servings:4
- ½ cup cake flour
- 1¼ cups all-purpose flour
- ¾ teaspoon baking powder
- ¼ cup + 2 tablespoons butter, cut into cubes
- ¾ cup buttermilk
- 1teaspoon granulated Sugar Salt, to taste

1. Preheat the air fryer to 400 o f and grease a pie pan lightly.
2. Sift together flours, baking soda, baking powder, Sugar and salt in a large bowl.
3. Add cold butter and mix until a coarse crumb is formed.
4. Stir in the buttermilk slowly and mix until a dough is formed.
5. Press the dough into ½ inch thickness onto a floured surface and cut out circles with a 1¾-inch round cookie cutter.
6. Arrange the biscuits in a pie pan in a single layer and brush butter
7. on them.
8. Transfer into the air fryer and cook for about 8 minutes until golden brown.

Coconut-Coated White Chocolate Cookies

Servings: 8
- 3½-ounce butter
- 1small egg
- 5-ounce self-rising flour
- 1¼-ounce white chocolate, chopped 3 tablespoons desiccated coconut 2¼-ounce caster Sugar
- 1teaspoon vanilla extract

1. Preheat the air fryer to 355 o f and grease a baking sheet lightly.
2. Mix Sugar and butter in a large bowl and beat till fluffy.
3. Whisk in the egg, vanilla extract, flour and chocolate and mix until well combined.
4. Place coconut in a shallow dish and make small balls from the mixture.
5. Roll the balls into coconut evenly and arrange them onto baking sheet.
6. Press each ball into a cookie-like shape and transfer into the air fryer.
7. Cook for about 8 minutes and set the air fryer to 320 o f.
8. Cook for about 4 minutes and dish out to serve.

Basic Butter Cookies

Servings: 8
- 4-ounce unsalted butter 1 cup all-purpose flour
- ¼ teaspoon baking powder 1¼-ounce icing Sugar

1. Preheat the air fryer to 340 o f and grease a baking sheet lightly.
2. Mix butter, icing Sugar, flour and baking powder in a large bowl.
3. Mix well until a dough is formed and transfer into the piping bag fitted with a fluted nozzle.

4. Pipe the dough onto a baking sheet and arrange the baking sheet in
5. the air fryer.
6. Cook for about 10 minutes until golden brown and serve with tea.

Tasty Lemony Biscuits

Servings: 10
- 8½ ounce self-rising flour 3½-ounce cold butter
- 1 small egg
- 1 teaspoon fresh lemon zest, grated finely 3½-ounce caster Sugar
- 1 tablespoons fresh lemon juice 1 teaspoon vanilla extract

1. Preheat the air fryer to 355 o f and grease a baking sheet lightly.
2. Mix flour and Sugar in a large bowl.
3. Add cold butter and mix until a coarse crumb is formed.
4. Stir in the egg, lemon zest and lemon juice and mix until a dough is formed.
5. Press the dough into ½ inch thickness onto a floured surface and cut dough into medium-sized biscuits.
6. Arrange the biscuits on a baking sheet in a single layer and transfer into the air fryer.
7. Cook for about 5 minutes until golden brown and serve with tea.

Perfect Apple Pie

Servings: 6
- frozen pie crust, thawed
- large apple, peeled, cored and chopped 1 tablespoon butter, chopped
- 1egg, beaten
- 3tablespoons Sugar, divided
- 1tablespoon ground cinnamon 2 teaspoons fresh lemon juice
- ½ teaspoon vanilla extract

1. Preheat the air fryer to 320 o f and grease a pie pan lightly.
2. Cut 2 crusts, first about 1/8-inch larger than pie pan and second, a little smaller than first one.
3. Arrange the large crust in the bottom of pie pan.
4. Mix apple, 2 tablespoons of Sugar, cinnamon, lemon juice and vanilla extract in a large bowl.
5. Put the apple mixture evenly over the bottom crust and top with butter.
6. Arrange the second crust on top and seal the edges.
7. Cut 4 slits in the top crust carefully and brush with egg.
8. Sprinkle with Sugar and arrange the pie pan in the air fryer basket.
9. Cook for about 30 minutes and dish out to serve.

Crispy Fruit Tacos

Servings: 2
- 2soft shell tortillas
- 4tablespoons strawberry jelly
- ¼ cup blueberries
- ¼ cup raspberries
- 2tablespoons powdered Sugar

1.Preheat the air fryer to 300 o f and grease an air fryer basket.
2.Put 2 tablespoons of strawberry jelly over each tortilla and top with blueberries and raspberries. Sprinkle with powdered Sugar and transfer into the air fryer basket. Cook for about 5 minutes until crispy and serve.

Healthy Fruit Muffins

Servings: 6
- 1cup milk
- 1pack oreo biscuits, crushed
- ¾ teaspoon baking powder
- 1banana, peeled and chopped
- 1apple, peeled, cored and chopped
- 1teaspoon cocoa powder - 1 teaspoon honey
- 1teaspoon fresh lemon juice Pinch of ground cinnamon

1.Preheat the air fryer to 320 o f and grease 6 muffin cups lightly.
2.Mix milk, biscuits, cocoa powder, baking soda and baking powder in a bowl until a smooth mixture is formed.
3.Divide this mixture into the prepared muffin cups and transfer into the air fryer basket.
4.Cook for about 10 minutes and remove from air fryer.
5.Mix banana, apple, honey, lemon juice and cinnamon in a bowl. Scoop out some portion from center of muffins and fill with the fruit mixture. Refrigerate for 2 hours and serve chilled.

Chocolate Lover's Muffins

Servings: 8
- 1½ cups all-purpose flour 2 teaspoons baking powder 1 egg
- 1cup yogurt
- ½ cup mini chocolate chips
- ¼ cup Sugar Salt, to taste
- 1/3 cup vegetable oil
- 2teaspoons vanilla extract

1.Preheat the air fryer to 355 o f and grease 8 muffin cups lightly.
2.Mix flour, baking powder, Sugar and salt in a bowl.
3.Whisk egg, oil, yogurt and vanilla extract in another bowl.
4.Combine the flour and egg mixtures and mix until a smooth mixture is formed.
5. Fold in the chocolate chips and divide this mixture into the prepared muffin cups.
6.Transfer into the air fryer basket and cook for about 10 minutes.
7.Refrigerate for 2 hours and serve chilled.

Delicate Pear Pouch

Servings: 4
- 2small pears, peeled, cored and halved 2 cups prepared vanilla custard
- 4puff pastry sheets 1 egg, beaten lightly 2 tablespoons Sugar
- Pinch of ground cinnamon
- 2tablespoons whipped cream

1.Preheat the air fryer to 330 o f and grease an air fryer basket.
2.Place a spoonful of vanilla custard and a pear half in the center of each pastry sheet.

3.Mix Sugar and cinnamon in a bowl and sprinkle on the pear halves.
4.Pinch the corners of sheets together to shape into a pouch and transfer into the air fryer basket.
5.Cook for about 15 minutes and top with whipped cream.
6.Dish out and serve with remaining custard.

Red Velvet Cupcakes

Servings:12
For cupcakes:
- 2cups refined flour
- ¾ cup peanut butter 3 eggs
- For Frosting:
- 1cup butter
- 1cup cream cheese For cupcakes:
- ¾ cup icing Sugar
- 2teaspoons beet powder 1 teaspoon cocoa powder

For frosting:
- ¾ cup icing Sugar
- ¼ cup strawberry sauce
- 1teaspoon vanilla essence

1.Preheat the air fryer to 340 o f and grease 12 silicon cups lightly.
For Cupcakes:
1.Mix all the Ingredients in a large bowl until well combined.
2.Transfer the mixture into silicon cups and place in the air fryer basket.
3.Cook for about 12 minutes and dish out.
For Frosting:
1.Mix all the Ingredients in a large bowl until well combined.
2.Top each cupcake evenly with frosting and serve.

Heavenly Tasty Lava Cake

Servings: 6
- 2/3 cup unsalted butter
- eggs
- 2/3 cup all-purpose flour
- cup chocolate chips, melted 1/3 cup fresh raspberries
- tablespoons Sugar Salt, to taste

1.Preheat the air fryer to 355 o f and grease 6 ramekins lightly.
2.Mix Sugar, butter, eggs, chocolate mixture, flour and salt in a bowl until well combined.
3.Fold in the melted chocolate chips and divide this mixture into the prepared ramekins.
4.Transfer into the air fryer basket and cook for about 3 minutes.
5.Garnish with raspberries and serve immediately.

Apple Cake

Servings: 6
- 1cup all-purpose flour
- ½ teaspoon baking soda 1 egg
- 2cups apples, peeled, cored and chopped
- 1/3 cup brown Sugar
- 1teaspoon ground nutmeg
- 1teaspoon ground cinnamon Salt, to taste
- 5tablespoons plus 1 teaspoon vegetable oil
- ¾ teaspoon vanilla extract

1. Preheat the air fryer to 355 o f and grease a baking pan lightly.
2. Mix flour, Sugar, spices, baking soda and salt in a bowl until well combined.
3. Whisk egg with oil and vanilla extract in another bowl.
4. Stir in the flour mixture slowly and fold in the apples.
5. Pour this mixture into the baking pan and cover with the foil paper.
6. Transfer the baking pan into the air fryer and cook for about 40 minutes.
7. Remove the foil and cook for 5 more minutes.
8. Allow to cool completely and cut into slices to serve.

Nutella And Banana Pastries

Servings: 4
- 1puff pastry sheet, cut into 4 equal squares
- ½ cup nutella
- 2bananas, sliced
- 2tablespoons icing Sugar

1. Preheat the air fryer to 375 o f and grease an air fryer basket.
2. Spread nutella on each pastry square and top with banana slices and icing Sugar.
3. Fold each square into a triangle and slightly press the edges with a fork.
4. Arrange the pastries in the air fryer basket and cook for about 12 minutes.
5. Dish out and serve immediately.

Perfect Cinnamon Toast

Servings: 6
- 2tsp. Pepper
- 1½ tsp. Vanilla extract 1 ½ tsp. Cinnamon
- ½ c. Sweetener of choice 1 c. Coconut oil
- 12slices whole wheat bread

1. Melt coconut oil and mix with sweetener until dissolved. Mix in remaining minus bread till incorporated.
2. Spread mixture onto bread, covering all area. Place coated pieces of bread in your air fryer.
3. Cook 5 minutes at 400 degrees.
4. Remove and cut diagonally. Enjoy!

Apple Dumplings

Servings: 4
- 2tbsp. Melted coconut oil 2 puff pastry sheets
- 1tbsp. Brown Sugar 2 tbsp. Raisins
- 2small apples of choice

1. Ensure your air fryer is preheated to 356 degrees.
2. Core and peel apples and mix with raisins and Sugar.
3. Place a bit of apple mixture into puff pastry sheets and brush sides with melted coconut oil.
4. Place into air fryer. Cook 25 minutes, turning halfway through. Will be golden when done.

Air Fryer Chocolate Cake

Servings: 8-10
- ½ c. Hot water 1 tsp. Vanilla
- ¼ c. Olive oil
- ½ c. Almond milk 1 egg

- ½ tsp. Salt
- ¾ tsp. Baking soda
- ¾ tsp. Baking powder
- ½ c. Unsweetened cocoa powder 2 c. Almond flour
- c. Brown Sugar

1. Preheat your air fryer to 356 degrees.
2. Stir all dry together. Then stir in wet . Add hot water last.
3. The batter will be thin, no worries.
4. Pour cake batter into a pan that fits into the fryer. Cover with foil and poke holes into the foil.
5. Bake 35 minutes.
6. Discard foil and then bake another 10 minutes.

Easy Air Fryer Donuts

Servings: 8
- Pinch of allspice
- 4tbsp. Dark brown Sugar
- ½ - 1 tsp. Cinnamon
- 1/3 c. Granulated sweetener 3 tbsp. Melted coconut oil 1can of biscuits

1. Mix allspice, Sugar, sweetener, and cinnamon.
2. Take out biscuits from can and with a circle cookie cutter, cut holes from centers and place into air fryer.
3. Cook 5 minutes at 350 degrees. As batches are cooked, use a brush to coat with melted coconut oil and dip each into Sugar mixture.
4. Serve warm!

Chocolate Soufflé For Two

Servings: 2
- 2tbsp. Almond flour
- ½ tsp. Vanilla
- 3tbsp. Sweetener
- 2separated eggs
- ¼ c. Melted coconut oil
- 3ounces of semi-sweet chocolate, chopped

1. Brush coconut oil and sweetener onto ramekins.
2. Melt coconut oil and chocolate together. Beat egg yolks well, adding vanilla and sweetener. Stir in flour and ensure there are no lumps.
3. Preheat fryer to 330 degrees.
4. Whisk egg whites till they reach peak state and fold them into chocolate mixture.
5. Pour batter into ramekins and place into the fryer.
6. Cook 14 minutes.
7. Serve with powdered Sugar dusted on top.

Apple Hand Pies

Servings: 6
- 15-ounces no-Sugar-added apple pie filling 1 store-bought crust

1. Lay out pie crust and slice into equal-sized squares.
2. Place 2 tbsp. Filling into each square and seal crust with a fork.
3. Place into the fryer. Cook 8 minutes at 390 degrees until golden in color.

Calories: 278 Fat: 10g Protein: 5g Sugar: 4g

Blueberry Lemon Muffins

Servings: 12
- 1tsp. Vanilla
- Juice and zest of 1 lemon 2 eggs
- 1c. Blueberries

- ½ c. Cream
- ¼ c. Avocado oil
- ½ c. Monk fruit
- 2½ c. Almond flour

1.Mix monk fruit and flour.

2.In another bowl, mix vanilla, egg, lemon juice, and cream. Add mixtures together and blend well.

3.Spoon batter into cupcake holders. Place in air fryer. Bake 10 minutes at 320 degrees, checking at 6 minutes to ensure you don't overbake them.

Sweet Cream Cheese Wontons

Servings: 16-20
- 1egg mixed with a bit of water Wonton wrappers
- ½ c. Powdered erythritol
- 8ounces softened cream cheese Olive oil

1.Mix sweetener and cream cheese together.

2.Lay out 4 wontons at a time and cover with a dish towel to prevent drying out.

3.Place ½ of a teaspoon of cream cheese mixture into each wrapper.

4.Dip finger into egg/water mixture and fold diagonally to form a triangle. Seal edges well.

5.Repeat with remaining .

6.Place filled wontons into air fryer and cook 5 minutes at 400 degrees, shaking halfway through Cooking .

Calories: 303 Fat: 3g Protein: 0.5g Sugar: 4g

Air Fryer Cinnamon Rolls

Servings: 8
- 1½ tbsp. Cinnamon
- ¾ c. Brown Sugar
- ¼ c. Melted coconut oil
- 1-pound frozen bread dough, thawed

Glaze:
- ½ tsp. Vanilla
- 1¼ c. Powdered erythritol 2 tbsp. Softened ghee
- 4ounces softened cream cheese

1.Lay out bread dough and roll out into a rectangle. Brush melted ghee over dough and leave a 1-inch border along edges.

2.Mix cinnamon and sweetener and then sprinkle over dough.

3.Roll dough tightly and slice into 8 pieces. Let sit 1-2 hours to rise.

4.To make the glaze, simply mix till smooth.

5.Once rolls rise, place into air fryer and cook 5 minutes at 350 degrees.

6.Serve rolls drizzled in cream cheese glaze. Enjoy!

French Toast Bites

Servings: 8
- Almond milk Cinnamon Sweetener
- 8 eggs
- 3 pieces wheat bread

1.Preheat air fryer to 360 degrees.

2.Whisk eggs and thin out with almond milk.

3.Mix 1/3 cup of sweetener with lots of cinnamon.

4.Tear bread in half, ball up pieces and press together to form a ball.

5.Soak bread balls in egg and then roll into cinnamon Sugar, making sure to thoroughly coat.

6.Place coated bread balls into air fryer and bake 15 minutes.

Baked Apple

Servings: 4
- ¼ c. Water
- ¼ tsp. Nutmeg
- ¼ tsp. Cinnamon
- 1½ tsp. Melted ghee 2 tbsp. Raisins
- **2**tbsp. Chopped walnuts 1 medium apple

1.Preheat your air fryer to 350 degrees.

2.Slice apple in half and discard some of the flesh from the center.

3.Place into frying pan.

4.Mix remaining together except water. Spoon mixture to the middle of apple halves.

5.Pour water over filled apples.

6.Place pan with apple halves into air fryer, bake 20 minutes.

Cinnamon Sugar Roasted Chickpeas

Servings: 2
- 1tbsp. Sweetener
- 1tbsp. Cinnamon
- 1c. Chickpeas

1.Preheat air fryer to 390 degrees.

2.Rinse and drain chickpeas.

3. Mix all together and add to air fryer.

4.Cook 10 minutes.

Cinnamon Fried Bananas

Servings: 2-3
- 1c. Panko breadcrumbs 3 tbsp. Cinnamon
- ½ c. Almond flour 3 egg whites
- 8ripe bananas
- 3tbsp. Vegan coconut oil

1.Heat coconut oil and add breadcrumbs. Mix around 2-3 minutes until golden. Pour into bowl.

2.Peel and cut bananas in half. Roll each bananas half into flour, eggs, and crumb mixture. Place into air fryer.

3.Cook 10 minutes at 280 degrees.

4.A great addition to a healthy banana split!

Brownies

Servings: 4

The Wet
- 1/4 cup almond milk 1/4 cup chickpeas liquid
- 1/2 teaspoon vanilla extract, unsweetened

The Dry
- 1/2 cup whole-wheat pastry flour 1/2 cup coconut Sugar
- 1/4 cup cocoa powder, unsweetened 1 tablespoon ground flax seeds
- 1/4 teaspoon salt

For The Mix-Ins:
- 2tablespoons chopped walnuts 2 tablespoons pecans
- 2tablespoons shredded coconut

1. Switch on the air fryer, insert the fryer basket, then shut it with the lid, set the frying temperature 350 degrees f, and let it preheat for 5 minutes.

2. Meanwhile, take a large bowl, add all the dry in it and
stir until mixed.

1. Take another bowl, place all the wet in it, whisk until combined, then gradually mix into the dry mixture until incorporated and mix the walnuts, pecans and coconut until combined.
2. Take a 5-inch round pan, line it with parchment paper, pour in prepared batter, smooth the top with a spatula.
3. Open the preheated fryer, place the prepared pan in it, close the lid and cook for 20 minutes until firm and a toothpick come out clean from the center of the pan.
4. When done, the air fryer will beep, open the lid, remove the pan from the fryer and cool for 15 minutes.
5. Then cut into brownies and serve.

Apple And Blueberries Crumble

Servings: 2
- 1/2 cup frozen blueberries
  - medium apple, peeled, diced 2 tablespoons coconut Sugar
- 1/4 cup and 1 tablespoon brown rice flour
- 1/2 teaspoon ground cinnamon 2 tablespoons almond butter

1. Switch on the air fryer, insert the fryer basket, then shut it with the lid, set the frying temperature 350 degrees f, and let it preheat for 5 minutes.
2. Meanwhile, take a large ramekin, place apples and berries in it, and stir until mixed.
3. Take a small bowl, add flour and remaining in it, stir until mixed, and then spoon this mixture over fruits.
4. Open the preheated fryer, place the prepared ramekin in it in, close
5. the lid and cook for 15 minutes until cooked and the top has turned golden brown.
6. When done, the air fryer will beep, then open the lid and remove ramekin from it.
7. Serve straight away.

Mug Carrot Cake

Servings: 1
- 2 tablespoons grated carrot
- 1/4 cups whole-wheat pastry flour 1/8 teaspoon ground dried ginger 2 tablespoons chopped walnuts 1/4 teaspoon baking powder
- 1 tablespoon coconut Sugar 1/8 teaspoon salt
- 1/4 teaspoon ground cinnamon 1 tablespoons raisin
- 1/8 teaspoon ground allspice
- 2 tablespoons and 2 teaspoons almond milk 2 teaspoons olive oil

1. Switch on the air fryer, insert the fryer basket, then shut it with the lid, set the frying temperature 350 degrees f, and let it preheat for 5 minutes.
2. Meanwhile, take an ovenproof mug, place flour in it, stir in ginger, baking powder, salt, Sugar, cinnamon, and allspice until mixed and then mix in carrots, raisins, nuts, oil, and milk until incorporated
3. Open the preheated fryer, place the prepared mug in it, close the lid and cook for 15 minutes until firm and a toothpick come out clean from the center of the cake.

4. When done, the air fryer will beep, then open the lid and take out the mug.
5. Serve straight away.

Peanut Butter Balls

Servings: 6
- 1/2 cup coconut flour
- tablespoons flaxseed 1/2 cup oats
- 1/2 teaspoon baking soda 1/3 cup maple syrup
- 1/2 teaspoon baking powder
- 1/2 cup peanut butter
- 5 tablespoons water, warmed

1. Prepare the flax egg and for this, place flax seeds a small bowl, stir in water until combined and let it stand for 5 minutes.
2. Then pour flax egg in a large bowl, add butter and maple syrup,
3. whisk until smooth and then whisk in baking powder and soda until well combined.
4. Stir in oats and flour until incorporated and dough comes together, place the dough into the refrigerator for 10 minutes until chilled,
5. and then shape the dough into twelve balls.
6. Meanwhile, switch on the air fryer, insert the fryer basket, then shut it with the lid, set the frying temperature 250 degrees f, and let it preheat for 5 minutes.
7. Open the preheated fryer, place balls in it in a single layer, close the lid and cook for 10 minutes until golden brown and cooked,
8. shaking halfway.
9. When done, the air fryer will beep, open the lid, and transfer balls to a dish.
10. Cook remaining balls in the same manner and then serve.

Cinnamon Churros

Servings: 4
For The Churros:
- 1 cup coconut flour
- 1/2 cup and 1 tablespoon coconut Sugar 2 teaspoons cinnamon
- 1/2 teaspoon vanilla extract, unsweetened 1/2 cup almond butter
- 3 flax eggs
- 1 cup of water

For The Chocolate Sauce:
- 1 teaspoon coconut oil
- 3/4 cup chocolate chips, unsweetened

1. Prepare churros and for this, take a medium saucepan, place it over medium heat, pour in water and bring it to a boil.
2. Stir in butter and 1 tablespoon Sugar, let it melts, switch heat to medium-low level and then fold in the flour until incorporated and the dough comes together, remove the pan from heat and set aside until required.
3. Take a medium bowl, place flax eggs in it and whisk in vanilla until combined.
4. Fold the flax egg mixture into the prepared dough until well combined and then let it stand 15 minutes until cooked.
5. Transfer cooled dough into a piping bag with a star-shaped tip, take a baking pan, line it with parchment

paper and pipe churros on it, about 6-inch long, and then chill them in the refrigerator for 30 minutes.

6.Meanwhile, switch on the air fryer, insert the fryer basket, then shut it with the lid, set the frying temperature 380 degrees f, and let it preheat.

7.Then open the preheated fryer, place churros in it in a single layer, close the lid and cook for 10 minutes until golden brown and cooked, shaking halfway.

8.Meanwhile, take a small bowl, place the cinnamon and remaining

9.Sugar in it and stir until mixed, set aside until required.

10.When done, the air fryer will beep, then open the lid, dredge churros into the cinnamon-Sugar mixture, place them on a wire rack and cook remaining churros in the same manner.

11.In the meantime, prepare the chocolate sauce and

12.for this, take a heatproof bowl, place chocolate chips in it, add oil and microwave for 30 seconds until chocolate has melted, and when done, stir well.

13.Dip churros into the chocolate sauce and serve.

Stuffed And Spiced Baked Apples

Servings: 4

- 1/3 cup rolled oats 4 medium apples
- 1/4 cup chopped pecans
- 1 teaspoon pumpkin spice seasoning 2 tablespoons raisins
- 1/4 cup maple syrup 2/3 cup water

1.Switch on the air fryer, insert the fryer basket, then shut it with the

2.lid, set the frying temperature 340 degrees f, and let it preheat for 5 minutes.

3.Meanwhile, prepare the apples and core them from the center but not through the bottom and scoop out the seeds by using a spoon.

4.Take a medium bowl, place remaining in it, except for water, stir until mixed and stuff this mixture into the apples.

5.Take a shallow heatproof dish that fits into the air fryer, pour water in it, and place prepared apples in it.

6.Open the preheated fryer, place the dish containing apples in it,

7.close the lid and cook for 15 minutes until fork-tender, turning and spraying with oil halfway.

8.When done, the air fryer will beep, then open the lid and take out the dish.

9.Serve straight away.

Sweet Potato Dessert Fries

Servings: 2

- 2medium sweet potatoes, peeled 1/4 cup coconut Sugar
- 1tablespoon cornstarch
- 2tablespoons cinnamon
- ½tablespoon coconut oil
- Powdered Sugar as needed for dusting

1.Switch on the air fryer, insert the fryer basket, then shut it with the lid, set the frying temperature 370 degrees f, and let it preheat for 5 minutes.

2.Meanwhile, cut peeled potatoes into ½-inch thick slices, place them in a bowl, add cornstarch and oil and toss until well coated.

3.Open the preheated fryer, place sweet potatoes in it in a single layer, close the lid, and cook for 18 minutes until golden brown and cooked, shaking halfway.

4.When all the fries have cooked, transfer them to a large bowl,

5.sprinkle them with remaining coconut Sugar and cinnamon and toss until coated.

6.Transfer potatoes to a dish, sprinkle with powdered Sugar, and then serve.

Donut Holes

Servings: 6

- 1cup almond flour
- 1teaspoon baking powder 1/2 teaspoon salt
- 1/4 cup and 2 tablespoons coconut Sugar, divided
- 21/4 teaspoons cinnamon, divided
- 1tablespoon melted coconut oil
- 2tablespoons chickpea liquid 1/4 cup soymilk

1.Take a large bowl, place flour in it, stir baking powder, salt, ¼ cup Sugar, and 2 teaspoons cinnamon.

2.Whisk in oil, milk and chickpea liquid until incorporated and the

3.dough comes together and then chill it in the refrigerator for 1 hour.

4.Take a shallow dish, place remaining Sugar and cinnamon in it and stir until mixed, set aside until required.

5.Switch on the air fryer, insert the fryer basket lined with parchment

6.Then, shut it with the lid, set the frying temperature 370 degrees f, and let it preheat for 5 minutes.

7.Meanwhile, remove chilled dough from the refrigerator, distribute it into twelve parts, shape each part into a ball, and dredge it with cinnamon-Sugar mixture.

8.Open the preheated fryer, place balls in it in a single layer, spray with olive oil, close the lid and cook for 6 minutes until golden brown and cooked, don't shake.

9.When done, the air fryer will beep, then open the lid, transfer balls to a dish and let them cool completely.

10.Cook remaining donut balls in the same manner and then serve.

Cake With Cream And Strawberries

Servings: 2

- 1pure butter puff pastry to stretch
- 500g strawberries (clean and without skin) 1 bowl of custard
- 3tbsp icing Sugar baked at 210°c in the air fryer

1. Unroll the puff pastry and place it on the baking sheet. Prick the bottom with a fork and spread the custard.

2. Arrange the strawberries in a circle and sprinkle with icing Sugar. Cook in a fryer setting a 210°c for 15 minutes.

3. Remove the cake from the fryer with the tongs and let cool. When serving sprinkle with icing Sugar. And why not, add some whipped cream.

Apple Pie

Servings: 3

- 600g flour 350g margarine 150g Sugar
- 2 eggs
- 50g breadcrumbs 3 apples
- 75g raisins 75g Sugar 1tsp cinnamon

1.Put the flour, Sugar, eggs, and margarine nuts in the blender just outside the refrigerator. Mix everything until you get a compact and quite flexible mixture.

2.Let it rest in the refrigerator for at least 30 minutes.

3. Preheat the air fryer at 1500c for 5 minutes.

4. Spread 2/3 of the broken dough mass in 3-4 mm thick covering the just-floured and floured tank and making the edges adhere well, which should be at least 2 cm.

5. Place the breadcrumbs, apple slices, Sugar, raisins, and cinnamon in the bottom; cover everything with the remaining dough and make holes in the top to allow steam to escape.

6.Cook for 40 minutes and then turn off the lower resistance. Cook for another 20 minutes only with the upper resistance on. Once it has cooled, put it on a plate and serve.

Apple Rotation

Servings: 6
- 1 roll of rectangular puff pastry 220g of apples
- 50g of Sugar 100g raisins 50g pine nuts
- To taste breadcrumbs Cinnamon powder to taste

1.Put the raisins in warm water for at least 30 min.

2. Meanwhile, peel the apples, remove the kernel, and cut them into thin slices.

3.Pour the apples into a large bowl and add the dried raisins. Add the cinnamon, Sugar and pine nuts, gently mix the and let stand.

4. Meanwhile, spread the puff pastry on a work surface with parchment paper. Sprinkle with the breadcrumbs, leaving a 2-3 cm border around. Place the mixture in the center of the dough and close the coating along.

5.Be careful not to tear the dough, close the sides tightly so that the contents do not come out during Cooking.

6. Place the liner on the air fryer and cook over low temperature for about 25 min. When finished Cooking , sprinkle the strudel with icing Sugar and serve warm sliced.

Fried Cream

Servings: 8

For the cream:
- 500ml of whole milk 3 egg yolks
- 150 g of Sugar 50 g flour
- 1envelope vanilla Sugar
- For The Pie:
- 2eggs

Unlimited breadcrumbs 1 tsp oil

1. First prepare the custard; once cooked, pour the cream into a dish just covered with a transparent film and level. Let cool at room temperature for about 2 hours. Grease the basket and distribute it all over. When the cream is cold, place it on a cutting board and cut it into dice; pass each piece of cream first in the breadcrumbs, covering the 4 sides well in the beaten egg and then in the pie. Place each part inside the basket. Set the temperature to 1500c. Cook for 10 to 12 minutes, turning the pieces after 6 to 8 minutes. The

doses of this cream are enough to make 2 or even 3 kitchens in a row.

Calories: 355 Fat: 18.37g Carb: 44.94g Sugar: 30.36g Protein: 4.81g Cholesterol: 45m

Apple, Cream, And Hazelnut Crumble

Servings: 6
- 4golden apples 100 ml of water
- 50g cane Sugar 50g of Sugar
- ½ tbsp cinnamon
- 200ml of fresh cream Chopped hazelnuts to taste

1.In a bowl, combine the peeled apples, cut into small cubes, cane Sugar, Sugar, and cinnamon. Pour the apples inside the basket, add the water.

2.Set the air fryer to 1800c and simmer for 15 minutes

3.depending on the type of apple used and the size of the pieces. At the end, divide the apples in the serving glasses, cover with

4.whipped cream and sprinkle with chopped hazelnuts.

Fregolotta (Venetian Puff Pastry Pie) With Hazelnuts

Servings: 8 people
- 200g of flour 150g of Sugar
- 100g melted butter 100g hazelnuts
- 1egg
- ½ sachet of yeast

1.Do not finely chop the hazelnuts. In a large bowl, pour all the (the butter once melted should be cooled before using), mix lightly, without the dough becoming too liquid.

2.Place parchment paper on the bottom of the basket and pour the mixture into it. Spread it evenly. Set the air fryer to 1800c and simmer for

15 minutes and then turn the cake.

Cook for an additional 5 minutes. Let cool and sprinkle the cake with icing Sugar.

Frozen Treats

Servings: 8

14 frozen pieces

1. Place the handles, placing them on the parchment paper and place them on the basket. Set the temperature to 1500c. Cook everything for 25 min.

Roscòn Of Reyes (Spanish King's Cake)

Servings: 4
- 2puff pastries 100g almond flour 1 egg
- 75g of Sugar 50g butter
- 1vial of almond aroma
- 1porcelain bean

1.First, prepare the filling: in a bowl mix the flour, egg, Sugar, butter at room temperature and almond extract. Stretch a puff pastry with the baking paper inside the basket. Prick with a fork and spread the filling well. Place the bean inside, choosing an external position for the cake.

2.Cover with the second roll of puff pastry and weld the edges well.

3. Brush the surface with an egg yolk diluted with milk and decorate with small incisions. Set the temperature to 1800c.

4. Bake the pie for

25 minutes turn the baking paper half a turn and cook for another 10 minutes. Tradition says that the person who finds the hidden bean becomes the "king" of the day.

Chocolate Muffins
Servings: 10
- 300g of flour 00:
- 300g of Sugar:
- 150g of butter
- 70g bitter cocoa powder 6g baking powder
- 180 ml of whole fresh milk 1g of salt
- Eggs
- 2g of baking soda 100g dark chocolate 1 vanilla pod

1.In a food processor, beat the butter of the ointment with the Sugar and then combine the seeds of a vanilla bean. When the mixture is clear and foamy enough, add the eggs at room temperature, one at a time.

2.Work all the for a few minutes and then add the flour, bitter cocoa, yeast, baking soda and salt (all sifted), alternating with milk at room temperature.

3. Finally, combine the dark chocolate chips. Fill the molds with the mixture and place them inside the air fryer (7 to 8 lots) preheated at 1800c.

4. Cook for about 25 minutes. In the end let cool. You can, at discretion, sprinkle with icing Sugar.

Nut Cake
Servings: 10
- 250g of walnuts 150g maïzena
- 4medium eggs
- 200g of butter (room temperature) 1 sachet of yeast
- sachet of vanilla Sugar 200g of Sugar

1.Chop the nuts with 50 g of Sugar. Using a food processor, beat the butter with the remaining Sugar until you get a shiny and foamy mixture.

2.Add the eggs one by one, making sure the mixture is still soft, then add the vanilla. Add the chopped nuts with the Sugar and then the cornstarch that will sift with the yeast. Butter and flour the basket, then pour the mixture in the center.

3. Set the air fryer at 180°c. Cook for 45 minutes (turn off the lower heating element 40 minutes later). Let cool before serving.

Italian Cake
Servings: 8
- 250g of potato starch
- 150g of flour 00 (flour 55)
- 250g of su
- 4 eggs
- 50 g butter
- sachet of yeast Powdered Sugar

1.Melt the butter in a small saucepan and let it cool. Beat the eggs with the fine Sugar until you get a light and frothy mixture. Add the flour, starch, sifted yeast, melted butter and mix until a homogeneous mixture is obtained.

2.Butter and flour the basket and pour the into it.

3.Set the temperature to 1800c and cook the cake for 35 min.

Marble Cake

Servings: 10
- 190g butter
- 1g bag of vanilla Sugar 12g baking powder 375g flour
- 22g cocoa powder
- 4g medium eggs 225g of Sugar 165 ml of milk Salt (a pinch)

1.Put the softened butter into small pieces in a bowl with the Sugar, mount the until a white and foamy cream forms. Add the eggs at room temperature, one by one, the salt and beat about 5 minutes until you get a mixture without lumps. Add the flour (except 30 g that will keep aside), the yeast and vanilla Sugar sifted alternately with the milk. Mix the well, divide them evenly, and add the remaining flour in a bowl and the sifted cocoa. Butter and flour the basket and first place the transparent mixture divided into three separate parts. Do the same with the dark mixture by filling the remaining gaps between the light mixture. To get the veined effect, rotate a fork from top to bottom through the mixture's two colors.

2.Set the air fryer to 1800c and cook for 40 minutes and then turn off the lower resistance. Cook for another 10 min. Control the baking

3.of the cake with the tip of a knife.

Genoves Cake
Servings: 10
- eggs
- 190g of Sugar
- 150g of flour 00 (flour 55) 75g potato starch
- 2g vanilla Sugar

1.In a bowl, beat the eggs with the Sugar until you get a light and smooth mixture. Add the sifted flour, starch and vanilla Sugar and mix with a whisk until a homogeneous mixture is obtained. Butter and flour the basket, then pour the mixture. Set the air fryer to 1800c and simmer for 35 minutes.

Creamy Cheesecake
Servings: 4
- ¾ cup sweetener, low Cal orie
- 16 ounces cream cheese, kept in room temperature 2 eggs
- teaspoon vanilla extract 2 tablespoons sour cream
- ½ teaspoon lemon zest
  1. Blend the eggs, vanilla, lemon juice, and sweetener in a blender or food processor to make a smooth mixture.
  2. Add the cream cheese, sour cream, and blend again.
  3. Grease a spring form pan (4 inch) with some Cooking spray. Add the mixture over it.
  4. Place instant pot air fryer crisp over kitchen platform. Press air fry set the temperature to 400°f and set the timer to 5 minutes to preheat. Press "start" and allow it to pre-heat for 5 minutes.
  5. In the inner pot, place the air fryer basket. In the basket, add the pan.
  6. Close the crisp lid and press the "bake" setting. Set temperature to 350°f and set the timer to 10 minutes. Press "start."
  7. Open the crisp lid after cooking time is over. Cooldown and refrigerate until chilled. Slice

and serve chilled.

Air Fried Bananas

Servings: 2-3
- ½ cup all-purpose flour 3 egg whites
- cup panko breadcrumbs 3 tablespoon cinnamon
- ripe bananas, peeled and halved 3 tablespoon canola oil

1. Place instant pot air fryer crisp over kitchen platform. Press
2. "sauté," select "hi" setting and press "start." In the inner pot, add the oil and allow it to heat.
3. Add the breadcrumbs and stir-cook for 2-3 minutes until evenly golden. Set aside in a bowl. Take two bowls, in one bowl beat the egg whites and in another, add the flour.
4. Coat the bananas with egg mixture, flour mixture, and then with the crumbs.
5. In the inner pot, place the air fryer basket. In the basket, add the bananas.
6. Close the crisp lid and press the "bake" setting. Set temperature to
7. 280°f and set the timer to 10 minutes. Press "start."
8. Open the crisp lid after Cooking time is over. Serve warm.

Delicious Apple Crisp

Servings: 4
- 5 apples, peel and cut into bite-size pieces 1 tsp maple syrup
- 1/4 cup brown Sugar 3/4 cup rolled oats 1/4 cup flour
- 1/4 cup butter
- 1/2 tsp cinnamon 1/4 tsp nutmeg
- 1/2 cup water 1/4 tsp salt

1. Spray instant pot duo crisp from inside with cooking spray.
2. Add apple pieces into the pot. Sprinkle nutmeg, cinnamon, and maple syrup on top of apples.
3. Pour water over apple mixture.
4. Add butter in microwave-safe bowl and microwave until butter is melted.
5. Add oats, brown Sugar, flour, and salt in melted butter and mix well.
6. Spread oat mixture evenly over apple mixture.
7. Seal the pot with pressure Cooking lid and cook on high pressure for 5 minutes.
8. Once done, allow to release pressure naturally. Remove lid.
9. Seal the pot with air fryer lid and select air fry for 4 minutes.
10. Top with vanilla ice-cream and serve immediately.

Calories 375 Fat 12 g Carbohydrates 66 g Sugar 39 g Protein 8 g Cholesterol 31 mg

Almond Coconut Cake

Servings: 8
- 2 eggs, lightly beaten
- 1/2 cup heavy whipping cream 1/4 cup butter, melted
- 1 tsp vanilla
- 1 tsp baking powder 1/3 cup swerve
- 1/2 cup shredded coconut 1 cup almond flour

1. Spray a 6-inch baking dish with Cooking spray and set aside.
2. In a mixing bowl, mix almond flour, shredded coconut, sweetener, and baking powder.
3. Add egg, heavy cream, butter, and vanilla and mix until well combined.
4. Pour batter into the prepared dish and cover dish with foil.
5. Pour 2 cups of water into the inner pot of instant pot duo crisp then place steamer rack in the pot.
6. Place baking dish on top of the steamer rack.
7. Seal the pot with pressure Cooking lid and cook on high pressure for 40 minutes.
8. Once done, allow to release pressure naturally for 10 minutes then
9. release remaining pressure using a quick release. Remove lid.
10. Carefully remove the baking dish from the pot and let it cool for 20 minutes.
11. 1 slice and serve.

Choco Coconut Cupcake

Servings: 4
- 1 egg, lightly beaten
- 2 tbsp coconut flour 2 tbsp cocoa powder 1/2 tsp vanilla
- 1/4 cup maple syrup 1/2 cup sun butter Pinch of salt

1. In a bowl, whisk together sun butter, egg, vanilla, maple syrup, and salt. Add coconut flour and cocoa powder and stir to combine. Pour batter into the silicone muffin molds and place in instant pot air fryer basket.
2. Place basket in the pot. Seal the pot with air fryer lid and select bake mode and cook at 350 f for 10 minutes. Serve and enjoy.

Creamy Choco Pots

Servings: 6
- 5 egg yolks
- 4 tbsp Sugar 1/2 cup milk
- 1 1/2 cups heavy cream 8 oz chocolate, melted Pinch of salt

1. Add milk and cream in a saucepan and bring to simmer over medium-low heat.
2. In a bowl, whisk together Sugar, egg yolks, and salt.
3. Slowly add egg yolks mixture in milk mixture and whisk constantly.
4. Add melted chocolate and whisk until combined.
5. Pour mixture into the 6 ramekins.
6. Pour 1 1/2 cups of water into the inner pot of instant pot duo crisp then place steamer rack in the pot.
7. Place ramekins on top of the steamer rack.
8. Seal the pot with pressure Cooking lid and cook on high for 6 minutes.
9. Once done, allow to release pressure naturally. Remove lid.
10. Remove ramekins from the pot and let it cool completely then place in the refrigerator for 4 hours.
11. Top with whipped cream and serve.

Apple Chips With Almond Dip

Servings: 4
- (8-oz.) Apple
- 1 teaspoon ground cinnamon 2 teaspoons canola oil Cooking spray

- 1/4 cup greek yogurt
- 1tablespoon almond butter
- 1 teaspoon honey

1. Pass the apple through a mandolin to get thin slices.
2. Add these slices to a bowl and add oil and cinnamon them toss well.
3. Place the slices in the air fryer basket in a single layer.
4. Set the air fryer basket in the instant pot duo.
5. Put on the air fryer lid and seal it.
6. Hit the "air fry button" and select 12 minutes of Cooking time, then press "start."
7. Flip the slices after every 4 minutes then resume Cooking .
8. Once the instant pot duo beeps, remove its lid.
9. Air fry the remaining slices in the same manner.
10. whisk yogurt with honey and almond butter in a bowl.
11. serve the apple crisp with yogurt on top.

Blueberry Cheesecake
Servings: 6
- 6digestives
- 2oz. Butter, melted 5 cups soft cheese
- 1½ cups caster Sugar 4 large eggs
- 5oz. Fresh blueberries
- 2tablespoon greek yogurt
- 1tablespoon vanilla essence 5 tablespoon icing Sugar

1. Take a 6-inch springform pan and dust it with flour.
2. Crush digestive biscuits in a food processor and mix with melted butter.
3. Spread the biscuit crumb in the pan and press it evenly.
4. Beat cream cheese with Sugar in an electric mixer until fluffy.
5. Stir in eggs, vanilla essence, and yogurt then mix well.
6. Fold in chopped berries and mix gently with the filling.
7. Spread the blueberry-cream filling in the crust evenly.
8. Place the prepared pan in the air fryer basket.
9. Set the air fryer basket in the instant pot duo.
10. Put on the air fryer lid and seal it.
11. Hit the "air fry button" and select 15 minutes of Cooking time, then press "start."
12. Once the instant pot duo beeps, remove its lid.
13. Allow the cake to cool down then transfer to the refrigerator for 4 hours.
14. Garnish with icing Sugar.
15. slice and serve.

Oats Sandwich Biscuits
Servings: 6
- 1½ cups plain flour
- 5oz. Butter
- 3oz. White Sugar
- ½ small egg beaten
- ¼ cup desiccated coconut
- ½ cup gluten-free oats 1/3 oz. White chocolate
- 1teaspoon vanilla essence

Filling:
- 5oz. Icing Sugar 2 oz. Butter

- 1/2 teaspoon lemon juice 1 teaspoon vanilla essence

1. Whisk butter with Sugar in an electric mixer until fluffy.
2. Stir in egg, vanilla essence, coconut, and chocolate then mix well.
3. Slow add flour and continue mixing until it forms a cookie dough.
4. Make medium-sized biscuits out of it then roll them in the oats to coat.
5. Place the cookies in the air fryer basket. Cook the cookies in batches to avoid overcrowding.
6. Set the air fryer basket in the instant pot duo.
7. Put on the air fryer lid and seal it.
8. Hit the "air fry button" and select 18 minutes of Cooking time, then press "start." Flip the cookies after 9 minutes then resume Cooking
9. . Once the instant pot duo beeps, remove its lid. Air fry the remaining cookies in the same manner. Meanwhile, beat butter with icing Sugar into a creamy mixture. Stir in vanilla and lemon juice, then mix well. Spread a tablespoon of this filling in between two cookies and make a sandwich out of them. Use the entire filling to make more cookie sandwiches. Serve.

Chocolate Smarties Cookies
Servings: 6
- 5oz. Butter
- 5oz. Caster Sugar
- 8oz. Self-rising flour
- 1teaspoon vanilla essence 5 tablespoon milk
- 3tablespoon cocoa powder
- 2oz. Nestle smarties

1. Whisk cocoa powder with caster Sugar and self-rising flour in a bowl.
2. Stir in butter and mix well to form a crumbly mixture.
3. Stir in milk and vanilla essence, then mix well to form a smooth dough.
4. Add the smarties and knead the dough well.
5. Roll this cookie dough into a 1-inch thick layer.
6. Use a cookies cutter to cut maximum cookies out of it.
7. Roll the remaining dough again to carve out more cookies.
8. Place half of the cookies in the air fryer basket.
9. Set the air fryer basket in the instant pot duo.
10. Put on the air fryer lid and seal it.
11. Hit the "bake button" and select 10 minutes of Cooking time, then press "start."
12. flip the cookies after 5 minutes then resume Cooking .
13. Once the instant pot duo beeps, remove its lid.
14. Similarly bake the remaining cookies.
15. Enjoy.

Pumpkin Cookies
Servings: 24
- 2and ½ cups flour
- ½ teaspoon baking soda
- 1tablespoon flax seed, ground 3 tablespoons water

- ½ cup pumpkin flesh, mashed
- ¼ cup honey
- 2 tablespoons butter
- 1 teaspoon vanilla extract
- ½ cup dark chocolate chips

1. In a bowl, mix flax seed with water, stir and leave aside for a few minutes.
2. In another bowl, mix flour with salt and baking soda.
3. In a third bowl, mix honey with pumpkin puree, butter, vanilla extract and flaxseed.
4. Combine flour with honey mix and chocolate chips and stir.
5. Scoop 1 tablespoon of cookie dough on a lined baking sheet that fits your air fryer, repeat with the rest of the dough, introduce them in your air fryer and cook at 350 degrees f for 15 minutes.
6. Leave cookies to cool down and serve.
7. Enjoy!

Figs And Coconut Butter Mix

Servings: 3
- 2 tablespoons coconut butter 12 figs, halved
- ¼ cup Sugar
- 1 cup almonds, toasted and chopped

1. Put butter in a pan that fits your air fryer and melt over medium high heat.
2. Add figs, Sugar and almonds, toss, introduce in your air fryer and cook at 300 degrees f for 4 minutes.
3. Divide into bowls and serve cold.
4. Enjoy!

Lemon Bars

Servings: 6
- 4 eggs
- 2 and ¼ cups flour Juice from 2 lemons 1 cup butter, soft
- 2 cups Sugar

1. In a bowl, mix butter with ½ cup Sugar and 2 cups flour, stir well, press on the bottom of a pan that fits your air fryer, introduce in the fryer and cook at 350 degrees f for 10 minutes.
2. In another bowl, mix the rest of the Sugar with the rest of the flour, eggs and lemon juice, whisk well and spread over crust.
3. Introduce the fryer at 350 degrees f for 15 minutes more, leave aside to cool down, cut bars and serve them.
4. Enjoy!

Pears And Espresso Cream

Servings: 4
- 4 pears, halved and cored
- 2 tablespoons lemon juice 1 tablespoon Sugar
- 2 tablespoons water
- 2 tablespoons butter

For The Cream:
- 1 cup whipping cream 1 cup mascarpone
- 1/3 cup Sugar
- 2 tablespoons espresso, cold

1. In a bowl, mix pears halves with lemon juice, 1 tablespoons Sugar, butter and water, toss well,

transfer them to your air fryer and cook at 360 degrees f for 30 minutes.
2. Meanwhile, in a bowl, mix whipping cream with mascarpone, 1/3 cup Sugar and espresso, whisk well and keep in the fridge until pears are done.
3. Divide pears on plates, top with espresso cream and serve them.
4. Enjoy!

Poppyseed Cake

Servings: 6
- 1 and ¼ cups flour
- 1 teaspoon baking powder
- ¾ cup Sugar
- 1 tablespoon orange zest, grated 2 teaspoons lime zest, grated
- ½ cup butter, soft 2 eggs, whisked
- ½ teaspoon vanilla extract 2 tablespoons poppy seeds 1 cup milk

For The Cream:
- 1 cup Sugar
- ½ cup passion fruit puree
- 3 tablespoons butter, melted 4 egg yolks

1. In a bowl, mix flour with baking powder, ¾ cup Sugar, orange zest and lime zest and stir.
2. Add ½ cup butter, eggs, poppy seeds, vanilla and milk, stir using your mixer, pour into a cake pan that fits your air fryer and cook at 350 degrees f for about 30 minutes.
3. Meanwhile, heat a pan with 3 tablespoons butter over medium
4. heat, add Sugar and stir until it dissolves.
5. Take off heat, add passion fruit puree and egg yolks gradually and whisk well.
6. Take cake out of the fryer, cool it down a bit and cut into halves horizontally.
7. Spread ¼ of passion fruit cream over one half, top with the other cake half and spread ¼ of the cream.
8. Serve cold.
9. Enjoy!

Sweet Squares

Servings: 6
- 1 cup flour
- ½ cup butter, soft 1 cup Sugar
- ¼ cup powdered Sugar
- 2 teaspoons lemon peel, grated 2 tablespoons lemon juice
- 2 eggs, whisked
- ½ teaspoon baking powder

1. In a bowl, mix flour with powdered Sugar and butter, stir well, press on the bottom of a pan that fits your air fryer, introduce in the fryer and bake at 350 degrees f for 14 minutes.
2. In another bowl, mix Sugar with lemon juice, lemon peel, eggs, baking powder, stir using your mixer and spread over baked crust.
3. Bake for 15 minutes more, leave aside to cool down, cut into medium squares and serve cold.
4. Enjoy!

Plum Bars

Servings: 8
- 2 cups dried plums 6 tablespoons water 2 cup rolled

- oats
- 1cup brown Sugar
- ½ teaspoon baking soda
- 1teaspoon cinnamon powder 2 tablespoons butter, melted 1 egg, whisked
- Cooking spray

1.In your food processor, mix plums with water and blend until you obtain a sticky spread.
2.In a bowl, mix oats with cinnamon, baking soda, Sugar, egg and butter and whisk well.
3.Press half of the oats mix in a baking pan that fits your air fryer sprayed with Cooking oil, spread plums mix and top with the other half of the oats mix.
4.Introduce in your air fryer and cook at 350 degrees f for 16 minutes.
5.Leave mix aside to cool down, cut into medium bars and serve.
6.Enjoy!

Plum And Currant Tart

Servings: 6
- For The Crumble:
- ¼ cup almond flour
- ¼ cup millet flour
- 1cup brown rice flour
- ½ cup cane Sugar
- 10tablespoons butter, soft 3 tablespoons milk

For The Filling:
- 1-pound small plums, pitted and halved 1 cup white currants
- 2tablespoons cornstarch
- 3tablespoons Sugar
- ½ teaspoon vanilla extract
- ½ teaspoon cinnamon powder
- ¼ teaspoon ginger powder 1 teaspoon lime juice

1.In a bowl, mix brown rice flour with ½ cup Sugar, millet flour, almond flour, butter and milk and stir until you obtain a sand like dough.
2.Reserve ¼ of the dough, press the rest of the dough into a tart pan that fits your air fryer and keep in the fridge for 30 minutes.
3.Meanwhile, in a bowl, mix plums with currants, 3 tablespoons
4.Sugar, cornstarch, vanilla extract, cinnamon, ginger and lime juice and stir well.
5.Pour this over tart crust, crumble reserved dough on top, introduce in your air fryer, and cook 350 degrees f for 35 minutes.
6.Leave tart to cool down, slice and serve.
7.Enjoy!

Tasty Orange Cookies

Servings: 8
- 2cups flour
- 1teaspoon baking powder
- ½ cup butter, soft
- ¾ cup Sugar
- 1egg, whisked
- 1teaspoon vanilla extract
- 1tablespoon orange zest, grated

For The Filling:
- 4ounces cream cheese, soft
- ½ cup butter

- 2cups powdered Sugar

1.In a bowl, mix cream cheese with ½ cup butter and 2 cups powdered Sugar, stir well using your mixer and leave aside for now.
2.In another bowl, mix flour with baking powder.
3.In a third bowl, mix ½ cup butter with ¾ cup Sugar, egg, vanilla extract and orange zest and whisk well.
4. Combine flour with orange mix, stir well and scoop 1 tablespoon of the mix on a lined baking sheet that fits your air fryer.
5.Repeat with the rest of the orange batter, introduce in the fryer and cook at 340 degrees f for 12 minutes.
6.Leave cookies to cool down, spread cream filling on half of them top with the other cookies and serve.
7.Enjoy!

Cashew Bars

Servings: 6
- 1/3 cup honey
- ¼ cup almond meal
- 1tablespoon almond butter
- 1and ½ cups cashews, chopped 4 dates, chopped
- ¾ cup coconut, shredded 1 tablespoon chia seeds

1.In a bowl, mix honey with almond meal and almond butter and stir well.
2.Add cashews, coconut, dates and chia seeds and stir well again.
3.Spread this on a lined baking sheet that fits your air fryer and press well.
4.Introduce in the fryer and cook at 300 degrees f for 15 minutes.
5.Leave mix to cool down, cut into medium bars and serve.
6.Enjoy!

Brown Butter Cookies

Servings: 6
- 1and ½ cups butter 2 cups brown Sugar 2 eggs, whisked
- 3cups flour
- 2/3 cup pecans, chopped
- 2teaspoons vanilla extract 1 teaspoon baking soda
- ½ teaspoon baking powder

1.Heat a pan with the butter over medium heat, stir until it melts, add brown Sugar and stir until these dissolves.
2.In a bowl, mix flour with pecans, vanilla extract, baking soda, baking powder and eggs and stir well.
3.Add brown butter, stir well and arrange spoonful of this mix on a lined baking sheet that fits your air fryer.
4.Introduce in the fryer and cook at 340 degrees f for 10 minutes.
5.Leave cookies to cool down and serve.
6.Enjoy!

Sweet Potato Cheesecake

Servings: 4
- 4tablespoons butter, melted 6 ounces mascarpone, soft 8ounces cream cheese, soft
- 2/3 cup graham crackers, crumbled
- ¾ cup milk
- 1teaspoon vanilla extract 2/3 cup sweet potato

puree
- ¼ teaspoons cinnamon powder

1.In a bowl, mix butter with crumbled crackers, stir well, press on the bottom of a cake pan that fits your air fryer and keep in the fridge for now.

2.In another bowl, mix cream cheese with mascarpone, sweet potato

3.puree, milk, cinnamon and vanilla and whisk really well.

4.Spread this over crust, introduce in your air fryer, cook at 300

5.degrees f for 4 minutes and keep in the fridge for a few hours before serving.

6.Enjoy!

Low Carb Dessert recipes

Angel Food Cake

Prep Time 10 m | **Cook Time** 30 m | 12 **Servings**
- ¼ cup butter, melted
- 1 cup powdered erythritol
- 1 teaspoon strawberry extract
- 12 egg whites
- 2 teaspoons cream of tartar
- A pinch of salt

1. Preheat the air fryer for 5 minutes.
2. Mix the egg whites with the cream of tartar.
3. Use a hand mixer and whisk until white and fluffy.
4. Add the rest of the ingredients except for the butter and whisk for another minute.
5. Pour into a baking dish.
6. Place in the oven basket and cook for 30 minutes at 4000F, or if a toothpick inserted in the middle comes out clean.
7. Drizzle with melted butter once cooled.

Per Serving: Calories 65|Carbohydrates 1.8g|Protein 3.1g|Fat 5g

Apple Pie in Air Fryer

Prep Time 15 m | **Cook Time** 35 m | 4 **Servings**

- ½ teaspoon vanilla extract
- 1 beaten egg
- 1 large apple, chopped
- 1 Pillsbury Refrigerator pie crust
- 1 tablespoon butter
- 1 tablespoon ground cinnamon
- 1 tablespoon raw sugar
- 2 tablespoon sugar
- 2 teaspoons lemon juice
- Baking spray

1. Lightly grease the baking pan of the air fryer with cooking spray. Spread the pie crust on the rare part of the pan up to the sides.
2. In a bowl, make a mixture of vanilla, sugar, cinnamon, lemon juice, and apples. Pour on top of pie crust. Top apples with butter slices.
3. Cover apples with the other pie crust. Pierce with a knife the tops of the pie.
4. Spread whisked egg on top of crust and sprinkle sugar.
5. Cover with foil.
6. For 25 minutes, cook at 3900F.
7. Remove foil cook for 10 minutes at 3300F until tops are browned.

Per Serving: Calories 372|Carbs 44.7g|Protein 4.2g|Fat 19.6g

Apple-Toffee Upside-Down Cake

Prep Time 10 m | **Cook Time** 30 m | 9 **Servings**
- ¼ cup almond butter
- ¼ cup sunflower oil
- ½ cup walnuts, chopped
- ¾ cup + 3 tablespoon coconut sugar
- ¾ cup water
- 1 ½ teaspoon mixed spice
- 1 cup plain flour
- 1 lemon, zest
- 1 teaspoon baking soda
- 1 teaspoon vinegar
- 3 baking apples, cored and sliced

1. Preheat the air fryer to 3900F.
2. In a skillet, melt the almond butter and 3 tablespoons of sugar. Pour the mixture over a baking dish that will fit in the air fryer. Arrange the slices of apples on top. Set aside.
3. In a mixing bowl, combine flour, ¾ cup sugar, and baking soda. Add the mixed spice.
4. In a different bowl, mix the water, oil, vinegar, and lemon zest. Stir in the chopped walnuts.
5. Combine the wet ingredients to the dry ingredients until well combined.
6. Pour over the tin with apple slices.
7. Bake for 30 minutes or until a toothpick inserted comes out clean.

Per Serving: Calories 335 |Carbohydrates 39.6g | Protein 3.8g | Fat 17.9g

Banana-Choco Brownies

Prep Time 15 m | **Cook Time** 30 m | 12 **Servings**
- 2 cups almond flour
- 2 teaspoons baking powder
- ½ teaspoon baking powder
- ½ teaspoon baking soda
- ½ teaspoon salt
- 1 over-ripe banana
- 3 large eggs
- ½ teaspoon stevia powder
- ¼ cup coconut oil
- 1 tablespoon vinegar
- 1/3 cup almond flour
- 1/3 cup cocoa powder

1. Preheat the air fryer for 5 minutes.
2. Add together all ingredients in a food processor and pulse until well combined.
3. Pour into a skillet that will fit in the deep fryer.
4. Place in the fryer basket and cook for 30 minutes at 3500F, or if a toothpick inserted in the middle comes out clean.

Per Serving: Calories 75|Carbohydrates 2.1g |Protein 1.7g|Fat 6.6g

Blueberry & Lemon Cake

Prep Time 10 m | **Cook Time** 17 m | 4 **Servings**
- 2 eggs
- 1 cup blueberries
- zest from 1 lemon
- juice from 1 lemon
- 1 tsp. vanilla

brown sugar for topping (a little sprinkling on top of each muffin-less than a teaspoon)

2 1/2 cups self-rising flour

1/2 cup Monk Fruit (or use your preferred sugar)

1/2 cup cream

1/4 cup avocado oil (any light cooking oil)

1. In a mixing bowl, beat well the wet ingredients. Stir in dry ingredients and mix thoroughly.
2. Lightly grease the baking pan of the air fryer with cooking spray. Pour in batter.
3. For 12 minutes, cook at 330F.
4. Let it stand in the air fryer for 5 minutes.

Per Serving: Calories 589|Carbs 76.7g|Protein 13.5g|Fat 25.3g

Bread Pudding with Cranberry

Prep Time 20 m | **Cook Time** 45 m | 4 **Servings**

1-1/2 cups milk

2-1/2 eggs

1/2 cup cranberries1 teaspoon butter

1/4 cup golden raisins

1/8 teaspoon ground cinnamon

3/4 cup heavy whipping cream

3/4 teaspoon lemon zest

3/4 teaspoon kosher salt

2 tbsp. and 1/4 cup white sugar

3/4 French baguettes, cut into 2-inch slices 3/8 vanilla bean, split and seeds scraped away

1. Lightly grease the baking pan of the air fryer with cooking spray. Spread baguette slices, cranberries, and raisins.
2. In a blender, blend well vanilla bean, cinnamon, salt, lemon zest, eggs, sugar, and cream. Pour over baguette slices. Let it soak for an hour.
3. Cover pan with foil.
4. For 35 minutes, cook at 330F.
5. Let it rest for 10 minutes.

Per Serving: Calories 581 |Carbs 76.1g|Protein 15.8g|Fat 23.7g

Cherries 'n Almond Flour Bars

Prep Time 15 m | **Cook Time** 35 m | 12 **Servings**

1/4 cup of water

1/2 cup butter softened

1/2 teaspoon salt

1/2 teaspoon vanilla

1 1/2 cups almond flour

1 cup erythritol

1 cup fresh cherries, pitted

1 tablespoon xanthan gum

2 eggs

1. In a medium bowl, make a mixture of the first 6 ingredients to form a dough.
2. Press the batter onto a baking sheet that will fit in the air fryer.
3. Place in the fryer and bake for 10 minutes at 375F.
4. Meanwhile, mix the cherries, water, and xanthan gum in a bowl.
5. Scoop out the dough and pour over the cherry.
6. Return to the fryer and cook for another 25 minutes at 3750F.

Per Serving: Calories 99 |Carbohydrates 2.1g |Protein 1.8g|Fat 9.3g

Cherry-Choco Bars

Prep Time 5 m | **Cook Time** 15 m | 8 **Servings**

1/4 teaspoon salt

1/2 cup almonds, sliced

1/2 cup chia seeds

1/2 cup dark chocolate, chopped

1/2 cup dried cherries, chopped

1/2 cup prunes, pureed

1/2 cup quinoa, cooked

3/4 cup almond butter

1/3 cup honey

2 cups old-fashioned oats

2 tablespoon coconut oil

1. Preheat the air fryer to 3750F.
2. In a bowl, combine the oats, quinoa, chia seeds, almond, cherries, and chocolate.
3. In a saucepan, heat the almond butter, honey, and coconut oil.
4. Pour the butter mixture over the dry mixture. Add salt and prunes.
5. Mix until well combined.
6. Pour over a baking dish that can fit inside the air fryer.
7. Cook for 15 minutes.
8. Allow settling for an hour before slicing into bars.

Per Serving: Calories 321|Carbohydrates 35g|Protein 7g|Fat 17g

Chocolate Chip in a Mug

Prep Time 10 m | **Cook Time** 20 m | 6 **Servings**

1/4 cup walnuts, shelled and chopped

1/2 cup butter, unsalted

1/2 cup dark chocolate chips

1/2 cup erythritol

1/2 teaspoon baking soda

1/2 teaspoon salt

1 tablespoon vanilla extract

2 1/2 cups almond flour

2 large eggs, beaten

1. Preheat the air fryer for 5 minutes.
2. Combine all ingredients in a mixing bowl.
3. Place in greased mugs.
4. Bake in the air fryer oven for 20 minutes at 3750F.

Per Serving: Calories 234|Carbohydrates 4.9g|Protein 2.3g|Fat 22.8g

Choco-Peanut Mug Cake

Prep Time 10 m | **Cook Time** 20 m | 6 **Servings**

1/4 teaspoon baking powder

1/2 teaspoon vanilla extract

1 egg

1 tablespoon heavy cream

1 tablespoon peanut butter

1 teaspoon butter, softened

2 tablespoon erythritol

2 tablespoons cocoa powder, unsweetened

1. Preheat the air fryer for 5 minutes.
2. Combine all ingredients in a mixing bowl.
3.Pour into a greased mug.
4. Place in the air fryer oven basket and cook for 20 minutes at 4000F, or if a toothpick inserted in the middle comes out clean.

Per Serving: Calories 293 |Carbohydrates 8.5g|Protein 12.4g|Fat 23.3g

Coco-Lime Bars

Prep Time 10 m | **Cook Time** 20 m | 3 **Servings**
- ¼ cup almond flour
- ¼ cup coconut oil
- ¼ cup dried coconut flakes
- ¼ teaspoon salt
- ½ cup lime juice
- ¾ cup coconut flour
- 1 ¼ cup erythritol powder
- 1 tablespoon lime zest
- 4 eggs

1. Preheat the air fryer for 5 minutes.
2. Combine all ingredients in a mixing bowl.
3. Place in the greased mug.
4. Bake in the air fryer oven for 20 minutes at 375F.

Per Serving: Calories 506 | Carbohydrates 21.9g| Protein 19.3g | Fat 37.9g

Coconut 'n Almond Fat Bombs

Prep Time 5 m | Cooking Time 15 m | 12 Servings
- ¼ cup almond flour
- ½ cup shredded coconut
- 1 tablespoon coconut oil
- 1 tablespoon vanilla extract
- 2 tablespoons liquid stevia
- 3 egg whites

1. Preheat the air fryer for 5 minutes.
2. Combine all ingredients in a mixing bowl.
3. Form small balls using your hands.
4. Place in the air fryer oven basket and cook for 15 minutes at 4000F.

Per Serving: Calories 23 |Carbohydrates 0.7g|Protein 1.1g|Fat 1.8g

Coconutty Lemon Bars

Prep Time 10 m | **Cook Time** 25 m | 12 **Servings**
- ¼ cup cashew
- ¼ cup fresh lemon juice, freshly squeezed
- ¾ cup coconut milk
- ¾ cup erythritol
- 1 cup desiccated coconut
- 1 teaspoon baking powder
- 2 eggs, beaten
- 2 tablespoons coconut oil
- A dash of salt

1. Preheat the air fryer for 5 minutes.
2. In a mixing bowl, combine all ingredients.
3. Use a hand mixer to mix everything.
4. Pour into a baking bowl that will fit in the air fryer.
5. Bake for 25 minutes at 350F or until a toothpick inserted in the middle comes out clean.

Per Serving: Calories 118|Carbohydrates 3.9g|Protein 2.6g |Fat 10.2g

Coffee 'n Blueberry Cake

Prep Time 15 m | **Cook Time** 35 m | 6 **Servings**
- 1 cup white sugar
- 1 egg
- 1/2 cup butter, softened
- 1/2 cup fresh or frozen blueberries
- 1/2 cup sour cream
- 1/2 teaspoon baking powder
- 1/2 teaspoon ground cinnamon
- 1/2 teaspoon vanilla extract
- 1/4 cup brown sugar
- 1/4 cup chopped pecans
- 1/8 teaspoon salt
- 1-1/2 teaspoons confectioners' sugar for dusting
- 3/4 cup and 1 tablespoon all-purpose flour

1. In a small bowl, whisk well pecans, cinnamon, and brown sugar.
2. In a blender, blend well all wet ingredients. Add dry ingredients except for confectioner's sugar and blueberries. Blend well until smooth and creamy.
3. Lightly grease the baking pan of the air fryer with cooking spray.
4. Pour half of the batter into the pan. Sprinkle a little of the pecan mixture on top. Pour the remaining batter and then top with the remaining pecan mixture.
5. Cover pan with foil.
6. For 35 minutes, cook at 3300F.
7. Serve and enjoy with a dusting of confectioner's sugar.

Per Serving: Calories 471|Carbs 59.5g|Protein 4.1g |Fat 24.0g

Coffee Flavored Cookie Dough

Prep Time 10 m | **Cook Time** 20 m | 12 **Servings**
- ¼ cup butter
- ¼ teaspoon xanthan gum
- ½ teaspoon coffee espresso powder
- ½ teaspoon stevia powder
- ¾ cup almond flour
- 1 egg
- 1 teaspoon vanilla
- 1/3 cup sesame seeds
- 2 tablespoons cocoa powder
- 2 tablespoons cream cheese, softened

1. Preheat the air fryer for 5 minutes.
2. Combine all ingredients in a mixing bowl.
3. Press into a baking dish that will fit in the air fryer.
4. Place in the air fryer oven basket and cook for 20 minutes at 4000F, or if a toothpick inserted in the middle comes out clean.

Per Serving: Calories 88|Carbohydrates 1.3g|Protein 1.9g|Fat 8.3g

Angel Food Cake

Prep Time 10 m | **Cook Time** 30 m | 12 **Servings**
- ¼ cup butter, melted
- 1 cup powdered erythritol
- 1 teaspoon strawberry extract
- egg whites
- teaspoons cream of tartar
- A pinch of salt

1. Preheat the air fryer for 5 minutes.
2. Mix the egg whites with the cream of tartar.
3. Use a hand mixer and whisk until white and fluffy.
4. Add the rest of the ingredients except for the butter and whisk for another minute.
5. Pour into a baking dish.
6. Place in the oven basket and cook for 30 minutes at 4000F, or if a toothpick inserted in the middle comes out clean.
7. Drizzle with melted butter once cooled.

Per Serving: Calories: 65 |Carbohydrates: 1.8g |Protein: 3.1g |Fat: 5g

Apple Pie in Air Fryer

Prep Time 15 m | **Cook Time** 35 m | 4 **Servings**

  ½ teaspoon vanilla extract
  1 beaten egg
  1 large apple, chopped
  1 Pillsbury Refrigerator pie crust
  1 tablespoon butter
  1 tablespoon ground cinnamon
  1 tablespoon raw sugar
  tablespoon sugar
  teaspoons lemon juice
  Baking spray

1.Lightly grease the baking pan of the air fryer with cooking spray. Spread pie crust on rare part of the pan up to the sides.
2.In a bowl, make a mixture of vanilla, sugar, cinnamon, lemon juice, and apples. Pour on top of pie crust. Top apples with butter slices.
3.Cover apples with the other pie crust. Pierce with a knife the tops of the pie.
4.Spread whisked egg on top of crust and sprinkle sugar.
5.Cover with foil.
6.For 25 minutes, cook on 3900F.
7.Remove foil cook for 10 minutes at 3300F until tops are browned.
Per Serving: Calories 372 |Carbs: 44.7g |Protein: 4.2g| Fat: 19.6g

Apple-Toffee Upside-Down Cake

Prep Time 10 m | **Cook Time** 30 m | 9 **Servings**

  ¼ cup almond butter
  ¼ cup sunflower oil
  ½ cup walnuts, chopped
  ¾ cup + 3 tablespoon coconut sugar
  ¾ cup water
  1 ½ teaspoon mixed spice
  1 cup plain flour
  1 lemon, zest
  1 teaspoon baking soda
  1 teaspoon vinegar
  baking apples, cored and sliced

1.Preheat the air fryer to 3900F.
2. In a skillet, melt the almond butter and 3 tablespoons of sugar. Pour the mixture over a baking dish that will fit in the air fryer. Arrange the slices of apples on top. Set aside.
3. In a mixing bowl, combine flour, ¾ cup sugar, and baking soda. Add the mixed spice.
4. In a different bowl, mix the water, oil, vinegar, and lemon zest. Stir in the chopped walnuts.
5. Combine the wet ingredients to the dry ingredients until well combined.
6. Pour over the tin with apple slices.
7. Bake for 30 minutes or until a toothpick inserted comes out clean.
Per Serving: Calories: 335| Carbohydrates: 39.6g |Protein: 3.8g| Fat: 17.9g

Banana-Choco Brownies

Prep Time 15 m | **Cook Time** 30 m | 12 **Servings**

  cups almond flour
  teaspoons baking powder
  ½ teaspoon baking powder
  ½ teaspoon baking soda
  ½ teaspoon salt
  1 over-ripe banana
  large eggs

  ½ teaspoon stevia powder
  ¼ cup coconut oil
  1 tablespoon vinegar
  1/3 cup almond flour
  1/3 cup cocoa powder

1. Preheat the air fryer for 5 minutes.
2. Add together all ingredients in a food processor and pulse until well combined.
3. Pour into a skillet that will fit in the deep fryer.
4. Place in the fryer basket and cook for 30 minutes at 3500F, or if a toothpick inserted in the middle comes out clean.
Per Serving: Calories: 75 |Carbohydrates: 2.1g| Protein: 1.7g |Fat: 6.6g

Blueberry & Lemon Cake

Prep Time 10 m | **Cook Time** 17 m | 4 **Servings**

  eggs
  1 cup blueberries
  Zest from 1 lemon
  Juice from 1 lemon
  1 tsp. vanilla
  Brown sugar for topping (a little sprinkling on top of each muffin-less than a teaspoon)
  1/2 cups self-rising flour
  1/2 cup Monk Fruit (or use your preferred sugar)
  1/2 cup cream
  1/4 cup avocado oil (any light cooking oil)

1.In a mixing bowl, beat well-wet Ingredients. Stir in dry ingredients and mix thoroughly.
2.Lightly grease the baking pan of the air fryer with cooking spray. Pour in batter.
3.For 12 minutes, cook on 3300F.
4.Let it stand in the air fryer for 5 minutes.
Per Serving: Calories: 589| Carbs: 76.7g |Protein: 13.5g |Fat: 25.3g

Chocolate Chip in a Mug

Prep Time 10 m | **Cook Time** 20 m | 6 **Servings**

  ¼ cup walnuts, shelled and chopped
  ½ cup butter, unsalted
  ½ cup dark chocolate chips
  ½ cup erythritol
  ½ teaspoon baking soda
  ½ teaspoon salt
  1 tablespoon vanilla extract
  ½ cups almond flour
  large eggs, beaten

1.Preheat the air fryer for 5 minutes.
2.Combine all ingredients in a mixing bowl.
3.Place in greased mugs.
4.Bake in the air fryer oven for 20 minutes at 3750F.
Per Serving: Calories: 234| Carbohydrates: 4.9g |Protein: 2.3g |Fat: 22.8g

Bread Pudding with Cranberry

Prep Time 20 m | **Cook Time** 45 m | 4 **Servings**

  1-1/2 cups milk
  2-1/2 eggs
  1/2 cup cranberries1 teaspoon butter
  1/4 cup golden raisins
  1/8 teaspoon ground cinnamon
  3/4 cup heavy whipping cream
  3/4 teaspoon lemon zest

3/4 teaspoon kosher salt

tbsp. and 1/4 cup white sugar

3/4 French baguettes, cut into 2-inch slices 3/8 vanilla bean, split and seeds scraped away

1. Lightly grease the baking pan of the air fryer with cooking spray. Spread baguette slices, cranberries, and raisins.
2. In a blender, blend well vanilla bean, cinnamon, salt, lemon zest, eggs, sugar, and cream. Pour over baguette slices. Let it soak for an hour.
3. Cover pan with foil.
4. For 35 minutes, cook on 3300F.
5. Let it rest for 10 minutes.

Per Serving: Calories: 581 |Carbs: 76.1g |Protein: 15.8g |Fat: 23.7g

Cherries 'n Almond Flour Bars

Prep Time 15 m | **Cook Time** 35 m | 12 **Servings**

¼ cup of water

½ cup butter softened

½ teaspoon salt

½ teaspoon vanilla

1 ½ cups almond flour

1 cup erythritol

1 cup fresh cherries, pitted

1 tablespoon xanthan gum

eggs

1. In a medium bowl, make a mixture of the first 6 ingredients to form a dough.
2. Press the batter onto a baking sheet that will fit in the air fryer.
3. Place in the fryer and bake for 10 minutes at 3750F.
4. Meanwhile, mix the cherries, water, and xanthan gum in a bowl.
5. Scoop out the dough and pour over the cherry.
6. Return to the fryer and cook for another 25 minutes at 3750F.

Per Serving: Calories: 99 |Carbohydrates: 2.1g |Protein: 1.8g |Fat: 9.3g

Cherry-Choco Bars

Prep Time 5 m | **Cook Time** 15 m | 8 **Servings**

¼ teaspoon salt

½ cup almonds, sliced

½ cup chia seeds

½ cup dark chocolate, chopped

½ cup dried cherries, chopped

½ cup prunes, pureed

½ cup quinoa, cooked

¾ cup almond butter

1/3 cup honey

cups old-fashioned oats

tablespoon coconut oil

1. Preheat the air fryer to 3750F.
2. In a bowl, combine the oats, quinoa, chia seeds, almond, cherries, and chocolate.
3. In a saucepan, heat the almond butter, honey, and coconut oil.
4. Pour the butter mixture over the dry mixture. Add salt and prunes.
5. Mix until well combined.
6. Pour over a baking dish that can fit inside the air fryer.
7. Cook for 15 minutes.
8. Allow settling for an hour before slicing into bars.

Per Serving: Calories: 321 |Carbohydrates: 35g |Protein: 7g |Fat: 17g

Choco-Peanut Mug Cake

Prep Time 10 m | **Cook Time** 20 m | 6 **Servings**

¼ teaspoon baking powder

½ teaspoon vanilla extract

1 egg

1 tablespoon heavy cream

1 tablespoon peanut butter

1 teaspoon butter, softened

tablespoon erythritol

tablespoons cocoa powder, unsweetened

1. Preheat the air fryer for 5 minutes.
2. Combine all ingredients in a mixing bowl.
3. Pour into a greased mug.
4. Place in the air fryer oven basket and cook for 20 minutes at 4000F, or if a toothpick inserted in the middle comes out clean.

Per Serving: Calories: 293 |Carbohydrates: 8.5g |Protein: 12.4g |Fat: 23.3g

Coco-Lime Bars

Prep Time 10 m | **Cook Time** 20 m | 3 **Servings**

¼ cup almond flour

¼ cup coconut oil

¼ cup dried coconut flakes

¼ teaspoon salt

½ cup lime juice

¾ cup coconut flour

1 ¼ cup erythritol powder

1 tablespoon lime zest

eggs

1. Preheat the air fryer for 5 minutes.
2. Combine all ingredients in a mixing bowl.
3. Place in the greased mug.
4. Bake in the air fryer oven for 20 minutes at 3750F.

Per Serving: Calories: 506 |Carbohydrates: 21.9g| Protein: 19.3g |Fat: 37.9g

Coconut 'n Almond Fat Bombs

Prep Time 5 m | **Cook Time** 15 m | 12 **Servings**

¼ cup almond flour

½ cup shredded coconut

1 tablespoon coconut oil

1 tablespoon vanilla extract

tablespoons liquid stevia

egg whites

1. Preheat the air fryer for 5 minutes.
2. Combine all ingredients in a mixing bowl.
3. Form small balls using your hands.
4. Place in the air fryer oven basket and cook for 15 minutes at 4000F.

Per Serving: Calories: 23 |Carbohydrates: 0.7g |Protein: 1.1g |Fat: 1.8g

Coconutty Lemon Bars

Prep Time 10 m | **Cook Time** 25 m | 12 **Servings**

¼ cup cashew

¼ cup fresh lemon juice, freshly squeezed

¾ cup coconut milk

¾ cup erythritol

1 cup desiccated coconut

1 teaspoon baking powder

eggs, beaten

tablespoons coconut oil
A dash of salt
1. Preheat the air fryer for 5 minutes.
2. In a mixing bowl, combine all ingredients.
3. Use a hand mixer to mix everything.
4. Pour into a baking bowl that will fit in the air fryer.
5.Bake for 25 minutes at 3500F or until a toothpick inserted in the middle comes out clean.
Per Serving: Calories: 118 |Carbohydrates: 3.9g |Protein: 2.6g| Fat: 10.2g

Coffee 'n Blueberry Cake

Prep Time 15 m | **Cook Time** 35 m | 6 **Servings**
1 cup white sugar
1 egg
1/2 cup butter, softened
1/2 cup fresh or frozen blueberries
1/2 cup sour cream
1/2 teaspoon baking powder
1/2 teaspoon ground cinnamon
1/2 teaspoon vanilla extract
1/4 cup brown sugar
1/4 cup chopped pecans
1/8 teaspoon salt
1-1/2 teaspoons confectioners' sugar for dusting
3/4 cup and 1 tablespoon all-purpose flour
1. In a small bowl, whisk well pecans, cinnamon, and brown sugar.
2. In a blender, blend well all wet Ingredients. Add dry ingredients except for confectioner's sugar and blueberries. Blend well until smooth and creamy.
3. Lightly grease the baking pan of the air fryer with cooking spray.
4. Pour half of the batter into the pan. Sprinkle small of the pecan mixture on top. Pour the remaining batter. And then topped with the remaining pecan mixture.
5. Cover pan with foil.
6. For 35 minutes, cook on 3300F.
7. Serve and enjoy with a dusting of confectioner's sugar.
Per Serving: Calories: 471|Carbs: 59.5g |Protein: 4.1g |Fat: 24.0g

Coffee Flavored Cookie Dough

Prep Time 10 m | **Cook Time** 20 m | 12 **Servings**
¼ cup butter
¼ teaspoon xanthan gum
½ teaspoon coffee espresso powder
½ teaspoon stevia powder
¾ cup almond flour
1 egg
1 teaspoon vanilla
1/3 cup sesame seeds
tablespoons cocoa powder
tablespoons cream cheese softened
1. Preheat the air fryer for 5 minutes.
2. Combine all ingredients in a mixing bowl.
3. Press into a baking dish that will fit in the air fryer.
4. Place in the air fryer oven basket and cook for 20 minutes at 4000F, or if a toothpick inserted in the middle comes out clean.
Per Serving: Calories: 88 |Carbohydrates: 1.3g |Protein: 1.9g| Fat: 8.3g

Sweet Potato Tater Tots

Prep Time 10 m | **Cook Time** 23 m | 4 **Servings**
1sweet potatoes, peeled
1/2 tsp. Cajun seasoning
Olive oil cooking spray
Sea salt to taste
1.Boil sweet potatoes in water for 15 minutes over medium-high heat.
2.Drain the sweet potatoes, then allow them to cool
3. Peel the boiled sweet potatoes and return them to the bowl.
4. Mash the potatoes and stir in salt and Cajun seasoning. Mix well and make small tater tots out of it.
5.Place the tater tots in the Air Fryer basket and spray them with cooking oil.
6.Place the Air Fryer basket inside the Air Fryer toaster and close the lid.
7. Select Air Frying mode at a temperature of 400 ° F for 8 minutes.
8. Turn the trays over and continue cooking for another 8 minutes.
Per Serving: Calories: 184 Cal |Protein: 9 g |Carbs: 43 g |Fat: 17 g

Fried Ravioli

Prep Time 10 m | **Cook Time** 15 m | 4 **Servings**
1 package ravioli, frozen
1 cup breadcrumbs
1/2 cup parmesan cheese
1 tbs. Italian seasoning
1 tbs. garlic powder
Eggs, beaten
Cooking spray
1. Mix breadcrumbs with garlic powder, cheese, and Italian seasoning in a bowl.
2. Whisk eggs in another bowl. Dip each ravioli in eggs first, then coat them with a crumbs mixture.
3. Place the ravioli in the Air Fryer basket. Place the air Fryer basket inside the oven and close the lid.
4. Select the Air Fry mode at 360°F temperature for 15 minutes.
5. Flip the ravioli after 8 minutes and resume cooking.
Per Serving: Calories: 124 Cal |Protein: 4.5 g | Carbs: 27.5 g| Fat: 3.5 g

Eggplant Fries

Prep Time 10 m | **Cook Time** 20 m | 4 **Servings**
1/2 cup panko breadcrumbs
1/2 tsp. salt
1 eggplant, peeled and sliced
1 cup egg, whisked
1. Toss the breadcrumbs with salt in a tray.
2. Dip the eggplant in the whisked egg and coat with the crumb's mixture.
3.Place the eggplant slices in the Air Fryer basket. Put the basket inside the Air Fryer toaster oven and close the lid.
4.Select the Air Fry mode at 400°F temperature for 20 minutes.
5. Flip the slices after 10 minutes, then resume cooking.
Per Serving: Calories: 110 Cal| Protein: 5 g |Carbs: 12.8 g | Fat: 11.9 g

Stuffed Eggplants

Prep Time 10 m | **Cook Time** 38 m | 4 **Servings**
Eggplants, cut in half lengthwise

1/2 cup shredded cheddar cheese
1/2 can (7.5 oz.) chili without beans
1 Tsp. kosher salt
FOR SERVING
Tbsp. cooked bacon bits
tbsp. sour cream
Fresh scallions, thinly sliced
1. Place the eggplants halves in the Air Fryer toaster oven and close the lid.
2. Select the Air Fry mode at 390°F temperature for 35 minutes.
3. Top each eggplant half with chili, cheese, and salt.
4. Place the halves in a baking pan and return to the oven. Select the Broil mode at 375°F temperature for 3 minutes.
5. Garnish with bacon bits, sour cream, and scallions.
Per Serving: Calories: 113 Cal |Protein: 9.2 g| Carbs: 13 g| Fat: 21 g

Bacon Poppers

Prep Time 10 m | **Cook Time** 15 m | 4 **Servings**
1 strips bacon, crispy cooked
Dough:
2/3 cup water
1 tbsp. butter
1 tbsp. bacon fat
1 tsp. kosher salt
2/3 cup all-purpose flour
Eggs
oz. Cheddar cheese, shredded
½ cup jalapeno peppers
A pinch pepper
A pinch of black pepper
1.Whisk butter with water and salt in a skillet over medium heat. Stir in flour, then stir cook for about 3 minutes.
2.Transfer this flour to a bowl, then whisk in eggs and the rest of the ingredients.
3.Fold in bacon and mix well. Wrap this dough in a plastic sheet and refrigerate for 30 minutes. Make small balls out of this dough.
4.Place these bacon balls in the Air Fryer toaster oven and close the lid.
5.Select the Air Fry mode at 390°F temperature for 15 minutes. Flip the balls after 7 minutes, then resume cooking. Serve warm.
Per Serving: Calories: 240 Kcal| Protein: 14.9 g |Carbs: 7.1 g |Fat: 22.5 g

Stuffed Jalapeno

Prep Time 10 m | **Cook Time** 10 m | 4 **Servings**
1 lb. ground pork sausage
1 (8 oz.) package cream cheese, softened
1 cup shredded Parmesan cheese
1 lb. large fresh jalapeno peppers halved lengthwise and seeded
1 (8 oz.) bottle Ranch dressing
1.Mix pork sausage ground with ranch dressing and cream cheese in a bowl.
2. But the jalapeno in half and remove their seeds.
3. Divide the cream cheese mixture into the jalapeno halves. Place the jalapeno pepper in a baking tray.
4. Set the Baking tray inside the Air Fryer toaster oven and close the lid.
5. Select the Bake mode at 350°F temperature for 10 minutes. Serve warm.

Per Serving: Calories: 168 Kcal |Protein: 9.4 g | Carbs: 12.1 g |Fat: 21.2 g

Creamy Mushrooms

Prep Time 10 m | **Cook Time** 15 m | 24 **Servings**
20 mushrooms
1 orange bell pepper, diced
1 onion, diced
Slices bacon, diced
1 cup shredded Cheddar cheese
1 cup sour cream
1.First, sauté the mushroom stems with onion, bacon, and bell pepper in a pan.
2.After 5 minutes of cooking, add 1 cup cheese and sour cream. Cook for 2 minutes.
3.Place the mushroom caps on the Air Fryer basket crisper plate.
4.Stuff each mushroom with the cheese-vegetable mixture and top them with cheddar cheese.
5.Insert the basket back inside and select Air Fry mode for 8 minutes at 350°F.
Per Serving: Calories: 101 Kcal |Protein: 8.8 g |Carbs: 25 g | Fat: 12.2 g

Italian Corn Fritters

Prep Time 10 m | **Cook Time** 3 m | 4 **Servings**
Cups frozen corn kernels
1/3 cup finely ground cornmeal
1/3 cup flour
½ tsp. salt
¼ tsp. pepper
½ tsp. baking powder
Onion powder, to taste
Garlic powder, to taste
¼ tsp. paprika
Tbsp. green chilies with juices
Tbsp. almond milk
¼ cup chopped Italian parsley
1.Beat cornmeal with flour, baking powder, parsley, seasonings in a bowl. Blend 3 tbsp. almond milk with 1 cup corn, black pepper, and salt in a food processor until smooth.
2.Stir in the flour mixture, then mixes until smooth. Spread this corn mixture in a baking tray lined with wax paper.
3.Set the baking tray inside the Air Fryer toaster oven and close the lid.
4.Select the bake mode at 350°F temperature for 2 minutes. Slice and serve.
Per Serving: Calories: 146 Kcal |Protein: 6.3 g| Carbs: 18.8 g| Fat: 4.5 g

Artichoke Fries

Prep Time 8 m | **Cook Time** 13 m | 6 **Servings**
1 oz. can artichoke hearts
1 cup flour
1 cup almond milk
½ tsp. garlic powder
¾ tsp. salt
¼ tsp. black pepper, or to taste
For Dry Mix:
1 ½ cup panko breadcrumbs
½ tsp. paprika
¼ tsp. salt
1.Whisk the wet ingredients in a bowl until smooth and mix the dry ingredients in a separate bowl.

2.First, dip the artichokes quarters in the wet mixture and then coat it with the dry panko mixture.

3.Place the artichokes hearts in the Air Fryer basket. Insert the basket inside the Air Fryer toaster oven and close the lid.

4.Select the Air Fry mode at 340°F temperature for 13 minutes. Serve warm.

Per Serving: Calories: 199 Cal |Protein: 9.4 g |Carbs: 15.9 g |Fat: 4 g

Crumbly Beef Meatballs

Prep Time 8 m | **Cook Time** 20 m | 6 **Servings**

 Lbs. of ground beef
 Large eggs
 1-1/4 cup panko breadcrumbs
 1/4 cup chopped fresh parsley
 1 tsp. dried oregano
 1/4 cup grated Parmigianino Regina
 1 small clove garlic chopped
 Salt and pepper to taste
 1 tsp. vegetable oil

1. Thoroughly mix beef with eggs, crumbs, parsley, and the rest of the ingredients.

2. Make small meatballs out of this mixture and place them in the basket.

3.Place the basket inside the Air Fryer toaster oven and close the lid.

4.Select the Air Fry mode at 350°F temperature for 13 minutes.

5.Toss the meatballs after 5 minutes and resume cooking.

Per Serving: Calories: 221 Cal |Protein: 25.1 g | Carbs: 11.2 g |Fat: 16.5 g

Pork Stuffed Dumplings

Prep Time 15 m | **Cook Time** 12 m | 3 **Servings**

 1 tsp. canola oil
 Cups chopped book Choy
 1 tbsp. chopped fresh ginger
 1 tbsp. chopped garlic
 Oz. ground pork
 1/4 tsp. crushed red pepper
 18 dumpling wrappers
 Cooking spray
 1 Tbsp. rice vinegar
 1 tsp. lower-sodium soy sauce
 1 tsp. toasted sesame oil
 1/2 tsp. packed light Sugar
 1 tbsp. finely chopped scallions

1.In a greased skillet, sauté bok choy for 8 minutes, then add ginger and garlic. Cook for 1 minute.

2.Transfer the bok choy to a plate.

3.Add pork and red pepper, then mix well. Place the dumpling wraps on the working surface and divide the pork fillings on the dumpling wraps.

4.Wet the edges of the wraps and pinch them together to seal the filling.

5.Place the dumpling in the Air Fryer basket.

6.Set the Air Fryer basket inside the Air Fryer toaster oven and close the lid.

7.Select the Air Fry mode at 375°F temperature for 12 minutes.

8.Flip the dumplings after 6 minutes, then resume cooking.

Per Serving: Calories: 172 Cal| Protein: 2.1 g |Carbs: 18.6 g |Fat: 10.7 g

Panko Tofu with Mayo Sauce

Prep Time 10 m | **Cook Time** 20 m | 4 **Servings**

 1 tofu cutlets
 For the Marinade
 1 tbsp. toasted sesame oil
 1/4 cup soy sauce
 1 tsp rice vinegar
 1/2 tsp garlic powder
 1 tsp. ground ginger
Make the Tofu:
 1/2 cup vegan mayo
 1 cup panko breadcrumbs
 1 tsp. of sea salt

1. Whisk the marinade ingredients in a bowl and add tofu cutlets. Mix well to coat the cutlets.

2. Cover and marinate for 1 hour. Meanwhile, whisk crumbs with salt and mayo in a bowl.

3. Coat the cutlets with crumbs mixture. Place the tofu cutlets in the Air Fryer basket.

4. Select the Air Fry mode at 370°F temperature for 20 minutes. Flip the cutlets after 10 minutes, then resume cooking.

Per Serving: Calories: 151 Cal |Protein: 1.9 g | Carbs: 6.9 g |Fat: 8.6 g

Garlicky Bok Choy

Prep Time 10 m | **Cook Time** 10 m | 2 **Servings**

 bunches baby book Choy
 Spray oil
 1 tsp. garlic powder

1.Toss bok choy with garlic powder and spread them in the Air Fryer basket.

2.Spray them with cooking oil.

3.Place the basket inside the Air Fryer toaster oven and close the lid.

4.Select the Air Fry mode at 350°F temperature for 6 minutes. Serve fresh.

Per Serving: Calories: 81 Cal |Protein: 0.4 g | Carbs: 4.7 g |Fat: 8.3 g

Walnut Brownies

Prep Time 15 m | **Cook Time** 35 m | 6 **Servings**

 Eggs 2
 Brown sugar 1 cup
 Vanilla ½ teaspoon
 Cocoa powder 1/4 cup
 Walnuts 1/2 cup, chopped
 All-purpose flour – 1/4 cup
 Butter – 1/2 cup, melted
 Pinch of salt

1.Sprinkle a baking dish with cooking spray and set aside. In a bowl, whisk together eggs, butter, cocoa powder, and vanilla. Add walnuts, flour, sugar, and salt and stir well. Pour batter into the baking dish. Place steam rack into the instant pot. Place baking dish on top of the steam rack. Seal pot with the air fryer lid. Select bake mode and cook at 320 F for 35 minutes. Serve.

Per Serving: Calories 340 Carbs 30g Fat 23g Protein 5g

Seasoned Cauliflower Chunks

Prep Time 10 m | **Cook Time** 15 m | 4 **Servings**

 1 cauliflower head, diced into chunks
 ½ cup unsweetened milk
 Tbsp. mayo

¼ cup all-purpose flour
¾ cup almond meal
¼ cup almond meal
1 tsp. onion powder
1 tsp. garlic powder
1 tsp. of sea salt
½ tsp. paprika
Pinch of black pepper
Cooking oil spray

1.Toss cauliflower with the rest of the ingredients in a bowl, then transfers to the Air Fryer basket.
2.Spray them with cooking oil.
3.Set the basket inside the Air Fryer toaster oven and close the lid.
4 Select the Air Fry mode at 400°F temperature for 15 minutes.
5 Toss well and serve warm.
Per Serving: Calories: 137 Cal |Protein: 6.1 g |Carbs: 26 g |Fat: 8 g

Almond Butter Brownies

Prep Time 10 m | **Cook Time** 15 m | 4 **Servings**
1/2 cup Almond butter
1/2 teaspoon Vanilla
1 tablespoon Almond milk
2 tablespoons Coconut sugar
2 tablespoons Applesauce
2 tablespoons Honey
1/4 teaspoon Baking powder
1/2 teaspoon Baking soda
2 tablespoons Cocoa powder
3 tablespoons Almond flour
1 tablespoon Coconut oil
1/4 teaspoon Sea salt

1.Sprinkle baking pan with cooking spray and set aside. In a small bowl, mix almond flour, baking soda, baking powder, and cocoa powder and set aside. Add coconut oil and almond butter into the microwave-safe bowl and microwave until melted. Stir. Add honey, milk, coconut sugar, vanilla, and applesauce into the melted coconut oil mixture and stir well. Add flour mixture and stir to combine. Pour batter into the baking pan. Place steam rack into the instant pot. Place baking pan on top of the steam rack. Seal pot with the air fryer lid. Select bake mode and cook at 350 F for 15 minutes. Serve.
Per Serving: Calories 170 Carbs 22g Fat 8g Protein 2g

Brownie Muffins

Prep Time 10 m | **Cook Time** 15 m | 6 **Servings**
1/4 cup Cocoa powder
1/2 cup Almond butter
1 cup Pumpkin puree
8 drops Liquid stevia
2 scoops of Protein powder

1.Mixed all the ingredients into the mixing bowl and beat until smooth. Pour batter into the 6 silicone muffin molds. Place the dehydrating tray into the multi-level air fryer basket and place the basket into the instant pot. Place muffin molds on a dehydrating tray. Seal pot with the air fryer lid. Select bake mode and cook at 350 F for 15 minutes. Serve.
Per Serving: Calories 70 Carbs 6g Fat 2g Protein 8g

Delicious Lemon Muffins

Prep Time 10 m | **Cook Time** 15 m | 6 **Servings**

1 Egg
3/4 teaspoon Baking powder
1 tsp. grated Lemon zest
1/2 cup Sugar
1/2 teaspoon Vanilla
1/2 cup Milk
2 tablespoons Canola oil
1/4 teaspoon Baking soda
1 cup Flour
1/2 teaspoon Salt

1.In a mixing bowl, beat egg, vanilla, milk, oil, and sugar until creamy. Add remaining ingredients and stir to combine. Pour batter into the 6 silicone muffin molds. Place the dehydrating tray into the multi-level air fryer basket and place the basket into the instant pot. Place muffin molds on a dehydrating tray. Seal pot with the air fryer lid. Select bake mode and cook at 350 F for 15 minutes. Serve.
Per Serving: Calories 202 Carbs 34g Fat 6g Protein 4g

Vanilla Strawberry Soufflé

Prep Time 10 m | **Cook Time** 15 m | 4 **Servings**
3 Egg whites
1 1/2 cup Strawberries
1/2 teaspoon Vanilla
1 tablespoon Sugar

1.Spray 4 ramekins with cooking spray and set aside. Add strawberries, sugar, and vanilla into the blender and blend until smooth. Add egg whites into the bowl and beat until medium peaks form. Add strawberry mixture and fold well. Pour egg mixture into the ramekins. Place the dehydrating tray into the multi-level air fryer basket and place the basket into the instant pot. Place ramekins on the dehydrating tray. Seal pot with the air fryer lid. Select bake mode and cook at 350 F for 15 minutes. Serve.
Per Serving: Calories 50 Carbs 8g Fat 0.5g Protein 3g

Healthy Carrot Muffins

Prep Time 15 m | **Cook Time** 20 m | 6 **Servings**
1 Egg
1 teaspoon Vanilla
1/4 cup Brown sugar
1/4 cup Granulated sugar
1/2 tablespoon Canola oil
1/4 cup Applesauce
1 cup all-purpose flour
1 1/2 teaspoons Baking powder
1/2 teaspoon Nutmeg
1 teaspoon Cinnamon
3/4 cup Grated carrots
1/4 teaspoon Salt

1.Into a large bowl, put all the ingredients, then mix until thoroughly combined. Pour batter into 6 silicone muffin molds. Place the dehydrating tray into the multi-level air fryer basket and place the basket into the instant pot. Place muffin molds on the dehydrating tray. Seal pot with the air fryer lid. Select bake mode and cook at 350 F for 20 minutes. Serve.
Per Serving: Calories 165 Carbs 33g Fat 2g Protein 3g

Cinnamon Carrot Cake

Prep Time 10 m | **Cook Time** 25 m | 4 **Servings**
1Egg
1/2 teaspoon Vanilla
1/2 teaspoon Cinnamon

1/2 cup Sugar
1/4 cup Canola oil
1/4, chopped Walnuts
1/2 teaspoon Baking powder
1/2 cup Flour
1/4 cup Grated carrot

1.Sprinkle a baking dish with cooking spray and set aside. In a mixing bowl, beat sugar and oil for 1-2 minutes. Add vanilla, cinnamon, and egg and beat for 30 seconds. Add remaining ingredients and stir to combine. Pour batter into the prepared baking dish. Place steam rack into the instant pot. Place baking dish on top of the steam rack. Seal pot with the air fryer lid. Select bake mode and cook at 350 F for 25 minutes. Serve.

Per Serving: Calories 340 Carbs 39g Fat 19g Protein 5g

Blueberry Muffins

Prep Time 15 m | **Cook Time** 20 m | 6 **Servings**
2 Eggs
1 1/2 cups Blueberries
1 cup Yogurt
1 cup Sugar
1 tablespoon Baking powder
2 cups Flour
2 teaspoons fresh lemon juice
2 tablespoons, grated Lemon zest
1 teaspoon Vanilla
1/2 cup Oil
1/2 teaspoon Salt

1.Using a small bowl, mix flour, salt, and baking powder. Set aside. In a large bowl, whisk together eggs, lemon juice, lemon zest, vanilla, oil, yogurt, and sugar. Add flour mixture and blueberries into the egg mixture and fold well. Pour batter into 9 silicone muffin molds. Place the dehydrating tray into the multi-level air fryer basket and place the basket into the instant pot. Place 6 muffin molds on the dehydrating tray. Seal pot with the air fryer lid. Select bake mode and cook at 375 F for 20 minutes. Cook remaining muffins. Serve.

Per Serving: Calories 343 Carbs 50g Fat 13g Protein 5.9g

Almond Raspberry Muffins

Prep Time 10 m | **Cook Time** 35 m | 6 **Servings**
2 Eggs
1 teaspoon Baking powder
5 ounces Almond meal
2 tablespoons Coconut oil
2 tablespoons Honey
3 ounces Raspberries

1.In a bowl, mix almond meal and baking powder. Add honey, eggs, and oil and stir until thoroughly combined. Add raspberries and fold well. Pour batter into the 6-silicone muffin molds. Place the dehydrating tray into the multi-level air fryer basket and place the basket into the instant pot. Place 6 muffin molds on the dehydrating tray. Seal pot with the air fryer lid. Select bake mode and cook at 350 F for 35 minutes. Serve.

Per Serving: Calories 227 Carbs 13g Fat 17g Protein 7g

Chocolate Butter Cake

Prep time: 20 m | **Cook time:**11 m | **Serves:** 4
4 ounces (113 g) butter, melted
4 ounces (113 g) dark chocolate
2 eggs, lightly whisked

2 tablespoons monk fruit
2 tablespoons almond meal
1 teaspoon baking powder
½ teaspoon ground cinnamon ¼ teaspoon ground star anise

1. Begin by preheating your Air Fryer to 370 degrees F (188ºC). Spritz the sides and bottom of a baking pan with nonstick cooking spray.
2. Melt the butter and dark chocolate in a microwave-safe bowl. Mix the eggs and monk fruit until frothy.
3. Pour the butter/chocolate mixture into the egg mixture. Stir in the almond meal, baking powder, cinnamon, and star anise. Mix until everything is well incorporated.
4. Scrape the batter into the prepared pan. Bake in the preheated Air Fryer for 9 to 11 minutes.
5. Let stand for 2 minutes. Invert on a plate while warm and serve.

Per Serving: calories: 408 | fat: 39g | protein: 8g | carbs: 7g | net carbs: 3g | fiber: 4g

Buttery Chocolate Cake

Prep time: 20 m | **Cook time:**11 m | **Serves:** 4
2½ ounces (71 g) butter, at room temperature 3 ounces (85 g) chocolate, unsweetened 2 eggs, beaten
½ cup Swerve
½ cup almond flour
1 teaspoon rum extract
1 teaspoon vanilla extract

1. Begin by preheating your Air Fryer to 370 degrees F (188ºC). Spritz the sides and bottom of four ramekins with cooking spray.
2. Melt the butter and chocolate in a microwave-safe bowl. Mix the eggs and Swerve until frothy.
3. Pour the butter/chocolate mixture into the egg mixture. Stir in the almond flour, rum extract, and vanilla extract. Mix until everything is well incorporated.
4. Scrape the batter into the prepared ramekins. Bake in the preheated Air Fryer for 9 to 11 minutes.
5. Let stand for 2 to 3 minutes. Invert on a plate while warm and serve. Bon appétit!

Per Serving: calories: 364 | fat: 33g | protein: 8g | carbs: 9g | net carbs: 4g | fiber: 5g

Chocolate Butter Cake

Prep Time:30 m | **Cook time:**22 m | **Serves:** 10
1 cup no-sugar-added peanut butter
1¼ cups monk fruit
3 eggs
1 cup almond flour
1 teaspoon baking powder
¼ teaspoon kosher salt
1 cup unsweetened bakers' chocolate, broken into chunks

1. Start by preheating your Air Fryer to 350 degrees F (180ºC). Now, spritz the sides and bottom of a baking pan with cooking spray.
2. In a mixing dish, thoroughly combine the peanut butter with the monk fruit until creamy. Next, fold in the egg and beat until fluffy.
3. After that, stir in the almond flour, baking powder, salt, and baker's chocolate. Mix until everything is well combined.
4. Bake in the preheated Air Fryer for 20 to 22 minutes. Transfer to a wire rack to cool before slicing and serving.

Per Serving: calories: 207 | fat: 17g | protein: 8g | carbs: 6g | net carbs: 3g | fiber: 3g

Butter Chocolate Cake with Pecan

Prep Time: 30 m | **Cook time:** 22 m | **Serves:** 6

- ½ cup butter, melted
- ½ cup Swerve
- 1 teaspoon vanilla essence
- 1 egg
- ½ cup almond flour
- ½teaspoon baking powder ¼ cup cocoa powder
- ½ teaspoon ground cinnamon ¼ teaspoon fine sea salt
- 1 ounce (28 g) bakers' chocolate, unsweetened ¼ cup pecans, finely chopped

1. Start by preheating your Air Fryer to 350 degrees F (180°C). Now, lightly grease six silicone molds.
2. In a mixing dish, beat the melted butter with the Swerve until fluffy. Next, stir in the vanilla and egg and beat again.
3. After that, add the almond flour, baking powder, cocoa powder, cinnamon, and salt. Mix until everything is well combined.
4. Fold in the chocolate and pecans; mix to combine. Bake in the preheated Air Fryer for 20 to 22 minutes.

Per Serving: calories: 253 | fat: 25g | protein: 4g | carbs: 6g | net carbs: 3g | fiber: 3g

Baked Cheesecake

Prep Time: 40 m | **Cook time:** 35 m | **Serves:** 6

- ½ cup almond flour
- 1½ tablespoons unsalted butter, melted
- 2 tablespoons erythritol
- 1 (8-ounce / 227-g) package cream cheese, softened
- ¼ cup powdered erythritol ½ teaspoon vanilla paste
- 1 egg, at room temperature

Topping:
- 1½ cups sour cream
- 3 tablespoons powdered erythritol
- 1 teaspoon vanilla extract

1. Thoroughly combine the almond flour, butter, and 2 tablespoons of erythritol in a mixing bowl. Press the mixture into the bottom of lightly greased custard cups.
2. Then, mix the cream cheese, ¼ cup of powdered erythritol, vanilla, and egg using an electric mixer at low speed. Pour the batter into the pan, covering the crust.
3. Bake in the preheated Air Fryer at 330 degrees F (166°C) for 35 minutes until edges are puffed and the surface is firm.
4. Mix the sour cream, 3 tablespoons of powdered erythritol, and vanilla for the topping; spread over the crust and allow it to cool to room temperature.
5. Transfer to your refrigerator for 6 to 8 hours.

Per Serving: calories: 306 | fat: 27g | protein: 8g | carbs: 9g | net carbs: 7g | fiber: 2g

Crusted Mini Cheesecake

Prep Time: 30 m | **Cook time:** 18 m | **Serves:** 8

For the Crust:
- ⅓ teaspoon grated nutmeg
- 1½ tablespoons erythritol
- 1½ cups almond meal
- 8 tablespoons melted butter
- 1 teaspoon ground cinnamon
- A pinch of kosher salt, to taste

For the Cheesecake:
- 2 eggs
- ½ cups unsweetened chocolate chips 1½ tablespoons sour cream

- 4 ounces (113 g) soft cheese
- ½ cup Swerve
- ½ teaspoon vanilla essence

1. Firstly, line eight cups of a mini muffin pan with paper liners.
2. To make the crust, mix the almond meal with erythritol, cinnamon, nutmeg, and kosher salt.
3. Now, add melted butter and stir well to moisten the crumb mixture.
4. Divide the crust mixture among the muffin cups and press gently to make even layers.
5. In another bowl, whip together the soft cheese, sour cream, and Swerve until uniform and smooth. Fold in the eggs and the vanilla essence.
6. Then, divide chocolate chips among the prepared muffin cups. Then, add the cheese mix to each muffin cup.
7. Bake for about 18 minutes at 345 degrees F (174°C). Bake in batches if needed. To finish, transfer the mini cheesecakes to a cooling rack; store them in the fridge.

Per Serving: calories: 314 | fat: 29g | protein: 7g | carbs: 7g | net carbs: 4g | fiber: 3g

Creamy Cheese Cake

Prep Time: 1 h | **Cook time:** 37 m | **Serves:** 8

- 1½ cups almond flour
- 3 ounces (85 g) Swerve
- ½ stick butter, melted
- 20 ounces (567 g) full-fat cream cheese
- ½ cup heavy cream
- 1¼ cups granulated Swerve
- 3 eggs, at room temperature
- 1 tablespoon vanilla essence
- 1 teaspoon grated lemon zest

1. Coat the sides and bottom of a baking pan with a little flour.
2. In a mixing bowl, combine the almond flour and Swerve. Add the melted butter and mix until your mixture looks like bread crumbs.
3. Press the mixture into the bottom of the prepared pan to form an even layer. Bake at 330 degrees F (166°C) for 7 minutes until golden brown. Allow it to cool completely on a wire rack.
4. Meanwhile, in a mixer fitted with the paddle attachment, prepare the filling by mixing the soft cheese, heavy cream, and granulated Swerve; beat until creamy and fluffy.
5. Crack the eggs into the mixing bowl, one at a time; add the vanilla and lemon zest and continue to mix until fully combined.
6. Pour the prepared topping over the cooled crust and spread evenly.
7. Bake in the preheated Air Fryer at 330 degrees F (166°C) for 25 to 30 minutes; leave it in the Air Fryer to keep warm for another 30 minutes.
8. Cover your cheesecake with plastic wrap. Place in your refrigerator and allow it to cool at least 6 hours or overnight. Serve well chilled.

Per Serving: calories: 245 | fat: 21g | protein: 8g | carbs: 7g | net carbs: 5g | fiber: 2g

Air Fried Chocolate Brownies

Prep Time: 40 m | **Cook time:** 35 m | **Serves:** 8

- 5 ounces (142 g) unsweetened chocolate, chopped into chunks
- 2 tablespoons instant espresso powder
- 1 tablespoon cocoa powder, unsweetened

½ cup almond butter

½ cup almond meal ¾ cup Swerve

1 teaspoon pure coffee extract

½ teaspoon lime peel zest

¼ cup coconut flour

2 eggs plus 1 egg yolk ½ teaspoon baking soda ½ teaspoon baking powder

½ teaspoon ground cinnamon ⅓ teaspoon ancho chile powder

For the Chocolate Mascarpone Frosting:

4 ounces (113 g) mascarpone cheese, at room temperature 1½ ounces (43 g) unsweetened chocolate chips 1½ cups Swerve

¼ cup unsalted butter, at room temperature

1 teaspoon vanilla paste A pinch of fine sea salt

1. First of all, microwave the chocolate and almond butter until completely melted; allow the mixture to cool at room temperature.

2. Then, whisk the eggs, Swerve, cinnamon, espresso powder, coffee extract, ancho chile powder, and lime zest.

3. Next step, add the vanilla/egg mixture to the chocolate/butter mixture. Stir in the almond meal and coconut flour along with baking soda, baking powder, and cocoa powder.

4. Finally, press the batter into a lightly buttered cake pan. Air-fry for 35 minutes at 345 degrees F (174⁰C).

5. In the meantime, make the frosting. Beat the butter and mascarpone cheese until creamy. Add in the melted chocolate chips and vanilla paste.

6. Gradually, stir in the Swerve and salt; beat until everything's well combined. Lastly, frost the brownies and serve.

Per Serving: calories: 363 | fat: 33g | protein: 7g | carbs: 10g | net carbs: 5g | fiber: 5g

Butter Cake with Cranberries

Prep Time:30 m | **Cook time:**20 m | **Serves:** 8

1 cup almond flour

⅓ teaspoon baking soda

⅓ teaspoon baking powder

¾ cup erythritol

½ teaspoon ground cloves

⅓ teaspoon ground cinnamon

½ teaspoon cardamom

1 stick butter

½ teaspoon vanilla paste

2 eggs plus 1 egg yolk, beaten

½ cup cranberries, fresh or thawed

1 tablespoon browned butter

For Ricotta Frosting:

½ stick butter

½ cup firm Ricotta cheese

1 cup powdered erythritol ¼ teaspoon salt

Zest of ½ lemon

1. Start by preheating your Air Fryer to 355 degrees F (181⁰C).

2. Combine the flour with baking soda, baking powder, erythritol, ground cloves, cinnamon, and cardamom in a mixing bowl.

3. In a separate bowl, whisk 1 stick butter with vanilla paste; mix in the eggs until light and fluffy. Add the flour/sugar mixture to the butter/egg mixture. Fold in the cranberries and browned butter.

4. Scrape the mixture into the greased cake pan. Then, bake in the preheated Air Fryer for about 20 minutes.

5. Meanwhile, in a food processor, whip ½ stick of the butter and Ricotta cheese until there are no lumps.

6. Slowly add the powdered erythritol and salt until your mixture has reached a thick consistency. Stir in the lemon zest; mix to combine and chill completely before using.

Per Serving: calories: 286 | fat: 27g | protein: 8g | carbs: 10g | net carbs: 5g | fiber: 5g

Buttery Monk Fruit Cookie

Prep time: 25 m | **Cook time:**20 m | **Serves:** 4

8 ounces (227 g) almond meal

2 tablespoons flaxseed meal

1 ounce (28 g) monk fruit

1 teaspoon baking powder

A pinch of grated nutmeg

A pinch of coarse salt

1 large egg, room temperature.

1 stick butter, room temperature

1 teaspoon vanilla extract

1. Mix the almond meal, flaxseed meal, monk fruit, baking powder, grated nutmeg, and salt in a bowl.

2. In a separate bowl, whisk the egg, butter, and vanilla extract.

3. Stir the egg mixture into a dry mixture; mix to combine well or until it forms a nice, soft dough.

4. Roll your dough out and cut out with a cookie cutter of your choice.

5. Bake in the preheated Air Fryer at 350 degrees F (180⁰C) for 10 minutes. Decrease the temperature to 330 degrees F (166⁰C) and cook for 10 minutes longer. Bon appétit!

Per Serving: calories: 388 | fat: 38g | protein: 8g | carbs: 7g | net carbs: 4g | fiber: 3g

Buttery Cookie with Hazelnut

Prep Time:20 m | **Cook time:**10 m | **Serves:** 6

1 cup almond flour

½ cup coconut flour

1 teaspoon baking soda

1 teaspoon fine sea salt

1 stick butter

1 cup Swerve

2 teaspoons vanilla

2 eggs, at room temperature

1 cup hazelnuts, coarsely chopped

1. Begin by preheating your Air Fryer to 350 degrees.

2. Mix the flour with baking soda and sea salt.

3. In the bowl of an electric mixer, beat the butter, Swerve, and vanilla until creamy. Fold in the eggs, one at a time, and mix until well combined.

4. Slowly and gradually stir in the flour mixture. Finally, fold in the coarsely chopped hazelnuts.

5. Divide the dough into small balls using a large cookie scoop; drop onto the prepared cookie sheets. Bake for 10 minutes or until golden brown, rotating the pan once or twice through cooking.

6. Work in batches and cool for a couple of minutes before removing to wire racks. Enjoy!

Per Serving: calories: 328 | fat: 32g | protein: 7g | carbs: 5g | net carbs: 3g | fiber: 2g

Hazelnut Butter Cookie

Prep Time:1 h | **Cook time:**20 m | **Serves:** 10

4 tablespoons liquid monk fruit

½ cup hazelnuts, ground

1 stick butter, room temperature
2 cups almond flour
1 cup coconut flour
2 ounces (57 g) granulated Swerve
2 teaspoons ground cinnamon

1. Firstly, cream liquid monk fruit with butter until the mixture becomes fluffy. Sift in both types of flour.
2. Now, stir in the hazelnuts. Now, knead the mixture to form a dough; place in the refrigerator for about 35 minutes.
3. To finish, shape the prepared dough into bite-sized balls; arrange them on a baking dish; flatten the balls using the back of a spoon.
4. Mix granulated Swerve with ground cinnamon. Press your cookies in the cinnamon mixture until they are completely covered.
5. Bake the cookies for 20 minutes at 310 degrees.
6. Leave them to cool for about 10 minutes before transferring them to a wire rack. Bon appétit!
Per Serving: calories: 246 | fat: 23g | protein: 5g | carbs: 7g | net carbs: 3g | fiber: 4g

Walnut Butter Cookie

Prep Time:40 m | **Cook time:**15 m | **Serves:** 8
½ cup walnuts, ground
½ cup coconut flour
1 cup almond flour
¾ cup Swerve
1 stick butter, room temperature
2 tablespoons rum
½ teaspoon pure vanilla extract
½ teaspoon pure almond extract

1. In a mixing dish, beat the butter with Swerve, vanilla, and almond extract until light and fluffy. Then, throw in the flour and ground walnuts; add in rum.
2. Continue mixing until it forms a soft dough. Cover and place in the refrigerator for 20 minutes. In the meantime, preheat the Air Fryer to 330 degrees F (166°C).
3. Roll the dough into small cookies, place them on the Air Fryer cake pan; gently press each cookie using a spoon.
4. Bake butter cookies for 15 minutes in the preheated Air Fryer. Bon appétit!
Per Serving: calories: 228 | fat: 22g | protein: 4g | carbs: 4g | net carbs: 2g | fiber: 2g

Buttery Almond Fruit Cookie

Prep Time:50 m | **Cook time:**13 m | **Serves:** 8
½ cup slivered almonds
1 stick butter, room temperature
4 ounces (113 g) monk fruit
⅔ cup blanched almond flour
⅓ cup coconut flour
⅓ teaspoon ground cloves
1 tablespoon ginger powder
¾ teaspoon pure vanilla extract

1. In a mixing dish, beat the monk fruit, butter, vanilla extract, ground cloves, and ginger until light and fluffy. Then, throw in the coconut flour, almond flour, and slivered almonds.
2. Continue mixing until it forms a soft dough. Cover and place in the refrigerator for 35 minutes. Meanwhile, preheat the Air Fryer to 315 degrees F (157°C).
3. Roll dough into small cookies and place them on the Air Fryer cake pan; gently press each cookie using the back of a spoon.
4. Bake these butter cookies for 13 minutes. Bon appétit!

Per Serving: calories: 199 | fat: 19g | protein: 3g | carbs: 4g | net carbs: 2g | fiber: 2g

Butter and Chocolate Chip Cookie

Prep time: 20 m | **Cook time:**11 m | **Serves:** 8
1 stick butter, at room temperature
1¼ cups Swerve
¼ cup chunky peanut butter
1 teaspoon vanilla paste
1 fine almond flour ⅔ cup coconut flour
⅓ cup cocoa powder, unsweetened 1 ½ teaspoons baking powder
¼ teaspoon ground cinnamon
¼ teaspoon ginger
½ cup chocolate chips, unsweetened

1. In a mixing dish, beat the butter and Swerve until creamy and uniform. Stir in the peanut butter and vanilla.
2. In another mixing dish, thoroughly combine the flour, cocoa powder, baking powder, cinnamon, and ginger.
3. Add the flour mixture to the peanut butter mixture; mix to combine well. Afterward, fold in the chocolate chips.
4. Drop by large spoonfuls onto a parchment-lined Air Fryer basket. Bake at 365 degrees F (185°C) for 11 minutes or until golden brown on the top. Bon appétit!
Per Serving: calories: 303 | fat: 28g | protein: 6g | carbs: 10g | net carbs: 5g | fiber: 5g

Blueberry Cream Flan

Prep Time:30 m | **Cook time:**25 m | **Serves:** 6
¾ cup extra-fine almond flour
1 cup fresh blueberries ½ cup coconut cream
¾ cup coconut milk
3 eggs, whisked
½ cup Swerve
½ teaspoon baking soda
½ teaspoon baking powder
⅓ teaspoon ground cinnamon
½ teaspoon ginger
¼ teaspoon grated nutmeg

1. Lightly grease 2 mini pie pans using a nonstick cooking spray. Lay the blueberries on the bottom of the pie pans.
2. In a saucepan that is preheated over a moderate flame, warm the cream and coconut milk until thoroughly heated.
3. Remove the pan from the heat; mix in the flour along with baking soda and baking powder.
4. In a medium-sized mixing bowl, whip the eggs, Swerve, and spices; whip until the mixture is creamy.
5. Add the creamy milk mixture. Carefully spread this mixture over the fruits.
6. Bake at 320 degrees (160°C) for about 25 minutes.
Per Serving: calories: 250 | fat: 22g | protein: 7g | carbs: 9g | net carbs: 6g | fiber: 3g

Air Fried Muffin

Prep Time:5 m | **Cook time:**25 m | **Serves:** 5
½ cup coconut flour
2 tablespoons cocoa powder
3 tablespoons erythritol
1 teaspoon baking powder
2 tablespoons coconut oil
2 eggs, beaten
½ cup coconut shred

1. In the mixing bowl, mix all ingredients.

2. Then, pour the mixture into the molds of the muffin and transfer it to the air fryer basket.
3. Cook the muffins at 350F (180ºC) for 25 minutes.
Per Serving: calories: 206 | fat: 16g | protein: 4g | carbs: 13g | net carbs: 6g | fiber: 7g

Homemade Muffin

Prep Time:10 m | **Cook time:**10 m | **Serves:** 5
    5 tablespoons coconut oil, softened
    1 egg, beaten
    1 teaspoon vanilla extract
    1 tablespoon poppy seeds
    1 teaspoon baking powder
    2 tablespoons erythritol
    1 cup coconut flour

1. In the mixing bowl, mix coconut oil with egg, vanilla extract, poppy seeds, baking powder, erythritol, and coconut flour.
2. When the mixture is homogenous, pour it into the muffin molds and transfer it to the air fryer basket.
3. Cook the muffins for 10 minutes at 365F (185ºC).
Per Serving: calories: 239 | fat: 17g | protein: 5g | carbs: 17g | net carbs: 7g | fiber: 10g

Creamy Pecan Bar

Prep Time:5 m | **Cook time:**40 m | **Serves:** 12
    2 cups coconut flour
    5 tablespoons erythritol
    4 tablespoons coconut oil, softened
    ½ cup heavy cream
    1 egg, beaten
    4 pecans, chopped
1. Mix coconut flour, erythritol, coconut oil, heavy cream, and egg.
2. Pour the batter into the air fryer basket and flatten well.
3. Top the mixture with pecans and cook the meal at 350F (180ºC) for 40 minutes.
4. Cut the cooked meal into the bars.
Per Serving: calories: 174 | fat: 12g | protein: 4g | carbs: 14g | net carbs: 5g | fiber: 9g

Lime Bar

Prep time: 10 m | **Cook time:**35 m | **Serves:** 10
    3 tablespoons coconut oil, melted
    3 tablespoons Splenda
    1½ cup coconut flour
    3 eggs, beaten
    1 teaspoon lime zest, grated
    3 tablespoons lime juice
1. Cover the air fryer basket bottom with baking paper.
2. Then, in the mixing bowl, mix Splenda with coconut flour, eggs, lime zest, and lime juice.
3. Pour the mixture into the air fryer basket and flatten gently.
4. Cook the meal at 350F (180ºC) for 35 minutes.
5. Then cool the cooked meal a little and cut it into bars.
Per Serving: calories: 144 | fat: 7g | protein: 4g | carbs: 16g | net carbs: 8g | fiber: 7g

Macadamia Bar

Prep time: 15 m | **Cook time:**30 m | **Serves:** 10
    3 tablespoons butter, softened
    1 teaspoon baking powder

    1 teaspoon apple cider vinegar
    1.5 cup coconut flour
    3 tablespoons Swerve
    1 teaspoon vanilla extract
    2 eggs, beaten
    2 oz macadamia nuts, chopped
    Cooking spray

1. Spray the air fryer basket with cooking spray.
2. Then mix all remaining ingredients in the mixing bowl and stir until you get a homogenous mixture.
3. Pour the mixture in the air fryer basket and cook at 345F (174ºC) for 30 minutes.
4. When the mixture is cooked, cut it into bars and transfer it to the serving plates.
Per Serving: calories: 158 | fat: 10g | protein: 4g | carbs: 13g | net carbs: 5g | fiber: 8g

Creamy Vanilla Scones

Prep Time:20 m | **Cook time:**10 m | **Serves:** 6
    4 oz coconut flour
    ½ teaspoon baking powder
    1 teaspoon apple cider vinegar
    2 teaspoons mascarpone
    ¼ cup heavy cream
    1 teaspoon vanilla extract
    1 tablespoon erythritol
    Cooking spray
1. In the mixing bowl, mix coconut flour with baking powder, apple cider vinegar, mascarpone, heavy cream, vanilla extract, and erythritol.
2. Knead the dough and cut it into scones.
3. Then, put them in the air fryer basket and sprinkle them with cooking spray.
4. Cook the vanilla scones at 365F (185ºC) for 10 minutes.
Per Serving: calories: 104 | fat: 4g | protein: 3g | carbs: 14g | net carbs: 6g | fiber: 8g

Homemade Mint Pie

Prep Time:15 m | **Cook time:**25 m | **Serves:** 2
    1 tablespoon instant coffee
    2 tablespoons almond butter, softened
    2 tablespoons erythritol
    1 teaspoon dried mint
    3 eggs, beaten
    1 teaspoon spearmint, dried
    4 teaspoons coconut flour
    Cooking spray
1. Spray the air fryer basket with cooking spray.
2. Then mix all ingredients in the mixer bowl.
3. When you get a smooth mixture, transfer it to the air fryer basket. Flatten it gently.
4. Cook the pie at 365F (185ºC) for 25 minutes.
Per Serving: calories: 313 | fat: 19g | protein: 16g | carbs: 20g | net carbs: 8g | fiber: 12g

Cheese Keto Balls

Prep Time:15 m | **Cook time:**4 m | **Serves:** 10
    2 eggs, beaten
    1 teaspoon coconut oil, melted
    9 oz coconut flour
    5 oz provolone cheese, shredded
    2 tablespoons erythritol
    1 teaspoon baking powder

¼ teaspoon ground coriander Cooking spray
1. Mix eggs with coconut oil, coconut flour, Provolone cheese, erythritol, baking powder, and ground cinnamon.
2. Make the balls and put them in the air fryer basket.
3. Sprinkle the balls with cooking spray and cook at 400F (205°C) for 4 minutes.
Per Serving: calories: 176 | fat: 7g | protein: 8g | carbs: 19g | net carbs: 8g | fiber: 11g

Pecan Butter Cookie

Prep Time:5 m | **Cook time:**24 m | **Makes** 12 cookies
    1 cup chopped pecans
    ½ cup salted butter, melted
    ½ cup coconut flour
    ¾ cup erythritol, divided
    1 teaspoon vanilla extract
1. In a food processor, blend pecans, butter, flour, ½ cup erythritol, and vanilla for 1 minute until a dough forms.
2. Form dough into twelve individual cookie balls, about 1 tablespoon each.
3. Cut three pieces of parchment to fit the air fryer basket. Place four cookies on each ungreased parchment and place one parchment piece with cookies into the air fryer basket. Adjust air fryer temperature to 325°F (163°C) and set the timer for 8 minutes. Repeat cooking with remaining batches.
4. When the timer goes off, allow cookies to cool for 5 minutes on a large serving plate until cool enough to handle. While still warm, dust cookies with remaining erythritol. Allow cooling completely, about 15 minutes, before serving.
Per Serving: calories: 151 | fat: 14g | protein: 2g | carbs: 13g | net carbs: 10g | fiber: 3g

Golden Doughnut Holes

Prep time: 10 m | **Cook time:**6 m | **Makes** 20 doughnut holes
    1 cup blanched finely ground almond flour
    ½ cup low-carb vanilla protein powder
    ½ cup granular erythritol
    ¼ cup unsweetened cocoa powder ½ teaspoon baking powder
    2 large eggs, whisked
    ½ teaspoon vanilla extract
1. Mix all ingredients in a large bowl until a soft dough forms. Separate and roll dough into twenty balls, about 2 tablespoons each.
2. Cut a piece of parchment to fit your air fryer basket. Working in batches if needed, place doughnut holes into air fryer basket on ungreased parchment. Adjust the temperature to 380°F (193°C) and set the timer for 6 minutes, flipping doughnut holes halfway through cooking. Doughnut holes will be golden and firm when done. Let cool completely before serving, about 10 minutes.
Per Serving: calories: 103 | fat: 7g | protein: 8g | carbs: 13g | net carbs: 11g | fiber: 2g

Chocolate Chips Soufflés

Prep Time:5 m | **Cook time:**15 m | **Serves:** 2
    2 large eggs, whites, and yolks separated
    1 teaspoon vanilla extract
    2 ounces (57 g) low-carb chocolate chips
    2 teaspoons coconut oil, melted
1. In a medium bowl, beat egg whites until stiff peaks form, about 2 minutes. Set aside. In a separate medium bowl, whisk egg yolks and vanilla together. Set aside.

2. In a separate medium microwave-safe bowl, place chocolate chips and drizzle with coconut oil. Microwave on high for 20 seconds, then stir and continue cooking in 10-second increments until melted, careful not to overheat the chocolate. Let cool for 1 minute.
3. Slowly pour melted chocolate into egg yolks and whisk until smooth. Then, slowly begin adding egg white mixture to chocolate mixture, about ¼ cup at a time, folding in gently.
4. Pour mixture into two 4-inch ramekins greased with cooking spray. Place ramekins into air fryer basket. Adjust the temperature to 400°F (205°C) and set the timer for 15 minutes. Soufflés will puff up while cooking and deflate a little once cooled. The center will be set when done. Let cool for 10 minutes, then serve warm.
Per Serving: calories: 217 | fat: 18g | protein: 8g | carbs: 19g | net carbs: 11g | fiber: 8g

Creamy Strawberry Pecan Pie

Prep time: 15 m | **Cook time:**10 m | **Serves:** 6
    1½ cups whole shelled pecans
    1 tablespoon unsalted butter, softened
    1 cup heavy whipping cream
    12 medium fresh strawberries, hulled
    2 tablespoons sour cream
1. Place pecans and butter into a food processor and pulse ten times until a dough forms. Press dough into the bottom of an ungreased 6-inch round nonstick baking dish.
2. Place dish into air fryer basket. Adjust the temperature to 320°F (160°C) and set the timer for 10 minutes. The crust will be firm and golden when done. Let cool for 20 minutes.
3. In a large bowl, whisk the cream until fluffy and doubled in size, about 2 minutes.
4. In a separate large bowl, mash strawberries until mostly liquid. Fold strawberries and sour cream into whipped cream.
5. Spoon mixture into cooled crust, cover, and place into the refrigerator for at least 30 minutes to set. Serve chilled.

Per Serving: calories: 340 | fat: 33g | protein: 3g | carbs: 7g | net carbs: 4g | fiber: 3g

Chocolate Chip Cookie Cake

Prep Time:5 m | **Cook time:**15 m | **Serves:** 8
    4 tablespoons salted butter, melted
    ⅓ cup granular brown erythritol
    1 large egg
    ½ teaspoon vanilla extract
    1 cup blanched finely ground almond flour
    ½ teaspoon baking powder
    ¼ cup low-carb chocolate chips
1. In a large bowl, whisk together butter, erythritol, egg, and vanilla. Add flour and baking powder, and stir until combined.
2. Fold in chocolate chips, then spoon batter into an ungreased 6-inch round nonstick baking dish.
3. Place dish into air fryer basket. Adjust the temperature to 300°F (150°C) and set the timer for 15 minutes. When edges are browned, a cookie cake will be made.
Per Serving: calories: 170 | fat: 16g | protein: 4g | carbs: 15g | net carbs: 11g | fiber: 4g

Homemade Pretzels

Prep Time:10 m | **Cook time:**10 m | **Serves:** 6
    1½ cups shredded Mozzarella cheese

1 cup blanched finely ground almond flour
2 tablespoons salted butter, melted, divided
¼ cup granular erythritol, divided
1 teaspoon ground cinnamon

1. Place Mozzarella, flour, 1 tablespoon butter, and 2 tablespoons erythritol in a large microwave-safe bowl. Microwave on high for 45 seconds, then stir with a fork until smooth dough ball forms.
2. Separate dough into six equal sections. Gently roll each section into a 12 -inch rope, then fold into a pretzel shape.
3. Place pretzels into an ungreased air fryer basket. Adjust the temperature to 370°F (188°C) and set the timer for 8 minutes, turning pretzels halfway through cooking.
4. In a small bowl, combine the remaining butter, remaining erythritol, and cinnamon. Brush ½ mixture on both sides of pretzels.
5. Place pretzels back into the air fryer and cook an additional 2 minutes at 370°F (188°C).
6. Transfer pretzels to a large plate. Brush on both sides with the remaining butter mixture, then let cool 5 minutes before serving.
Per Serving: calories: 223 | fat: 19g | protein: 11g | carbs: 13g | net carbs: 11g | fiber: 2g

Pecan Chocolate Brownies

Prep Time:10 m | **Cook time:** 20 m | **Serves:** 6
½ cup blanched finely ground almond flour
½ cup powdered erythritol
2 tablespoons unsweetened cocoa powder ½ teaspoon baking powder
¼ cup unsalted butter softened
1 large egg
¼ cup chopped pecans
¼ cup low-carb, sugar-free chocolate chips

1. In a large bowl, mix almond flour, erythritol, cocoa powder, and baking powder. Stir in butter and egg.
2. Fold in pecans and chocolate chips. Scoop mixture into 6 - inch round baking pan. Place pan into the air fryer basket.
3. Adjust the temperature to 300°F (150°C) and set the timer for 20 minutes.
4. When fully cooked, a toothpick inserted in the center will come out clean. Allow 20 minutes to fully cool and firm up.
Per Serving: calories: 215 | fat: 18g | protein: 4g | carbs: 22g | net carbs: 19g | fiber: 3g

Butter Cheesecake

Prep Time:20 m | **Cook time:**35 m | **Serves:** 6
½ cup blanched finely ground almond flour
1 cup powdered erythritol, divided
2 tablespoons unsweetened cocoa powder
½ teaspoon baking powder
¼ cup unsalted butter softened
2 large eggs, divided
8 ounces (227 g) full-fat cream cheese, softened
¼ cup heavy whipping cream
1 teaspoon vanilla extract
2 tablespoons no-sugar-added peanut butter

1. In a large bowl, mix almond flour, ½ cup erythritol, cocoa powder, and baking powder. Stir in butter and one egg.
2 Scoop mixture into 6-inch round baking pan. Place pan into the air fryer basket.
3. Adjust the temperature to 300°F (150°C) and set the timer for 20 minutes.
4. When fully cooked, a toothpick inserted in the center will come out clean. Allow 20 minutes to fully cool and firm up.

5. In a large bowl, beat cream cheese, remaining ½ cup erythritol, heavy cream, vanilla, peanut butter, and remaining egg until fluffy.
6. Pour mixture over cooled brownies. Place pan back into the air fryer basket.
7. Adjust the temperature to 300°F (150°C) and set the timer for 15 minutes.
8. Cheesecake will be slightly browned and mostly firm with a slight jiggle when done. Allow to cool, then refrigerate 2 hours before serving.
Per Serving: calories: 347 | fat: 30g | protein: 8g | carbs: 30g | net carbs: 28g | fiber: 2g

Golden Cheese Cookie

Prep Time:10 m | **Cook time:**7 m | **Serves:** 6
½ cup blanched finely ground almond flour
½ cup powdered erythritol, divided
2 tablespoons butter, softened
1 large egg
½ teaspoon unflavored gelatin
½ teaspoon baking powder
½ teaspoon vanilla extract
½ teaspoon pumpkin pie spice
2 tablespoons pure pumpkin purée
½ teaspoon ground cinnamon, divided
¼ cup low-carb, sugar-free chocolate chips
3 ounces (85 g) full-fat cream cheese, softened

1. In a large bowl, mix almond flour and ¼ cup erythritol. Stir in butter, egg, and gelatin until combined.
2. Stir in baking powder, vanilla, pumpkin pie spice, pumpkin purée, and ¼ teaspoon cinnamon, then fold in chocolate chips.
3. pour batter into a 6-inch round baking pan. Place pan into the air fryer basket.
4. Adjust the temperature to 300°F (150°C) and set the timer for 7 minutes.
5. When fully cooked, the top will be golden brown, and a toothpick inserted in the center will come out clean. Let cool for at least 20 minutes.
6. Make the frosting: mix cream cheese, remaining ¼ teaspoon cinnamon and remaining ¼ cup erythritol in a large bowl. Using an electric mixer, beat until it becomes fluffy. Spread onto the cooled cookie. Garnish with additional cinnamon if desired.
Per Serving: calories: 199 | fat: 16g | protein: 5g | carbs: 22g | net carbs: 20g | fiber: 2g

Toasted Coconut Flakes

Prep Time:5 m | **Cook time:**3 m | **Serves:** 4
1 cup unsweetened coconut flakes
2 teaspoons coconut oil
¼ cup granular erythritol ⅛ teaspoon salt

1. Toss coconut flakes and oil in a large bowl until coated. Sprinkle with erythritol and salt.
2. Place coconut flakes into the air fryer basket.
3. Adjust the temperature to 300°F (150°C) and set the timer for 3 minutes.
4. Toss the flakes when 1 minute remains. Add an extra minute if you would like a more golden coconut flake.
5. Store in an airtight container for up to 3 days.
Per Serving: calories: 165 | fat: 15g | protein: 1g | carbs: 20g | net carbs: 17g | fiber: 3g

Cheesy Cream Cake

Prep Time:10 m | **Cook time:**25 m | **Serves:** 6

 1 cup blanched finely ground almond flour
 ¼ cup salted butter, melted ½ cup granular erythritol
 1 teaspoon vanilla extract
 1 teaspoon baking powder ½ cup full-fat sour cream
 1 ounce (28 g) full-fat cream cheese, softened 2 large eggs

1. In a large bowl, mix almond flour, butter, and erythritol.
2. Add in vanilla, baking powder, sour cream, and cream cheese and mix until well combined. Add eggs and mix.
3. Pour batter into a 6-inch round baking pan. Place pan into the air fryer basket.
4. Adjust the temperature to 300°F (150°C) and set the timer for 25 minutes.
5. When the cake is made, a toothpick inserted in the center will come out clean. The center should not feel wet. Allow it to cool completely, or the cake will crumble when moved.

Per Serving: calories: 253 | fat: 22g | protein: 7g | carbs: 25g | net carbs: 23g | fiber: 2g

Cheese Monkey Bread

Prep Time:15 m | **Cook time:**12 m | **Serves:** 6

 ½ cup blanched finely ground almond flour
 ½ cup low-carb vanilla protein powder
 ¾ cup granular erythritol, divided ½ teaspoon baking powder
 8 tablespoons salted butter, melted and divided 1 ounce (28 g) full-fat cream cheese, softened 1 large egg
 ¼ cup heavy whipping cream ½ teaspoon vanilla extract

1. In a large bowl, combine almond flour, protein powder, ½ cup erythritol, baking powder, 5 tablespoons butter, cream cheese, and egg. A soft, sticky dough will form.
2. Place the dough in the freezer for 20 minutes. It will be firm enough to roll into balls. Wet your hands with warm water and roll into twelve balls. Place the balls into a 6-inch round baking dish.
3. In a medium skillet over medium heat, melt the remaining butter with remaining erythritol. Lower the heat and continue stirring until the mixture turns golden, then add cream and vanilla. Remove from heat and allow it to thicken for a few minutes while you continue to stir.
4. While the mixture cools, place the baking dish into the air fryer basket.
5. Adjust the temperature to 320°F (160°C) and set the timer for 6 minutes.
6. When the timer beeps, flip the monkey brvad over onto a plate and slide it back into the baking pan. Cook an additional 4 minutes until all the tops are brown.
7. Pour the caramel sauce over the monkey bread and cook an additional 2 minutes. Let cool completely before serving.

Per Serving: calories: 322 | fat: 24g | protein: 20g | carbs: 34g | net carbs: 32g | fiber: 2g

Cheesy Cream Puffs

Prep Time:15 m | **Cook time:**6 m | **Makes** 8 puffs

 ½ cup blanched finely ground almond flour
 ½ cup low-carb vanilla protein powder
 ½ cup granular erythritol
 ½ teaspoon baking powder
 1 large egg
 5 tablespoons unsalted butter, melted
 2 ounces (57 g) full-fat cream cheese
 ¼ cup powdered erythritol
 ¼ teaspoon ground cinnamon
 2 tablespoons heavy whipping cream
 ½ teaspoon vanilla extract

1. Mix almond flour, protein powder, granular erythritol, baking powder, egg, and butter in a large bowl until a soft dough forms.
2. Place the dough in the freezer for 20 minutes. Wet your hands with water and roll the dough into eight balls.
3. Cut a piece of parchment to fit your air fryer basket. Working in batches as necessary, place the dough balls into the air fryer basket on top of the parchment.
4. Adjust the temperature to 380°F (193°C) and set the timer for 6 minutes.
5. Flip cream puffs halfway through the cooking time.
6. When the timer beeps, remove the puffs and allow them to cool.
7. In a medium bowl, beat the cream cheese, powdered erythritol, cinnamon, cream, and vanilla until fluffy.
8. Place the mixture into a pastry bag or a storage bag with the end snipped. Cut a small hole in the bottom of each puff and fill with some of the cream mixtures.
9. Store in an airtight container for up to 2 days in the refrigerator.

Per Serving: calories: 178 | fat: 12g | protein: 15g | carbs: 22g | net carbs: 21g | fiber: 1g

Zucchini Bread

Prep Time:10 m | **Cook time:**40 m | **Serves:** 12

 2 cups coconut flour
 2 teaspoons baking powder
 ¾ cup erythritol
 ½ cup coconut oil, melted
 1 teaspoon apple cider vinegar
 1 teaspoon vanilla extract
 3 eggs, beaten
 1 zucchini, grated
 1 teaspoon ground cinnamon

1. In the mixing bowl, mix coconut flour with baking powder, erythritol, coconut oil, apple cider vinegar, vanilla extract, eggs, zucchini, and ground cinnamon
2. Transfer the mixture to the air fryer basket and flatten it in the bread's shape.
3. Cook the bread at 350F (180°C) for 40 minutes.

Per Serving: calories: 179 | fat: 12g | protein: 4g | carbs: 15g | net carbs: 7g | fiber: 8g

Orange Cinnamon Cookies

Prep Time:15 m | **Cook Time:** 24 m | **Servings:**10

 3 tablespoons cream cheese
 3 tablespoons Erythritol
 1 teaspoon vanilla extract
 ½ teaspoon ground cinnamon
 1 egg, beaten
 1 cup almond flour
 ½ teaspoon baking powder
 1 teaspoon butter, softened
 ½ teaspoon orange zest, grated

Put the cream cheese and Erythritol in the bowl. Add vanilla extract, ground cinnamon, and almond flour. Stir the mixture with the help of the spoon until homogenous. Then add egg, almond flour, baking powder, and butter. Add orange zest and stir the mass until homogenous. Then knead it with the help of the fingertips. Roll up the dough with the help of the rolling pin. Then make the cookies with the help of the cookie cutter. Preheat the air fryer to 365F. Line the air fryer basket with baking paper. Put the cookies on the baking paper and cook them for 8 minutes. The time of cooking depends on the cooking size

Per Serving: calories 38, fat 3.3, fiber 0.4, carbs 1, protein 1.4

Mini Almond Cakes

Prep Time:10 m | **Cook Time:** 20 m | **Servings:**4
    3 ounces dark chocolate, melted
    ¼ cup coconut oil, melted
    2 tablespoons swerve
    2 eggs, whisked
    ¼ teaspoon vanilla extract
    1 tablespoon almond flour
    Cooking spray

In a bowl, combine all the ingredients except the cooking spray and whisk well. Divide this into 4 ramekins greased with cooking spray, put them in the fryer, and cook at 360 degrees F for 20 minutes. Serve warm.

Per Serving: calories 161, fat 12, fiber 1, carbs 4, protein 7

Chia Bites

Prep Time:15 m | **Cook Time:** 8 m | **Servings:** 2
    ½ scoop of protein powder
    1 egg, beaten
    3 tablespoons almond flour
    1 oz hazelnuts, grinded
    1 tablespoon flax meal
    1 teaspoon Splenda
    1 teaspoon butter, softened
    1 teaspoon chia seeds, dried
    ¼ teaspoon ground clove

In the mixing bowl, mix up protein powder, almond flour, ground hazelnuts, flax meal, chia seeds, ground clove, and Splenda. Then add egg and butter and stir it with the spoon's help until you get a homogenous mixture. Cut the mixture into pieces and make 2 bites of any shape with the help of the fingertips. Preheat the air fryer to 365F. Line the air fryer basket with baking paper and put the protein bites inside. Cook them for 8 minutes.

Per Serving: calories 433, fat 35.5, fiber 7, carbs 15.6, protein 20.2

Espresso Cinnamon Cookies

Prep Time:5 m | **Cook Time:** 15 m | **Servings:** 12
    8 tablespoons ghee, melted
    1 cup almond flour
    ¼ cup brewed espresso
    ¼ cup swerve
    ½ tablespoon cinnamon powder
    2 teaspoons baking powder
    2 eggs, whisked

In a bowl, mix all the ingredients and whisk well. Spread medium balls on a cookie sheet lined with parchment paper, flatten them, put the cookie sheet in your air fryer and cook at 350 degrees F for 15 minutes. Serve the cookies cold.

Per Serving: calories 134, fat 12, fiber 2, carbs 4, protein 2

Turmeric Almond Pie

Prep Time:20 m | **Cook Time:** 35 m | **Servings:**4
    4 eggs, beaten
    1 tablespoon poppy seeds
    1 teaspoon ground turmeric
    1 teaspoon vanilla extract
    1 teaspoon baking powder
    1 teaspoon lemon juice
    1 cup almond flour

    2 tablespoons heavy cream
    ¼ cup Erythritol
    1 teaspoon avocado oil

Put the eggs in the bowl. Add vanilla extract, baking powder, lemon juice, almond flour, heavy cream, and Erythritol. Then add avocado oil and poppy seeds. Add turmeric. With the help of the immersion blender, blend the pie batter until it is smooth. Line the air fryer cake mold with baking paper. Pour the pie batter into the cake mold. Flatten the pie surface with the help of the spatula if needed. Then preheat the air fryer to 365F. Put the cake mold in the air fryer and cook the pie for 35 minutes. When the pie is cooked, cool it completely and remove it from the cake mold. Cut the cooked pie into the servings.

Per Serving: calories 149, fat 11.9, fiber 1.2, carbs 3.8, protein 7.7

Sponge Cake

Prep Time:5 m | **Cook Time:** 30 m | **Servings:** 8
    1 cup ricotta, soft
    1/3 swerve
    3 eggs, whisked
    1 cup almond flour
    7 tablespoons ghee, melted
    1 teaspoon baking powder
    Cooking spray

In a bowl, combine all the ingredients except the cooking spray and stir them very well. Grease a cake pan that fits the air fryer with the cooking spray and pour the cake mix inside. Put the pan in the fryer and cook at 350 degrees F for 30 minutes. Cool the cake down, slice, and serve.

Per Serving: calories 210, fat 12, fiber 3, carbs 6, protein 9

Cinnamon and Butter Pancakes

Prep Time:10 m | **Cook Time:** 12 m | **Servings:** 2
    1 teaspoon ground cinnamon
    2 teaspoons butter, softened
    1 teaspoon baking powder
    ½ teaspoon lemon juice
    ½ teaspoon vanilla extract
    ¼ cup heavy cream
    4 tablespoons almond flour
    2 teaspoons Erythritol

Preheat the air fryer to 325F. Take 2 small cake molds and line them with baking paper. After this, mix up ground cinnamon, butter, baking powder, lemon juice, vanilla extract, heavy cream, almond flour, and Erythritol in the mixing bowl. Stir the mixture until it is smooth. Then pour the mixture into the prepared cake molds. Put the first cake mold in the air fryer and cook the pancake for 6 minutes. Then check if the pancake is cooked (it should have light brown color) and remove it from the air fryer. Repeat the same steps with the second pancake. It is recommended to serve the pancakes warm or hot.

Per Serving: calories 414, fat 37.4, fiber 6.7, carbs 14.7, protein 12.4

Strawberry Cups

Prep Time:5 m | **Cook Time:** 10 m | **Servings:** 8
    16 strawberries, halved
    2 tablespoons coconut oil
    2 cups chocolate chips, melted

In a pan that fits your air fryer, mix the strawberries with the oil and the melted chocolate chips, toss gently, put the pan in the air fryer, and cook at 340 degrees F for 10 minutes. Divide into cups and serve cold.

Per Serving: calories 162, fat 5, fiber 3, carbs 5, protein6

Cardamom Squares

Prep Time:15 m | **Cook Time:** 20 m | **Servings:** 4

- 4 tablespoons peanut butter
- 1 tablespoon peanut, chopped
- 1 teaspoon vanilla extract
- ½ cup coconut flour
- 1 tablespoon Erythritol
- ½ teaspoon ground cardamom

Put the peanut butter and peanut in the bowl. Add vanilla extract, coconut flour, and ground cardamom. Then add Erythritol and stir the mixture until homogenous. Preheat the air fryer to 330F. Line the air fryer basket with baking paper and pour the peanut butter mixture over it. Flatten it gently and cook for 20 minutes. Then remove the cooked mixture from the air fryer and cool it completely. Cut the dessert into squares.

Per Serving: calories 181, fat 11.7, fiber 7.2, carbs 12.8, protein 7.6

Made in the USA
Monee, IL
13 November 2021